# Financial Models of Insurance Solvency

# Huebner International Series on Risk, Insurance, and Economic Security



Previously published books in the series:

Cummins, J. David; Smith, Barry D.; Vance, R. Neil; VanDerhei, Jack L.; *Risk Classification in Life Insurance*
Mintel, Judith; *Insurance Rate Litigation*
Cummins, J. David: *Strategic Planning and Modeling in Property-Liability Insurance*
Lemaire, Jean: *Automobile Insurance: Actuarial Models*
Rushing, William.: *Social Functions and Economic Aspects of Health Insurance*
Cummins, J. David and Harrington, Scott E.: *Fair Rate of Return in Property-Liability Insurance*
Appel, David and Borba, Philip S.: *Workers Compensation Insurance Pricing*
Cummins, J. David and Derrig, Richard A.: *Classical Insurance Solvency Theory*

The objective of the series is to publish original research and advanced textbooks dealing with all major aspects of risk bearing and economic security. The emphasis is on books that will be of interest to an international audience. Interdisciplinary topics as well as those from traditional disciplines such as economics, risk and insurance, and actuarial science are within the scope of the series. The goal is to provide an outlet for imaginative approaches to problems in both the theory and practice of risk and economic security.

# Financial Models of Insurance Solvency

edited by

**J. David Cummins**
The Wharton School
University of Pennsylvania
Philadelphia, Pennsylvania

and

**Richard A. Derrig**
Massachusetts Rating Bureau
Boston, Massachusetts

**Kluwer Academic Publishers**
Boston/Dordrecht/London

**Distributors**

for North America: Kluwer Academic Publishers, 101 Philip Drive, Assinippi Park, Norwell, Massachusetts 02061, USA

for all other countries: Kluwer Academic Publishers Group, Distribution Centre, Post Office Box 322, 3300 AH Dordrecht, THE NETHERLANDS

**Library of Congress Cataloging-in-Publication Data**

Financial models of insurance solvency / edited by J. David Cummins and Richard A. Derrig.
p. cm. — (Huebner International series on risk, insulrance, and economic security)
Vol. 2 of the proceedings of the 1st International Conference on Insurance Solvency held in Philadelphia, 1986 and published under the title Classical insurance solvency theory.
Includes index.
ISBN 0-7923-9018-0
1. Insurance—Finance—Congresses. I. Cummins, J. David. II. Derrig, Richard A. III. International Conference on Insurance Solvency (1st : 1986 : Philadelphia, Pa.) IV. Classical insurance solvency theory. V. Series.
HG8026.I58 1989
368'.01—dc20 89-2725
CIP



Printed in the United States of America

# Contents

## FINANCIAL MODELS OF INSURANCE SOLVENCY

Edited by J.D. Cummins and R.A. Derrig

Volume II of the Proceedings of the First International Conference on Insurer Solvency

# ABOUT THE AUTHORS

**Stewart Coutts,** International Actuarial Consultants, 8 St. Martins' -le-Grand, London ECIA 4ED, England

Stewart Coutts is a partner with International Actuarial Consultants in London, England. He holds a Doctorate in Actuarial Mathematics from the City University in London, and is Fellow of the Institute of Actuaries. He has published a wide range of research papers from motor-rating to probabilistic models for measuring the Solvency of Insurance Companies.

**J. David Cummins,** Department of Insurance, Wharton School, University of Pennsylvania, 3641 Locust Walk, Philadelphia, PA. U.S.A. 19104-6218

J. David Cummins is the Harry J. Loman Professor of Insurance and Executive Director of the S. S. Huebner Foundation for Insurance Education at the Wharton School. Dr. Cummins has served as President of the American Risk and Insurance Association and is a member of ASTIN, the American Economic Association, and the American Finance Association. His primary research interests are the financial pricing of insurance, financial management of insurance companies, and the economics of property-liability insurance markets. Dr. Cummins is the author or editor of ten books on risk and insurance. His numerous articles have appeared in journals such as the ASTIN Bulletin, the Bell Journal, the Journal of Finance, International Journal of Forecasting, and the Journal of Risk and Insurance. Dr. Cummins consulting clients have come from the Insurance industry, business and government.

**Richard A. Derrig,** Massachusetts Rating Bureaus, 40 Broad Street, Boston, Massachusetts U.S.A. 02109

Dr. Richard A. Derrig is Vice President for Research with the actuarial staff of the Massachusetts Automobile and Workers' Compensation Insurance Rating Bureaus. He joined the Bureaus in 1976 after teaching mathematics at the collegiate and graduate levels at Brown University, Villanova University and Wheaton College in Massachusetts.

In his current position, Dr. Derrig oversees several on-going actuarial research projects in such diverse area as investment income and profitability, requirements for solvency, pricing tax-exempt securities, and claim cost containment. Dr. Derrig has authored several research papers on ratemaking and has provided expert testimony in public hearings. He is a member of the American Risk and Insurance Association, Mathematical Association of America and the American Statistical Association.

**Russell Devitt,** NEL Britannia Group of Companies, Nilton Court Dorking, Surrey, ENGLAND RH4 3LZ

Russell Devitt is Director of Business Development for the NEL Britannia Group of Companies. He holds a masters degree in financial management from the City University in London, and is a Fellow of the Chartered Association of Certified Accountants and a Fellow of the Chartered Insurance Institute.

**R. Dixit,** School of Management, Rensselaer Polytechnic Institute, Troy, NY 12180

R. Dixit is systems designer for CAMEX Enterprises of Ballston Lake, NY. Mr. Dixit holds master degrees in power engineering and operations research and statistics from Rensselaer Polytechnic Institute. He has published several articles in the areas of risk management and statistics. His current interests are cash flow and yield curve modeling, and statistical methods for risk management.

**Neil A. Doherty,** Department of Insurance, Wharton School, University of Pennysivania, 3641 Locust Walk, Philadelphia, Pennysivania U.S.A. 19104-6218

Neil A. Doherty is Professor of Insurance at the Wharton School of the University of Pennsylvania. His papers on financial and economic aspects of insurance markets have appeared in Journals such as the Journal of Risk and Insurance, The Journal of Finance, The Journal of Political Economy and The Economic Journal. His books include *Corporate Risk Management: A Financial Exposition, Insurance Pricing and Loss Prevention*, and, with S. D'Arcy, *The Financial Theory of Insurance Pricing.* He has consulted with various firms on issues such as insurance rate regulation, the harmonization of insurance services in the European community and the taxation of captive insurance companies. Dr. Doherty has also acted as an economic adviser to the U. K. government on social security and pension issues.

**James R. Garven,** College of Business Administration, Department of Finance, The Pennsylvania State University, University Park, Pennsylvania U.S.A. 16802

James R. Garven, Assistant Professor of Finance at The Pennsylvania State University, holds a Ph.D. in Finance from the University of Illinois.

His current research interests include the economics of regulation and the application of contingent claims analysis to insurance and securities markets. He has published articles in journals such as the Financial Review, the Journal of Business Finance and Accounting, the Journal of Finance, and the Journal of Financial Services Research. He is a member of the American Finance Association, the Financial Management Association, the American Risk and Insurance Association, and the Risk Theory Seminar.

**Yehuda Kahane,** Academic Director, Erhard Insurance Center, Faculty of Management, Tel-Aviv University, Ramat-Aviv, Israel 69978

Dr. Kahane, who is a member of the International Association of Actuaries, is active in both the academic and business environments. Since 1967, he has taught at the Hebrew University of Jerusalem, the University of Florida, the University of Toronto, the Wharton School, the Instituto of Estudios Superiores De Administracion, Caracas and has recently served as the Visiting Blades Professor of

Insurance at the Department of Finance, Insurance and Actuarial Studies of the University of Texas at Austin. He is currently Professor of Insurance and Finance and Academic Director of the Erhard Insurance Center at Tel-Aviv University.

His career includes a period spent in business and in consulting activities on risk management, insurance and actuarial topics, to large organizations and major companies in Israel and Europe. Dr. Kahane is the author of several books and numerous articles. He is Associate Editor of Insurance Mathematics and Economics, Insurance Abstracts and Reviews, and the Journal of Finance Services Research. His studies focus on financial and actuarial aspects of the insurance business: inflation, portfolio optimization, reserving and ratemaking, pensions, no-fault auto insurance, and natural catastrophes.

**Laurent L. Jacque,** Curtis L. Carlson School of Management, University of Minnesota, 271 19th Avenue So., Minneapolis, MN 55455

Laurent L. Jacque received his M.A., MBA and PhD from the Wharton School where he taught International Management and International Finance prior to joining the Carlson School of Management (University of Minnesota) as an Associate Professor of International Management. His research centers on risk management in an international setting, and he has published in the Journal of International Business Studies, Journal of Operational Research Society, Journal of Risk and Insurance, the Scandanavian Actuarial Journal etc. His book *Management of Foreign Exchange Risk* was first published in 1978 and is now in its sixth printing.

**Albert S. Paulson**, School of Management, Rensselear Polytechnic Institute, Troy, New York, U.S.A. 12181

Albert S. Paulson is Professor of Management, Professor of Operations Research and Statistics and Director of Doctoral Programs in Management at Rensselaer Polytechnic Institute.

He has published extensively in the areas of risk management, economics, financial modeling, forecasting and control, engineering management, and statistics. His current interests center on (1) the use of cash flow simulation models in quantifying premium amount, risk, reward, solvency, tax, size of firm, and investment issues in the operation of a risk business, and (2) the evolution into the future of yield curves given a window of historical data and given volatility expectations for the spectrum of maturities.

**Jukka Rantala,** The Ministry of Social Affairs and Health, Insurance Department, Bulevardi 28, SF - 00120 Helsinki Finland

Since 1983, Dr. Rantala has been Chief Director of the Insurance Department in the Finnish Ministry of Social Affairs and Health, the insurance supervisory office in Finland. His department is also responsible for drafting insurance legislation. He has been Lecturer in mathematical statistics in the University of Tampere, Actuary in Mutual Insurance Company Sampo and Actuary in the Insurance Department of the Ministry of Social Affairs and Health. Dr. Rantala has published several articles in actuarial journals on solvency issues and on the applications of stochastic control theory in the insurance business. He is the co-author of the book *The Solvency of Insurers and Equalization Reserves* with Teivo Pentikainen. That book was awarded the Clarence Arthur Kulp Memorial Award in 1984.

**Charles S. Tapiero,** Graduate School of Business, University of Washington, Seattle, Washington 98122

Professor Tapiero is currently the Kermit O. Hanson Visiting Professor of Management Science in the Graduate School of Business, University of Washington, Seattle. He was from 1969 to 1974 an Assistant and Associate Professor at Columbia University and has lectured throughout Europe, and Israel. He has also been at the Hebrew University of Jerusalem, Graduate School of Business since 1974. Professor Tapiero has published several books and numerous articles in stochastic models applications and optimization in management science, operations management, insurance and marketing. His more recent book, *Applied Stochastic Models and Control in Management*, was published in January 1988 by North Holland. Professor Tapiero's contributions to insurance include applications of stochastic dynamic systems to insurance problems and mutual insurance problems. Current research interests of Professor Tapiero in insurance include the design of insurance pools, intra-corporate insurance and incentive plans for loss prevention.

**U. K. Solvency Working Party,** Institute of Actuaries, Staple Inn Hall, High Holburn, London, WCIV 7QJ England

The authors of the "Emerging Costs" paper in this volume, are members of the Solvency Working Party of the General Insurance Study Group of the Institute of Actuaries - six actuaries and one accountant. Chris Daykin, the Chairman, works for the Government Actuary's Department in London. Geoffrey Bernstein was a Research Fellow at the City University and is now in private practice. Stewart Coutts is a consultant with International Actuarial Consultants, while Russell Devitt is Director of Business Development for the NEL Brittannia Group of Companies. Brian Hey retired a few years ago from the Co-operative Insurance Society. Ian Reynolds is with City University, London and Peter Smith works for the Excess Insurance Group.

**Howard R. Waters,** Department of Actuarial Mathematics and Statistics, Heriot - Watt University, Riccarton, Edinborough EH 14 4AS Scotland

Howard Waters received his doctorate from Oxford University. After working for two years with Duncan C. Fraser and Co., consulting actuaries, he joined the Department of Actuarial Mathematics and Statistics at Heriot-Watt University in 1975. He qualified as a Fellow of the Institute of Actuaries in London in 1976. He has been at Heriot-Watt University since 1975, apart from the year 1981 when he worked at the Laboratory of Actuarial Mathematics, University of Copenhagen. His publications have been in the areas of Risk Theory, life assurance mathematics and, most recently, health insurance.

PHOTO IDENTIFICATION

Participants: First International Conference on Insurance Solvency

Left to Right. First Row Neil A. Doherty, Brian Hey, Tapan S. Roy, Teivo Pentikainen, Richard A. Derrig, J. David Cummins, Chris D. Daykin. Second Row Gregory C. Taylor, Dongsae Cho, Ben Zehnwirth, Howard R. Waters, Ian Reynolds, Yahuda Kahane, Nathan F. Jones. Third Row Albert S. Paulson, Jukka Rantala, Alan Brender, Glenn Meyers, Walter T. Karten, Edward W. Frees, John S. McGuiness. Fourth Row Stewart M. Coutts, Richard Woll, David Appel, Peter D. Smith, James R. Garven, James Gerofsky. Fifth Row Philippe Artzner, Thomas Kozik, Robert A. Buchanan, Leonard Freifelder, Robert Bailey, Terrie E. Troxel.

Not shown Geoffrey D. Bernstein, Russell Devitt, Scott E. Harrington, Roger S. Lawson, Stephen J. Ludwig, Charles A. Tapiero.

# CONTRIBUTORS


Stewart Coutts
*International Actuarial Consultants*
*8 St. Martin'-le-Grand*
*London EC1A 4ED*
*ENGLAND*

J. David Cummins
*Department of Insurance,*
*The Wharton School*
*3641 Locust Walk*
*University of Pennsylvania,*
*Philadelphia, PA 19104-6218*

Richard A. Derrig
*Massachusetts Rating Bureaus,*
*40 Broad Street*
*Boston, MA 02109*

Russell Devitt
*NEL Britannia Group of Companies*
*Nilton Court Dorking*
*Surrey RH4 3LZ,*
*ENGLAND*

R. Dixit
*School of Management*
*Rensselaer Polytechnic Institute*
*Troy, NY 12180*

Neil Doherty
*The Wharton School*
*University of Pennsylvania*
*3641 Locust Walk*
*Philadelphia, PA 19104-6218*

James R. Garven
*Department of Finance*
*College of Business Administration*
*The Pennsylvania State University*
*University Park, PA 16802*

Yehuda Kahane
*M. W. Erhard Center for Higher Education and Research in Insurance*
*Tel-Aviv University*
*P. O. Box 39010*
*Ramat-Aviv, Tel-Aviv*
*ISRAEL*

Laurent Jacque
*University of Minnesota*
*271 19th Avenue S*
*Minneapolis, MN 55455*

Albert S. Paulson
*School of Management*
*Rensselear Polytechnic Institute*
*Troy, NY 12181*

Jukka Rantala
*Ministry of Social Affairs & Health*
*Insurance Department*
*Bulevardi 28*
*SF - 00120 Helsinki, FINLAND*

Charles S. Tapiero
*Department of Management Science*
*Graduate School of Business*
*University of Washington*
*Seattle, WA 98195*

U.K. Solvency Working Party
*Institute of Actuaries*
*Staple Hall Inn*
*High Holburn, London WCIV 7QJ*
*ENGLAND*

Howard R. Waters
*Department of Actuarial Mathematics and Statistics*
*Heriot - Watt University*
*Riccarton*
*Edinborough EH 14 4AS*
*SCOTLAND*

## CONTRIBUTING ORGANIZATIONS

Allstate Insurance Companies

American Risk and Insurance Association

Center for Research on Risk and Insurance, The Wharton School, University of Pennsylvania

Geneva Association

Government Office of New South Wales

Hartford Accident and Indemnity Company

Institute of Actuaries of Australia

LIberty Mutual Insurance Companies

London Institute of Actuaries

Massachusetts Rating Bureaus

Mercantile Mutual Holdings Limited

Prudential Insurance Company of America

# PREFACE

The First International Conference on Insurance Solvency was held at the Wharton School, University of Pennsylvania from June 18th through June 20th, 1986. The conference was the inaugural event for Wharton's Center for Research on Risk and Insurance. In attendance were thirty-nine representatives from Australia, Canada, France, Germany, Israel, the United Kingdom, and the United States.

The papers presented at the Conference are published in two volumes, this book and a companion volume, *Classical Insurance Solvency Theory*, J. D. Cummins and R. A. Derrig, eds. (Norwell, MA: Kluwer Academic Publishers, 1988). The first volume presented two papers reflecting important advances in actuarial solvency theory. The current volume goes beyond the actuarial approach to encompass papers applying the insights and techniques of financial economics. The papers fall into two groups. The first group consists of papers that adopt an essentially actuarial or statistical approach to solvency modelling. These papers represent methodology advances over prior efforts at operational modelling of insurance companies. The emphasis is on cash flow analysis and many of the models incorporate investment income, inflation, taxation, and other economic variables. The papers in second group bring financial economics to bear on various aspects of solvency analysis. These papers discuss insurance applications of asset pricing models, capital structure theory, and the economic theory of agency.

A common theme expressed by the papers in the first group is that the traditional accounting approach to solvency measurement embodied in the insurance regulations of most Western nations is outmoded. This approach is essentially static, relying on accounting ratios and reflecting a liquidation rather than going-concern view of the insurance firm. In contrast, most of the models presented in this book reflect a *cash flow* approach to measuring insurance solvency, with the relevant cash flows modelled as stochastic processes. Cash inflows include premiums, investment income, and capital contributions; while cash outflows encompass loss payments, expenses, and taxes.

All of the components of the net cash flow are potentially stochastic. The firm is defined to be solvent if the present market value of cash inflows exceeds the present market value of cash outflows, where the market values reflect both the expected value and risk of the flows. As Kahane, Tapiero, and Jacque point out (chapter 7), in perfect markets this definition of solvency is the same as the requirement that the market value of assets exceed the market value of liabilities. This approach is markedly different from the usual requirement that the book value of assets exceed the book value of liabilities. It also leads naturally to the concept of *firm-specific* capital margins, which depend upon the overall risk of the firm's underwriting and investment portfolio.

The financial economic approach reflected in the second part of the book places the insurance firm in a more general context than envisioned by traditional actuarial models. Actuarial models typically assume that the level of capital is determined exogenously. It is then the role of the actuary to determine the probability that this capital will be sufficient to meet the company's obligations. The actuary also is assumed to have control over most of the key stochastic processes affecting the firm, such as the premium rate. The traditional approach ignores the company's investment activities and the attendant risks.

In contrast to the actuarial approach, financial models view the firm in the context of the economy in general and financial markets in particular. Insurers are providing a type of financial product—a contingent claim on their assets, analogous to a bond or an option. The price for this product is set in competitive financial markets and not by the actuary. The price reflects both expected value and risk, and the product is priced at market equilibrium rates that reflect both demand and supply. The firm's capital structure (e.g., ratio of market value of liabilites to the market value of equity) is determined endogenously by the market and the payments to the providers of equity capital reflect the market equilibrium price for risk-bearing (the *cost of capital*).

While the preceding discussion suggests a wide gulf between the actuarial and financial approaches, the gap is beginning to close. The papers in the first half of this book reflect a growing recognition among actuaries that the traditional view of insurance and insurance markets is no longer viable. These papers take a major step towards providing a sophisticated modelling framework which can be used to establish linkages between actuarial and financial models. The papers in the second half suggest ways in which financial theories of market equilibrium, asset pricing, and capital structure can be integrated into insurance analysis.

Although the papers in this book represent an important step towards the development of a fully integrated approach to modelling the insurance firm, much work remains to be done. Both actuaries and financial economists need to gain a greater appreciation of the contributions to be made by the other field. The reference lists in this book are symptomatic: the papers written by actuaries almost exclusively cite other actuaries, while the papers written by economists almost exclusively cite economists. Both groups need to become more aware that significant research exists outside of their own literature.

Chapter 1 by Stewart Coutts and Russell Devitt advocates the use of cash flows rather than balance sheet ratios to assess solvency. The authors argue for the development of a unified theory of insurance solvency, which would apply to all types of insurance. They propose a stochastic theory of insurance that considers both asset and liability risk. Such a model would be valuable both for solvency assessment and financial management of insurers. Coutts and Devitt illustrate their ideas by providing case-study simulations of general insurance and pension insurance.

In chapter 2, Albert S. Paulson and R. Dixit present an overview of a sophisticated insurance company simulation model they have developed. The objective of their research is to integrate the underwriting and financial sides of the insurance business to facilitate the examination of premium adequacy, rates of return, and solvency. The model allows for multiple lines of insurance, multiple investment types, taxes, and either multiple or single period planning horizons. The analysis focuses on cash flows, and results are summarized as internal rates of return. Among the innovative features are confidence limits for the simulated results.

Chapter 3, by Howard A. Waters, focuses on the investment risk in a cohort of endowment insurance policies. Investment risk is modelled using the Wilke [1986] model. Waters simulates the impact of investment strategies, terms to maturity, and premium rate levels on the present value of profits.

The conclusions of the British Institute of Actuaries Working Party on Insurance Solvency are presented in Chapter 4. The authors utilize a simulation model that focuses on insurance cash flows and "emerging costs." They argue that the model could be used by actuaries to evaluate the solvency of each company on an individual basis, thus providing more accurate solvency assessments than traditional regulatory ratios. Rather than focusing on the book values of assets and liabilities they point out that "what is important is whether the proceeds of the assets, both capital and income, will prove sufficient to meet the liabilities as they emerge." An important principle is that the totality of the company's operations be considered. Case simulations are provided to illustrate the Working Party's simulation model.

In Chapter 5, Albert S. Paulson and R. Dixit discuss the solution of one of the classic problems of collective risk theory, the calculation of the total loss distribution and the probability of ruin. They utilize an approach that was pioneered by Paulson, inversion of the characteristic function of the total claims distributions. Two algorithms are used, adaptive quadrature and the Fast Fourier Transform. The results are compared to those obtained with the four moment form of the Normal Power approximation. Surprisingly, tests based on a large number of simulated distributions reveal that both characteristic function inversion and the Normal Power method give reasonable approximations to the tail of the loss distribution.

Chapter 6, by Jukka Rantala, proposes the use of *stochastic control theory* for the modelling of insurance solvency. In his model, the insurer is viewed as a filter, transforming the claims process, with the most important outputs being the claims reserve, accumulated profit, and future premium rates. The company exercises control over the process by adapting future premiums based upon past outcomes of the claims process and the level of surplus. Both feedback and feedforward (forecasting) controls are proposed. The concepts are illustrated by an application to Finnish workers' compensation data.

Chapter 7, by Yehuda Kahane, Charles Tapiero, and Laurent Jacque, provides a review of some key concepts of financial theory and a discussion of their applicability to insurance. They stress the importance of basing solvency analyses on "the overall performance of the insurance company . . . which is a function of both underwriting and investment income and their risks." Solvency is viewed as depending upon the entire operation of the firm, including pricing, managerial expenses, reinsurance, dividend policy, and external conditions such as inflation and economic growth. Three primary areas of finance are proposed as having important implications for insurance: mean-variance portfolio theory, capital structure theory, and the theory of agency.

In chapter 8, James Garven discusses the implications of financial theory for the analysis of the insurance firm. He points out that traditional finance theory shows that capital structure is irrelevant, absent taxes and bankruptcy costs. Thus, one of the first tasks of the financial theorist is to explain why capital structure matters, or seems to matter, in insurance. Garven argues that capital structure and ruin probabilities matter under a number of conditions, including the presence of redundant tax shields, bankruptcy costs, and agency costs. Agency costs may be particularly important. These are costs incurred in resolving or avoiding incentive conflicts among parties involved in the insurance enterprise, i.e., owners, managers, and policyholders. An important finding is that, even in an unregulated market, insurers may voluntarily limit their premium to capital ratios in order to economize on agency and other contracting costs.

Chapter 9, by Neil Doherty, also deals with the issue of capital structure. Doherty uses an options pricing model to investigate the impact of the insurance product market on capital structure. He contends that, in a perfect market, the optimal solution is for the insurer to operate with no capital (i.e., be totally debt financed). However, he points out that certain types of market imperfections may invalidate the zero capital solution. Among these are costly monitoring and imperfectly elastic demand for insurance. Doherty also identifies certain "time-inconsistent incentives" inherent in the insurance transaction, namely, the insurer's incentive to increase its equity value following policy issue date by increasing asset and insurance risk.

The issue of insurance insolvency (guaranty) funds is addressed in Chapter 10, by J. David Cummins. Cummins points out that the provision of insolvency insurance with flat (non-risk-based) premiums may cause the number of insolvencies to rise. This is because the presence of insolvency insurance greatly reduces the market penalty (in the form of lower premiums) that would otherwise be incurred by high-risk insurers. A type of "lemons" problem is created, whereby companies have an incentive to increase risk since they are not penalized by the market and are penalized through higher guaranty fund premiums only on the average. The solution is to adopt risk-based premiums, which replace the market penalty with a regulatory penalty. Market equilibrium risk-based premium formulae are derived using conventional options theory, options models with jumps (catastrophes), and a perpetual options (cohort) model. Although these models are presented in the context of the guaranty fund problem, they also can serve as financial pricing models for insurance contracts.

In chapter 11, Richard A. Derrig examines the issue of the allocation of surplus by line and proposes a new definition of solvency and a corresponding technique for establishing fair premiums. Derrig shows that, under the capital asset pricing model (CAPM), the appropriate basis for allocation of surplus is in proportion to the market value of reserves rather than premiums or book values of reserves. Derrig points out that the insurer possesses an insolvency-put-option which will be exercised to the disadvantage of the policyholders if assets are less than promised claim payments at the option "exercise date." The company is defined to be *solvent at level* if the value of the put is less than some specified value. He proposes that the loading for "fully" guaranteed loss payouts be set equal to the value of the put at an asset to liability ratio of 1. Illustrations of required risk premia and "safe" premium to capital ratios are derived for the automobile and workers' compensation lines of insurance, utilizing these concepts and the Cummins cohort-options model. The results indicate that premiums-to-capital ratios should vary by line.

A unified theory of insurance should integrate and reconcile the conflicting and seemingly inconsistent results of actuarial science and financial economics. Conventional financial economics insists that asset prices (including insurance policies) depend solely upon *systematic* or non-diversifiable risk and that capital structure is irrelevant, i.e., that ruin probabilities do not matter. Actuarial science, on the other hand, assumes that exogenously-given ruin probabilities are important and that insurance companies have a high degree of control over prices and profits. The options models presented in this book provide a partial reconciliation of these theoretical results by developing equilibrium premia that depend upon capital structure and total, rather than just non-diversifiable, risk. The simulation models presented elsewhere in the book provide the level of institutional and statistical sophistication needed to arrive at an operational model of the insurance enterprise. The task that remains is to effect a synthesis of these two areas of research.

## Acknowledgements

The editors gratefully acknowledge the conference coordination and production assistance of Lesley Phipps and Sonia Dunbar of the Massachusetts Rating Bureaus and the invaluable support of the Conference by the insurance organizations listed on page xv.

# Financial Models of Insurance Solvency

# 1

# THE ASSESSMENT OF THE FINANCIAL STRENGTH OF INSURANCE COMPANIES BY A GENERALIZED CASH FLOW MODEL

Stewart M. Coutts and Russell Devitt

## 1. Introduction

This paper is concerned with the assessment of the financial strength of insurance enterprises of various kinds. This is of concern to many parties - not only shareholders and the supervisory authorities but also management, policyholders, potential investors and financial analysts are among those who require information about it. The aim of this paper is to develop a general framework that may be employed in producing information in assessing capital adequacy for published accounts prepared for shareholders, for the financial statements required by supervisory authorities and for management accounts.

A central concept of this paper is that the subject of financial solidity within the insurance industry can be dealt with in terms of one integrated model which is applicable to all types of insurance operations. Redington (1951) suggested that the matching of assets and liabilities should be looked at in terms of the cash inflows for assets and the cash outflows for liabilities. It is our contention that the correct way to approach the determination of the financial strength of an insurance company is to look in terms of the relationship between the projected cash inflows and outflows of that insurance company. In this context, insolvency, for example, can be defined as the state which exists when cash inflows from assets are no longer adequate to meet the required outflows for liabilities. This basic statement will be true for all types of insurance, even though the parameters may differ between life, pensions or general business.

Further, the projection of future cash flows cannot be made with certainty. These streams of future income and outgo therefore have to be modelled. Any realistic model must take account of the variability inherent in such projections and a practical way to address this problem is through the use of simulation techniques.

Our approach to assessing capital adequacy has a number of consequences which are as follows:

(1) The underlying financial strength of a company can be judged.

(2) Different investment strategies can be investigated or reviewed.

(3) Probability statements may be made concerning the company's ability to meet the outgoings to which it is committed in respect of its liabilities.

(4) Those responsible for the preparation and publication of financial statements are compelled to make detailed disclosure of the assumptions upon which those statements are based.

The structure of this paper is as follows. Section 2 reviews the current literature on the subject. Section 3 puts the case for cash flow models and in Section 4 the case for an integrated insurance model is made. Section 5 describes the model algorithm, Section 6 examines the practical implications of the model and Section 7 gives some illustrative examples. Section 8 considers how our approach could be used to report on an insurance company's financial strength. Section 9 looks at the question of solvency and the insurance supervisor. Section 10 examines the implications for financial management of an insurance company. Finally, Section 11 describes the research that has still to be done.

## 2. Literature Review

The following section reviews some of the major contributions to the literature concerned with assessing the financial strength of insurance companies.

Perhaps the first major contribution by a UK author was a little known paper by Beard (1964). He started from the point of view that an insurance company can be regarded as collection of liabilities, against which a group of assets is held.

In addition to considering the margin required for the various components of liabilities, he also drew attention to the fact that an additional item may be required to provide against assets having to be realised when investment markets are depressed. Thus he argued that both assets and liabilities must be considered when assessing capital strength.

Benjamin (1976) examined profit and other financial concepts in insurance. His conclusions may be paraphrased by saying that he found the accountant's model of income and capital to be inadequate. His ideas were developed further in a later paper, Benjamin (1980), which spelt out that the premium basis in non-life business is an 'anticipated actual' basis. The reserving basis, however, is more stringent and capital is therefore required to finance the resulting strain. Thus, he was demonstrating that the need for capital in both life and non-life business arises from the same underlying cause.

Kahane (1979) used econometric models to establish relationships between solvency margins, underwriting results and return on investment. However, his paper is little known within the actuarial world.

Recognition that the need for capital in both types of business arises from the same cause is absent in the statutory minimum solvency requirements which have to be met by insurance companies trading in the UK, which are derived from those which are in force in the E.E.C. (1961). These regulations treat long term business, that is life and pensions business, and general business as being separate categories, quite independent of each other. In addition, they have the following serious failings:

(1) They are conceived from a viewpoint which is quite static, in the sense that they regard the company as having notionally ceased to trade at the balance sheet date and ignores the effect of future new business.

(2) They are based on research which is both out of date and related to industry averages, thereby failing to take account of the different characteristics of individual companies.

A more dynamic approach has been advocated in the pioneering work of Pentakainen and Rantala (1980, 1981) in their studies of the solvency of general insurance companies.

This approach does take account of the future trading of the company, that is, it makes the assumption that new business is written. It is based on simulation models which allow characteristics of individual companies to be taken into account. These models are derived from the basic principles of risk theory and are stochastic rather than deterministic. It is primarily concerned with solvency, but the basic principles can be generalised to the overall question of financial strength.

However, the work of Pentakainen and Rantala can also be subjected to some criticisms. It is restricted to general insurance only, whereas we will argue for a general model for all types of insurance business. Because of the peculiarities of the insurance market in Finland, the model takes limited account of asset risks. This is clearly inappropriate for companies operating in markets such as the UK, where the asset risk is likely to be substantial. Further, the model looks at extended periods without taking account of the ability of management to react to developments, with the result that the requirements it suggests are excessive.

Another paper which takes account of the stochastic nature of solvency is the recently published paper on the solvency of life assurance companies, by a Working Party of the Faculty of Actuaries chaired by Limb (1984). This paper also points out the need to take account of future new business. However, as its name implies, it is concerned only with life business. Ryan (1980, 1984) has treated the solvency of general insurance companies in a stochastic way.

An issue which is raised in the Limb paper is the question of matching assets and liabilities. This issue has also been dealt with by Wise (1984). However, once again, this paper deals only with life and pensions business, although the principles would seem capable of extension to general business.

The UK literature on the financial strength of insurance companies has concentrated exclusively on the amount of capital required to support a given volume of business. It has ignored the question of the cost associated with the use of the capital in that way. However, this question has attracted rather more interest in the US. A recent review by Cummins and Paulson (1984) summarises the current state of thinking.

From the above, we draw a number of conclusions as follows:

(1) There is a need to integrate the theory relating to capital strength of insurance companies, which has developed separately in the different branches of insurance.

(2) Any model used to examine capital strength must look at both assets and liabilities and their interaction.

(3) Any model used in this context must be stochastic in that it takes account of the variability inherent in the business.

(4) Any model used must also be dynamic, in the sense that it takes account of future new business, rather than assuming that the company notionally ceases to trade.

(5) Attention must be paid to the amount of capital required to support a given volume of business and the return on that capital.

This paper deals with items (1) and (2) in detail. The remaining problems are left to a future paper.

## 3. The Case for Cash Flow Models

Traditionally the assessment of an insurance company's financial strength has been based on accounting statements. In financial accounting it is axiomatic that reporting cash flows is inadequate and that some form of accrual accounting is appropriate. The accruals concept demands that revenue and costs are recognised as they are earned or incurred, not as the cash is received or paid and that they are matched with one another insofar as their relationship can be established or justifiably assumed. However, the accrual process is ambiguous and not well defined because there exists a variety of alternative methods for matching costs and revenues. In addition, there are departures from historical cost accounting, such as the use of market values for certain assets, which further increase the alternatives available. Nevertheless, as the FASB (1982) point out

> "...financial reporting should provide information to help investors, creditors and others assess the amounts, timing and uncertainty of prospective net cash inflows to the...enterprise"

The use of conventional accounting statements implicitly accepts the traditional accounting concepts of income and capital. Lee (1980) has examined these concepts and points out that the accountant is concerned to measure performance for a defined past period of time. Accounting income is therefore an "ex-post" measure, that is, it is measured after the event. Further, the accountant measures capital in terms of the residual equity of the business identifying the various assets net of liabilities. Accounting capital is traditionally conceived as a set of goods and services expressed in aggregate money terms, an expression of the property rights of the business in its net assets. It is therefore transaction based, derived from the process of determining income from recorded transactions and consequently dependent on the nature of the transactions recorded.

In assessing the financial strength, however, we are essentially concerned with whether the cash inflows generated by the assets held by the business are adequate to meet the cash outflows required by the liabilities. In the first place, we are concerned with income that will arrive in the future (an "ex-ante" measure) not that which has arisen in the past (an "ex-post" measure). Secondly, we are concerned with measuring capital directly rather than as a residual. Thirdly, capital should be regarded as a stream of future benefits rather than the results of a series of past transactions. There exists a model of income and capital which satisfies all these requirements known as the economists "ex-ante" model. It regards capital as the present value of future net cash flows and income as the difference between the company's opening and closing capital after adjusting for any capital subscribed or withdrawn during the period.

An interesting analogy may be drawn between this model and the methods employed by the life actuary. Like the economist the actuary is concerned with future cash flows. The measure of income he employs is a residual from the direct measurement of capital at the start of the period. Capital is measured by finding the present value of the future cash flows. Hence the valuation of a life fund can be described as an example of the economists' "ex-ante" model in action.

The future cash flows of an insurance company are a series of uncertain events. Hence, the model which projects them can show only the range of possible outcomes.

In such circumstances, it seems to us discounting to give a single value is inappropriate. Rather, it is necessary to present the results in the form of "stochastic bundles" as employed by Pentakainen and Rantala (1981) or to express them as a probability statement. This argument is similar to that used to justify profit testing in life assurance.

Further, a distinction can be drawn between those uncertainties which are beyond management control e.g. the variation in claim frequency and those which management can dictate, such as investment policy. Ideally, the cash flow model should be of the form which allows different sets of assumptions relating to factors under management control to be evaluated and compared.

It is our submission therefore that the model to be employed in measuring financial strength must be "ex-ante". Since it is concerned with future events which are uncertain, it must also contain a stochastic element, we contend. It must deal with future cash flows, since these will be of interest to all users of financial reports. Rather than using theoretically dubious discounting methods, however, it must deal in projections of the future cash flows. It should allow different policy options to be explored. The availability of modern computing power now makes this a practical possibility.

## 4. The Case for an Integrated Model of Insurance

The classical model of a life assurance company can be conceived in terms of a company writing conventional non-profit business. The assessment of the financial strength of such an office involves the use of traditional actuarial methods which are concerned with projecting future cash flows in respect of sums assured payable on death or maturity and estimating their present values. The projections here involve a relatively high degree of certainty. The future premium and the benefits payable under the policy are fixed and the existence of life tables makes the estimation of future payments relatively exact. Hence, the payments to be made in the future in respect of liabilities can be assessed with relative certainty.

Under the classical model, the funds of the office will be invested in fixed interest bonds with a high degree of security, for example, Government securities. Such securities will have a fixed rate of interest and a determinate repayment date and, because of the high degree of security, the risk of default is practically negligible.

Hence, the future returns on assets can be assessed with relative certainty. Redington (1951) demonstrated that by considering the projected future cash flows it is possible to test whether a fund is protected against developing a deficiency in the event of the assets and liabilities being mismatched and the occurrence of a general change in interest rates. This theory of immunisation has been developed further by authors such as Boyle (1979). The important consequence of Redington's work was that it established that liabilities cannot be considered in isolation from the associated assets.

The classical model described above has had to be modified to take into account developments in both the types of contracts now issued by life offices and the change in the structure of their investment portfolios. Since the classical model has been developed, with profit business has taken precedence over non-profit business in the UK. This has the result of introducing a new element of uncertainty into the projection of future cash outflows in respect of liabilities.

Recent years have seen the development of the unit-linked contract. The assets in which the fund under the policy is invested can consist entirely of equity type assets with a consequent increase in volatility, but the future benefits payable under the policy are linked to the value of the associated assets and consequently the main uncertainty relates to any guarantees given under the contract with respect to maturity values. The Maturity Guarantee Working Party (1980) developed a method for forecasting the possible future values of the assets associated with such contracts so that the assessment of future cash flows was possible. The nature of the processes involved here often makes the use of simulation models desirable but the underlying technique is the same. A further technique which uses cash flow is profit testing. Whilst this method takes into account expected cash flow, it ignores variation in asset values.

Turning now to pension business, we find that the classical actuarial approach to immunisation is not employed here. This is due to the fact that the liabilities with which we are concerned are necessarily stretching far into the future and are, at present, not guaranteed. A member joining a pension scheme may not retire for another 40 years and could be drawing benefits from the fund for a further 40 years. As a consequence of this, it has been considered necessary to invest to a large extent in equity type assets in order to ensure achievement of the real growth necessary to meet the eventual liabilities.

The liabilities themselves are subject to many uncertainties. The death risk can be assessed with reasonable certainty, as with life assurance. The same is true to a lesser extent with the risk of ill health. The future level of salaries, which will determine the amount of benefits payable, is much more difficult to estimate with any degree of certainty, and the level of benefits may also be affected by events such as the marriage of a scheme member or the size of the member's family.

As a result, there has relatively recently been developed a technique of valuing liabilities on an emerging cost basis. Essentially this can be characterised as assessing the future cash outflows in respect of liabilities. Assets are valued not on their market values but in terms of a stream of future income. In other words, this involves projecting the future cash inflows which these assets will generate and relating them to the cash flow projections for liabilities by discounting them at a rate equal to the difference between the rate at which liabilities are expected to inflate and the expected rate of return on assets. Thus, it can be seen that the basic model used in this approach to assessing the strength of pension fund is the same as the one identified in valuing a life fund, since both are involved in examining the relationship between future cash inflows in respect of assets and outflows in respect of liabilities.

Turning now to the question of general insurance, the traditional method of assessing capital strength has been to look at the solvency margin, that is the excess of assets over liabilities. However, if we consider general insurance in relation to the types of insurance which have been discussed so far, we can establish a number of common factors. The liabilities of a non-life insurer are an estimate of future cash outflows to be made to policyholders in respect of claims. In general insurance, there is a further order of uncertainty because not only the amount to be paid to the policyholder but also the timing of the payment are both uncertain.

However, we would argue that the difference is merely one of degree rather than principle. As far as assets are concerned, a non-life office will use investments of the same types, even if the proportions of the different types vary.

The analysis of this section can be summarised in Table 1 overleaf.

**Table 1**

| | Liabilities | Assets |
|---|---|---|
| **Life Assurance** | | |
| Non profit business | Relatively predictable in both time & amount. | Mainly predictable in time & amount. |
| With profit business | Timing relatively predictable, amount uncertain. | Some uncertainty in respect of time and amount. |
| Unit linked business | Timing relatively predictable, amount highly uncertain, but linked to assets. | Predominantly uncertain in respect of time and amount for guarantees. |
| **Pension Business** | Timing uncertain, amount highly uncertain. | Significant proportion uncertain in respect of time and amount. |
| **General Insurance** | Timing & amount highly uncertain. | Significant proportion uncertain in respect of time and amount. |

In summary, we would argue that there is an underlying structure which is common to all types of insurance contract, be they life, pensions or general business. In all cases, the insurer is involved in entering into a contract which commits him to make certain future payments to policyholders under certain conditions. The insurer invests in assets, which entitles him to a future stream of income. Since the concept of capital adequacy is concerned with the ability of the insurer to meet his liabilities in the future, in all cases, we may form a judgement on his ability to do this by making a projection of his cash outflows in respect of liabilities and his inflows in respect of assets and then examining the relationship between these two flows.

## 5. The Model Algorithm

In looking at the financial strength of an insurance company we are concerned with the probability that the company has sufficient funds to meet its liabilities when they fall due. If the payment pattern of the company's liabilities were known exactly, it would be possible to arrange its assets in such a way that the stream of income generated by those assets would match the cash outflows of liabilities. However, we are not in a position of perfect information. The liabilities will be subject to random fluctuation and to influences such as inflation. Hence, it is possible to make only probability statements about the future cash outflows. Consequently, it is possible to arrange assets to generate a stream of income which is only approximately equal to the amount required. Although absolute matching in this sense is not possible, we are concerned to ensure that cash inflows are at all times at least adequate to meet the cash outflows.

Consider in simple terms a model of an insurance operation. At time 0 it will hold a set of investments, in order to support its liabilities. In year 1, there would be income in the form of the yield on investments held, plus the maturity of dated securities falling due in that year. Out of this income, claim payments would have to be made. If these claim payments exceed the income, then further assets would have to be realised. On the other hand, if income exceeded outgo, the surplus would be re-invested. Hence, at the start of year 2, there would be a different set of assets and a different set of liabilities. The process would then be repeated for each year until all liabilities had been run off. If at any stage the claim payments were so large that they could not be met from the cash inflows plus the realisation of all investments then the company is insolvent in the strictest sense.

It can be seen therefore that we are faced with having to model a complex sequential decision problem, namely, the determination of the optimal strategy for investment, dis-investment and re-investment.

The complex nature of this problem means that it is almost mathematically intractable. However, Tapeiro and Zuckerman (1983) have suggested an approach using some simple mathematical functions. Pentakainen and others have shown that such complex problems can be investigated using simulation techniques. In order to do this, it is necessary to specify a simulation model, such as that advocated in Coutts et al (1980).

Such a model would require the following assumptions to be made:

A.1 A probability distribution of future claim payments from time zero by time and amount.

A.2 The present asset portfolio, showing, for fixed interest securities, details of maturity dates, nominal amount held and coupon rates and, for equities, market values yields and dividends.

A.3 A set of decision rules defining future strategy for re-investment and dis-investment.

A.4 A model for predicting the selling price of fixed interest securities (where sold before maturity) and for equities future prices, dividends and yields.

The algorithm for the model is as follows:

Step 1 Generate total claim payments for each future year, using the probability distribution in assumption A.1

Step 2 From assumption A.2, generate the first year cash inflows of interest plus maturities from Government bonds plus dividends from equities, using the model in assumption A.4. Compare the total cash inflow with claim payments.

Step 3 If claim payments exceed cash inflow, apply dis-investment strategy; otherwise go to Step 4. This will lead to a new set of assets at the end of year 1. Pass to step 5.

Step 4 If claim payments are less than income, apply re-investment strategy. This will lead to a new set of assets at the end of year 1. Pass to Step 5.

Step 5 Repeat the process from Stage 2 for remaining years until all liabilities have run-off. If at any stage the claim payments are so large that they cannot be met from cash inflows plus the realisation of all investments then the company is strictly insolvent.

If on the other hand there are no further claim payments due to be made, the value of the remaining assets is a measure of the company's strength.

Step 6 Repeat process 1,000 times (say) from the start, to build up a distribution of possible values of the strength of the company. The proportion of the occasions when assets prove inadequate will enable an estimate to be made of the probability of ruin.

## 6. Practical Implications

In the previous sections, we set out the algorithm for the application of the model which we advocate and four assumptions which would have to be made. In this section we consider the practical implications of those assumptions.

The first assumption which is required is a probability distribution of future claim payments by time and amount. For conventional life assurance business, this would be the equivalent of the mortality table. The amounts payable will be fixed and the timing of the payments relatively predictable. Traditionally, little regard has been paid to the variation inherent in such data. In the past, a conservative approach was used in applying this data, with the consequence that profit margins have been very comfortable. Increasing competition in the marketplace has led to a revision of these attitudes and, as a result, pressure on profit margins.

Similar considerations apply in pensions business. Again, the timing and amount of the payments will be relatively predictable, though there will be some variation. The principal source of this variation will be fluctuations in the rate of inflation and particularly the rate of earnings inflation. Wise (1984) has shown how this may be treated in a stochastic way.

For general business, the modelling process is more complicated. The uncertainty about future cash outflows in respect of liabilities, both reported and unreported, exists in two dimensions, the amount of payment and the time at which that payment is made. The degree of uncertainty for either dimension may well be significantly different for individual classes of business.

Account also needs to be taken of inflation. We suggest therefore that what is required in this instance therefore is a bivariate distribution of cash flows by time and amount. This is a difficult process to model but Reid (1978) suggests one possible approach and Daykin et al (1985) another.

The second assumption that requires to be made is the opening asset portfolio. This will need to distinguish between fixed interest securities and equity type investments. For fixed interest securities, details will be required of the nominal amount held, the coupon rate and maturity dates (if any). For equity type investments, details will be required of market values at the valuation date, together with current yields and rate of dividend.

There is also required a set of decision rules defining future strategy for re-investment and dis-investment. These could be relatively straight-forward, for example, buying or selling in proportion to current market values or aiming to maintain the initial asset mix. More complex strategies could involve reference to the relationship between liabilities and shareholders' funds or relating the strategy to the performance of the different types of assets. More than one set of such decision rules may be identified, in order to test the sensitivity of the model to different investment strategies. Dickinson and Roberts (1984) for example have suggested that conventional investment strategies might not be the most optimal and the model would be used to investigate such propositions.

The final set of assumptions relates to the models for predicting the income and capital values of the assets. For equity type investments, we require future prices, dividends and yields. A suitable model might be that proposed by Wilkie (1984). For fixed interest securities, the model must enable us to predict the selling price where the security has to be sold before maturity. Wilkie has also proposed a model for undated Government Bonds. This could be extended to dated bonds fairly easily by making assumptions about redemption yields and, yield the curve, as has been done by Daykin et al (1985).

An important aspect of this model is that it forces management to think about the future behaviour of variables which are the essential dynamics of its business. In addition, the output of the model leads to explicit rather than implicit measures of financial strength. Hence, it is possible to test the variation in different sets of assumptions. For example it may be important for management to understand the differing degrees of uncertainty associated with various investment strategies.

But the most important feature of the approach which we advocate is that it requires the cash flows relating to both assets and liabilities to be modelled and their interaction considered.

Whilst the specific models that we have proposed in this section may be felt to be inappropriate, such a criticism does not question the validity of the basic concept. Indeed, there will be aspects of the models where complete specification is not possible. In such circumstances, the approach adopted enables the decision makers to investigate the consequences of different options before choosing one strategy or another.

## 7. Examples

In this section of the paper, we set out a number of examples to illustrate the algorithm which was outlined in the previous section. As a matter of deliberate policy, we have chosen simple examples, in order to demonstrate the principles of the method in operation.

Our first example is one that has already been published by Daykin et al (1985). This paper describes the work of the Institute of Actuaries' General Insurance Solvency Working Party, of which both the authors of the current paper are also members. The example refers to the run-off of a general insurance portfolio. The assumptions required by the model are as follows:

A1 The probability distribution of outstanding claims. The Company is assumed to write six classes of business, three short-tailed and three long-tailed. The volume of business in each class is assumed to be such as will require equal reserves at the end of the year in which business is written. The claims are assumed to be settled in accordance with the following run-off patterns, suggested for illustrative purposes by Abbott, et al (1981), and shown in Table 2 overleaf.

**Table 2**

| Duration from Year of Origin | Short-tailed (Percent) | Long-tailed (Percent) |
|---|---|---|
| 0 | 61.2 | 5.6 |
| 1 | 24.1 | 25.3 |
| 2 | 5.2 | 18.7 |
| 3 | 3.7 | 13.2 |
| 4 | 2.7 | 10.4 |
| 5 | 2.2 | 7.9 |
| 6 | 0.9 | 6.4 |
| 7 | - | 4.6 |
| 8 | - | 3.8 |
| 9 | - | 3.0 |
| 10 | - | 1.1 |

Apart from the effect of inflation, the actual outstanding claims settled in each year in respect of each year of origin were assumed to be distributed about the estimate of outstanding claims in accordance with a log normal distribution, with a mean equal to the estimate and standard deviation of 30% of the outstanding claims estimate. It was assumed that, when the reserves were set, an expected inflation rate of 5% was used. The reserves were not discounted.

A stochastic inflation model was employed, based on that proposed by Wilkie (1984). The development of the model is described in Wilkie's paper. One of the assumptions required by the model is an expected rate of inflation and this was taken to be 5%.

A2 The distribution of the present asset portfolio.
The opening asset portfolio is assumed to be 115% of total liabilities. The liabilities were assumed to be covered half by cash and half by Government securities. The excess of assets over liabilities was assumed to be invested in ordinary shares.

A3 Investment Strategy.
The strategy assumed was that equities are sold first, then Government securities, with cash being utilised last of all. Where there was an excess of income over expenditure, this was held in cash.

A4 Model for determining Investment Values.
The model employed was that proposed by Wilkie (1984) for Government securities and ordinary shares. Although there is no specific provision within this model for cash as an investment, it was assumed that the return on cash for any year is the yield obtainable on Government securities at the start of the year less one percentage point, since the returns on cash deposits are likely to be closely correlated to interest rates in general.

The simulation shows the ultimate net worth, once the business concerned has run off. When the value of the company's assets prove insufficient, insolvency occurs. Where this happens prior to completion of simulation the company is treated as holding negative cash. The results of the simulation are shown in Table 3 overleaf.

This distribution shows that the expected net worth under these assumptions is about 37% of the initial outstanding claims, compared to an initial margin of 15%. Hence, it tells something about the expected return on capital under this scenario. However, the mean ultimate net worth does not, in isolation, convey much information about capital adequacy. For this, we need to have regard to the dispersion of outcomes from the simulation model.

It can be seen that, of the 5,000 simulations undertaken, 29 resulted in an insolvency. A judgement now has to be made whether the resulting probability of ruin of 0.58% is regarded as appropriate. If it is not, then the model may be further employed in order to determine the amount of capital that is required to support the business in order to obtain a specified probability of ruin.

Essentially, the approach being employed in the foregoing example involves specifying the amount of capital at the outset and employing the model to determine a range of possible outcomes for the capital remaining when the liabilities have been run off.

**Table 3**

| Remaining Assets as % of initial outstanding claims | Number of cases out of 5000 simulations |
|---|---|
| Less than 0 | 29 |
| 0-10 | 65 |
| 10-20 | 309 |
| 20-30 | 992 |
| 30-40 | 1576 |
| 40-50 | 1438 |
| 50 and Over | 591 |
| | 5000 |

However, this is not the only possible approach. Particularly in cases where liabilities are being run off to extinction, an equally valid approach is to stipulate an amount of closing capital required, say zero, and use the model to determine the distribution of opening capital. A possible method would involve the following steps:

(1) Determine an amount of opening capital in some random manner.

(2) Perform the simulation process.

(3) If the closing capital is arbitrarily close to zero, record the amount of opening capital. If not, return to Step 1.

(4) Repeat steps (1) - (3) until a specified number of simulation results have been recorded.

This is the approach used in the following example, taken from pensions business. The required assumptions are as follows:

A1 Liabilities are determined by reference to the following simplified demographic model, taken from the paper by Wise (1984) as follows:

(1) Minimum entry age is 45 and retirement age is 65.
(2) Probability of reaching retirement age is 100%.
(3) Term of pension payments is 10 years certain.

The rate of inflation is measured by the RPI each year is derived from the Wilkie model to which reference has already been made. The rate of increase in earnings is precisely 1.5% more than the increase in the RPI. All pensions in payment increase at a fixed 3% per annum, in accordance with the rules of the scheme.

A2 Present asset portfolio.
This is assumed to be 50% Government securities and 50% ordinary shares.

A3 Investment strategy.
Where re-investment is necessary, the amount available is divided equally between Government securities and ordinary shares. Similarly, where disinvestment is necessary, the amount to be realised is raised equally from Government securities and ordinary shares.

A4 Model for determining investment values.
The model is that described by Wilkie (1984).

The results of the simulation are shown in Figure 1 overleaf.

From this it can be seen that the expected level of capital required is 702. Again, this does not mean much in isolation but in practice could be usefully compared with the actual amount of capital being held. For capital adequacy purposes, what is important is the distribution of outcomes and a striking feature is the relative variability exhibited in the histogram. The standard deviation is, in fact, 245. From the histogram we can see that to achieve a probability of ruin smaller than 1%, opening capital of 1500 is required.

A similar approach is obviously applicable to life business. In this example, we consider a block of 10-year non-profit endowment assurances. Premium rates are based on the assumption that expenses are fixed at 20% and an interest rate of 6% per annum net. The assumptions required by the model are as follows:

A1 The probability distribution of future claims payments is determined by a Poisson distribution which approximates to the A.67/70 ult mortality table.

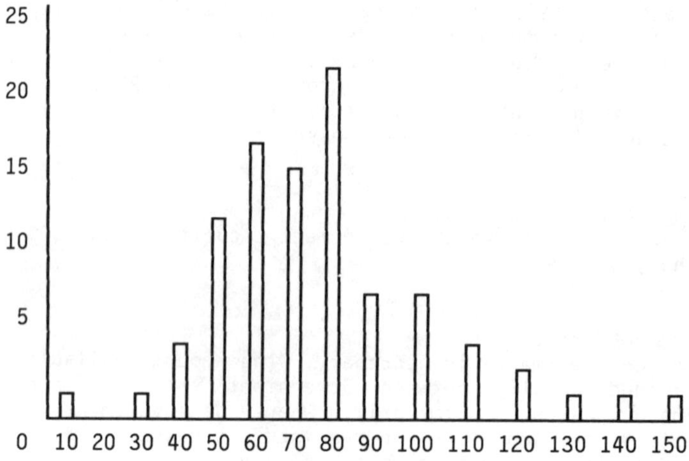


Class Intervals(10's)

Mean 702, Standard Deviation 245

Figure 1

**Distribution of Original Capital for Pension Business**

Assumptions A2, A3 and A4 are the same as those employed in the pensions example. The results of the simulation are shown in Figure 2 overleaf.

We stress once again that we have deliberately chosen simple examples to demonstrate our method in operation. The models themselves are relatively unimportant. What is important is that the method provides a result in the form of a distribution, based on assumptions relating to the individual company under consideration, and provides the facility to explore the results to be expected under different scenarios.

## 8. Reporting on Financial Evaluation of an Insurance Company

In this section, we suggest the form of report which could be the output of the approach we have advocated to the evaluation of an insurance company. An example of such a report for general insurance is included as an appendix to this paper.

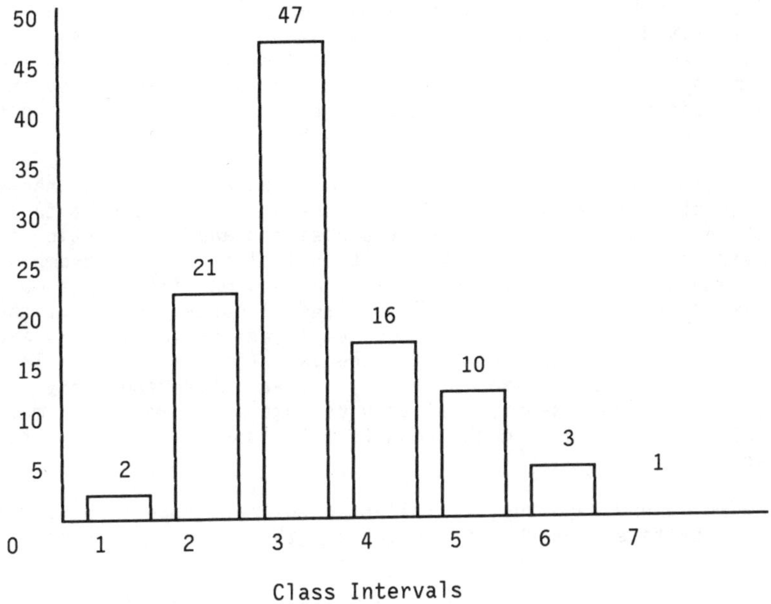


Mean 2.73, Standard Deviation 1.098

Figure 2

**Distribution of Original Capital for Life Business**

The format of a report would need to start by stating the assumptions that have been made. In Section 5 of this paper, we set out the four basic types of assumptions that would be necessary. In the report, the details of these assumptions would need to be set out together with other important assumptions, such as inflation, where appropriate. In many cases, this involves the use of some type of stochastic model. In such instances the model must be described and the parameters set out so that the user of the report can form a judgement on them. The data which has been employed must also be summarised, possibly on a computer tape.

The results of the simulation exercise must then be summarised. Effectively, this involves making probability statements about the future financial strength of the company. There should also be some sort of commentary by the professional person, whether accountant or actuary, who has prepared the report.

In the UK for life and pension business some of these assumptions are listed. However, there is no account taken of the stochastic nature of the business and no attention is paid to alternative investment policies. For example, Schedules 4 and 5 of the returns which a UK life office must make to the Department of Trade and Industry set out the valuation basis which has been employed by the actuary and summarises the data upon which the valuation is based. This allows the supervisor, or any other interested party, to employ his own assumptions to undertake his own approximate valuation and compare the results with those of the appointed actuary.

We would envisage that a similar approximate assessment could be undertaken by the recipient of the report which we are outlining.

There would be clear benefits in such a form of reporting to all those who are interested in the future progress of the company. The ability to undertake an independent check in the way described would be important to all such parties. The shareholder, for example, would have important information to enable his to form a judgement on the probable future performance of his investment. The policyholder and supervisor will be able to form judgments on the probability of the company remaining solvent in the foreseeable future.

The discipline exerted by the ability to undertake such an independent check would be an important part in maintaining the credibility of such a report. However, we must not allow ourselves to be carried away with the notion that such reports would solve all the problems which are inherent in financial reporting. The purpose of financial reports is to provide decision makers with information which is relevant to the decisions which they have to make. The decision itself, whether it is a shareholder deciding to dispose of an investment or a supervisor withdrawing a company's licence because of impending insolvency, is still a question of judgement. This is inevitably so, because such decisions have to be made in a situation of partial knowledge. There are certain aspects of the future which can never be foreseen.

A good example of this is the asbestosis claims which have been hitting the market in recent years. Nevertheless, we feel that our approach will result in a significant improvement in the quality of financial information available to decision makers.

A report of this type is capable of adaptation to a number of different tasks. It can be used by management to establish the capital requirements of different lines of business. It can be used by outside analysts to assess a company's performance and financial position. It can be used by the supervisor to assess the solvency of companies for which he is responsible. In the following sections, we consider such applications in more detail.

## 9. Financial Management of an Insurance Company

The method which we have advocated in this paper is applicable to life, pensions and general insurance. Since it is concerned with the essential dynamics of the business, it is ideally suited to use by the management of the company. Decisions which the management will have to make, such as which lines of business to emphasise or their future investment strategy, are issues which can be explored using the type of model which we have described.

For example, Daykin et al (1985) have shown that the amount of capital required is very much dependent on the type of asset held. For an otherwise fixed set of standard assumptions, they achieved the results shown in Table 4 overleaf.

The model which we have described allows management to explore different investment strategies with a view to evaluating the return on capital available and the associated degree of risk.

It needs to be emphasised, however, that, in making financial management decisions, we are no longer concerned with the static situation of a company's assets and liabilities at a particular point in time and how these will run off. In other words, we are concerned with the future cash flows not only from the business currently on the company's books but also with the business that it will write in future.

An important aspect which is not of direct concern to the supervisor but which will be vitally important to management is the role of capital in such decisions. Capital is available as a buffer against future variability.

**Table 4**

**Required Margin (as % of outstanding claims)**

| Initial Asset Distribution | Probability of Ruin 1/100 | 1/1000 |
|---|---|---|
| 100% cash | 5% | 20% |
| 100% government securities | 20% | 35% |
| 100% ordinary shares | 45% | 75% |

It is the function of management to deploy the capital available in the optimal manner. Hence the return on capital, and the associated degree of risk, are key items of information in making such decisions.

So far, we have concerned ourselves only with existing business on the books. To model a company which remains open to new business, certain additional assumptions are required. We need to estimate the volumes of business to be written in the future and the associated claims experience. We also have to consider to what extent, if any, the assumptions A1 to A4 concerning cash flows arising from the existing assets and liabilities new business to be changed when applied to assets and liabilities arising from the need to be written. These assumptions can then be overlaid on those made in respect of the existing business and the modelling process carried out as before. The model is structured to allow different sets of assumptions to be evaluated.

It is not the intention that assumptions are made for extended periods into the future. To do so would give meaningless results. Rather, the modelling process should become integrated into the management control cycle of the company. The model provides the information to enable the appraisal value of the company's business to be determined. The actual results of trading can be compared with those used in the model. As a result of this, the assumptions can be updated, the model run again and the cycle can restart. The link with the profit testing approach nowadays employed is life assurance is obvious (Goford 1985).

Capital is required because there is a probability of ruin associated with any given block of business. The similarity between life and non-life business in their need for capital was pointed out by Benjamin (1980).

The model will provide a probability distribution of the outcomes involved. This will enable the degree of risk to be gauged. By breaking the business down into homogenous blocks, the relative riskiness of different parts of the business can be assessed. Further, the impact of different scenarios can be explored.

For each additional block of business that is written, there will need to be an increment in the minimum capital required. The model can be used to determine what this amount should be, given a stipulated probability of ruin. Further, it may be used to determine the amount by which the capital used to support a given block of business is likely to grow over a period and this the likely return on capital.

Hence, for each individual line of business, management will have information about both risk and return, both necessary for decisions on the allocation of capital.

An important feature of the model which we have advocated is its probablistic nature. This introduced the additional dimension of variability into the results which from the output of the model. It has been seen that this is of key importance in making decisions about the allocations of capital. It does, however, require that management is willing and able to interpret data presented in the form of probability statements. The presentation and interpretation of data in this form is a subject to which comparatively little attention has been devoted.

There are, however, some examples in the literature, e.g. Coutts and Devitt (1980), Devitt (1982). Nevertheless, more attention needs to be paid to how such data should be presented and communicated to management.

## 10. Solvency and the Supervisor

The function of the supervisor is to regulate the insurance industry in such a way that consumers are protected from potential insolvencies of life, pension and general insurers. The supervisor is consequently concerned with a special case of the assessment of the capital adequacy of insurers. Hence, the approach which we advocate is clearly relevant to the problem that the supervisor must address.

The following sections investigate solvency as an integrated approach. However, the actual examples are only drawn from a general insurance scenario.

The traditional approach to solvency involves looking at the balance sheet, to ascertain the extent to which assets exceed liabilities. However, such an approach takes a deterministic approach to the amount and timing of the cash flows in respect of both assets and liabilities. It is our firm conviction that this approach is incorrect. The assets and liabilities in the balance sheet represent a valuation of future cash flows. These cash flows are uncertain both in their amount and their timing. They therefore have to be modelled in a stochastic way. The approach we advocate is similar to that of Coutts et al (1984) and Daykin et al (1985).

The objective of the insurance supervisor is to avoid, as far as possible, the companies under his supervision from becoming unable to meet their commitments. The risk of this happening arises from the uncertainty in relation to the amount and timing of the future cash flows of those companies. It is for this reason that the supervisor requires a margin by which assets must exceed liabilities. The fact that such a margin no longer exists enables the supervisor to be given early warning of the impending inability to meet commitments and therefore to arrange for the appropriate action to be taken.

reasons

However, the practical realities of the situation dictate that there will inevitably be a time delay between the submission of returns to the supervisor and the end of the period to which they relate. The traditional view of solvency, because it is concerned with assets and liabilities at a point in time, is inadequate for the assessment of solvency. It is necessary for account to be taken of future new business, as Pentakainen and Rantala (1982) have agreed.

We have argued that the financial strength of a company may be measured using stochastic models of future cash flows and simulation techniques. It is necessary to demonstrate the relevance of such an approach to the insurance supervisor. In the first case, it is important to note that the supervisor will be in possession of information relating to the whole of the industry, through aggregation of the returns made by individual companies. In one sense, therefore, he has the macro-economic view. The returns of an individual company, on the other hand, have the micro-economic view, since they relate to one enterprise only. Important information may be gathered by examining the relationship between the macro-economic and the micro-economic. The supervisor will be able to establish the deviation views of the individual company's return from that of the industry as a whole and hence judge where he needs to act.

The position which existed in 1974, when many companies were shown under the prevailing legislation to be technically insolvent, would not have arisen if a cash flow approach had been employed.

Daykin et al (1985) argue that the appropriate asset margin requirements for different companies could differ considerably according to the nature of the business written and the investments held. A solvency system which does not take this into account is clearly defective. A full application of the simulation approach to establishing solvency standards would imply that each company's solvency margin should be separately assessed. This would necessitate a suitably qualified professional person within each company who could perform this function.

We envisage that the return to the supervisor should contain a detailed report on the company's solvency of the form described in Section 8. This will therefore include the following.

(1) Detailed data relating to the company's asset portfolio and the distribution of its liabilities.

(2) The assumptions and parameters employed in the evaluation of the company's financial strength.

(3) A detailed account of the models used to project the future cash inflows from assets and cash outflows for liabilities.

(4) A summary of the data output from the models, showing the inter-action of assets and liabilities and the impact of different investment strategies.

(5) A professional interpretation by a suitably qualified person of the results obtained.

Some of these points are already necessary in the UK for life and pension reports. However, even for these reports there are major omissions.

There are a number of important consequences of this approach. Firstly, it will provide a comprehensive profile of the company's financial strength, in a way which is not available from the present conventional returns. Secondly, it will take account of the fact that the solvency margin which a company reports in its returns is not a deterministic quantity, but behaves in a stochastic fashion. Hence, it needs to be reported in terms of probability statements, rather than point estimates.

The position of small or new companies demands consideration. Such companies will be in possession of either no data whatsoever or insufficient data on which to draw up a report of the type envisaged. In such cases, we would see there being extensive consultation with the supervisor. This would enable appropriate data to be made available based on the macro-economic picture which the supervisor has assembled. It would also be possible for advice to be given on the selection of appropriate models to use for the simulation process.

## 11. Future Research

The approach which we have advocated in this paper is at an early stage of development. There are still many problems which have yet to be resolved. The purpose of this section is to identify some of those problems and indicate where further research is necessary.

A major problem is the availability of data in the form in which it is required. Our experience suggests for example that not many companies could readily produce an analysis of cash flows in respect of claims, analysed by amount and time. The provision of such data is of course not without cost. It is necessary to demonstrate that the benefits to be obtained in providing this data outweigh the costs involved. However, the point must be made that we live in the computer age. More importantly, computers are increasingly being used not only for high volume processing tasks but also for the provision and analysis of data for management purposes. Our approach to the assessment of the financial strength of a company should have the benefit that it leads to better understanding by management of the dynamics of its business. It should also be borne in mind, when we refer to the provision of data, for example to the insurance supervisor, that this data need not necessarily be provided in the form of hard copy.

The essence of the approach which we have advocated is that it is based on stochastic simulation models. In the case of the models required for cash outflows in respect of liabilities, the methodology for life and pensions business is well established. This is not so, however, in the case of general business, where the methodology is seriously under-developed. Considerable work needs to be done here. The Working Party whose work is reported in Daykin et al (1985) have produced a version of the model which can be run on a personal computer which, it is hoped, will encourage research in this area. In addition, the inter-action of asset and liability models requires more attention.

On the asset side, there is also need for work to be done. We have been able to take advantage of the pioneering work of Professor Wilkie in this respect, but his research has related primarily to equities and undated Government Bonds and is also concerned with time scales that are appropriate to life rather than non-life business. There is need, therefore, for more research into models of returns on other types of assets and for techniques which are suitable for the time scales involved in general business.

Traditional financial reports are based on point estimates and therefore assume that the underlying data is deterministic. It is characteristic of the method which we advocate that the underlying variables are in fact probabilistic. It is for this reason that we suggest that the most appropriate form for reporting the results is that of probability statements. Because such statements represent a departure from the norm, managers accustomed to conventional financial reports will find them difficult to interpret. There is need for research, therefore, into ways of presenting such probabilistic information in a way which is meaningful to the layman.

An important characteristic of international general insurance activities which we have ignored is that they are carried on in many currencies. This creates many problems for management, for example in the matching of assets and liabilities and the possibilities for hedging. There is an obvious analogy between the concept of matching here and that which we have discussed in the context of investments. However, very little work has been done, as far as we are aware, in the area of modelling currency fluctuations and further research is obviously necessary here.

Perhaps the major omission in our work is the subject of reinsurance. This was intentional on our part, because we feared that the complex nature of the subject could obscure our underlying message. Nevertheless, it has to be admitted that reinsurance has a major impact on the financial results of an insurance company and it is an issue that therefore has to be addressed. However, its complexity is such that it really merits a paper of its own.

As far as outward reinsurance is concerned, this is comparatively easy to model at least for companies transacting personal lines business.

It should not be too difficult to take account of a company's reinsurance protection when modelling the cash flows in respect of liabilities. The major uncertainty for which it is difficult to make provision is the security of the reinsurers who are providing the protection.

The real problems arise when the question of inward reinsurance is considered. The difficulties are caused by the paucity of information and the volatility of the variables concerned. So far as we are aware, there is no-one who has provided any sort of satisfactory answer to the modelling of this type of business. In addition, there are the difficulties created by occurrences exemplified by the current developments in respect of asbestosis. Once again, it is clear that considerable work is required in this area.

Another factor which we have glossed over is the impact of tax. Once again, there was the danger that the complexities this would impart would obscure the underlying message. However, it is a factor of critical importance in the real world, not least because of its impact on investment strategy and cash flow.

Finally another area where we have barely scratched the surface is that of return on capital. The literature on capital adequacy focuses almost entirely on the amount of capital required. However, capital decisions are management decisions and it is the function of management to deploy resources in such a way as to maximise the return on them. There is, therefore, considerable scope for further work in this area.

## 12. Acknowledgements

We would like to thank numerous colleagues for the help in fashioning these arguments, in particular the late Bobby Beard, who planted the embryo of these ideas. We would also like to thank Mrs Claire Rogers for her patience and willingness in helping us prepare innumerable drafts of this paper. Finally, we would like to thank Geoffrey Bernstein for his assistance in the computing work connected with this paper.

## References

The following abbreviations of Journals have been used:
JIA - Journal of the Institute of Actuaries
JSS - Journal of the Students' Society of Actuaries

Abbott WM, Clarke TG and Treen WR 'Some financial aspects of a general insurance company' JIA 108 (1981)

Beard RE 'Some Thoughts on the Solvency of Insurance Companies' Algemene Reinsurance Companies Jubilee Letter No.1 (1964)

Benjamin S 'Profit and other financial concepts in insurance' JIA 103 (1976)

Benjamin S 'Solvency and profitability in insurance' Paper submitted to 21st International Congress of Actuaries (1980)

Boyle PP 'Immunisation under stochastic models of the term structure' JIA 105 (1978)

Coutts SM, and Devitt ER 'Introducing probability statements to the revenue account: confidence limits for outstanding claims' Paper submitted to ASTIN Conference (1981)

Coutts SM, Devitt ERF and Ross GAF 'A probabilistic approach to assessing the financial strength of a general insurance company' Paper submitted to 22nd International Congress of Actuaries (1984)

Cummins JD and Paulson AS 'An Investigation of Fair Rate of Return in Property-Liability Insurance' Massachusetts (1984)

Daykin CD and Bernstein G 'A Simulation Model to examine questions of Solvency in the light of asset and run-off risks' Paper submitted to ASTIN Conference (1985)

Daykin CD, Devitt ER, Khan MR and McCaughan JP 'The Solvency of general insurance companies' JIA 111 (1984)

De Campagne C 'Minimum Standards of Solvency for Insurance Firms - Report of the ad hoc Working party on Minimum Standards of Solvency' OEEC (1961)

Devitt ERF 'The Construction of Probabilistic Accounting Statements for an Insurance Company' Unpublished (1982)

Dickinson GM and Roberts LA 'Capital Management in UK General Insurance Companies' British Insurance Association (1984)

Financial Accounting Standards Board 'Statement of Financial Accounting Concepts No. 1 FASB (1978)

Goford J 'The Control Cycle - Financial Control of a Life Assurance Company' JSS 28 (1985)

Kahane Y 'Solidity, Leverage and the Regulation of Insurance Companies' The Geneva Papers on Risk and Insurance No. 14 December (1979)

Lee TA 'Income and Value Measurement - Theory & Practice' Van Nostrand Rheinhold (1974)

Limb AP (Chairman) 'The Solvency of Life Assurance Companies' Report of Working Party to the Faculty of Actuaries (1984)

Report of the Maturity Guarantees Working Party JIA 107 (1980)

Pentakainen T & Rantala J 'Solvency of Insurers and Equalisation Reserves' Helsinki (1982)

Redington FM 'Review of the principles of Life office valuations' JIA 78 (1952)

Reid DH 'Claims reserves in General Insurance' JIA 105 (1978)

Ryan JP 'An Application of Model Office Techniques to the Solvency Question' Paper submitted to the 21st International Congress of Actuaries (1980)

Ryan JP 'Application of Simulation Techniques to Solvency Testing for a Non-Life Office' Paper submitted to the 22nd International Congress of Actuaries (1984)

Tapeiro CS and Zuckerman D'Optimal Investment Policy of an Insurance Firm' Insurance: Mathematics & Economics Vol. 2 (1983)

Wilkie AD 'A Stochastic Investment Model for Actuarial use' Paper presented to Faculty of Actuaries (1984)

Wise AJ 'The Matching of Assets to Liabilities' JIA 111 (1984).

## APPENDIX

## SAMPLE REPORT ON FIANCIAL STRENGTH OF AN INSURANCE COMPANY

In this Appendix, we illustrate a report on the financial strength of an insurance company, in the format suggested in Section 8 of the paper. The data upon which this report is based is taken from Daykin et al (1985).

### 1. Existing Liabilities and Assets

The company has six classes of business, three classes with an identical short-tailed settlement pattern and three with an identical long-tailed settlement pattern. The volume of business in each class is such as will require equal technical provisions at the end of the year in which the business is written. The amount of business written in past years has remained constant in real terms.

(In practice, details would be given of the amount of the technical provisions for each class of business, together with triangulation data showing past settlement patterns).

Assets are held to the value of 115% of the liabilities. Their initial distribution is as follows:-

| | |
|---|---|
| Cash | $\frac{1}{2}$ L |
| Government Securities | $\frac{1}{2}$ L |
| Ordinary Shares | S |

where L is the amount of assets covering the liabilities, S is the asset margin in excess of the liabilities.

### 2. Assumptions and Parameters

Claims are assumed to be settled in accordance with the following two run-off patterns in Table 5 overleaf.

Table 5

| Duration from year of origin | Proportion of claims amounts settled | |
|---|---|---|
| | Short-tailed | Long-tailed |
| 0 | 61.2% | 5.6% |
| 1 | 24.1 | 25.3 |
| 2 | 5.2 | 18.7 |
| 3 | 3.7 | 13.2 |
| 4 | 2.7 | 10.4 |
| 5 | 2.2 | 7.9 |
| 6 | 0.9 | 6.4 |
| 7 | - | 4.6 |
| 8 | - | 3.8 |
| 9 | - | 3.0 |
| 10 | - | 1.1 |

Technical provisions were set up assuming 5% inflation and without discounting.

The mean rate of future inflation is assumed to be 5%. The initial dividend yield on equities is assumed to be 4% and the initial yield on assets 3.5%.

The future investment strategy is assumed to be one where equities are sold first, then government securities, with cash being used last of all. Reinvestment is assumed to be in cash.

## 3. Models Employed

The claims settled in each accounting year for each year of origin are assumed to be distributed about the estimate of outstanding claims in accordance with a log-normal distribution, with mean equal to the estimate and standard deviation of 30% of the outstanding claims estimate.

Asset values, investment income and inflation are projected using the models proposed by Wilkie (1984), using the parameters he suggests.

The simulation model starts with the existing assets and liabilities as specified and generates a large number of run-off scenarios, assuming the claim settlement distribution and inflation assumptions mentioned above. The values of the assets are assumed to vary in accordance with the investment model.

**Table 6**

| **Remaining assets as % of initial outstanding claims** | **Number of cases out of 5,000 simulations** |
|---|---|
| Less than 0 | 29 |
| 0-10 | 65 |
| 10-20 | 309 |
| 20-30 | 992 |
| 30-40 | 1576 |
| 40-50 | 1438 |
| 50 and over | 591 |
| | 5000 |
| Mean assets remaining (as % of initial outstanding claims) | 36.6% |

Where investment income falls short of simulated out-go assets are realised to meet the liabilities as they fall due. Where investment income exceeds similulated out-go, the excess is reinvested. The decision rules for asset realisation and reinvestment are as stated above. The simulation process continues until either all the liabilities have been paid or when insolvency occurs because the assets are exhausted.

4. **Data Output**

Using the models and assumptions specified above, 5,000 simulations were performed. The results obtained were as follows in table 6 above.

Different initial asset distributions (with unchanged investment strategy) were investigated, with the following results shown in table 7 overleaf.

5. **Professional Opinion**

I have carried out the appropriate tests to satisfy myself that the existing liabilities of the Company and its current holding of assets are correctly stated above.

The assumptions and parameters made are, in my opinion, reasonable and the models employed I consider to be appropriate.

Table 7

| Initial asset Distribution | | | No. of Movements out of 5000 simulations | Mean assets remaining as % of initial outstanding claims |
|---|---|---|---|---|
| Cash | Gilts | Equities | | |
| L+S | | | 2 | 34.8 |
| | L+S | | 113 | 39.8 |
| L | .5S | .5S | 7 | 35.2 |
| .5L+5S | .5L | .5S | 13 | 35.9 |
| .5L | .5L-.5S | .5S | 15 | 36.1 |
| L | | S | 8 | 35.5 |
| | L | S | 117 | 40.4 |
| .5L | | .5L+S | 103 | 39.1 |
| | | L+S | 349 | 59.0 |

The simulations suggest a probability of ruin of 0.5%, which, given that the company is not writing new business, I consider to be acceptable.

The proposed investment strategy is, in my opinion, a reasonable one. The investigation of alternative initial asset distribution suggests that the current distribution is appropriate, in my opinion.

# 2

# CASH FLOW SIMULATION MODELS FOR PREMIUM AND SURPLUS ANALYSIS

Albert S. Paulson and R. Dixit

**Abstract**

This paper summarizes some typical results generated from a set of general cash flow simulation models which were produced to mimic a statutory insurance company operating in a general economic environment. The flows resulting from the underwriting and investment sides of the business are treated in an integrated and dynamic fashin. A large number of economic, company-specific, tax-specific, surplus-specific, and other factors are allowed in these models. Several results concerning the influence of size of underwriting firm, combined ratio, variability of losses, impairment of capital and probability of insolvency are given.

## 1. Introduction

An early and somewhat abstract examination of solvency of an insurance business is embodied in the so-called probability of ruin problem. Suppose a pool of assets is created by an insurer who contributes an initial risk reserve $R \geq 0$, and who receives payments (premiums) uniformly in time. After an interval of time of length t the fund will have had inputs amounting to R+pt. Claims $x_1, x_2, \ldots, x_{N(t)}$ against the fund are made over the interval of time of length t. The $x_i$ are independent with a common severity distribution; the total number of claims N(t) against the fund is random with a frequency distribution which depends on the length of the time interval. At the end of the period of time of length t, the fund contains an asset amount of

$$Z(t) = R + pt - \sum_{j=1}^{N(t)} x_j. \tag{1}$$

A measure of solvency of the fund or the insurer is captured in the probability of ruin index

$$\rho(t,R,G,S,p) = \Pr(Z(t) < 0). \tag{2}$$

This probability clearly depends on the length of the time interval t, the size of the initial reserve, the distribution function of the frequency of claims G, the premium p and the distribution function of claim severity S. Only recently has it become possible to numerically determine $\rho$ for virtually any R,t,G, and S. In addition, it is possible to get numerical estimates of $\rho$ for virtually any R,t, and G when only grouped or ungrouped severity data is available [Paulson and Dixit, 1988, or PD for brevity]. Other quantities of interest are the probability of capital impairment and the probability of profit

$$\Pr(Z(t) < R) \text{ and } \Pr(Z(t) > R),$$

respectively. Given that impairment occurs, the distribution of amount of impairment or proportion of impairment would be of considerable interest. It seems that the algorithm of Heckman and Myers [1983] and the approach of Pentikainen and Rantala [1982] should also be useful in many probability of ruin problems.

The probability of ruin problem takes on a different character if we allow the initial asset reserve R to fluctuate in value over time according to market conditions, such as would be the case for a reserve consisting of common stocks and bonds. If R(t) denotes the asset value of the reserve at time t, then (1) becomes

$$Z^*(t) = R(t) + pt - \sum_{j=1}^{N(t)} x_j. \tag{3}$$

One form of R(t) which has received considerable attention in the literature is a version of the random walk given by

$$R(t) = R + \sum_{j=1}^{M(t)} y_j, \tag{4}$$

where R>0, M(t) is the number of re-valuations of the initial assets up to time t, M(t) has distribution function H, and the $y_j$ are independent with common distribution J. The $x_j$, the $y_j$, M(t), and N(t) are all mutually independent. The number of re-valuations of the initial assets may be on a periodic basis, for example monthly in which case M(t) is deterministic, or random. For model (4), the results of PD [1988] may be readily modified to determine numerically

$$\rho^*(t,R,G,S,H,J,p) = \Pr(Z^*(t) < 0) \tag{5}$$

If for fixed t, E(R(t)) = R, the probability of ruin $\rho^*$ will be greater than $\rho$ when Pr(M(t)>0) = 1, perhaps dramatically so, since there will be intervals of time when R(t) may be small while $\sum_{j=1}^{N(t)} x_j$ may be large, thus swamping out effect of the constant input of operating funds pt.

While the model (5) more realistically embodies the needs of a real-world risk business than (1), it still fails to capture more than a few of the characteristics required for a realistic representation. Even so, $\rho^*$ is already a function of seven variables, some of which are themselves functions which may depend on two or more parameters. And we have not yet even considered other important factors such as interest rates, discount rates, timing of flows, taxes, inflation, etc. Determination of $\rho^*$ by numerical methods is possible in this case, but the addition of additional complexity for the ensurance of realism or the addition of more factors in augmentation to the probability of ruin problem (5), apart from special structural cases, will result in the need to resort to computer simulation in combination with numerical methods to obtain estimates of the probability of ruin. Indeed, realistic versions of the probability of ruin problem are more correctly called solvency problems.

The expression (5) as a function of seven variables provides an immediate glimpse of some major difficulties in examination of issues of solvency. Any realistic model of an insurance business will embody a large number of factors and possibly a large number of timing decisions as well. The large number of resulting variables lead to great difficulties in summarization and communication of the results of a solvency study. Summaries of a marginal nature, i.e., results as a function of one factor only, all others held fixed, are generally unsatisfactory. The presence of a large number of factors allows for a multitude of choices, e.g., investment strategies, and interpretations, e.g., accounting valuations of liabilities. How many choices does one examine in an investigation of solvency? In any sound investigation of solvency it seems necessary to (1) try to keep at a minimum the number and the impact of assumptions made, (2) try to use actual company, industry-wide, etc. data as much as possible, (3) try to identify information that should be incorporated in prospective studies if it is not currently available, and (4) try to effect an integration of salient factors and timing aspects into a cash flow model which faithfully captures the essential character of an insurance firm subject to market and regulatory behavior. Accounting procedures and interpretations can be a source of serious difficulty in an empirical investigation of solvency. It seems that, in some cases at least, market valuations are preferable to accounting valuations but considerable research may be needed to determine in which cases and how this should be done.

We have constructed a number of cash flow-simulation models with a large number of decision points to enable an investigation of a variety of issues centering around solvency and rates of return. The models we have developed are computer-, numeric-, and simulation-based because this is the only combination of techniques that is capable of permitting a realistic investigation of problems concerning solvency. The models allow for extensive complexity in order to produce realism and integration of a large number of factors. In particular, we have allowed for the integration into dynamic models the following features: multiple lines of insurance, multiple investment types, taxes, cohort analysis for one accounting period and cohort analysis over many accounting periods. There are many issues and many structures that are worth investigation, many more than we can address in this paper. We therefore shall concern ourselves only with the presentation of some methodology and an examination of a few cases.

## 2. Framework for Theory and Practice of Forecasting Rates of Return

Our main objective is to integrate the underwriting and financial sides of an insurance business in order to examine premium adequacy, rates of return and, ultimately, solvency.

In many settings the following data will be available by quarter or year, as appropriate: total losses, total expenses, total premiums, dividend payments, individual or grouped loss data, pay-out patterns, premium pay-in patterns, yield curves for various debt instruments, maturity patterns for outstanding claims, the structure of an embedded portfolio, and current portfolio acquisitions.

Suppose that five years of total loss data are available. Figure 1 provides bodily injury liability losses for 1981, 1982, 1983, 1984, 1985(estimated). Suppose also that individual or finely grouped loss data corresponding to the total losses of Figure 1 are also available. First a forecast of the total loss for 1986 is developed by simple linear regression. If L(t) represents the total loss at time t and $L_t$ the observed total loss at time t, we fit

$$L(t) = a+bt+\epsilon_t, \quad t=1,2,\ldots,5 \tag{6}$$

by ordinary least squares to get $\hat{L}(t) = \hat{a} + \hat{b}t$. The estimate of total loss for 1986 is thus $\hat{L}(6)$. The estimates $\hat{L}(6)$ and error structure of this estimate play fundamental roles in determining a fair premium and a fair rate of return and in addressing many issues of solvency. We shall now develop a method for getting at this error structure. The next step is to compute the total loss distribution for each of the years 1981-1985. The non-parametric or the normal powers method of PD [1988] can be used for this purpose. If the sample skewness and sample kurtosis for each of the years 1981-1985 lie within the region of admissible approximation, then the approximate total loss distribution for each year t may be written in terms of the PD [1988] case 4 approximation

$$\frac{z_\beta - E(z)}{\sigma(z)} = y_\beta + \frac{1}{6}\gamma_1(y_\beta^2-1) + \frac{1}{24}\gamma_2(y_\beta^3-3y_\beta) - \frac{1}{36}\gamma_1^2(2y_\beta^3 - 5y_\beta) \, . \tag{7}$$

Given a set of total loss distributions for years one to five, a reasonable forecast for 1986 could be developed from the previous total loss distributions by forecasting the 1 percent point, the 2

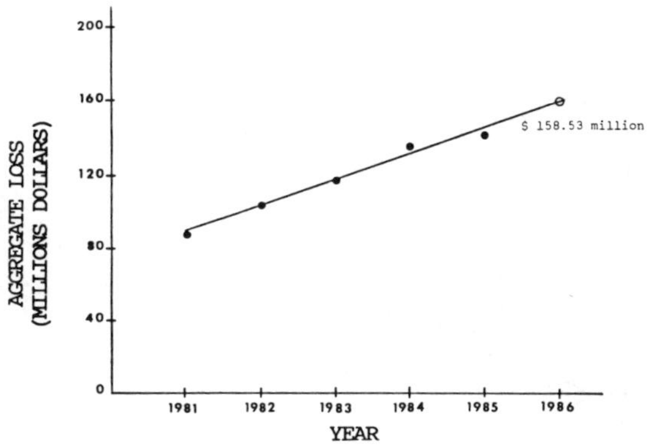


Forecast:

Error = $5.45 million  L(t) = a + bt

c.v. = 3.4 %  a = 75.7 million

b = 138.0 million

FIGURE 1: Total Bodily Injury Liability Losses for 1981 - 85

percent point,..., the 99 percent point. This construction clearly indicates that the forecast of the total loss distribution is uncertain over the entire range of the distribution, as one would expect, since the total loss distribution embodies the uncertainty present in the frequency of loss distribution, severity of loss distribution, the coefficients of the linear model structure, and the linear model itself. A "point" forecast of the total loss distribution in our case is given by

$$z_{\beta,\text{forecast}} = \frac{1}{5}\sum_{j=1}^{5}\left(z_{\beta j}+(6-j)\hat{b}\right). \tag{8}$$

The result of this construction leads to the situation depicted in Figure 2. This figure clearly captures the character of the forecast of the total loss for the 1986 accounting period. The dashed lines show "more or less" the spread of values that the total loss distribution may take on, "more or less" because one more consideration regarding the forecast is still necessary. The spread of values that the total loss may take on is in fact greater than that conveyed by Figure 2. The reason is that, in a forecast of the value of total loss, the variance of the forecast consists of two components, the variance of the sampling distribution of $\hat{L}(6)$ and the variance of the distribution of the total losses

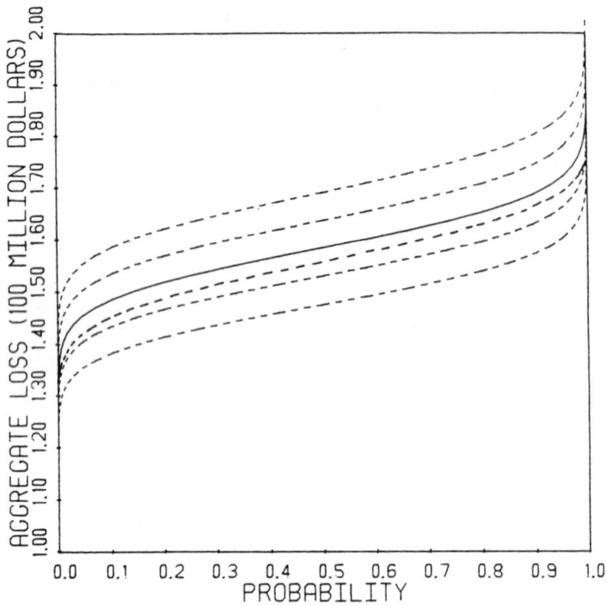


FIGURE 2: Total Loss Profiles For Six Years "Centered" at L(6)

[Neter and Wasserman, 1974, pp. 71-73]. If the spread is greater than Figure 2 may indicate, the element of risk associated with the error of the forecast is not usually allowed for in producing forecasts of internal rate of return or premium requirements. An effective and accurate model for the total loss can be developed as follows. The variance of the point forecast for each $0<\beta<1$ will be

$$\hat{\sigma}^2_{\beta,\text{forecast}} = \hat{\sigma}^2_{\beta}\left\{1 + \frac{1}{n} + \left(\frac{1}{2}(n+1)\right)^2 \Big/ \sum_{t=1}^{n} (t - \tfrac{1}{2}(n+1))^2\right\} \qquad (9)$$

$$\hat{\sigma}^2_{\beta} = \frac{1}{n-2}\sum_{t=1}^{n} (z_{\beta t} - \hat{a}_{\beta} - \hat{b}_{\beta}t)^2, \qquad (10)$$

where $a_\beta$ and $b_\beta$ represent the coefficients for a linear model in the percentiles of the total loss distribution.
Here $n = 5$ and $\hat{a}_\beta$ and $\hat{b}_\beta$ are the least squares estimates of $a_\beta$ and $b_\beta$, $0<\beta<1$. Several approaches for obtaining total loss variations are now possible. The simplest is to ignore the skewness and kurtosis and approximate, for fixed $\beta$, the spread in total loss by a normal variate centered at $z_{\beta,\text{forecast}}$ with variance $\hat{\sigma}^2_{\beta,\text{forecast}}$.

(One could argue that the use of a t variate is the variate is the technically correct approach but such refinement is of second order at most.) A more complex approach is to use the normal powers method again to develop the distribution of variation around $z_{\beta,\text{forecast}}$ for fixed $\beta$. The more complex normal powers approach is approximately a non-parametric procedure and thus almost entirely reflects the character of the data (or information) available for making a forecast. If this forecast is made in the presence of an assumed financial structure encompassing investment behavior, surplus considerations, and timing and structure of cash flows, we can examine the cash flow results to assess a number of solvency and capital impairment issues as well as premium rates.

The methodology of this section may be applied in a wide variety of settings. While the methodology was presented in terms of linear regression, it is clear that linearity is not required. Further, the total losses depicted in Figure 1 have not been adjusted for maturity of development. The total loss, and the corresponding total loss distribution, generally change substantially with maturity of development. Indeed, the total loss distributions for bodily injury liability for years previous to those covered for the example of section 2 exhibit a marked upward change in amount of total loss and an increased spread with increasing maturity, the net result being that the situation was markedly riskier to the underwriter than the original data would have implied. Finally, the character of the total loss distribution depends on the number of losses, i.e., the size of the firm. The bodily injury liability data discussed in the previous section is state-wide data and may be regarded as losses incurred by a firm writing 100% of the state's business. For firms writing any fraction of the state's business, it would be useful to have an index by which to compare the fluctuations in total losses to which the firms are subject.

## 3. Size of Firm: Some Considerations

The coefficient of variation of a firm's total loss distribution is a reasonable index of potential for fluctuation or riskiness although other indexes could be advanced. For example, an index which focuses on the spread of the upper portion of the total loss distribution is somewhat more appealing than the coefficient of variation itself since total loss distributions are almost always skewed to the right. Such a coefficient of variation may be defined as the total loss at the 84th percentile minus the total loss at the 50th percentile all divided by the total loss at the 50th percentile, i.e.

$$\text{c.v.} = (z_{0.84} - z_{0.50})/z_{0.50}.$$

This definition coincides with the usual coefficient of variation when the total loss z is normal. It is more useful, however, in the presence of skewness and kurtosis. Another measure which provides a useful index is the (upper) tail weight measure

$$\tau = \frac{(z_{0.99} - z_{0.50})}{(z_{0.75} - z_{0.50})} \Big/ \frac{(y_{0.99} - y_{0.50})}{(y_{0.75} - y_{0.50})} ,$$

where $y_{\beta}$, $0 \le \beta \le 1$ is the $\beta$th percentile of the normal distribution. Heavy tail distributions have $\tau > 1$; short tail distributions have $\tau < 1$; the normal distribution has $\tau = 1$. The measure c.v. is particularly useful because the more usual variant of it is often used in the financial literature as a measure of risk.

Suppose that the frequency of loss distribution at the statewide level of an insurance line is negative binomial with mean m and variance m(1+m/N*). (This is a very mild assumption; however, with more sophistication even this assumption need not be made. Results based on the weaker assumption would still be similar to those that follow.) Then the empirical characteristic function for the total loss distribution at the statewide level will give

$$\hat{\psi}(u) = (1 - \frac{m}{N*} (\hat{\phi}(u)-1))^{-N*}, \tag{11}$$

where $\hat{\phi}(u)$ is the empirical characteristic function [see PD [1988]. The total loss profile corresponding to (11), together with the 16th, 50th and 84th percentiles is given in Figure 3. Since this characteristic function is infinitely divisible [Lukacs, 1970, Ch. 12, p. 318], total loss distribution of a risk business writing 10% of the total will have empirical total loss characteristic function

$$[\hat{\psi}(u)]^{1/10} = \hat{\psi}_{.10}(u) = \left(1 - \frac{m/10}{N*/10} (\hat{\phi}(u)-1)\right)^{-N*/10} \tag{12}$$

The total loss profile corresponding to (12) will exhibit much more pronounced skewness than that corresponding to (11). The coefficient of variation of the total loss distribution for the 100% firm is 0.013, for the 10% firm it is 0.158; for a 2.5% firm it is 0.373. The 100% firm is clearly much less susceptible to fluctuations than the 10% firm; the 10% firm is much less susceptible to fluctuation than the 2.5% firm. Moreoever, not only does the coefficient of variation increase with decreasing size of firm (relative to state totals), but the (positive) skewness also increases with decreasing size so the smaller firms are relatively more likely to experience total losses in the right hand tail of the total loss distribution which is appropriate for the size of the firm. Thus solvency or stability requirements such as premium to surplus ratio of 2 to 1 will provide less security for a smaller firm than for a larger firm since excursions far from expected are much more likely for the smaller firm than for the larger firm, relatively speaking. Thus, the use of ratios and normalized quantities, common in the insurance business, in the absence of

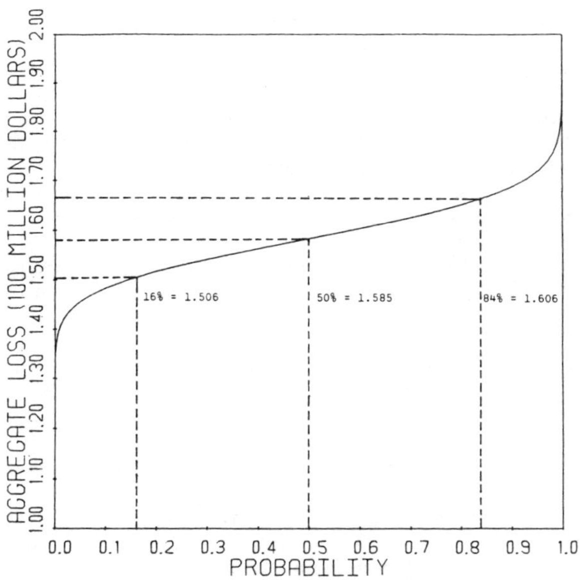


**FIGURE 3: Total Loss Profile for Bodily Injury Liability - Statewide**

additional information may be misleading in many cases.

If size of firm writing a line of business is a determinant of its rate of return or the fluctuation in its rate of return, the determination of fair rate of return across an industry where size of firm varies widely becomes particularly difficult. We shall examine the issues of size, rate of return, probability of capital impairment, and solvency in greater detail in the subsequent sections.

## 4. Flow Models

In order to investigate issues of solvency, rates of return, the setting of premiums, among others, we have developed a number of cash flow models which integrate the underwriting and financial sides of the insurance business. The influence of re-insurance on solvency has not yet been addressed. The cash flow simulation and forecasting models consist of a very extensive set of algorithms. These algorithms are capable of generating far more in the way of results than it is possible to express in this paper. We shall therefore just focus on providing a limited set of results concerning solvency and forecasts of rates of return as functions of underwriting flows and investment flows. Many of the results will focus on surplus flows and will be expressed in terms of the internal rate of return, a convenient index of the joint magnitude and timing of cash flows. The results reported here are indicative of those which can be obtained from use of the cash flow simulation models.

The flow models incorporate a wide variety of financial and operational inputs. Manipulations with claim severity data, claim frequency data, forecasts, loss distributions and the like are accomplished outside the flow models; only the required quantities are input into the flow model.

The major charateristics of the flow models are described immediately below. Flow diagrams are provided in the working paper of Paulson and Dixit [1986]. The details of the computations will not be given here. The flow models:

1) are capable of performing single or multiple year cohort analyses.
2) are capable of representing the behavior of up to seven lines of business.
3) are capable of determining the influence of any number of investment types.
4) impose taxation marginally as appropriate on all investment types and all underwriting operations. Tax carry-forwards and carry-backs are not presently within the capabilities of the models.
5) allow for evolution, or drift, of value of assets through time.
6) allow for a wide variety of surplus and asset scenarios.
7) incorporate as an input empirically developed pay-out and pay-in patterns. Theoretical patterns are easily substituted
8) permit a variety of timing scenarios.
9) summarize the cash flows of underwriting and investment in terms of the internal rate of return.
10) allow for cohort analyses subject to initial conditions concerning state of business by line, subject to embedded portfolio of investments, and evolution to a new investment portfolio.

A number of difficulties arose in the construction and evolution of the flow models. Insurance exists primarily because events rarely occur as expected. However, many flow models are based on expected losses, expected premiums, expected flows, etc. in spite of the fact that there must be substantial non-expected and random components on both the underwriting and financial sides of the insurance business. The introduction of random and non-expected structure into a flow model of the business leads to great difficulty in

1) specifying how surplus should be handled. What should the timing patterns of surplus contributions be? Should surplus be returned dollar for dollar as liabilities are liquidated? Or proportionately in terms of the payout pattern? In a long term cohort study, should additional surplus be added as required? or quarterly? or yearly? Random timing of surplus additions

or withdrawals leads to extremely intricate cash flow algorithms.

2) determining to what extent accounting practices should be built into the flow models.
3) determining the extent to which operational realism should be imbedded in the flow models. This is a delicate modeling question.
4) bounding the number of models and situations to be examined. There are an enormous number of reasonable models that can and should be examined. Many of these flow models will require separate programs.
5) communicating results. There are large number of structural factors and timing factors which are worthy of detailed analysis, singly and in combination. How does one summarize and present the results of the responses of, say, internal rate of return as a function of all interesting factors? This issue is further complicated by the random character of the responses which leads to the necessity for replication. We have found considerable success in use of response surface techniques but these require that responses of interest be expressed in empirical equation format, sometimes a disadvantage for communication of results.
6) evolving a future business, economic, and underwriting environment. There are a variety of ways of imposing an economic environment on the cash flow models. Which way is appropriate? The way in which asset values are evolved is crucial in the evaluation of solvency so some approach, possibly the random walk model (see also Ibbotson and Singuefield, 1982) for evolution in value of assets, must be adopted. Equity valuation is particularly difficult since gains or losses are not really well-defined until realized.
7) constructing models which are controversy-free. Given the great complexity of solvency issues, the wide range of accounting interpretations, the unbounded number of investment strategies, even useful models can be subject to considerable criticism. There can be no optimal models.

We now indicate the process of forecasting internal rates of return for the bodily injury liability line discussed earlier and whose relevant data is given in Figures 1-3. Suppose that an analysis of statewide bodily injury liability data results in a forecast of a mean 194,636 losses for the year 1986. Suppose further that the frequency of loss distribution is negative binomial and that the coefficient of variation of the frequency distribution is 0.05, i.e., $m = 194{,}636$ and $N^* = 400$ [see PD, 1988]. The 5% coefficient of variation represents a relatively innocuous condition for a situation in which an average of approximately 194,000 claims are expected to be incurred, i.e., 194,000 $\pm$ 20,000 claims with probability about 95%. Nevertheless, it is instructive to determine the influence of such an asumption on the result of the simulation and forecast. In actuality, such an assumption need not be made since information systems should be in place to capture the relevant statistical or accounting information. Based on past loss data, we forecast that the mean size of the bodily injury liability claim will be \$813; the standard deviation of the severity of loss distribution will be \$14,738; the skewness coefficient will be 187; the coefficient of kurtosis will be 61,190. These summary statistics imply that the severity distribution is very heavy tailed and embodies considerable risk well beyond that which would be characterized by coefficient of variation or standard deviation measures alone. The Lorenz curve summary, given in Figure 4, provides a clear indication of this. For example, this figure shows that approximately 50% of the total loss is expected to be accounted for by 20% of the claims, approximately 40% of the total loss by 10% of the claims.

While considerable fluctuations in total losses are possible on the underwriting side of the bodily injury liability line, the investment side of the business is also subject to sizeable fluctuations in returns. A proper forecast of rates of return, required premium, probability of ruin, etc. must consider fluctuations in investment return jointly with fluctuations in underwriting results. For example, if a much larger total loss than expected occurs over an underwriting period when investment results are much lower than expected, then the combined result from underwriting and investment could result in severe impairment of capital or insolvency. The probability of this result is not at all remote since, for example, returns on many financial instruments have historically had coefficients of variation well in excess of unity. (For example, the historical per annum return on large common stocks has a coefficient of variation of approximately 2.5 [Ibbotson and Sinquefield, 1982].) Certainty-equivalent cash flow models are simply not capable of capturing the correct interplay and interaction of flows and are very likely to understate the true degree of riskiness in a forecast, even though these models incorporate nominal adjustments for variability, i.e., they are nominally risk-adjusted.

The cash flow simulation models allow for a wide variety of investment strategies. Indeed, they could be used to explore a response surface of returns over many different factors to determine an optimal investment strategy although that is not our purpose here. Our goal is to illustrate the results of the use of the models under a simple investment strategy. Other strategies of interest are the forecast of rates of return under an investment strategy which constrains investments to be made in accordance with a state-wide or industry-wide statutory portfolio.

We have examined the influence of several factors as they influence internal rates of return; these factors are premium to surplus (P/S) ratio, size of firm, loss plus expenses to premium ratio, (L+E)/P, one year cohorts and cohorts consisting of twenty years of business. The flow models operate in the following way.

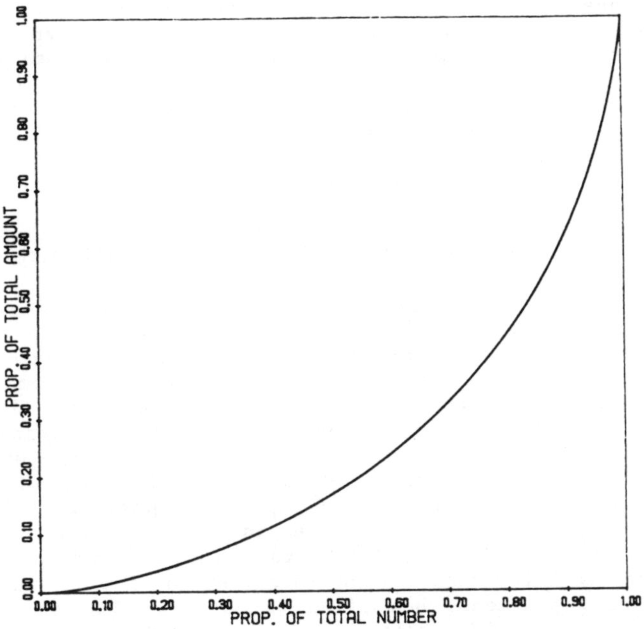


FIGURE 4: Lorenz-type Curve for 194,636 Bodily Injury Liability Claims

1) For the one year cohorts, supporting surplus is put in place at the beginning of each quarter, for four quarters.
2) An estimate of total losses and total loss distribution is available. From this we examine after-tax internal rates of return as a function of loss plus expense to premium ratios. Expenses have been determined in a prior empirical study as a proportion of premium. Expense flows, premium pay-in flows, claim payout flows, and dividend flows have been determined for each line of insurance in a previous empirical study. Tax flows are a function of randomly occurring claims, earned premium flows, expense flows, and investment income flows. The tax flows are determined by the provisions of the 1986 Tax Law.
3) For this paper investment income is determined from the 3 month yield in T-bills, credited quarterly and compounded as appropriate. This risk-free yield is hardly appropriate over the horizon of flow activity but it will suffice for the points to be made.
4) Total losses are developed quarterly from the total loss profiles. We do not make use of the total loss envelope at this time.
5) The structure of (1)-(4) is used for the multi-year cohorts.
6) Surplus is returned in proportion to the satisfaction of liabilities.

Simulations were conducted to determine the influence of size and premium to surplus ratio on internal rate of return for the bodily injury liability line when the loss plus expense to premium ratio was centered around 1.1. The standard error of the forecast is \$5.45 x $10^6$ and the coefficient of variation at the forecast value for the state-wide firm (at $\beta = 0.5$) is

$$\hat{\sigma}_{.5,\text{forecast}}/z_{.5} = 0.034 ,$$

not an insignificant quantity when compared with the coefficient of variation of the total loss distribution at the 100% firm level, namely 0.013.

Thus the use of a total loss forecast envelope may make a difference in assessment of premium adequacy and solvency. Table 1 summarizes the results concerning mean internal rate of return, standard deviation of rate of return, and the fraction of impairments and technical ruin. The determination of the internal rate of return at the statewide level (i.e., a 100% of-state-firm) leads at P/S = 2 to an after (federal and state) tax internal rate of return of 5.50%. The standard deviation of this rate of return is 2.18% so that some impairment of capital is possible. Indeed, one impairment was actually experienced in this case as may be seen from the table. At P/S = 4, the average internal rate of return has increased to 6.18% with a standard deviation of 4.13% while the percentage of impairments has risen to 4.9%%. Thus there is a greater risk to the policyholder and the statewide "firm" at P/S = 4 and this is reflected in the higher rate of return.

For a firm which underwrites 2.5% of the total statewide business the mean rates of return for fixed P/S ratio are higher than for the 10% firm, again reflecting greater expected returns in exchange for the greater risk due to size of underwriting firm. At 2.5% size and P/S = 4 we find that 2.8% of the firms can expect to experience ruin. However, the expected internal rate of return at 2.5% size and P/S = 4 is about 112% with a standard deviation of about 600%. The internal rate of return distribution for this case is heavily skewed right with some very large positive internal rates of return. Table 2 provides information concerning the mean and standard deviations of the amount of impairment for the ratio of losses plus expenses to premium, i.e., k = (L+E)/P and P/S = 2, for the 100% and the 10% firm. At k = 1.2 the impairments are becoming undesirably sizeable.

The results of this simulation are presented in Tables 1,2, and 3. Different simulations under different factor settings produce results with essentially the same character. The conclusions of the study are that

(1) as P/S increases, the mean rate of return increases. The variability of the rate of return also increases and thus signifies a riskier capital structure for the line of business.
(2) the mean rate of return is a rapidly decreasing function of k = (L+E)/P.

TABLE 1.

Average internal rates of return, standard deviation of rates of return, percent of cohorts for which insurer's capital was impaired, and percent of cohorts for which insurer was impaired or ruined. Number of cohorts put at risk is 1000. The size of firms considered were 100% (statewide), 10% and 2.5%. The line of insurance considered is Bodily Injury Liability.

Size = 100%

| | | | | |
|---|---|---|---|---|
| P/S | 1.0 | 2.0 | 3.0 | 4.0 |
| IRR (mean after tax) | 5.18 | 5.50 | 5.83 | 6.18 |
| IRR (S.D.) | 1.13 | 2.18 | 3.18 | 4.13 |
| Impaired | 0 | 0.1 | 2.5 | 4.9 |

Size = 10%

| | | | | |
|---|---|---|---|---|
| P/S | 1.0 | 2.0 | 3.0 | 4.0 |
| IRR (mean after tax) | 5.89 | 6.51 | 8.03 | 10.19 |
| IRR (S.D.) | 3.48 | 7.25 | 13.38 | 17.51 |
| Impaired | 5.7 | 16.8 | 23.2 | 27.6 |

Size = 2.5%

| | | | | |
|---|---|---|---|---|
| P/S | 1.0 | 2.0 | 3.0 | 4.0 |
| IRR (mean after tax) | 6.29 | 10.03 | 20.32 | 111.59 |
| IRR (S.D.) | 7.13 | 16.85 | 53.61 | 598.2 |
| Impaired | 18.6 | 28.6 | 33.6 | 37.0 |
| Ruined | 0 | 0 | 0.2 | 2.8 |

(3) the rate of capital impairment is a rapidly increasing function of k=(L+E)/P for firms 10% of the size of the 100% firm.

(4) the twenty year cohort of business has a lower mean rate of return than the one-year cohort, given that the two types of cohorts are characterized by the same P/S ratio and the same size as a percentage of the 100% firm. At the same time, the standard deviation around the mean rate of return is effectively that of the standard deviation of an average of twenty-one year cohorts. The policy implications of this are that if an identical internal rate of return is expected over the long run, year after year, then the risk characteristic of a small firm will approximate those of a larger firm, provided capital impairment and ruin do not occur first. Table 3 summarizes some 20 year cohort simulations.

(5) when coefficient of variation of the negative binomial distribution at the 100% firm level is 10% instead of 5%, the

mean internal rates of return are about the same but the variation about these means are larger for the greater coefficient of variation.

TABLE 2a

Solvency results for 100% and 10% firms for several loss plus expense to premium ratios when P/S = 2. The forecast losses are $158535.8 (thousand). The number of losses are negative binomial with mean m = 194,636 and N* = 400. The line of insurance considered is Bodily Injury Liability. All dollar amounts are in thousands.

Size = 100%

| $\frac{L+E}{P} = k$ | 0.8 | 0.9 | 1.0 | 1.1 | 1.2 |
|---|---|---|---|---|---|
| IRR | 26.73 | 17.40 | 10.67 | 5.50 | 1.15 |
| IRR (S.D.) | 2.98 | 2.70 | 2.38 | 2.19 | 2.02 |
| P | 276676 | 235566 | 205092 | 181500 | 162935 |
| Surplus | 138338 | 117783 | 102546 | 90750 | 81467 |
| Impaired | 0 | 0 | 0 | 1 | 26 |
| Mean | | | | -942.23 | -2733.11 |
| S.D. | | | | 812.50 | 2492.82 |
| Ruined | 0 | 0 | 0 | 0 | 0 |

TABLE 2b

Solvency results for 100% and 10% firms for several loss plus expense to premium ratios when P/S = 2. The forecast losses are $158535.8 (thousand). The number of losses are negative binomial with mean m = 194,636 and N* = 400. The line of insurance considered is Bodily Injury Liability. All dollar amounts are in thousands.

Size = 10%

| $\frac{L+E}{P} = k$ | 0.8 | 0.9 | 1.0 | 1.1 | 1.2 |
|---|---|---|---|---|---|
| IRR (after tax) | 26.93 | 19.44 | 11.47 | 6.72 | 1.28 |
| IRR (S.D.) | 10.04 | 8.26 | 7.27 | 6.80 | 6.08 |
| P | 276686 | 23556 | 20509 | 18150 | 16293 |
| Surplus | 13838 | 11778 | 10254 | 90750 | 8146 |
| Impaired | 0 | 0 | 6% | 15% | 42% |
| Mean | | | -438.37 | -527.25 | -895.06 |
| S.D. | | | 399.74 | 640.13 | 753.30 |
| Ruined | 0 | 0 | 0 | 0 | 0 |

TABLE 3

Comparison of average after tax internal rate of returns for 20 year accounting cohorts, for P/S = 2, and P/S = 4 for size of firm of 100%, 10%, 2.5%. The line of insurance considered is Bodily Injury Liability. The number of cohorts considered were 100.

| | P/S = 2 | | P/S = 4 | |
|---|---|---|---|---|
| Size | Mean | Standard Deviation | Mean | Standard Deviation |
| 2.5% | 5.73% | 3.16% | 7.61% | 8.51% |
| 10 | 5.69 | 1.64 | | |
| 100 | 5.49 | 0.50 | 5.73 | .93 |

## 5. Discussion

We have focused mainly on the behavior of rates of return, capital impairments and ruin in order to illustrate the interrelationship among P/S ratios, size of firm, loss plus expense to premium ratios, and coefficient of variation of the compounding distribution at the 100% firm level. We have not presented in this paper the time series character of quantities such as asset to liability ratios, total cash flow, net underwriting cash flow, etc. although we have a number of results concerning these quantities. We have not presented results based on multiple lines of insurance and multiple investment types although, again, we have a few results concerning rates of return and solvency for this situation. The basic problem at this stage is one of presentation: given several possible portfolio compositions, several possible levels of number of lines to be included, several levels of P/S ratio (or several levels of asset to liability ratios A/L, fixed at the beginning of the cohort study or to be maintained through the duration of the cohort study), several levels of size of firm, several levels of (L+E)/P ratio, etc. to be examined, not only for a single year's cohort, but through time, it is difficult to first understand and next communicate the effects of the individual factors and their interactions. A response surface technique is the only method of summarization which is capable of capturing the information available in the responses. However, since not all the responses behave in a polynomial fashion there is a further complication in that non-linear response surfaces, through time, would have to be fit. An extensive account of these difficulties will be addressed in a forthcoming manuscript.

## 6. Acknowledgment

We are pleased to acknowledge our considerable indebtedness to the Massachusetts Rating Bureaus and the U.S. Army Research Office (under contract DAAG29-81-K-0110) for the support under which this research was undertaken and completed.

References

1. Heckman, P.E. and Meyers, G. [1983]. The Calculation of Aggregate Loss Distributions from Claim Severity and Claim Count Distributions. *Proceedings of the Casulty Actuarial Society*, Vol. LXX.

2. Ibbotson, R.G. and Sinquefield, R.A. [1983]. Stocks, Bonds, Bills and Inflation: The Past and The Future. *The Financial Analyst Research Foundation*, Charlottesville, Virginia.

3. Lukacs, E. [1970]. *Characteristic Functions*. Griffin, London.

4. Neter, J. and Wasserman, W. [1974]. *Applied Linear Statistical Models*. Richard D. Irwin, Inc., Homewood, Illinois.

5. Paulson, A.S. and Dixit, R. [1986]. Some General Approaches to Computing Total Loss Distributions and the Probability of Ruin. Troy, N.Y.: Rensselaer Polytechnic Institute, School of Management Working Paper.

6. Pentikainen, T. and Rantala, J. (1982). *Solvency of Insurers and Equalization of Reserves*, Vol. I and II, Insurance Publishing Company Ltd., Helsinki.

STV

# 3

# SOME ASPECTS OF LIFE ASSURANCE SOLVENCY

Howard R. Waters

**ABSTRACT**

This paper uses a stochastic investment model developed by Professor A.D. Wilkie to study in probabilistic terms the investment risk to the solvency of a life assurance company. Two probabilities are considered for a cohort of policies:

i) the probability that the premiums paid together with investment income and any initial reserve will be insufficient to pay for the claims,
ii) the probability that at any time during the term of the policies the investment experience will have been sufficiently bad for a valuation to produce a deficit.

These probabilities are studied numerically for different investment strategies.

A version of this paper was published in *Astin Bulletin,* Volume 17, Number 1, pp. 86–132.

## 1. INTRODUCTION

In 1980 the Council of the Faculty of Actuaries in Scotland set up a Working Party to:

> *"...investigate the criteria by which the solvency of life assurance companies should be assessed and to determine the amount of the solvency margin which should be required in practice by supervisory authorities."*

The Working Party submitted their report to the Faculty of Actuaries in 1984 and this report has been published in the Transactions of the Faculty of Actuaries, Volume 39, (RFASWP [1986]). (The above quotation is taken from paragraph 1.1.1 of the report.)

Section 2 of the report discusses in general terms the meaning of solvency, the possible causes of solvency and the approach to solvency adopted by the Working Party. The Working Party took the view that:

> *"...solvency must be a matter of probability. ...Determining whether a life company is solvent means... in practice fixing a probability of ruin and thereafter attempting to determine whether or not the situation of that company appears to be such that the probability of its ruin is lower than the selected probability."*

(RFASWP [1986, paragraph 2.2.7.].) Section 3 of the report is a critical review of current legislation regarding solvency in the European Economic Community. The main part of the report, Section 4, describes what it calls:

> *"...a fresh approach to the determination of solvency..."*

(RFASWP [1986, paragraph 1.3.1.] ). This approach uses a stochastic model office technique to assess the investment risk to the company and the approach is illustrated by numerical examples which are summarized in Appendices 5 and 6 of the report. Each of these numerical examples summarizes the results of simulations for a single cohort of identical 20-year endowment assurances by annual premiums and takes account of different investment strategies and, for the with profit policies, different bonus distribution strategies. The investment model used for these simulations is a stochastic model developed by Wilkie [1986]. The Working Party expressed the hope that by analyzing the results of their simulations, they could:

> *"...arrive at a relatively simple set of rules by which the probability of ruin of a particular office could be estimated..."*

(RFASWP [1986, paragraph 4.1.1.]). This was an ambitious aim and it is neither surprising nor discreditable that they were:

> *"...obliged to admit that...[they] have found no such rules..."*

(RFASWP [1986, paragraph 2.4.13.]).

This present paper represents a (modest) step in the direction indicated by the Faculty of Actuaries' Working Party. We shall be concerned solely with the investment risk to the insurance company and we shall study this numerically by simulating the experience of a single cohort of identical endowment assurance policies using Wilkie's stochastic investment model [1986]. We shall be particularly concerned with the distribution of the present value of the profit from the cohort of policies, or, equivalently the distribution of the amount of capital required to ensure, with a given probability, that the office does not make a loss. We are interested in the shape of this distribution and how it is affected by:

i) changing the investment strategy,
ii) changing the term to maturity of the contracts, and, to a lesser extent
iii) changing the premium.

Although our primary concern is with the eventual profit when all the contracts have terminated, expressed in present value terms, we shall also consider the probability that at some time during the term of the policies a valuation produces a deficit. This probability is very much a function of the valuation basis and the basis we shall use is a particularly weak one, for reasons that will be explained later in the paper.

In carrying out our simulations we shall make many simplifying assumptions, notably:

i) we shall consider a single cohort of identical policies rather than a succession of cohorts of identical, or even different, policies,
ii) we shall ignore the insurance company's expenses,
iii) we shall ignore dealings costs for investments,
iv) we shall assume mortality follows a deterministic model, and
v) we shall consider only non-profit policies.

Given the nature and aims of this study it is inevitable that some simplifying assumptions should be made relating to factors other than the investment risk, but even so (v) above is rather unfortunate in the sense that for with profit policies it could be argued that the bonus distribution strategy is at least as important as the investment strategy in relation to the solvency of the company. Nevertheless, it is our hope that by studying in some detail one or two particular points, even though we make many simplifying assumptions, our understanding of the investment risk to life assurance companies will be increased, and, perhaps equally important, our understanding of the behaviour of Wilkie's investment model, which is the central pillar both of this study and of the Report of the Faculty of Actuaries' Solvency Working Party, will also be increased.

In the following section of this paper we give a very brief description of Wilkie's investment model and also of the four different investment strategies we shall consider. It is our intention that this paper should be, as far as possible, self contained and for this reason we give, in Appendix 1, the formulae determining the investment model even though the model is well documented elsewhere. Three of our four investment strategies are very simply explained; the fourth requires a more detailed explanation and this is included as Appendix 2.

In §3 we consider the present value of the profit from a single cohort of identical endowment assurances. We start by giving details of the policies and the way in which we have carried out the simulations and then we present and discuss the results of the simulations. In Appendix 3 we give the cash flow, premiums minus claims, for one of the cohorts we consider. In §4 we consider the probability that a valuation, using a particular basis, will produce a deficit.

## 2. THE INVESTMENT MODEL AND THE INVESTMENT STRATEGIES

In this section we give a very brief description of Wilkie's stochastic investment model and also describe the four different investment strategies used later in the paper.

### 2.1 The investment model.

The investment model is described in great detail in Wilkie [1986] where Wilkie says it seems to him to be:

> *"...the minimum model that might be used to describe the total investments of a life office or a pension fund."*

(Wilkie [1986, paragraph 1.1].) The model is essentially four inter-related time series:

- Q(t) the Retail Prices Index,
- D(t) an index of equity dividends,
- Y(t) the dividend yield on the same equities (i.e. the dividend index divided by the appropriate price index),
- C(t) the yield on (irredeemable) fixed interest securities.

The formulae defining these time series and the parameter values are given, for completeness, as Appendix 1.

From the basic elements given above, three more time series can be derived: P(t) the equity price index,

- PR(t) the "rolled up" equity price index including net reinvested dividends,
- CR(t) the "rolled up" index for fixed interest securities.

These are defined as follows:

$$P(t) = D(t)/Y(t)$$

$$PR(t) = PR(t-1)\{P(t) + D(t)[1-T1]\}/P(t-1)$$

$$CR(t) = CR(t-1)\{1/C(t) + 1-T2\}C(t-1)$$

where T1 and T2 are the appropriate rates of tax on income from equities and fixed interest securities respectively. It can be seen that PR(t+s) represents the accumulated amount at time (t+s) of an amount PR(t) invested at time t, where the investment is all in equities and all the dividend payments, net of tax, are reinvested in equities. A similar interpretation can be given of CR(t).

The investment model we use is the same as that used by the Faculty of Actuaries' Solvency Working Party. This model is the simpler of the two models described by Wilkie [1986] and is termed the "reduced standard model". The other model, the "full standard model", has been used by Daykin and Bernstein [1985] in a study of the solvency of general insurance companies. Using either model, with parameter values as in Appendix 1, Wilkie [1986, Tables 2 and 3] shows that the mean annual rate of inflation is a little over 5% for the terms in which we shall be interested.

Throughout the remainder of this paper we shall assume that equity dividends are taxed at 30% and that fixed interest security dividends are taxed at 37½%, as was assumed by the Faculty of Actuaries' Solvency Working Party (RFASWP [1986, Appendix 5]). Using these rates of taxation we have estimated the mean and standard deviation of the random variables

$$GPR(t) = 100\{(PR(t)/PR(0))^{1/t} - 1\}$$

$$GCR(t) = 100\{(CR(t)/CR(0))^{1/t} - 1\}$$

for various values of t, i.e. the mean and standard deviation of the rate of money return on equities and fixed interest securities respectively. These quantities have been estimated by simulating one thousand values of each random variable and the results are given in Table 1. (Wilkie [1986, Table 3] gives figures corresponding to those in Table 1 but assuming no taxation.)

### 2.1 The investment strategies.

We are interested in the effects of different investment strategies and the four strategies we shall consider are described below; we also give the abbreviations that will be used to identify them subsequently:

EQ 100% investment in equities.
For this strategy we assume all money, including dividends, is invested in equities. Hence PR(t+s)/PR(t) represents the accumulated amount at time (t+s) of a unit amount invested at time t, and, conversely, PR(t)/PR(t+s) is the amount that should be invested at time t in order that it accumulate to a unit amount at time (t+s).

FI 100% investment in fixed interest securities.
For this strategy we assume all money, including dividends, is invested in fixed interest securities so that, for example, CR(t)/CR(t+s) is the amount that should be invested at time t in order that it accumulate to a unit amount at time (t+s).

FE Investment in both fixed interest securities and equities.
For this strategy money is invested partly in fixed interest securities and partly in equities according to the following two rules:

i) investment income is reinvested in the type of investment, fixed interest securities or equities, from which it came,
ii) "new money", i.e. the excess of premiums over claims, is invested in fixed interest securities and equities in proportion to the relative past performance of these sectors. Of a unit of "new money" invested at time t an amount

$$CR(t)/\{CR(t) + PR(t)\}$$

will be invested in fixed interest securities, and the remainder

$$PR(t)/\{CR(t) + PR(t)\}$$

will be invested in equities. Hence at time (t+s) this unit will have accumulated to an amount

$$\{CR(t+s) + PR(t+s)\} / \{CR(t) + PR(t)\}$$

and, conversely, the amount that should be invested at time t in order that it accumulate to a unit amount at time (t+s) is

$$\{CR(t) + PR(t)\}/\{CR(t+s) + PR(t+s)\}$$

of which an amount

$$CR(t)/\{CR(t+s) + PR(t+s)\}$$

should be invested in fixed interest securities and the remainder in equities. In the remainder of this paper we shall take both CR(0) and PR(0) to be 1 so that the present value of a unit payable at time t, using this investment strategy, is

$$1/\{½(CR(t) + PR(t)\}$$

Strategies EQ and FI represent, in an obvious sense, two extremes. It is not claimed that FE has any merits other than that, in some sense, it represents a compromise between the two extremes and, as we have seen, it leads to very simple calculation of present values. Both EQ and FI are entirely passive strategies in the sense that if they are adopted, the way in which money is invested in future does not depend on subsequent events. Strategy FE is somewhat less passive in that subsequent events will affect the proportion of new money to be invested in equities and in fixed interest securities. However, none of the three strategies described so far takes any account of the nature of the liabilities of the company. The final investment strategy is included to add a little variety and also to go some way towards answering this last criticism.

IM Investment in fixed interest securities using an "immunization" strategy. For this strategy investment is solely in fixed interest securities. Unlike FI, where it was tacitly assumed that all fixed interest securities were irredeemable, we now assume that securities of different terms are available. Broadly speaking, each time the insurance company receives premiums or pays claims we assume it realises all its assets and then reinvests them in a single fixed interest security. The calculation of the term of this security takes into account the current yield on securities and the future liabilities of the company. This calculation is rather lengthy and the details are included, for completeness, as Appendix 2. It can be seen from Appendix 2 that the calculation of the term of the security is based loosely, but only loosely, on the classical concept of immunization. (See, for example, Redington [1952].) However, we must stress that we are not claiming any special merits for this strategy other than that it does take some (small) account of the company's liabilities and that it is superficially attractive in some sense.

## 3. NUMERICAL RESULTS I

In this section we consider the profit, expressed in present value terms, resulting from a single cohort of identical endowment assurance policies and, in particular the relationship between the distribution of this profit and the company's investment strategy. We start by giving details of the cohort of policies; we then give some details of the simulations and finally we discuss the results of the simulations, which are summarised in Tables 2-5.

### 3.1 The cohort of policies

For all the numerical examples considered in this and the following section we consider a single cohort of 1000 identical endowment assurances issued simultaneously to lives aged 35. Each policy has level annual premiums payable throughout the term and sum assured $10,000 payable at the end of the year of death or at the end of the term. We make no allowance for expenses, we assume there are no withdrawals and we assume mortality is deterministic, following the A1967-70 Ultimate mortality table published by the Faculty of Actuaries and the Institute of Actuaries. We consider 10-, 15- and 25- year terms for the policies with annual premiums $765, $450 and $215 respectively which are approximately the correct net premiums given the above mortality table and 5% interest. (In one example later in this section we consider the effect of increasing the premium for the 15-year endowment to $550.) In Appendix 3 we give the cash flow, premiums minus claims, for a cohort of 25-year endowments with annual premiums $215. It is clearly possible to derive the cash flow for all the other combinations of term and premium from these figures and this Appendix has been included solely for the sake of completeness. One feature of our assumptions, which is readily apparent from Appendix 3, is that by having deterministic mortality, premiums payable throughout the term and involving no ages greater than 60, the net cash flow is always into the company until the end of the term of the policies. Hence, if, as in this section, we are concerned with the possibility of the insurance company's bankruptcy, i.e. the possibility that it will be unable to pay a claim which is due, then the only time at which this can happen is at the end of the term of the policies.

3.2 **The simulations.**

Wilkie's [1986] investment model lends itself very easily to simulation (but not to exact analysis). In Appendix 1 we give a list of starting values for the various parameters. These values are either arbitrary or neutral in the sense that they do not imply any carried forward effects from before the policies were issued and they have been used as the starting values for all of our simulations. See Wilkie [1986, §4]. By generating four random unit normal variates, QZ(1), YZ(1), DZ(1) and CZ(1), we can use the given starting values to calculate all the elements of the model at time 1, in particular, C(1), CR(1) and PR(1). By generating another four random unit normal variates we can then move forward to time 2, and so on.

To simulate the present value of the profit from our cohort of policies we have:

- generated a simulation of the investment experience as described above
- using the chosen investment strategy, rolled up the premiums minus claims to the end of the term of the policies to obtain the accumulated profit
- then divided by an appropriate discount factor to get the present value of the profit.

The appropriate discount factors are PR(N), CR(N) and {CR(N) + PR(N)}/2 for strategies EQ, FI and FE respectively where N is the term of the endowments. For strategy IM the discount factor is the accumulation to time N of a unit invested at time 0; this unit is invested in a fixed interest security and at yearly intervals this security is converted into cash and then reinvested in a fixed interest security whose term is as calculated in Appendix 2.

The results of our simulations of the present value of the profit on a cohort of policies are summarised in Tables 2-5. For each of the four investment strategies we have considered three different policy terms and four combinations of policy term and premium. For each combination of investment strategy, policy term and premium we have performed 10,000 simulations. We have then calculated the mean value, standard deviation, coefficient of skewness and coefficient of kurtosis from each set of 10,000 values and the results of the simulations have been summarised in frequency distributions where the class intervals are measured in numbers of standard deviations from the mean, in steps of one half of a standard deviation. For the purposes of comparison Table 2 also includes the relevant figures for a normal distribution. (Note that the means and standard deviations in Tables 2-5 have been rounded to the nearest $100.)

3.3 **Discussion of Tables 2-5.**

3.3.1 **Initial reserves.**

Let us suppose that the insurance company wishes to know how much capital it should have when this cohort of policies is issued in order that the probability of its not requiring to use any further capital to finance the cohort is to be, say, 99%. If we consider, for example, the figures in

Table 2 for strategy EQ we see that 86 out of the 10,000 simulations had a (present value of) profit more than 3½ standard deviations below the mean. Working in very round figures, this implies that an initial capital of about \$6.5 million, or \$6,500 per policy, is required. The corresponding figures for the other strategies, also using Table 2, are:

FE \$2 million
FI \$2 million
IM \$0.8 million

(It is interesting that the lower 1% points of the frequency distributions in Tables 2-5, which are the basis for the above calculations, are consistently about 3½ standard deviations below the mean for strategy EQ and consistently about 2 to 2½ standard deviations below the mean for the other three strategies.) Two points should be noted about these calculations:

- we have talked about this capital being available when the policies are issued but it cannot be needed until the end of the term of the policies. However, it seems sensible to require it to be available when the policies are issued since it is at this point that the (possible future) liability is incurred.

- we have completely ignored the important question of where this initial capital comes from and, in particular, how it is serviced. The only assumption we have made is that it is invested in the same way as the excess of premiums over claims for the policies, an assumption of dubious realism.

3.3.2 **Means and standard deviations.**

If we look at the means and standard deviations in Tables 2-5 a consistent pattern emerges:

- the means for EQ and FE are of approximately the same size and considerably more than the means for FI and IM

- the means for IM are somewhat higher than those for FI

- the standard deviations for EQ are about twice as large as those for FE, which are in turn a little larger, but not much larger, than those for FI, which are in turn about twice as large as those for IM, although somewhat less than twice in Table 5.

Given the figures in Table 1, the differences between the means and standard deviations for EQ and FI are not at all surprising. What does seem surprising is the performance of FE compared to both EQ and FI. FE seems to have the best of both worlds in the sense that its means are as high as those of EQ and its standard deviations are (nearly) as low as those of FI. Presumably the explanation for this is that FE is an investment strategy that "backs winners" (see §2.2) and by doing so it avoids getting caught in a run of poor investment performance for either equities or fixed interest securities. The performance of IM compared with that of FI is interesting. Not only does IM have higher means but also considerably lower standard deviations.

### 3.3.3 Other comments.

The coefficients of skewness and kurtosis are useful summaries of the "shape" of a distribution. In the case of EQ these figures show, as do the frequency distributions themselves, that the distribution is highly non-normal and has a very long left hand tail, i.e. has the possibility of very large losses. It is noticeable that, in the case of EQ, the left hand tail of the distribution gets fatter as the term of the endowment increases. In the cases of FE and FI the shape of the distribution seems very little affected by either the term of the endowment or the premium; in all cases the distribution is not too different from a normal but does have a slightly fatter left hand tail. The shape of the distribution for IM is somewhat less stable. In Tables 2,3, and 5 it is not too dissimilar to those for FE and FI but in Table 4 it has fatter tails in both directions and is the only one of the sixteen distributions with a positive coefficient of skewness. We can get some idea of the effect of changing the premium by comparing Tables 3 and 4; for the "passive" investment strategies, EQ, FE and FI, the only effect is a change in the mean value but for strategy IM the resulting distributions are somewhat different in shape.

Three points seem to emerge from this discussion:

- the mean and standard deviation of the present value of the profit are affected by the term of the endowments, the premium and, in particular, the investment strategy

- if we ignore EQ, the shape of the distribution is not much affected by the term of the endowments, the premium or, apart from IM in Table 4, the investment strategy. In all cases the distribution is rather like a normal with a fatter left hand tail.

- it is noticeable how many extreme values occur in the left hand tail, up to 5, 6 or more standard deviations below the mean. There are far more of these values than there are correspondingly high values in the right hand tail.

## 4. NUMERICAL RESULTS II

### 4.1 The problems.

In the previous section we were concerned with the present value of the profit on a portfolio of policies. A question of obvious interest, which was discussed briefly in the previous section, is "How much capital should the company have when the policies are issued in order that, with some pre-assigned probability, it can meet all the claims when they become due (without having to call on further capital)?" In practice, a supervisory authority will wish to test for solvency not only when the policies are issued but also at intervals during the term of the policies and to do this it is natural to consider, among other factors, the valuation reserve for the policies. (Note that the current solvency margins specified by the European Economic Community for non-linked assurance and annuity funds are expressed partly in terms of valuation reserves and partly in terms of sums at risk. See RFASWP [1986, §3].)

In this section we shall consider valuation reserves for the (very simple) portfolio of policies considered in the previous section. This immediately raises two questions:

i) on what basis should we calculate the reserves?

ii) which particular events, or quantities, are we concerned with?

Since we are carrying out a valuation to test the solvency of a closed portfolio of non-profit policies, it is appropriate to use a realistic assessment of the future levels of the factors involved, in our case mortality and interest rates. (See Fisher and Young [1965, §10.4].) Mortality is not a problem; we use the same mortality table as was used, in a deterministic manner, to calculate the cash flow for our portfolio. The interest rate used is, in a sense which will be explained more fully in the next section, the expected future rate of interest given by the investment model. The quantity we are interested in is the (tail of the) distribution of the present value of valuation results throughout the term of the policies. Our reasons for choosing this particular quantity are explained in the next section but we recognise that there may well be other quantities of at least equal importance in relation to solvency.

### 4.2 The simulations.

Throughout the remainder of this section we consider a portfolio consisting of a single cohort of 1000 identical 15-year endowment assurances issued simultaneously to lives aged 35. The annual premium for each policy is \$450 and the other assumptions are as in §3. As in the previous section we are interested in the effects of different investment strategies but in this section we shall consider only the strategies FE, FI and IM. (It was always clear that 100% investment in equities was an unsuitable strategy for a portfolio of non-profit assurances and the poor performance of EQ is demonstrated in Tables 2-5.)

The numerical results discussed in this section are summarised in Tables 6,7 and 8, each table relating to a different investment strategy, and the different entries in these tables are explained in the remainder of §4.2.

#### 4.2.1 $U_1$

The figure given for $U_1$ is (an estimate of) the amount of capital, expressed in \$'000's, the company should have when the policies are issued in order that it will be able to pay all the claims when they arise with the probability given in the first column (as a percentage), assuming that this initial capital is invested in the same way as the excess of premiums over claims, i.e. according to the strategy given at the head of the table. For example, from Table 6 we see that if the company starts with capital \$1,180,000 and follows strategy FE there is a 97% probability that the company will be able to pay all the claims when they become due. The figures for $U_1$ have been taken from the same set of 10,000 simulations for each investment strategy which were summarized in Table 3. For example, - \$2,032,000 was the 50-th lowest present value of profit in the 10,000 simulations using strategy FE.

### 4.2.2 $U_2$

The figure given for $U_2$ is (an estimate of) the amount of capital the company should have when the policies are issued in order that with the probability given in the first column no valuation, on a basis specified below, during the term of the policies will result in a deficit. For each investment strategy the figures for $U_2$ are derived from a set of 1,000 simulations carried out independently of the simulations used to derive the corresponding figures for $U_1$. Each simulation proceeds as follows:

i) at duration t, t = 0,1,...,15, we have a value for the accumulation to time t, using a single simulation of the investment experience up to time t and the specified investment strategy, of the excess of premiums over claims invested at durations up to but not including time t; denote this amount $A_t$

ii) we also have at time t values for the various elements of the investment model for times up to and including time t, e.g. Q(t-1), C(t) and PR(t).

iii) using the starting values given in ii) we carry out twenty separate simulations of the future investment experience until the end of the term of the policies, i.e. we calculate Q(s), PR(s) etc. for s = t+1, t+2,...,15, and for each of these twenty simulations we calculate the value at time t of the excess of claims over premiums payable at and after time t; let $V_t$ denote the arithmetic average of these twenty values

iv) then $V_t$ is (an estimate of) the expected value of the present value at time t of the excess of claims over premiums payable from time t onwards given all the relevant information we have at time t, i.e. given the values for the elements of the investment model up to and including time t; note that we have estimated this expected value by simulating twenty values of the variable concerned and taking the mean of these values

v) hence $V_t$ can be regarded as the mathematical reserve for the portfolio calculated at time t on a basis which uses a realistic assessment of future mortality and interest rates and includes no hidden margins

vi) hence $(V_t-A_t)$ is the valuation deficit at time t calculated on the above basis

vii) now let $D_t$ be the value of $(V_t-A_t)$ discounted from time t to time 0 using an appropriate discount factor as described in §3

viii) for each simulation we record

$$\max_{0 \leq t \leq 15} D_t \tag{4.2.2.1}$$

which represents the maximum valuation deficit, in present value terms, during the term of the policies.

Hence, looking at Table 7, we see that the fifth largest valuation deficit during the term of the policies was \$1,936,000, or, to put it another way, if the company had started with initial capital \$1,936,000, had invested this capital 100% in (irredeemable) fixed interest securities and had included this capital in its valuations, then 995 of the 1000 simulations would have shown no valuation deficits at any time during the term of the policies, 4 of the simulations would have shown a deficit at least once during the term of the policies and the remaining simulation would have shown a valuation surplus of zero at least once during the term of the policies ( but no deficits).

### 4.2.3 $U_3$

There is a (rather tenuous) theoretical link between $U_1$ and $U_2$ which is provided by the following result:

- let M be a random variable representing the present value of the eventual loss on the portfolio (ignoring any initial capital), so that M is the random variable whose quantiles are denoted $U_1$. Then

$$1-p \leq \min_{r>0}(E[\exp\{rM\}].\exp\{-rU_2\}) \qquad (4.2.3.1)$$

where p is the probability given in the first column of Tables 6,7 and 8 and $U_2$ is the corresponding value in the third column.

(This result can be found in Papatriandafylou and Waters [1984, Result 3]. The proof requires only that the moment generating function of M is reasonably well behaved and that the valuation basis used to determine $U_2$ is as described in §4.2.2.) The random variable whose distribution was discussed in §3 is the present value of the profit on the portfolio, which is (-M), and we concluded that for strategies FE, FI and IM the distribution of (-M) was not too different from a normal, although with a somewhat fatter left hand tail. If we assume (-M), and hence M, has a normal distribution, (4.2.3.1) simplifies to:

$$1-p \leq \exp\{-[(\mu+U_2)/\sigma]^2\} \qquad (4.2.3.2)$$

where $\mu$ and $\sigma^2$ are the mean and variance of (-M). Re-arranging (4.2.3.2) we get:

$$U_2 \leq \sigma\sqrt{-2\log(1-p)} - \mu \qquad (4.2.3.3)$$

In Tables 6, 7 and 8 the figure for $U_3$ is calculated as the right hand side of (4.2.3.3) using the appropriate value of p as given in the table and taking the appropriate estimates of $\mu$ and $\sigma$ from Table 3. (For example, in Table 8 the figure of \$974,000 for $U_3$ is calculated from the right hand side of (4.2.3.3) using:

$p$ = 0.995

$\mu$ = 252,700 (Taken from Table 3)

$\sigma$ = 3736,800 (Taken from Table 3) )

4.3 **Discussion of Tables 6, 7 and 8.**

The amounts $U_1$, $U_2$ and $U_3$ in Tables 6, 7 and 8 all refer to amounts of capital which are required when the cohort of policies is issued and we would justify our decision to work in terms of present values by saying, as we did earlier, that it is when the policies are issued that the (future) liability is incurred. As far as solvency is concerned, the important question when the policies are issued is:

> "Will the company be able to pay the claims?"

or, since this canot be a matter of certainty:

> "What capital does the company need now in order that some pre-assigned probability it will be able to pay the claims (without having to call on additional capital)?"

It is this last question that is answered by $U_1$, and in this sense $U_1$ is the most important column of figures in each of Tables 6, 7 and 8.

The purpose of testing solvency at regular intervals during the term of the policies by taking account of, among other factors, valuation reserves, is to provide an "early warning signal" of possible problems in the future. (See RFASWP[1986, §2] for a discussion of this point.) If this early warning signal is activated by a valuation on a specified basis producing a deficit, or rather the company not having sufficient assets at the time of the valuation to cover the expected future liabilities, it is reasonable to ask,

> "How much capital should the company have when the policies are issued in order that with some pre-assigned probability the early warning signal is never activated during the term of the policies?"

The answer to this question depends on the basis used for the valuations. On the basis outlined in §4.2 above, the answer to this question is provided by $U_2$ in Tables 6, 7 and 8. Note that $U_2$ has been calculated using a valuation basis with no hidden margins; a stronger valuation basis would produce larger values for $U_2$. For a given probability level, $\epsilon$, the value of $U_2$ must be at least as large as the value of $U_1$. This follows from (4.2.2.1) since $D_{15}$ represents the present value of the eventual loss on the portfolio so that $U_1$ is the $\epsilon$-quantile of $D_{15}$ and $U_2$ is the $\epsilon$-quantile of the maximum of all the $D_t$'s from $t = 0$ to $t = 15$. The reason why in Tables 6, 7 and 8 some values of $U_1$ exceed the corresponding value of $U_2$ is that the figures for $U_1$ and $U_2$ in these tables have been derived from independent sets of simulations and are subject to random errors.

One noticeable feature of Tables 6 and 7, i.e. for strategies FE and FI, is how close the values of $U_2$ are to the corresponding values of $U_1$; from the figures shown, the value of $U_2$ never exceeds that of $U_1$ by more than

15% of the value of $U_1$. The obvious, but not necessarily correct, conclusion from this is that relatively little extra capital is required if we want our portfolio to pass "repeated solvency tests" during the term of the policies rather than a single solvency test when the policies are issued. Unfortunately, this conclusion is not very well supported by the figures in Table 8. In this table the value of $U_2$ exceeds the corresponding value of $U_1$ by up to 25% of the value of $U_1$. This is particularly unfortunate because IM is the most "active" of our investment strategies and, arguably, the most realistic.

Before trying to draw too many conclusions from the values of $U_1$ and $U_2$ in Tables 6, 7 and 8 a little caution should be exercised. The tabulated values of $U_1$ and $U_2$ are order statistics taken from sets of simulated values. To get an idea of the random error introduced by using simulations, consider, for example, Table 6. The figure \$2,032,000 for $U_1$ is, as explained in §4.2.1, the 50-th highest value of 10,000 simulated values. Using a normal approximation to what is really a binomial probablity, see, for example, David [1970, §2.5], the probability is about 0.75 that the true 0.995 quantile of the distribution will lie between the 59-th and 41-st highest of the 10,000 simulated values; these values are \$1,952,000 and \$2,127,000 respectively. Similarly an approximate 95% confidence interval for the 0.995 quantile is:

$$\$1,921,000 \rightarrow \$2,202,000 \ .$$

Approximate 75% and 95% confidence intervals for the 0.95 quantile of $U_1$ in Table 6, estimated as \$951,000, are:

$$\$927,000 \rightarrow \$969,000$$

$$\text{and } \$910,000 \rightarrow \$989,000$$

respectively. Approximate 75% and 95% confidence intervals for the 0.995 quantile of $U_2$ in Table 6, estimated as \$1,989,000, are, using a Poisson approximation:

$$\$1,922,000 \rightarrow \$2,697,000$$

$$\text{and } \$1,790,000 \rightarrow \$2,783,000$$

respectively. Approximate 75% and 95% confidence intervals for the 0.95 quantile of $U_2$ in Table 6, estimated as \$1,087,000, are, using a normal approximation again:

$$\$1,050,000 \rightarrow \$1,155,000$$

$$\text{and } \$1,009,000 \rightarrow \$1,229,000$$

respectively.

A (tentative) conclusion drawn from Tables 2-5 in §3.3 was that the distribution of the present value of the eventual profit on the portfolio is not too different from a normal, at least for strategies FE, FI and IM. In these circumstances the attraction of formula (4.2.3.3) is that it gives an upper bound for $U_2$ in terms of just the mean and variance of the present value of the eventual profit, i.e. the mean and variance of the distribution from which $U_1$ is obtained. This would be particularly useful if the upper bound, $U_3$, were close to the corresponding value of $U_2$. It can be seen from Tables 6, 7 and 8 that $U_3$ does indeed exceed $U_2$, as it should, but the relative difference ranges from about 20% for the high probabilities to about 45% for the lower probabilities in Tables 6 and 7 and as high as 64% for the lowest probability in Table 8. Perhaps it is a little optimistic to expect an inequality as general in its application as, say, Chebyshev's inequality, to provide sharp estimates of the quantity it is bounding!

## APPENDIX OF TABLES

**Table 1**

Rates of Money Return on Equities and Fixed Interest Securities

| Term t (years) | 1<br>% | 5<br>% | 10<br>% | 15<br>% | 20<br>% | 25<br>% |
|---|---|---|---|---|---|---|
| E[GPR(t)] | 9.96 | 9.18 | 8.68 | 8.38 | 8.57 | 8.57 |
| SD[GPR(t)] | 22.23 | 7.70 | 5.50 | 4.57 | 3.94 | 3.49 |
| E[GCR(t)] | 4.97 | 5.17 | 5.32 | 5.47 | 5.44 | 5.49 |
| SD[GCR(t)] | 7.64 | 3.07 | 1.89 | 1.29 | 1.06 | 0.90 |

**Table 2**

Present Value of Profit. Term 10 years. Premium $765 .

| Investment strategy | Normal distribution | EQ | FE | FI | IM |
|---|---|---|---|---|---|
| Mean $ | - | 645,400 | 632,500 | 115,800 | 220,500 |
| St. deviation $ | - | 2,065,500 | 1,060,600 | 824,500 | 383,800 |
| Skewness | 0 | -1.631 | -0.272 | -0.209 | -0.077 |
| Kurtosis | 3 | 8.869 | 3.175 | 3.272 | 4.947 |

Frequency distribution : class invervals expressed in numbers of standard deviations from the mean.

| Class interval | Normal distribution | EQ | FE | FI | IM |
|---|---|---|---|---|---|
| → -7 | | 2 | | | 1 |
| -7 → -6½ | | 2 | | | 0 |
| -6½ → -6 | | 5 | | | 0 |
| -6 → -5½ | | 3 | | | 1 |
| -5½ → -5 | | 14 | | | 5 |
| -5 → -4½ | | 7 | 3 | | 5 |
| -4½ → -4 | | 27 | 1 | 1 | 8 |
| -4 → -3½ | 2 | 26 | 7 | 10 | 16 |
| -3½ → -3 | 11 | 55 | 25 | 33 | 34 |
| -3 → -2½ | 49 | 95 | 73 | 63 | 69 |
| -2½ → -2 | 166 | 204 | 176 | 169 | 142 |
| -2 → -1½ | 440 | 335 | 424 | 436 | 203 |
| -1½ → -1 | 919 | 545 | 859 | 835 | 517 |
| -1 → -½ | 1498 | 993 | 1415 | 1407 | 1821 |
| -½ → 0 | 1915 | 1782 | 1865 | 1926 | 2743 |
| 0 → ½ | 1915 | 2609 | 1962 | 1987 | 1842 |
| ½ → 1 | 1498 | 2227 | 1618 | 1597 | 1018 |
| 1 → 1½ | 919 | 896 | 978 | 960 | 783 |
| 1½ → 2 | 440 | 154 | 423 | 382 | 486 |
| 2 → 2½ | 166 | 17 | 155 | 147 | 206 |
| 2½ → 3 | 49 | 2 | 16 | 41 | 76 |
| 3 → 3½ | 11 | | | 3 | 18 |
| 3½ → 4 | 2 | | | 3 | 5 |
| 4 → 4½ | | | | | 1 |
| 4½ → 5 | | | | | |
| 5 → | | | | | |

**Table 3**

Present Value of Profit. Term 15 years. Premium $450 .

| Investment strategy | EQ | FE | FI | IM |
|---|---|---|---|---|
| Mean $ | 719,300 | 679,000 | 166,200 | 252,700 |
| St. deviation $ | 1,779,400 | 925,800 | 758,300 | 376,800 |
| Skewness | -2.381 | -0.396 | -0.185 | -0.142 |
| Kurtosis | 14.954 | 3.232 | 3.370 | 3.913 |

Frequency distribution : class invervals expressed in numbers of standard deviations from the mean.

| Class interval | EQ | FE | FI | IM |
|---|---|---|---|---|
| → -7 | 13 | | | |
| -7 → -6½ | 2 | | | |
| -6½ → -6 | 5 | | | |
| -6 → -5½ | 9 | 1 | | 1 |
| -5½ → -5 | 11 | 0 | 1 | 1 |
| -5 → -4½ | 12 | 0 | 2 | 7 |
| -4½ → -4 | 16 | 4 | 5 | 6 |
| -4 → -3½ | 37 | 10 | 6 | 15 |
| -3½ → -3 | 61 | 27 | 22 | 19 |
| -3 → -2½ | 87 | 80 | 54 | 51 |
| -2½ → -2 | 159 | 180 | 172 | 134 |
| -2 → -1½ | 292 | 463 | 430 | 299 |
| -1½ → -1 | 465 | 808 | 854 | 781 |
| -1 → -½ | 933 | 1382 | 1391 | 1838 |
| -½ → 0 | 1807 | 1772 | 1989 | 2017 |
| 0 → ½ | 2840 | 1979 | 1993 | 1719 |
| ½ → 1 | 2505 | 1694 | 1564 | 1491 |
| 1 → 1½ | 658 | 1078 | 885 | 950 |
| 1½ → 2 | 78 | 420 | 424 | 468 |
| 2 → 2½ | 8 | 92 | 165 | 153 |
| 2½ → 3 | 2 | 9 | 35 | 32 |
| 3 → 3½ | | 1 | 8 | 9 |
| 3½ → 4 | | | | 6 |
| 4 → 4½ | | | | 3 |
| 4½ → 5 | | | | |
| 5 → | | | | |

**Table 4**

Present Value of Profit. Term 15 years. Premium $550 .

| Investment strategy | EQ | FE | FI | IM |
|---|---|---|---|---|
| Mean $ | 1,648,600 | 1,684,800 | 1,253,500 | 1,307,100 |
| St. deviation $ | 1,831,000 | 913,100 | 794,200 | 349,200 |
| Skewness | -2.259 | -0.339 | -0.161 | 0.275 |
| Kurtosis | 14.865 | 3.213 | 3.349 | 6.133 |

Frequency distribution : class invervals expressed in numbers of standard deviations from the mean.

| Class interval | EQ | FE | FI | IM |
|---|---|---|---|---|
| → -7 | 12 | | | |
| -7 → -6½ | 2 | | | 1 |
| -6½ → -6 | 5 | | | 0 |
| -6 → -5½ | 9 | | | 2 |
| -5½ → -5 | 11 | | | 3 |
| -5 → -4½ | 16 | 1 | | 9 |
| -4½ → -4 | 17 | 2 | 1 | 7 |
| -4 → -3½ | 26 | 9 | 12 | 11 |
| -3½ → -3 | 63 | 29 | 31 | 15 |
| -3 → -2½ | 93 | 79 | 62 | 27 |
| -2½ → -2 | 150 | 192 | 154 | 73 |
| -2 → -1½ | 236 | 434 | 409 | 289 |
| -1½ → -1 | 511 | 843 | 842 | 848 |
| -1 → -½ | 973 | 1326 | 1466 | 1667 |
| -½ → 0 | 1870 | 1834 | 1955 | 2206 |
| 0 → ½ | 3080 | 2066 | 1936 | 2167 |
| ½ → 1 | 2058 | 1629 | 1586 | 1431 |
| 1 → 1½ | 670 | 990 | 954 | 605 |
| 1½ → 2 | 166 | 433 | 405 | 298 |
| 2 → 2½ | 24 | 113 | 125 | 172 |
| 2½ → 3 | 8 | 17 | 49 | 94 |
| 3 → 3½ | | 2 | 8 | 40 |
| 3½ → 4 | | 1 | 4 | 20 |
| 4 → 4½ | | | 1 | 7 |
| 4½ → 5 | | | | 4 |
| 5 → | | | | 4 |

**Table 5**

Present Value of Profit. Term 25 years. Premium $215 .

| Investment strategy | EQ | FE | FI | IM |
|---|---|---|---|---|
| Mean $ | 621,900 | 631,700 | 195,400 | 286,400 |
| St. deviation $ | 1,244,700 | 649,200 | 587,500 | 385,900 |
| Skewness | -3.001 | -0.749 | -0.345 | -0.139 |
| Kurtosis | 20.464 | 3.909 | 3.468 | 3.517 |

Frequency distribution : class invervals expressed in numbers of standard deviations from the mean.

| Class interval | | | | |
|---|---|---|---|---|
| → -7 | 16 | | | |
| -7 → -6½ | 2 | | | |
| -6½ → -6 | 6 | | | 1 |
| -6 → -5½ | 11 | 1 | 2 | 0 |
| -5½ → -5 | 18 | 4 | 0 | 0 |
| -5 → -4½ | 15 | 2 | 1 | 0 |
| -4½ → -4 | 19 | 6 | 2 | 2 |
| -4 → -3½ | 37 | 20 | 8 | 5 |
| -3½ → -3 | 63 | 46 | 29 | 23 |
| -3 → -2½ | 90 | 98 | 78 | 68 |
| -2½ → -2 | 129 | 201 | 208 | 183 |
| -2 → -1½ | 265 | 412 | 409 | 434 |
| -1½ → -1 | 420 | 771 | 811 | 817 |
| -1 → -½ | 758 | 1201 | 1347 | 1308 |
| -½ → 0 | 1736 | 1733 | 1885 | 1920 |
| 0 → ½ | 3502 | 2094 | 2039 | 2258 |
| ½ → 1 | 2381 | 1923 | 1651 | 1653 |
| 1 → 1½ | 466 | 1153 | 980 | 641 |
| 1½ → 2 | 57 | 304 | 403 | 436 |
| 2 → 2½ | 7 | 31 | 118 | 189 |
| 2½ → 3 | 2 | | 24 | 46 |
| 3 → 3½ | | | 4 | 10 |
| 3½ → 4 | | | 1 | 6 |
| 4 → 4½ | | | | |
| 4½ → 5 | | | | |
| 5 → | | | | |

**Table 6**

Investment Strategy FE

(See §4.2 for details.)

| Probability % | $U_1$ \$'000 | $U_2$ \$'000 | $U_3$ \$'000 |
|---|---|---|---|
| 99.5 | 2,032 | 1,989 | 2,335 |
| 99 | 1,693 | 1,790 | 2,131 |
| 98.5 | 1,538 | 1,599 | 2,004 |
| 98 | 1,398 | 1,472 | 1,911 |
| 97.5 | 1,278 | 1,360 | 1,836 |
| 97 | 1,180 | 1,286 | 1,773 |
| 96.5 | 1,103 | 1,247 | 1,718 |
| 96 | 1,049 | 1,190 | 1,670 |
| 95.5 | 993 | 1,124 | 1,627 |
| 95 | 951 | 1,087 | 1,587 |

**Table 7**

Investment Strategy FI

(See §4.2 for details.)

| Probability % | $U_1$ \$'000 | $U_2$ \$'000 | $U_3$ \$'000 |
|---|---|---|---|
| 99.5 | 1,948 | 1,936 | 2,302 |
| 99 | 1,687 | 1,797 | 2,135 |
| 98.5 | 1,547 | 1,554 | 2,031 |
| 98 | 1,456 | 1,435 | 1,955 |
| 97.5 | 1,369 | 1,349 | 1,893 |
| 97 | 1,315 | 1,318 | 1,842 |
| 96.5 | 1,247 | 1,297 | 1,797 |
| 96 | 1,198 | 1,243 | 1,758 |
| 95.5 | 1,153 | 1,168 | 1,722 |
| 95 | 1,110 | 1,141 | 1,690 |

**Table 8**

Investment Strategy IM

(See §4.2 for details.)

| Probability % | $U_1$ \$'000 | $U_2$ \$'000 | $U_3$ \$'000 |
|---|---|---|---|
| 99.5 | 877 | 799 | 974 |
| 99 | 693 | 697 | 891 |
| 98.5 | 613 | 608 | 839 |
| 98 | 541 | 537 | 801 |
| 97.5 | 476 | 524 | 771 |
| 97 | 439 | 500 | 745 |
| 96.5 | 409 | 472 | 723 |
| 96 | 377 | 458 | 703 |
| 95.5 | 351 | 425 | 686 |
| 95 | 327 | 408 | 670 |

**REFERENCES**


David, H.A. 1970. *Order Statistics.* John Wiley. New York.

Daykin, C.D. and Bernstein, G.D. 1985. A Simulation Model to Examine Questions of Solvency in the Light of Asset and Run-Off Risks. Paper presented at the ASTIN Colloquium, Biarritz.

Fisher, H.F. and Young, J. 1965. *Actuarial Practice of Life Assurance.* Published by the Faculty of Actuaries and the Institute of Actuaries. Edinburgh and London.

Papatriandafylou, A. and Waters, H.R. 1984. Martingales in Life Insurance. *Scandinavian Actuarial Journal* : 210-230.

Redington, F.M. 1952. Review of the Principles of Life Office Valuations. *Journal of the Institute of Actuaries*, 78: 286-315.

RFASWP 1986. The Solvency of Life Assurance Companies. Report of the Faculty of Actuaries Solvency Working Party. *Transactions of the Faculty of Actuaries*, 39: 251-317.

Wilkie, A.D. 1986. A Stochastic Investment Model for Actuarial Use. *Transactions of the Faculty of Actuaries*, 39: 341-373.

**APPENDIX 1**

In this Appendix we give the formulae defining the four basic time series, Q(t), Y(t), D(t) and C(t), of the investment model. In these definitions {QZ(t)}, {YZ(t)}, {DZ(t)} and {CZ(t)} are sequences of independent and identically distributed unit normal variates. The defining formulae are:

$$\log[Q(t)/Q(t-1)] = 0.05 + 0.6\{\log[Q(t-1)/Q(t-2)] - 0.05\} + 0.05\ QZ(t) \qquad (A.1.1)$$

$$\log[Y(t)] = 1.35\ \log[Q(t)/Q(t-1)] + YN(t) \qquad (A.1.2)$$

where

$$YN(t) = \log[0.04] + 0.6\{YN(t-1) - \log[0.04]\} + 0.175\ YZ(t) \qquad (A.1.3)$$

$$\log[D(t)/D(t-1)] = 0.8DM(t) + 0.2\ \log[Q(t)/Q(t-1)] - 0.0525\ \ YZ(t-1) + 0.1\ DZ(t) \qquad (A.1.4)$$

where

$$DM(t) = 0.2\ \log[Q(t)/Q(t-1)] + 0.8\ DM(t-1) \qquad (A.1.5)$$

$$C(t) = CM(t) + CN(t) \qquad (A.1.6)$$

where

$$CM(t) = 0.05\ \log[Q(t)/Q(t-1)] + 0.95\ CM(t-1) \qquad (A.1.7)$$

and

$$\log[CN(t)] = \log[0.035] + 0.91\ \log[CN(t-1)/0.035] + 0.165\ CZ(t) \qquad (A.1.8)$$

It is possible for C(t), as defined above, to take negative values, which makes no sense in practice. For this reason the value of C(t) is taken to be the maximum of the value given by (A.1.6) → (A.1.8) and ½%.

Starting values (see §3.2):

$Q(0) = 1$

$\log[Q(0)/Q(-1)] = 0.05$

$YN(0) = \log[0.04]$

(The above values imply that $Y(0) = 0.04\ \exp[0.0675]$.)

$D(0) = Y(0)$ (which implies that $P(0) = 1$)

$DM(0) = 0.05$

$YZ(0) = 0$

$C(0) = 0.085$

$CM(0) = 0.05$

$PR(0) = 1$

$CR(0) = 1$

## APPENDIX 2

In this Appendix we give the details of the investment strategy IM which was introduced in §2. We shall work in discrete time, $t = 0,1,2,\ldots$, measured in some units, in practice years, from an arbitrary origin, in practice the time of issue of the cohort of policies, (see §3). We assume the insurance company has a known net liability, claims minus premiums, of amount $L_t$ at time t, $t = 0,1,2,\ldots,N$.

Now let us suppose we are at time t, $t = 0,1,2,\ldots,N-2$. The investment model described in §2 and Appendix 1 gives us a value of C(t), the gross yield on fixed interest securities at time t. Provided t is not equal to zero we will be holding at time t a fixed interest security of some term which provides future net dividend payments and redemption money at the end of the term. Let $A_t$ denote the value at time t and at (net) rate of interest 0.625C(t) of these future payments. We assume we can realise these assets to give an amount of cash $A_t$ at time t, i.e. we assume no dealings costs, which after deducting $L_t$ gives us an amount $(A_t-L_t)$ to be invested at time t. We assume that this amount will be invested in a fixed interest security with term M. At time t all fixed interest securities are assumed to stand at par, to be redeemable at par and to have gross dividend rates of C(t) with dividends payable annually at the end of each year. All integer terms of investment, up to 100 years, are available as well as irredeemable securities.

The parameter to be chosen is M and we do this by considering the function $V_t(i,M)$ defined by:

$$V_t(i,M) = \sum_{n=0}^{N-t-1} (1+i)^{-n} L_{n+t+1} - (A_t-L_t)\left\{\sum_{n=0}^{M-1} 0.625C(t)(1+i)^{-n} + (1+i)^{-M+1}\right\} \qquad \text{(A.2.1)}$$

Hence, $V_t(i,M)$ represents the valuation deficit, at time (t+1), at rate of interest i assuming we invest at time t in a security of term M. Note that if i is equal to 0.625C(t), then $V_t(i,M)$ is independent of M. We now choose M, if possible, so that $V_t(i,M)$, regarded as a function of i alone, has a local maximum at $i = 0.625C(t)$. Sufficient, but not strictly necessary, conditions for this are:

$$\frac{d}{di} V_t(i,M) = 0 \quad \text{at } i = 0.625C(t) \qquad \text{(A.2.2)}$$

$$\frac{d^2}{di^2} V_t(i,M) < 0 \quad \text{at } i = 0.625C(t) \qquad \text{(A.2.3)}$$

The decision process for choosing M can now be summarised as follows:

1. Find the value of M which satisfies (A.2.2). (It can be shown that there is at most one such M.) If this value exceeds 100, put it equal to infinity.

2. If the value of M found in 1. satisfies (A.2.3) then this is the value of M to be used. (In this case it can be shown that for this value of M, $V_t(i,M)$ has a global maximum at $i = 0.625C(t)$.)

3. If there is no value of M which satisfies (A.2.2) or the solution to (A.2.2) does not satisfy (A.2.3) we choose M as follows:

   i) calculate CM(t+1) and CN(t+1) as in Appendix 1 but assuming QZ(t+1) and CZ(t+1) are both zero, and denote them CM* and CN*,

   ii) let EC be defined by

   $$EC = CM^* + CN^* \exp\{0.0136125\}$$

   iii) if EC is less than C(t), choose M to be infinity, otherwise choose M to be one.

4. Finally, the above decision process applies for values of t up to and including (N-2). For t equal to (N-1) we always choose M to be one.

The rationale behind this decision process is as follows:

- at time t the gross yield on fixed interest securities is C(t)

- we wish to choose the term of our investments in such a way as to minimize losses or maximize profits in some sense

- it is convenient to alter this objective slightly to choosing M in such a way that a change in the yield on fixed interest securities results in a smaller valuation deficit at some time

- the time of the valuation we consider is one year from now rather than now because the current yield on fixed interest securities, C(t), is known and it makes little sense to consider the possibility of a different value for C(t)

- hence we are, in effect, immunizing the company one year into the future against a change in the gross yield from the current value of C(t)

- by considering the formulae in Appendix 1 it can be seen that, given the elements of the investment model up to and including time t, CM(t+1) has a normal distribution with mean value CM* and logCN(t+1) has a normal distribution with mean value logCN* and standard deviation 0.165; hence EC is the conditional expected value of C(t+1) given what we know at time t

- hence if the "immunization" calculation does not give a value for M, we will invest long, i.e take M to be infinity, if yields are expected to fall in the coming year, i.e. if EC is less than C(t), and invest short, i.e. take M to be one, otherwise.

**APPENDIX 3**

Net cash flow for 1000 25-year endowment assurances with annual premium \$215. See §3.1 for details.

| Duration years | Premiums - Claims \$ |
|---|---|
| 0 | 215,000 |
| 1 | 206,258 |
| 2 | 205,257 |
| 3 | 204,070 |
| 4 | 202,682 |
| 5 | 201,069 |
| 6 | 199,211 |
| 7 | 197,085 |
| 8 | 194,663 |
| 9 | 191,918 |
| 10 | 188,821 |
| 11 | 185,340 |
| 12 | 181,440 |
| 13 | 177,087 |
| 14 | 172,241 |
| 15 | 166,864 |
| 16 | 160,913 |
| 17 | 154,345 |
| 18 | 147,116 |
| 19 | 139,179 |
| 20 | 130,490 |
| 21 | 121,004 |
| 22 | 110,677 |
| 23 | 99,467 |
| 24 | 87,338 |
| 25 | -9,026,049 |

# 4

# THE SOLVENCY OF A GENERAL INSURANCE COMPANY IN TERMS OF EMERGING COSTS

C.D. Daykin, G.D. Bernstein, S.M. Coutts, E.R.F. Devitt, G.B. Hey, D.I.W. Reynolds and P.D. Smith (U.K. Solvency Working Party)

ABSTRACT

The authors challenge the traditional balance sheet concept of the solvency of a general insurance company and put forward an emerging cost concept, which enables the true nature of the assets and liabilities to be taken into account, including their essential variability. Simulation is suggested as a powerful tool for use in examining the financial strength of a company. A simulation model is then used to explore the resilience of a company's financial position to a variety of possible outcomes and to assess the probability that the assets will prove adequate to meet the liabilities with or without an assumption of continuing new business. This suggests the need for an appropriate asset margin assessed individually for each company. The implications for the management and supervision of general insurance companies are explored. The suggestion is made that the effectiveness of supervision based on the balance sheet and a crude solvency margin requirement is limited. More responsibility should be placed on an actuary or other suitably qualified professional individual to report on the overall financial strength of the company, both to management and to the supervisory authorities.

1. The nature of solvency

1.1 The financial position of a general insurance company is normally disclosed through annual accounts for shareholders and through returns to relevant supervisory authorities. Solvency is demonstrated by showing that the assets exceed the liabilities. To a large degree the bases are chosen by the company. For supervisory purposes it is not just a question of the assets exceeding the liabilities. The assets must normally exceed the liabilities by a specified margin.

1.2 In life assurance there is a report by the actuary on the valuation of the liabilities. By contrast the basis on which general insurance liabilities have been assessed is not usually stated. Furthermore, whereas in life assurance actuaries take account of the assets and effectively advise on the total financial strength of the company, there is no one with this role in a general insurance company. It is frequently the case that no specific account is taken of the suitability of the assets to match the expected liabilities nor of the resilience of the balance sheet position disclosed to the inherent uncertainty in both assets and liabilities.

1.3 In principle, the balance sheet represents no more than the Directors' opinion about the financial position of the company. There is considerable uncertainty about the true amount of the liabilities and the realizable value of the assets. The auditors may place some restraints on how the Directors present the position but their role is largely confined to ensuring that what the Directors have done is reasonable.

1.4 There is in fact no single correct value that can be ascribed to either assets or liabilities. Different values may be appropriate according to one's perspective. Shareholders want a "true and fair" view, authorities want a cautious assessment of the position and tax authorities want as little as possible to be offset against taxable profits, to name but three interested parties. A balance sheet which shows a solvent position should reflect an expectation that the assets will be adequate, but it may, either deliberately or inadvertently, present a misleading picture. It certainly does not give any idea of the probability that the assets may prove to be inadequate to meet the liabilities.

1.5 In most countries a general insurance company is permitted by the supervisory authority to carry on writing business only if it has some specified excess of the value of the assets over the liabilities. This clearly increases the probability that the assets will prove sufficient to meet the liabilities, but most solvency margin requirements pay little or no attention to the differing degrees of uncertainty inherent in different types of business, nor do they distinguish adequately between the risks of running off the claim payments on the existing portfolio of business and the risks involved in continuing to write further business.

1.6 Reserving standards are frequently ill-defined or non-existent and do not require special provision to be made to cover the effects of changes in the value of assets on their adequacy to meet the liabilities. Problems may arise from some or all of the following :

* adverse run-off of existing business
* poor underwriting experience
* failure to recover from reinsurers
* falls in asset values
* excessive expenses
* mismanagement, negligence or fraud

A more extended description of the factors affecting solvency and a discussion of the interaction between solvency margin requirements and standards for technical provisions may be found in a paper by Daykin et al (1984).

1.7 The object of a statutory solvency margin is two-fold. It reduces the probability that the assets will prove inadequate to meet the liabilities and it provides a buffer against further deterioration in a company's financial position which can occur in the period before its authorization to write new business can be withdrawn. The effect of a statutory minimum requirement is in practice also to set a somewhat higher formal standard in the market place.

1.8 A solvency margin is not required of other trading companies, but this can be said to reflect not only the nature of the business but also the extent of the insured's interest in the continued viability of the company. In many cases the insured can be exposed to quite serious liabilities in the event of the insurer failing to meet a claim. He cannot limit his liability in the way that he can with a trading company.

1.9 A company can carry on writing business only if the supervisory authority says that it meets the solvency requirements (c.f. Stewart (1971)). The way in which they lay down requirements for this purpose will differ from the criteria which would be used by a Court in determining whether a company should be wound up. It is in fact relatively rare for insurance companies to be wound up by the Courts. It is more normal for the existing business to be run off to extinction or be transferred to another company. The latter procedure is more common in some countries than others.

## 2. Break-up or going-concern?

2.1 The concern with safeguarding the position should the company cease trading is peculiarly the preserve of the supervisory authority. It arises because one of the main weapons available to the supervisory authority is the possibility of preventing a company from writing any further business. The supervisory authority will be subject to criticism if it stops a company from taking on any further business only when the position has been reached that the company cannot even meet its liabilities in respect of business already on its books. The consequence of this is that the supervisory authority will seek to close a company to new business when it can still be expected that the run-off of the existing liabilities will give rise to a surplus of assets, in other words the company is de facto solvent.

2.2 In order to achieve their objective of a "satisfactory" run-off, the supervisory authority is likely to take the view that outstanding claim provision should be sufficient to enable all claims to be met with a reasonably high degree of probability. Failure to maintain an additional solvency margin over and above the outstanding claim provision would not then imply that the company is unable to meet its existing liabilities, but that it does not have sufficient free resources to satisfy the supervisory authority that it should be permitted to continue writing business. Supervisory authorities using this approach are using what might be termed a "break-up" basis, i.e it is assumed that no further business is written but existing business is run off to extinction.

2.3 In the EEC a two-stage solvency margin trigger has been adopted. The higher level is referred to as the required solvency margin and the lower is termed the guarantee fund. The origins of the EEC requirements have been described by Daykin (1984). If an insurer fails to maintain its required solvency margin it must provide to the supervisor a plan for the restoration of a sound financial position, which may include demonstration that on a properly drawn-up business plan, and with realistic assumptions about profitability, the solvency margin will be restored within a reasonably short space of time. Only if the company fails to maintain the guarantee fund, set at one-third of the solvency margin, with a specified minimum in absolute terms, is immediate action to inject additional capital required in order to stave off withdrawal of authorization.

2.4 This approach is in practice not very different from one which assesses the company on a "going-concern" basis. Theoretically, the main differences will be in relation to the provision for outstanding claims, where a "going-concern" basis might include less of a margin than a "break-up" basis, and the provision for expenses, where a strict "break-up" basis would require a technical provision to be made to cover all the costs of running off the existing business. On a "going-concern" basis these costs may be set against the continuing business of the company and it is probable that the past liabilities may be able to be run off for a lesser sum than on the break-up basis. Yet another possible basis of assessment would be a "winding-up" basis, in which the assets are divided up and distributed on the basis of an estimate of the liabilities. This requires the assets to be realized at an early date, which in practice may have the effect of depressing market values.

2.5 A key objective of the management of an insurance company is to ensure that it does not have to cease trading. The accounts prepared for shareholders will reflect this by being prepared, as is the normal convention, on a going-concern basis. Whilst continuing solvency is also a concern of the shareholders, in most cases this will be taken for granted, and the objective of the accounts should be to provide a true and fair view of the financial position of the company. For this purpose, technical provisions should not be overestimated or contain cautious margins and any adverse development of outstanding claims will emerge in due course and affect future profitability. In spite of the differences in the purposes for which the provisions are required, however, most companies adopt the same provisions for their accounts as they do for their statutory returns.

2.6 Whether seen from the viewpoint of the supervisory authority, from that of the shareholder or from that of an outside analyst, a common problem is the uncertainty as to the strength of the technical provisions. This might be helped by more clearly defined reserving standards and by more disclosure of the basis for the provisions, but there is still the fundamental weakness that the assets and the liabilities are not being valued on consistent bases and variability is not taken into account.

2.7 The division of a company's resources into technical provisions and "free" assets is not necessarily helpful from the point of view of establishing the true financial strength of the company. Most of the so-called surplus or "asset margin" (the excess of assets over liabilities) may in fact be needed to reduce the probability of being unable to meet the liabilities to an acceptably low level, particularly if the provisions are only "best estimates". To examine financial strength, all of the resources of the company need to be brought into consideration.

## 3. Emerging costs

3.1 Although the current market value of the investments is increasingly coming to be disclosed in shareholders' accounts, at least in the UK, and is required by supervisory authorities for the statutory returns, its advantages are mainly in relation to its objectivity as a value to be placed on the company's investments, rather than in relation to its relevance to the ability of the company to meet its liabilities, even in the context of the break-up basis.

3.2 The assets will not in practice have to be realized on a particular date and, in any case, by the time the accounts or returns have been prepared, the market value at the date to which those accounts relate is a matter of no more than historical interest. What is important is whether the proceeds of the assets, both capital and income, will prove sufficient to meet the liabilities as they emerge. This is true solvency.

3.3 The concept of projecting the emerging costs of the liabilities to which an enterprise is subject and placing them alongside the expected pattern of income is one which is familiar to actuaries in the life assurance and pensions contexts and is also fundamental to investment appraisal by economists in many other spheres of industry. However, little work seems to have been done on the application of the concept to general insurance companies.

3.4 There has been some theoretical consideration by Kahane (1979) and Kahane and Biger (1979). Actuarial concepts of looking at the company as a whole were applied to general insurance in a paper by Benjamin (1980) and the use of emerging costs was implicit in papers by Ryan (1980,1984), on the use of simulation techniques in general insurance. Coutts et al (1984) set out more fully the fundamental concepts of the emerging costs of a general insurance company and a practical example was presented in a paper by Daykin and Bernstein (1985) on run-off and asset risks.

3.5 The concept is a simple one. It involves analysing the inflows and outflows of actual cash in each successive year. The inflows may consist of some or all of the following:

* premium income
* interest and dividends on assets
* maturity proceeds of assets
* reinsurance recoveries in respect of claims

The outflows may consist of the following:

* claims settled or amounts paid on account
* reinsurance premiums
* expenses
* tax
* dividends

3.6 The effect of the various items in each year will be either a net amount available for investment or a shortfall. In the latter case assets need to be sold to meet the deficit. So long as there are sufficient assets available to enable all the outflows to be met as they arise, the company is solvent in an absolute sense, whatever the balance sheet may have shown. If all the assets have been realized but net liabilities still remain, the situation is one of de facto insolvency.

3.7 An emerging cost analysis should be carried out on the totality of the assets and liabilities of the company. For this purpose the dividing line between technical provisions and asset margin is of no real importance, although estimates of future claim payments are necessary. The uncertainties of general insurance are such that it will not generally be sufficient to use deterministic values for the liabilities and the assets. Some measures of variability need to be introduced. However, this should not be allowed to detract from the essential simplicity of the concept. It only means that some or all of the items listed above should be treated as random variables. To handle this the emerging costs can be examined using simulation.

3.8 A single simulation is one realization of a random process in which each of the required quantities is assigned a value. By examining a large number of simulations a picture can be obtained of the likely pattern of development resulting from the interaction of the various variables. Simulation permits the use of stochastic models for the investment processes and allows the uncertainty in the outstanding claims and in the profitability of new business to be taken into account. The approach has much in common with the ideas developed by the Finnish Solvency Working Party (Pentikäinen and Rantala (1982)) and extended to cover run-off risk by Pentikäinen and Rantala (1986), although they did not use a stochastic approach for the investments.

3.9 In practice the various elements may be modelled in a variety of different ways. For some purposes very complex models may be desirable; for others a simpler model may suffice, although any model which is going to give a reasonably realistic representation of the real world is bound to be fairly complex. The important principle is that the totality of the company's operations is being considered.

3.10 The procedure is very flexible. It might enable, for example, questions to be asked about the impact of alternative strategies for premium rating or investment and about the effect of possible adverse claim development or failure to recover from reinsurers. It provides a management tool and also seems to offer a way forward for more rational supervision. This would involve the submission to the authorities of a report on total financial strength by an actuary or other suitably qualified expert, as a supplement to minimum balance sheet requirements. The result would be a system much better able to take account of the true position of each company, having regard to the specific risks to which it is subject and the inherent uncertainties of both assets and liabilities.

## 4. The simulation model

### 4.1 General structure

4.1.1 In order to demonstrate the potential of the emerging costs approach we present here a model which provides a representation of the dynamics of a general insurance operation. In order to be reasonably realistic the model is quite complex but, however complicated the model, it is essential that the concepts should be capable of being put across in a straightforward way and the results must be capable of being presented in ways that can be directly related to management concerns such as corporate strategy and decision-making.

4.1.2 At its most basic, the model is a projection of cash flow, bringing together income from premiums and from assets and outgo in respect of expenses, tax, dividends and claims, determining the net balance for each year, investing or disinvesting as the case may be and proceeding similarly for as many years into the future as one wishes. It may be considered more fully in terms of three separate components:

* liabilities arising from existing business

* future premiums and the liabilities resulting from the risks underwritten

* asset returns and asset value movements

4.1.3 A mathematical formulation of the model is given in Appendices 1 and 2 and a description of the computer program in Appendix 3.

### 4.2 Existing liabilities

4.2.1 The existing liabilities, as shown in the balance sheet, consist of estimates of outstanding claims, including IBNR, and unearned premium reserves (including any additional amount for unexpired risks). Unearned premiums can be dealt with along similar lines to new written premiums (see section 4.3) since the uncertainty includes uncertainty about the adequacy of premium rates in relation to events which have not yet occurred.

4.2.2 As far as outstanding claims are concerned, there is uncertainty about the amounts of claims and about when they will be settled. The model needs to provide an adequate representation of this uncertainty. We make the simplifying assumption that the variability in rates of settlement can be subsumed into a variation in the amount of claims settled in each period.

4.2.3 The first stage is to estimate the expected claim payments in each successive year for each year of origin. In order to do this, fixed settlement patterns have to be specified in constant money terms. The model permits different run-off patterns to be assumed for different types of business. Inflation then has to be allowed for. Future inflation is generated by a stochastic model and this is combined with the expected settlements in constant money terms to give the expected development of claim amounts. The inflation model is an integral part of the models used for the assets (see paragraph 4.4.4).

4.2.4 The variability of claim amounts payable in each period can be dealt with in a variety of ways. In an earlier paper describing the application of a similar model to a run-off situation, Daykin and Bernstein (1985) proposed that the actual outstanding claims settled in each year in respect of each year of origin should be varied. They assumed that each separate entry in the run-off triangle was distributed about the mean estimate of claims settled at that particular duration for that year of origin in accordance with a log normal distribution. This was attractive as a means of simulating the interaction between different years of origin and different classes of business, but it resulted in a somewhat lengthy simulation process.

4.2.5 In order to simplify the model and allow account to be taken of different sizes of company, the model presented here uses an aggregate approach, whereby the amount that is varied is the total amount of claims settled in a particular period, for all years of origin combined. This aggregate figure is assumed to vary according to a normal distribution with a standard deviation of the type:

$$aX + b\sqrt{X}$$

where X is the mean estimate of total claim payments in the year and a and b are suitably chosen constants. We understand that a similar formula is used by the Finnish supervisory authority for their statutory minimum solvency margin (see Appendix 5 for discussion of this formula which can be considered to be an approximation to the formula derived by Buchanan and Taylor (1986)).

4.2.6 The amounts payable in future years in respect of risks arising from future written premiums and from unearned premium reserves are included with the amounts payable in respect of existing liabilities before applying the overall variability formula. The extent of the assumed variability can be adjusted by varying the constants a and b in the formula above. For a standard basis we have assumed that they take the values 0.15 and 75 respectively, with claim amounts being expressed in £ sterling. The amounts payable in successive years are assumed to vary independently of each other. The variability is intended to cover not only stochastic variability of claim amounts, but also uncertainty about the expected run-off model in constant money terms. Uncertainty about future inflation is dealt with separately.

4.2.7 Two typical run-off patterns have been assumed, characterized as short and long-tailed. Details are given in Appendix 3. In order to place a value on the technical provisions which would be established at the outset in respect of the outstanding claims, it has been assumed that inflation would be allowed for at 5% a year and that the resulting outstanding claims would not be discounted. (For further discussion on the interaction between the reserving basis and the solvency margin, see paragraph 5.2).

4.2.8 In practice an actual outstanding claim portfolio could be used as the basis for the input to the model in respect of existing liabilities. It would need to be expressed as an expected run-off in constant money terms. For illustrative purposes, however, we have assumed that the outstanding claims have been generated as a result of a past pattern of business. The existing liabilities at the base date have been generated in a similar way to the liabilities in respect of future written premiums, by specifying a rate of real premium growth and claim ratios. For the purpose of generating the outstanding claims at the base date no variability was assumed in the historic claim ratios, in contrast to the process described in section 4.3. In conjunction with the specified run-off patterns and the inflation model, the liabilities generated in this way give rise to estimates of outstanding claims payable in each future year in respect of each past year of origin.

### 4.3 Future written premiums

4.3.1 Future premiums are generated from an assumed initial premium level and an assumed real annual growth rate. The effects of inflation are then built in explicitly. Although the existing portfolio of business is generated by assuming a past pattern of premium growth, as described in paragraph 4.2.8 above, a different growth rate assumption may be made for the future. The proportions of written premiums which are assumed to relate to different types of business can be specified. The written premiums are taken to be net of commission and initial expenses.

4.3.2 For each year for which additional premiums are assumed to be written, a ratio of claims to premiums net of commission and expenses is generated for each type of business. The ratio is assumed to be normally distributed with mean and standard deviation to be specified. The resulting ratio is applied to the assumed net written premiums to produce an initial estimate of total claims in respect of that business, without any allowance for future inflation or for discounting. This ratio is such that a value of 100% implies break-even if future investment income exactly balances inflation. The assumed proportions of claims settled in each future year are then applied to obtain uninflated estimates of expected claim payments. Future inflation, as generated by the model described below (paragraph 4.4.4), is incorporated when the expected claim payments in terms of constant money have been aggregated with the corresponding estimates in respect of the existing liabilities. The combined estimates are then varied as described in paragraph 4.2.5 above.

4.3.3 Since the claim ratios generated are ratios of claims to written premiums net of commission and expenses, no explicit allowance needs to be made for these items of outgo. Expenses of claim settlement are assumed to be included in the costs of settled claims.

4.3.4 This relatively simple approach has been used as a practical expedient in view of the complexity of the underlying risk process. An alternative approach, described by Beard et al (1984) and developed in the Report of the Finnish Solvency Working Party (Pentikäinen and Rantala (1982)), would be to treat the basic claim process as a Poisson process and then build on a series of "structure variables" to take account of:

* trends in claim frequency

* long term variations in premium rate adequacy

* year to year fluctuations in mean claim frequency

Further assumptions then have to be made about the claim size distribution.

4.3.5 Whilst it is clearly possible to specify a model which takes explicit account of each of these, the added complexity can only be justified if the parameters of the model can be satisfactorily determined. We have not as yet been able to assemble data in a suitable form for calibrating such a model. The problem of calibration still arises with the simpler model, but it is intuitively more accessible and enables judgement to be applied in the area which is probably of the greatest importance, i.e. changes in the relationship between premium levels prevailing in the market and the underlying risk premium. This is the factor described as "long-term cycles" by Pentikäinen and Rantala (1982).

4.3.6 Although the adequacy of premium rates does exhibit the characteristics of a business cycle, experience seems to show that the variation does not have a regular periodicity or a constant amplitude. A considerable degree of judgement is needed to decide where in the "cycle" the industry finds itself at any particular moment. Our model allows for the user to give explicit consideration to this and requires the mean claim ratio for the next couple of years to be estimated. If the model were to be used to examine the effects of future written premiums over a longer period than 2 years, further consideration would need to be given to modelling this component. The assumption of a normal distribution of claim ratios about the mean is a not unreasonable approximation, bearing in mind the large numbers of claims involved.

### 4.4 Asset variability

4.4.1 The variability inherent in the asset portfolio of a company depends on the nature and distribution of the assets. The realizable value of many assets will vary from day to day as market conditions change. In our model, the initial distribution of the assets by category has to be specified and the various components of the asset distribution are then analysed separately, simulating the income generated and the capital value of each type of asset for each future year. Rules need to be specified for investment and disinvestment.

4.4.2 Three different types of asset are assumed: cash, irredeemable Government securities and ordinary shares. A more realistic model would replace investment in irredeemable Government securities with short, medium and long-dated securities. In practice, however, short-dated securities behave somewhat like cash and long-dated securities like irredeemables, so the model can be regarded as a tolerable proxy and gets round the problem of the reducing life of dated stocks over time. Allowance has not been made for a proportion of the assets being effectively non-interest-bearing (eg agents' balances) but this could easily be done.

4.4.3 The development of the various components of the asset distribution has been represented by a series of interrelated stochastic processes, suggested by Wilkie (1984, 1986), which generate future scenarios for the values of different types of asset and the income from them. Although Wilkie's models were not originally intended to be used for relatively short-term simulations such as those with which we are concerned, we have adopted them as a readily available and coherent model of asset movements and inflation. Further work is needed on suitable asset models and the sensitivity of the results to the particular models used. Our results show that this is a most important aspect of the whole simulation model.

4.4.4 The models are described in detail in Appendix 2. In addition to the models of asset returns and asset values, the Wilkie models include a model for inflation and this has been used where it is needed in the simulation of the liabilities.

4.4.5 The initial asset mix is based on assets covering the technical provisions and assets representing the asset margin. Different distributions may be specified for each. A variety of different investment and disinvestment strategies may be applied to the total funds.

4.5 Results of the simulations

4.5.1 The number of potential combinations of variables is vast, even allowing each variable to take only three or four different values. We have limited our considerations by adopting a standard set of parameters and normally varying only one parameter at a time.

4.5.2 The simulation process involves sampling scenarios from an infinite set and the results are necessarily subject to statistical error. For any particular case which is of interest more simulations can be carried out in order to improve the accuracy of the estimate. In order to illustrate the results on a large number of scenarios, we have limited our considerations to 1000 simulations for each. For each parameter combination the same 1000 sets of random numbers are used, so that the comparisons are not significantly affected by any bias in the particular sets of random numbers chosen.

4.5.3 Figure 1 shows, for illustrative purposes, the results of 100 simulations, assuming no new business. This demonstrates the general shape of the results, which is common to all the scenarios, although the variability differs greatly. The graph shows the assets of the model company year by year throughout the run-off of the business.

4.5.4 When a line goes below the x-axis, this implies that all the assets have been exhausted on that particular simulation. If that should occur before the end of the run-off, true insolvency has occurred. In describing the results of the simulations, insolvency is used in this sense, without regard to the way in which the financial position of the company might be presented in the accounts or statutory returns at the base date or at any later date.

4.5.5 We thus define:

* an insolvency occurs when the assets run out before all the liabilities have been met (on an emerging cost basis)

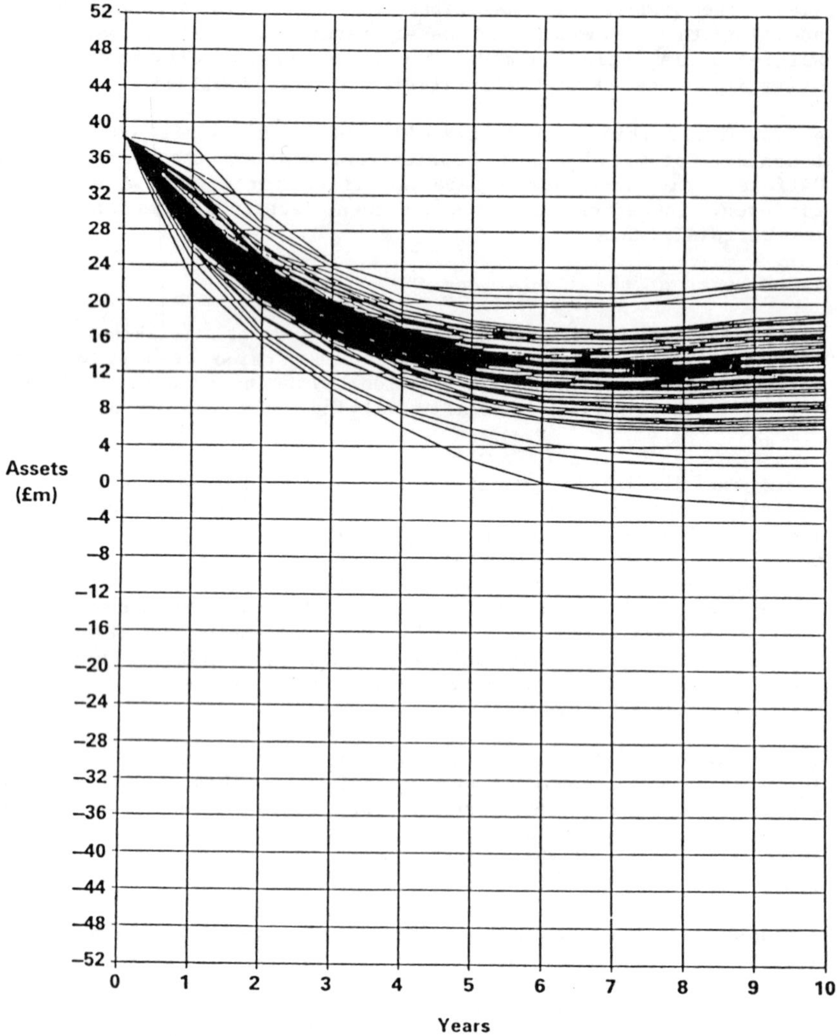


Run-off of assets assuming no new business (100 simulations)

Figure 1

In the simulations a realization which runs into insolvency is allowed to continue by borrowing (at the rate of interest on cash plus a margin of 3 per cent); this permits one to see how insolvent it becomes.

4.5.6 On the standard basis insolvency in this sense occurred in 8 cases out of 1000 with no new business and 50 cases out of 1000 with 2 years' new business. The distribution of assets at the end of the run-off, deflated to the date of assessment using the retail prices index, is summarized in Table 1. The written premiums in question are those in the year before the base date. It should be recalled that the written premiums are net of commission and expenses. Results expressed as percentages of net written premiums can be rated down (say, by applying a factor of 75% or 80%, depending on the type of business) to obtain comparable results in terms of gross written premiums. The mean level of remaining assets for the 1000 simulations was 112% of net written premiums with no new business and 144% with 2 years' new business, with standard deviations of 70% and 109% respectively of net written premiums.

**Table 1**

**Distribution of Assets at End of Run-off from 1000 Simulations on Standard Basis**

| Remaining assets as % of net written premiums | Number of cases<br>Pure run-off | Number of cases<br>2 years' new business |
|---|---|---|
| less than 0% | 8 | 50 |
| 0-20 | 31 | 34 |
| 20-40 | 67 | 62 |
| 40-60 | 128 | 65 |
| 60-80 | 124 | 81 |
| 80-100 | 136 | 78 |
| 100-120 | 128 | 93 |
| 120-140 | 104 | 91 |
| 140-160 | 69 | 84 |
| 160 and over | 205 | 362 |
| Mean | 112 | 144 |

Notes: The remaining assets at the end of the run-off are deflated to the date of assessment using the retail prices index. Premiums are net of commission and initial expenses.

4.5.7 Full details of the assumptions underlying the standard basis are given in Appendix 4. However, we will return to the results after commenting on the application of the model.

4.6 Application of the model

4.6.1 A simulation model of the insurance company, based on the emerging cost concept, provides a powerful and flexible tool for examining the dynamics of an insurer's operation, for exploring the effects of uncertainty and for developing the financial aspects of corporate strategy within a logical framework. This should be of value both to management and to the supervisory authorities. Crucial to this process would be the presence of a suitably qualified actuary or other expert within the company, or acting as consultant, who could develop a suitable model and apply the necessary judgement to the use of the model in the circumstances of the particular company. The responsible expert would report to management on the financial strength of the company, taking all relevant factors into account.

4.6.2 The simulation approach would also enable the actuary to advise management on the potential effects of different new business and investment strategies, the risks involved and the return on capital which might be expected if additional capital is injected to enable a particular strategy to be adopted.

4.6.3 A report on the financial strength of the company could accompany the statutory returns to the supervisory authority. The actuary would be answerable to the supervisor on the details of this report. One could envisage this leading to an informed dialogue between the supervisory authority and the company under scrutiny on the nature of the proposed corporate strategy, whether in relation to investment policy, growth or premium levels. The supervisor could then ask for an assessment of the effect of alternative strategies and seek agreement with the company on appropriate changes to its strategy as a condition for being permitted to continue writing business.

5. Solvency considerations

5.1 The results of the simulations can be presented in terms of numbers of insolvencies out of a given number of simulations. This is an estimate of the probability of ruin. Each result derives from an assumption about the excess of assets over technical provisions (the "asset margin") and a specified basis for calculating the latter. Given a basis for the technical provisions, the process can be used to derive the required initial asset margin in order to achieve a specified probability of ruin in a particular case.

5.2 The required asset margin will clearly differ according to differing definitions of the technical provisions. Table 2 illustrates this point. The table shows the technical provisions on the standard basis described above and the technical provisions on alternative bases as to inflation and discounting, but for the same set of outstanding claims. The table shows what asset margins would be necessary, expressed both as a percentage of technical provisions and as a percentage of net written premiums, in order to achieve the same degree of overall security as the technical provisions on the standard basis. Technical provisions on the standard basis are calculated assuming 5% inflation and no discounting. Thus if the reserves do not allow for any future inflation, or have been discounted using a rate of interest equal to the assumed rate of inflation, an asset margin of 21% of net written premiums or 9% of technical provisions would be needed to produce the same level of total assets as the technical provisions alone on the standard basis. The figures in this table underline the arbitrary nature of a statutory solvency requirement unless standards of technical provisions can be adequately specified.

**Table 2**

**Technical Provisions and Asset Margins**

| Reserving basis (net inflation assumed) | Technical provisions | Asset margin to achieve same security as standard: | |
|---|---|---|---|
| | | percentage of net written premiums | percentage of technical provisions |
| -5% | £20450 | 39% | 19% |
| 0 | 22264 | 21 | 9 |
| 5 | 24364 | 0 | 0 |
| 10 | 26805 | -24 | -9 |
| 15 | 29656 | -53 | -18 |

Notes: Premiums are net of commission and initial expenses. Technical provisions are based on 40% long-tailed business and 60% short-tailed.

5.3 First we give some results for a pure run-off, i.e. with no future premiums assumed to be written. The outstanding claims and unexpired risks are allowed to emerge and the adequacy of the total assets (technical provisions and asset margin) is examined. Table 3 shows the number of insolvencies and the mean assets remaining at the end of the run-off and the standard deviation of the assets remaining on some alternative bases. Table 4 gives a similar set of results with the inclusion of 2 further years' written premiums. Appendix 4 gives details of all the assumptions and a full set of results.

5.4 Tables 5 and 6 show the asset margins required to achieve a probability of ruin of 1 in 100 for each of the combinations of assumptions in Tables 3 and 4 respectively, assuming that the technical provisions are established on the standard basis of 5% inflation and no discounting. The asset margins are shown in terms of both net written premiums in the year before the base date and as a percentage of technical provisions at the base date. The results can be expressed in terms of net written premiums even for the pure run-off case, since these are the premiums in the year before the base date when premiums are assumed to cease. As described in paragraph 4.2.8, we have in fact generated the outstanding claims from past premiums. The difference between Tables 5 and 6 provides a measure of the additional capital needed in order to go on writing business for two more years.

5.5 It is clear that the results obtained depend critically on the models used and the parameters assumed. More work is needed on a number of different aspects. However, the results presented do appear consistent and sensible and variations in relation to changing parameter values conform with general reasoning.

5.6 It is difficult from these results to draw conclusions about an appropriate level of a minimum statutory solvency margin. In fact we have avoided using the term solvency margin in this section because of its special significance in statutory terms and have referred to the necessary margin as the asset margin. Our asset margins relate to particular assumptions about the basis for the technical provisions and provide a defined degree of security in relation to specified scenarios on the basis of our model. A statutory solvency margin, in the sense in which it is usually used, provides a general level of security, independent of the particular circumstances of the company, against all possible future scenarios, including the effect of unquantifiable risks such as fraud, mismanagement and the failure of reinsurers.

5.7 A starting point for consideration of an appropriate level of statutory solvency margin might be to look at the asset margin for a company with a fairly standard distribution of business, a

**Table 3**

**Summary of Results for Pure Run-off of Business (with 1000 simulations)**

| Assumptions | | | No of insol-vencies | Mean assets remaining | Standard deviation of assets remaining |
|---|---|---|---|---|---|
| Standard basis | | | 8 | 112% | 79% |
| 1. Net written premiums: | | | | | |
| £1m a year | | | 20 | 113 | 75 |
| £10m a year (s) | | | 8 | 112 | 70 |
| £100m a year | | | 6 | 112 | 69 |
| 2. Proportion of long-tailed business: | | | | | |
| 20% of net written premiums | | | 3 | 94 | 55 |
| 40% of net written premiums (s) | | | 8 | 112 | 70 |
| 60% of net written premiums | | | 13 | 130 | 85 |
| 3. Initial asset distribution: | | | | | |
| Cash | Gilts | Equities | | | |
| TP+AM | - | - | 3 | 95 | 53 |
| - | TP+AM | - | 20 | 120 | 98 |
| - | - | TP+AM | 49 | 136 | 115 |
| ½TP | ½TP | AM (s) | 8 | 112 | 70 |
| 4. Initial asset margin: | | | | | |
| 0% of net written premiums | | | 134 | 52 | 55 |
| 20% of net written premiums | | | 36 | 83 | 62 |
| 40% of net written premiums (s) | | | 8 | 112 | 70 |
| 60% of net written premiums | | | 2 | 147 | 80 |
| 80% of net written premiums | | | 0 | 180 | 90 |
| 5. Asset selling rules: | | | | | |
| Equities; gilts; cash | | | 9 | 102 | 66 |
| Cash; gilts; equities | | | 7 | 123 | 79 |
| In proportion to holdings (s) | | | 8 | 112 | 70 |
| Sell best performer first | | | 14 | 108 | 70 |

Notes: The remaining assets at the end of the run-off are deflated to the date of assessment using the retail prices index and expressed as a percentage of net written premiums in the year before the date of assessment (See App 3.6.8). Premiums are net of commission and expenses.
(s) indicates the assumption made for the standard basis.
TP = technical provisions, AM = asset margin.

**Table 4**

**Summary of Results with 2 Further Years' Business (with 1000 simulations)**

| Assumptions | No of insol-vencies | Mean assets remain-ing | Standard deviation of assets remaining |
|---|---|---|---|
| Standard basis | 50 | 144% | 109% |
| 1. Net written premiums: | | | |
| £1m a year | 61 | 144 | 117 |
| £10m a year(s) | 50 | 144 | 109 |
| £100m a year | 43 | 144 | 107 |
| 2. Proportion of long-tailed business: | | | |
| 20% of net written premiums | 48 | 120 | 91 |
| 40% of net written premiums (s) | 50 | 144 | 109 |
| 60% of net written premiums | 52 | 168 | 130 |
| 3. Real growth rate (past and future): | | | |
| -20% a year | 53 | 171 | 134 |
| No growth(s) | 50 | 144 | 109 |
| +50% a year | 83 | 144 | 121 |
| 4. Mean claim ratio (short-tailed): | | | |
| 80% of net written premiums | 7 | 187 | 117 |
| 100% of net written premiums (s) | 50 | 144 | 109 |
| 125% of net written premiums | 165 | 90 | 103 |
| 5. Variability of claim ratio (short-tailed): | | | |
| Standard variation 5% NWP | 49 | 144 | 109 |
| Standard deviation 10% NWP (s) | 50 | 144 | 109 |
| Standard deviation 15% NWP | 48 | 144 | 111 |
| 6. Mean claim ratio (long-tailed): | | | |
| 80% of net written premiums | 17 | 163 | 106 |
| 100% of net written premiums (s) | 50 | 144 | 109 |
| 125% of net written premiums | 105 | 120 | 114 |
| 7. Variability of claim ratio (long-tailed): | | | |
| Standard deviation 10% NWP | 50 | 144 | 109 |
| Standard deviation 15% NWP (s) | 50 | 144 | 109 |
| Standard deviation 20% NWP | 49 | 144 | 110 |

**Table 4 (cont.)**

**Summary of Results with 2 Further Years' Business (with 1000 simulations)**

| Assumptions | No of insol- vencies | Mean assets remain- ing | Standard deviation of assets remaining |
|---|---|---|---|
| Standard basis | 50 | 144% | 109% |
| 8. Initial asset distribution: | | | |
| Cash Gilts Equities | | | |
| TP+AM - - | 46 | 118 | 86 |
| - TP+AM - | 79 | 155 | 152 |
| - - TP+ AM | 86 | 181 | 172 |
| ½TP ½TP AM (s) | 50 | 144 | 109 |
| 9. Initial asset margin: | | | |
| 0% of net written premiums | 196 | 74 | 98 |
| 40% of net written premiums (s) | 50 | 144 | 109 |
| 80% of net written premiums | 11 | 216 | 133 |

Notes: The remaining assets at the end of the run-off are deflated to the date of assessment using the retail prices index and expressed as a percentage of net written premiums in the year before the date of assessment (See App 3.6.8). Premiums are net of commission and expenses. The mean claim ratio is the ratio of claims (including claim settlement expenses), without allowance for future inflation or for discounting, to premiums net of commission and expenses (see paragraph 4.3.2).
(s) indicates the assumption made for the standard basis.
TP = technical provisions, AM = asset margin.

**Table 5**

**Asset Margins Required to Achieve 1/100 Probability of Ruin - No Future Business**

| Assumptions | Asset margin as % of NWP | Asset margin as % of TP |
|---|---|---|
| Standard basis | 40% | 15% |
| 1. Net written premiums: | | |
| £1m a year | 55 | 25 |
| £10m a year (s) | 40 | 15 |
| £100m a year | 35 | 15 |
| 2. Proportion of long-tailed business: | | |
| 20% of net written premiums | 30 | 15 |
| 40% of net written premiums (s) | 40 | 15 |
| 60% of net written premiums | 45 | 15 |
| 3. Initial asset distribution: | | |
| Cash Gilts Equities | | |
| TP+AM - - | 30 | 10 |
| - TP+AM - | 60 | 25 |
| - - TP+AM | 80 | 35 |
| ½TP ½TP AM (s) | 40 | 15 |
| 4. Asset selling rules: | | |
| Equities; gilts; cash | 40 | 15 |
| Cash; gilts; equities | 35 | 15 |
| In proportion to holdings (s) | 40 | 15 |
| Sell best performer first | 55 | 25 |

Notes: Premiums are net of commission and expenses.
(s) indicates the assumption made for the standard basis.
NWP = net written premiums, TP = technical provisions, AM = asset margin.

**Table 6**

**Asset Margins Required to Achieve 1/100 Probability of Ruin - Two Years' New Business**

| Assumptions | Asset margin as % of NWP | Excess margin as compared to run-off (as % of NWP) |
|---|---|---|
| Standard basis | 90% | 50% |
| 1. Net written premiums: | | |
| £1m a year | 100 | 45 |
| £10m a year (s) | 90 | 50 |
| £100m a year | 80 | 45 |
| 2. Proportion of long-tailed business: | | |
| 20% of net written premiums | 80 | 50 |
| 40% of net written premiums (s) | 90 | 50 |
| 60% of net written premiums | 95 | 50 |
| 3. Real growth rate (past and future): | | |
| -20% a year | 100 | 35 |
| No growth (s) | 90 | 50 |
| +50% a year | 115 | 85 |
| 4. Mean claim ratio (short-tailed): | | |
| 80% of net written premiums | 30 | 0 |
| 100% of net written premiums (s) | 90 | 50 |
| 125% of net written premiums | 125 | 75 |
| 5. Variability of claim ratio (short-tailed): | | |
| Standard deviation 5% NWP | 80 | 45 |
| Standard deviation 10% NWP (s) | 90 | 50 |
| Standard deviation 15% NWP | 85 | 45 |
| 6. Mean claim ratio (long-tailed): | | |
| 80% of net written premiums | 50 | 20 |
| 100% of net written premiums (s) | 90 | 50 |
| 125% of net written premiums | 115 | 60 |
| 7. Variability of claim ratio (long-tailed) | | |
| Standard deviation 10% NWP | 85 | 50 |
| Standard deviation 15% NWP | 90 | 50 |
| Standard deviation 20% NWP | 90 | 50 |

**Table 6 (cont.)**

**Asset Margins Required to Achieve 1/100 Probability of Ruin - Two Years' New Business**

| Assumptions | | | | Asset margin as % of NWP | Excess margin as compared to run-off (as % of NWP) |
|---|---|---|---|---|---|
| Standard basis | | | | 90% | 50% |
| 8. Initial asset distribution: | | | | | |
| Cash | Gilts | Equities | | | |
| TP+AM | - | - | | 85 | 55 |
| - | TP+AM | - | | 110 | 50 |
| - | - | TP+AM | | 135 | 55 |
| ½TP | ½TP | AM | (s) | 90 | 50 |

Notes: Premiums are net of commission and expenses. The mean claim ratio is the ratio of claims (including claim settlement expenses), without allowance for future inflation or for discounting, to premiums net of commission and expenses (see paragraph 4.3.2). (s) indicates the assumption made for the standard basis. NWP = net written premiums, TP = technical provisions, AM = asset margin.

moderate growth rate and investment entirely in cash. In our view the resulting margin ought to be in two parts:

* a percentage of the technical provisions at the assessment date;

* a percentage of written premiums.

The former represents the margin required in respect of the run-off risks and the latter the margin required in respect of writing up to two years' further new business. To the new business margin might be added a contingency loading to cover other unquantifiable risks.

5.8 This would provide a basic safety net for an average company, assuming that technical provisions were at least up to the standard envisaged. Statutory reserving standards might be necessary to achieve this, since it has to be recognised that a solvency margin requirement based on technical provisions has a similar weakness to one based on written premiums. If the provisions are understated the requirement is reduced, whereas it should in fact be higher.

5.9 Alongside such a basic solvency requirement would be a requirement for a report by an actuary or other expert on the overall financial strength of the company. This would transcend the arbitrary dividing line between technical provisions and solvency margin and would take specific account of the nature of the business written by the company, the proportions of different types of business, the assets held, and all other relevant factors, including the nature of and the security of the reinsurance programme.

5.10 If a requirement for an actuarial report is not introduced, then further consideration would need to be given to whether the solvency margin requirement should include components relating to the assets held and the reinsurance recoveries expected. Regard should also be had to the nature of the outstanding claims portfolio and the type of business being written. However, such a solution would be far from ideal.

## 6. Reinsurance

6.1 Reinsurance business accepted may be regarded as another class of business, which is often particularly volatile and unpredictable. Appropriate reserving levels for casualty reinsurance business are likely to present particular problems, since it can take many years for the liabilities (including IBNR) to develop fully. Solvency margins certainly ought to have regard to this uncertainty. In principle there seems no reason why the simulation approach should not also provide some insights in this area of an insurer's portfolio.

6.2 Much more difficult to handle in the context of the assessment of financial strength is the security of reinsurance cessions. Many insurers are critically dependent on their ability to recover from reinsurers, since the size of the risks they write is such as to bankrupt or cripple them if they had to bear the liability alone. One safeguard against reinsurance failure is to spread reinsurance cessions widely, so that there is not any great dependence on particular reinsurers. However, this does not remove the need to look carefully at the security of individual reinsurers chosen for the programme.

6.3 From the reserving point of view, a decision has to be made on the extent to which reinsurance recoveries can be relied on. Extreme caution might point towards reserving for the full gross liability but this is not a practical commercial possibility in most cases. Clearly recoveries from reinsurance companies already known to be in trouble should be ignored or heavily discounted, but it is more difficult to know what should be done when there are no specific known problems. In accounting terms it may be difficult to set up a provision against an unseen and unquantifiable possibility of reinsurance failure. On the other hand the accountancy concept of prudence would preclude taking credit in advance for receipts which are uncertain, so it would be possible to justify taking only partial credit for reinsurance recoveries, depending on an assessment of the viability of the reinsurers.

6.4 The issue is of particular importance in considering the overall financial strength of the company. This would be one aspect which the actuary would need to cover in his report. Different approaches may be acceptable in different circumstances but simulation does seem to offer a promising way forward. Further work is clearly needed in this area to develop ways of modelling reinsurance recoveries. It has been assumed in our model that all claims are net of reinsurance. This may be good enough for many companies, with relatively little dependence on reinsurance. However, it will be far from adequate for other companies for which the possibility of failure to recover from reinsurers is a significant one and the potential impact disastrous in solvency terms. Some tentative ideas of a possible way of tackling this are set out in Appendix 6.

6.5 A detailed examination of the reinsurance programme can hardly be practicable for the supervisory authorities and here again it seems that an actuary's report would help. No general solvency requirement can be a substitute for this. The practice adopted for the EEC solvency margins of reducing the solvency margin requirement calculated on the basis of gross written premiums to allow for reinsurance based on actual recoveries in the past three years, but with a maximum reduction of 50%, is a very rough and ready solution and does not have any regard to the actual dependence on reinsurers for future recoveries. With non-proportional reinsurance the premium can be very small in relation to the potential liability, so no simple percentage of premium is likely to make sense as a solvency margin. A percentage of anticipated recoveries from reinsurers would have a stronger rationale, but it would be difficult to find a logical basis for any particular percentage.

## 7. CONCLUSIONS

7.1 We have outlined the weaknesses in the traditional balance sheet concept for describing the true financial strength of a general insurance company. Assets and liabilities should not be treated as independent aspects and much more attention needs to be focussed on the uncertainties and on the company's resilience in the face of such uncertainties. Appropriate techniques have been developed by actuaries for dealing with these problems in the life and pensions areas and similar principles can be used to begin to tackle the general insurance problem. The parallels are drawn in a paper by Coutts and Devitt (1986).

7.2 However, there are also differences, arising mainly from the greater volatility of claim amounts in general insurance. The problem of variability can be explored by means of simulation. A simulation model of a general insurance company provides a powerful tool for analysing the impact of all types of uncertainty and assessing the true financial strength of the company.

7.3 A solvency margin requirement expressed in terms of a simple percentage of written premiums (or in terms of a percentage of technical provisions, which might be more appropriate to cover the run-off risk) cannot have proper regard to the risks to which each company is subject, whether as regards the assets or liabilities. It must, therefore, be seen as a general underlying safety net, providing a margin against the effects not only of stochastic variations but also of mismanagement, fraud or simply error, and permitting the statutory authority to operate a satisfactory control system.

7.4 Despite our strong belief that the solvency margin should relate to the various risks affecting the financial position of an insurance company, we acknowledge that there will be interest in the use of our model to provide a rationale for a minimum statutory solvency margin. Time has so far prevented us from carrying out sufficient simulations to explore the full implications of the assumptions made and, in particular, the response of the Wilkie model to changes in parameters. We have also only shown the results for a probability of ruin of one per cent and this level is of course crucial to the resulting asset margins.

7.5 Nevertheless at this level of security Table 5 shows that, for a moderate sized company, writing £100m of net premiums but otherwise on our standard basis, the margin necessary to cover the run-off risks would be 15% of technical provisions, assuming that the provisions for outstanding claims are set up on an undiscounted basis with allowance for inflation at 5% (the mean value used in the Wilkie model). The margin might be reduced to 10% if all the investments are assumed to be held in cash. Such a margin may be over-stringent as a minimum for larger companies but Table 5 indicates that it should be higher for small companies. A similar standard to a 10% margin would be obtained for the mix of business considered here by setting up provisions for outstanding claims allowing for inflation at 10% with no discounting.

7.6 Care has to be taken in interpreting the extra margin implied to be necessary to allow for the risks contingent on writing new business for two years. The margins to cover the run-off risk have been expressed for this purpose in terms of net written premiums and these margins (for the respective sets of assumptions) have then been subtracted from the margins obtained assuming two further years in business. It could be argued that if the risks of new business and run-off are to be provided for independently, then the model should be run with no past business in order to assess the appropriate margin for new business risks. We have not done this as we do not believe that the two issues are independent, there being interactions in regard to both assets and the variability of the run-off of claims. Assuming that the margins expressed as a percentage of net written premiums are additive, Table 6 indicates a margin of 50% of premiums net of commission and expenses for a £100m company, otherwise on our standard basis apart from investment being entirely in cash. This might be equivalent to 35-40% of actual gross written premiums.

7.7 Such a solvency margin requirement appears rather high and it is worth considering briefly some of the major factors which give rise to it. A significant part arises from the effect of simulated future inflation and the possibility that returns on cash will not be adequate to compensate for it. This suggests that the risks might be reduced with greater use of index-linked stocks.

7.8 Much of it also arises from the assumption on the standard basis of a mean claim ratio of 100% of net written premiums. As described in paragraph 4.3.2, this implies break-even if future investment income exactly balances inflation. Thus the assumption is that business is written on a basis where the only profit on an expected value basis is to the extent that a positive real rate of return can be obtained. This might be perceived as too stringent for a minimum solvency margin requirement, although it is not unrealistic in current conditions. The requirement could be reduced by about 1% of actual written premiums for every percentage point by which the expected claim ratios are reduced below 100%.

7.9 Any general solvency requirement will have its limitations. Apart from the points mentioned in paragraph 7.3, there is also the problem of relating the requirement to written premiums or to technical provisions, which may themselves be more adequate for some companies than for others. The adequacy of the technical provisions is of particular importance (c.f. paragraph 5.2), since they determine what assets are apparently available as a margin. There is, therefore, a need for consistent standards to be applied in setting technical provisions, suggesting that there would be considerable advantages in requiring the provisions to be established on the basis of advice from an actuary or other claims reserving expert, acting within the framework of an appropriate professional standard. However, it has to be acknowledged that there is always likely to be some uncertainty about the strength of technical provisions.

7.10 We have also argued that a crude minimum solvency margin requirement cannot adequately have regard to the true level of risk for a particular company. The supervisory authority is not well-placed to assess each company's risk situation in detail on an individual basis and the answer would seem to be to rely on an appointed actuary or other similarly qualified person within the company (or acting as a consultant to the company). The actuary would be responsible for reporting both to management and to the supervisory authority on the financial strength of the company, taking all relevant factors into account. A summary of the actuary's report could appear in the statutory returns, with full details being available to the supervisory authority on request. The supervisory authority would be able to question the actuary on the effects of alternative assumptions and could then discuss with management an appropriate strategy for reducing the risk profile to an acceptable level.

7.11 The actuary would need to use simulation techniques in performing his duties. There is plenty of scope for developing appropriate simulation models for this task and one such model is presented here as an example of what can be done. Apart from providing a framework for analysing the existing position of the company, such models could be powerful tools for answering a wide variety of "what if?" questions, such as:

* what changes do there need to be to premium rates to make a particular line of business worth writing?

* is the investment strategy too risky with the present asset margin?

* what additional capital would be needed to pursue a particular strategy?

* will the strategy give a reasonable expected return on the additional capital?

## 8. ACKNOWLEDGEMENTS

8.1 The Working Party wishes to acknowledge a debt of gratitude to the members of the Finnish Solvency Working Party for starting them off along the lines of this paper and, in particular, to Professor Teivo Pentikäinen for his advice and encouragement. Our thanks are also due to many UK actuaries who commented on the work at different stages.

REFERENCES

Abbott W M, Clarke T G and Treen W R (1981) Some Financial Aspects of a General Insurance Company. **Journal of the Institute of Actuaries** 108:119 - 187

Beard R E, Pentikäinen T and Pesonen E (1984) **Risk Theory** (3rd edition). London & New York: Chapman and Hall.

Benjamin S (1980) Solvency and Profitability in Insurance. **Transactions of the 21st International Congress of Actuaries** 1:33 - 46

Buchanan R A and Taylor G C (1986) The Management of Solvency. **Proceedings of the First International Conference on Insurance Solvency.**

Coutts S M and Devitt E R F (1986) The Assessment of the Financial Strength of Insurance Companies - A Generalised Cash-flow Model. **Proceedings of the First International Conference on Insurance Solvency.**

Coutts S M, Devitt E R F and Ross G A F (1984) A Probabilistic Approach to Assessing the Financial Strength of a General Insurance Company. **Transactions of the 22nd International Congress of Actuaries** 3:129 - 136

Daykin C D (1984) The Development of Concepts of Adequacy and Solvency in Non-life Insurance in the EEC. **Transactions of the 22nd International Congress of Actuaries** 3:299 - 309

Daykin C D and Bernstein G D (1985) A Simulation Model to Examine Questions of Solvency in the Light of Asset and Run-off Risks. Presented to ASTIN Colloquium, Biarritz, October 1985

Daykin C D, Devitt E R, Khan M R and McCaughan J P (1984) The Solvency of General Insurance Companies. **Journal of the Institute of Actuaries** 111:279 - 319

Kahane Y (1979) Solidity, Leverage and the Regulation of Insurance Companies. **The Geneva Papers on Risk and Insurance**, 14

Kahane Y and Biger N (1977) Balance Sheet Optimisation in Inflationary Circumstances - The Case of Non-Life Insurance Companies. **The Journal of Insurance Issues and Practices** 1 No. 2, 15 - 27

Pentikäinen T and Rantala J (1982) **Solvency of Insurers and Equalization Reserves.** Helsinki: Insurance Publishing Company Ltd.

Pentikäinen T and Rantala J (1985) Run-off Risks as a Part of Claims Fluctuation. Presented to ASTIN Colloquium, Biarritz, October 1985.

Ryan J P (1980) An Application of Model Office Techniques to the Solvency Question. **Transactions of the 21st International Congress of Actuaries** 1:403 - 410

Ryan J P (1984) Application of Simulation Techniques to Solvency Testing for a Non-life Office. **Transactions of the 22nd International Congress of Actuaries** 3:269 - 277.

Stewart C M (1971) The Assessment of Solvency. **ASTIN Bulletin** 6:79 - 85

Wilkie A D (1984) Steps towards a Comprehensive Stochastic Investment Model. **Occasional Actuarial Research Discussion Paper** 36, Institute of Actuaries.

Wilkie A D (1986) A Stochastic Investment Model for Actuarial Use. **Transactions of the Faculty of Actuaries** 39:341 - 373

## Appendix 1 DESCRIPTION OF SIMULATION MODEL OF GENERAL INSURANCE COMPANY

A1.1 In standard risk theory the year to year transition formula is of the form:

$$\Delta U = B + I - X - C - T$$

where $\Delta U$ is the change in the solvency margin U
B is the earned premium income, including safety and expense loadings but net of reinsurance premiums
I is the net income from investments
X is incurred claims net of reinsurance recoveries
C is the cost of administration, reinsurance etc
T is dividends, tax, etc

By implication, incurred claims includes changes to estimates of outstanding claims generated in previous years and included in the technical provisions at the start of the year in question. This formulation is also deficient in that changes in the values of investments are ignored.

A1.2 GENERAL FORMULA

More generally, we define:

$$\Delta A(j) = A(j) - A(j-1)$$

$$= \sum_k A_k(j) - \sum_k A_k(j-1)$$

$$= \sum_k A_k(j-1)[(1+y_k(j-1))(1+g_k(j-1))-1] + \{B(j)-C(j)-T(j)-\sum_{i\leq j} X(i;j)\}$$

where A(j) is the total value of the assets at the end of year j.
$A_k(j)$ is the total value of component k of the asset portfolio at the end of year j (In our model k=1 for cash, 2 for redeemable government securities, 3 for ordinary shares).

$y_k(j)$ is the yield on asset component k at the end of year j. In particular, in our model:

$$y_1(j) = c(j) - .01$$

$$y_2(j) = c(j)$$

$$y_3(j) = y(j)$$

where $c(j)$ is the yield on 2.5% Consols;
$y(j)$ is the dividend yield on the Financial Times Actuaries All-Share Index.

$g_k(j)$ is the proportionate change in capital values between the end of years j and (j+1). In particular, in our model:

$$g_1(j) = 0$$

$$g_2(j) = \frac{c(j)}{c(j+1)}$$

$$g_3(j) = \frac{d(j+1)y(j)}{d(j)y(j+1)}$$

where $d(j)$ is an index of share dividends (= dividend yield x price index) corresponding to $y(j)$;

$B(j)$ is the <u>written</u> premium income in year j including safety and expense loadings;

$C(j)$ is the cost in year j of administration, commission, reinsurance etc;

$T(j)$ is the amount paid out in dividends and tax in year j;

$X(i;j)$ is the amount settled in year j (net of reinsurance recoveries)in respect of claims arising in year i.

We now define $B'(j)(=B(j)-C(j))$ as the written premiums in year j net of commission and all expenses other than claim settlement expenses and $X(i;j)$ as including claim settlement expenses.

## A1.3 ASSET AND INFLATION MODELS

The asset components $A_k(j)$ can be defined in a variety of ways relative to the total $\sum_k A_k(j)$. For example, if investment or disinvestment is proportional to the value of assets brought forward to the end of the year from the previous year-end,

$$A_k(j) = \frac{A(j)}{A(j-1)} A_k(j-1)$$

If proportions $p_k$ ($\sum_k p_k = 1$) are specified such that $p_k$ of any new investment is invested in component k:

$$A_k(j) = A_k(j-1)[1+y_k(j-1)][1+g_k(j-1)] + p_k\{B(j)-C(j)-T(j)-\sum_{i\leq j} X(i;j)\}$$

We also define q(j) as the retail price index at the end of year j and r(j) as the price growth in year j:

$$r(j) = \frac{q(j)}{q(j-1)} - 1$$

The variables q(j), d(j), y(j) and c(j) are defined by an interrelated set of autoregressive models, described in detail in Appendix 2.

## A1.4 TAX AND DIVIDENDS MODEL

The dividends and tax term is expressed in terms of the investment income and an input parameter (t), representing the proportion of investment income absorbed by tax and dividends paid to shareholders, by the following:

$$T(j) = t \sum_k A_k(j-1) y_k(j-1)$$

## A1.5 MODEL OF CLAIM GENERATION PROCESS

We define written premiums in the year prior to the date of assessment (taken as the time j = 0) as B'(0) and the rate of growth of written premiums before and after that date as $e_1$ and $e_2$. Then:

$$B'(j) = B'(0)\,(1 + e_1)^j \quad (j<0)$$

$$\phantom{B'(j) =} B'(0)\,(1 + e_2)^j \quad (j\geq 0)$$

and $B'_k(j) = f_k B'(j)$ for k=1,2

where $f_k$ is the proportion of written premiums in respect of type of business k (k=1 for short-tailed, 2 for long-tailed).

Claims are assumed to be generated from written premiums by means of a variable claim ratio and specified proportions settled in each year of the run-off. Thus the estimated payment in year j in respect of premiums written in year i is given by:

$$X(i;j) = \sum_k s^k(j) \;\; R_k(i)\; B'_k(i) \prod_{\ell=i+1}^{j} (1+r(\ell))$$

where $R_k(i)$ is the uninflated, undiscounted claims ratio in year i, assumed to be normally distributed with mean $R_k$ and standard deviation $\sigma_r^k$. For $i \leq 0$, $R_k(i) = R_k$

$s^k(j)$ is the proportion of uninflated, undiscounted claims from type of business k that are assumed to be settled in development year j.

A1.6 MODEL OF CLAIM SETTLEMENT

Claims settled in each year of development are aggregated from all the separate years of origin, whether before or after the date of assessment. The total amount of claims settled in year j ($X(j)$) is assumed to be normally distributed with mean $\bar{X}(j)$ and standard deviation $a\,\bar{X}(j) + b\sqrt{\bar{X}(j)}$ where a and b are specified constants and $\bar{X}(j)$ is defined as:

$$\bar{X}(j) = \sum_{i \le j} \sum_{k} s^k(j-i)\, R_k(i) B'_k(i) \prod_{\ell=i+1}^{j} (1+r(\ell))$$

A1.7 TECHNICAL RESERVES

The technical reserves ($TR(0)$) at the date of assessment are calculated from the estimates of claims to be settled in future years arising from premiums earned prior to the date in question. They allow for inflation at a specified rate (r) and discounting at a specified rate (d). They can be expressed as follows:

$$TR(0) = \tfrac{1}{2}\sum_{k} B'_k(0)\, R_k \sum_{j=0}^{20} s^k(j)\, (1+r)^j (1+d)^{-j}$$

$$+ \sum_{k} R_k \sum_{i=20}^{-1} B'_k(i) \sum_{j=-1}^{20} s^k(j)\, (1+r)^j (1+d)^{-j} + \tfrac{1}{2}\, B'_k(0)$$

The initial asset margin ($AM(0)$) is defined as a function of written premiums in the year before the date of assessment:

$$AM(0) = \alpha\, B'(0)$$

The initial assets are thus given by:

$$A(0) = TR(0) + AM(0)$$

## Appendix 2 DESCRIPTION OF STOCHASTIC MODELS USED FOR ASSETS AND INFLATION

A2.1 The investment and inflation models used are those proposed by Wilkie (1984,1986). A summary of the specification of the model is given below. The variables used are:

q(t) The UK retail prices index

d(t) An index of share dividends.

y(t) The dividend yield on these same share indices, that is, the dividend index at the specified date divided by the share price index at that date.

c(t) The yield on 2.5% Consols (irredeemable), which is taken as a measure of the general level of fixed interest yields in the market.

A2.2 The model used for q(t) is:

$$\nabla \ln\{q(t)\} = \mu_q + \alpha_q (\nabla \ln \{q(t-1)\} - \mu_q) + \sigma_q z_q(t)$$

where the backwards difference operator $\nabla$ is defined by

$$\nabla x(t) = x(t) - x(t-1)$$

and $z_q(t)$ is a sequence of independent identically distributed unit normal variates.

The values adopted for the parameters are:

$\mu_q = 0.05$, $\alpha_q = 0.6$, $\sigma_q = 0.05$.

A2.3 The model for y(t) is:

$$\ln \{y(t)\} = \omega_y \nabla \ln\{q(t)\} + y_n(t)$$

where $y_n(t) = \ln\{\mu_y\} + \alpha_y (y_n(t-1) - \ln\{\mu_y\}) + \sigma_y z_y(t)$

and $Z_y(t)$ is a sequence of independent identically distributed unit normal variates.

The values adopted for the parameters are:

$\mu_y = 0.04$, $\alpha_y = 0.6$, $\omega_y = 1.35$, $\sigma_y = 0.175$.

A2.4 The model for d(t) is:

$$\nabla \ln\{d(t)\} = \omega_d\left(\frac{\delta_d}{1-(1-\delta_d)\overline{B}}\right) \nabla \ln\{q(t)\} + \alpha_d \nabla \ln\{q(t)\}$$

$$+\beta_d \sigma_y z_y (t-1) + \sigma_d z_d(t) + \gamma_d \sigma_d z_d(t-1)$$

where the backwards step operator $\overline{B}$ is defined by

$$\overline{B}\, x(t) = x(t-1)$$

and hence $\overline{B}^n x(t) = x(t-n)$

and $z_d(t)$ is a sequence of independent identically distributed unit normal variates.

The term in parentheses above involving $\delta_d$ represents an infinite series of lag effects, with exponentially declining coefficients:

$\delta_d$,

$\delta_d(1-\delta_d)$,

$\delta_d(1-\delta_d)^2$, etc

The sum of these coefficients is unity, so this part of the formula represents the lagged effect of inflation, with unit gain. This means that if retail prices rise by 1% this term will also, eventually, rise by 1%. We can alternatively describe it as the "carried forward" effect of inflation m(t), where

$$m(t) = \delta_d \nabla \ln\{q(t)\} + (1-\delta_d)\, m(t-1),$$

from which we see that the amount that enters the dividend model each year is $\delta_d$ times the current inflation rate, plus $(1-\delta_d)$ times the amount brought forward from the previous year, and that this total is then carried forward to the next year.

The values adopted for the parameters are:

$\omega_d = 0.8$, $\delta_d = 0.2$, $\alpha_d = 0.2$, $\beta_d = -0.2$,

$\gamma_d = 0.375$, $\sigma_d = 0.075$.

A2.5 The model for c(t) is:

$$c(t) = \omega_c\left(\frac{\delta_c}{1-(1-\delta_c)\overline{B}}\right) \nabla \ln\{q(t)\} + n(t),$$

where $\ln\{n(t)\} = \ln\{\mu_c\}$

$$+ \alpha_c\overline{B} + \beta_c\overline{B}^2 + \gamma_c\overline{B}^3)\ (\ln\{n(t)\} - \ln\{\mu_c\})$$

$$+ \phi_c\sigma_y\ z_y(t) + \sigma_c\ z_c(t),$$

where $z_c(t)$ is a sequence of independent identically distributed unit normal variates.

The term in parentheses in $\delta_c$ has a similar form to the $\delta_d$ term in the dividend model, though the parameter value is different. It represents the current value of expected future inflation as an exponentially weighted moving average of past rates of inflation.

The values adopted for the parameters are:

$\omega_c = 1.0$, $\delta_c = 0.045$, $\mu_c = 0.035$, $\alpha_c = 1.20$,

$\beta_c = -0.48$, $\gamma_c = 0.20$, $\phi_c = 0.06$, $\sigma_c = 0.14$.

A2.6 Interested readers are referred to Wilkie (1986) for interpretation of what the model implies and how it can be used. A fuller description of the derivation of the model is given in by Wilkie (1984).

A2.7 There is no specific provision in Professor Wilkie's model for cash as an investment. We have assumed that the return on cash for any year is the Consols yield at the start of the year less one percentage point.

## APPENDIX 3 THE SIMULATION PROGRAM

### A3.1 Introduction

A3.1.1 In order to simulate the run-off of an insurance company it is necessary to make decisions in regard to a large number of parameters. The program is written in such a way as to allow for a range of values of each of the parameters. As there are at least 20 parameters or values that may vary, and several may have up to 8 or 9 values, it would not be sensible to provide for every possible combination of values of the parameters. The program would take too long to run and the volume of output could not be assimilated.

A3.1.2 The program is written, therefore, to allow each of the parameters to vary in turn over its whole range, whilst the others are kept constant at a "normal" or standard level. It also permits an analysis by two parameters at a time, for every possible combination of the various levels of those two parameters.

A3.1.3 The same set of random numbers has been used for each different parameter combination, so that the comparisons are not affected by any bias in the particular sets of random numbers chosen.

A3.2 The basis of the simulations

A3.2.1 The program works from a series of written premiums, going back sufficiently far into the past to include every year for which claims are still to be run off. Provision is made for three alternative bases for the future:

1 A wind-up - an assumed return of the unearned premium reserve (UPR) as the policyholders claim on the liquidator for the unearned part of their premiums.
2 A run-off - the UPR is translated into a pattern of future claim payments and included with payments in respect of the outstanding claims.
3 A continuing business - the future period of writing premiums can be selected and after that there is a run-off as in 2 above.

A3.2.2 It is necessary to generate claim ratios for each type of business and for provision to be made for the claim ratios to vary stochastically. The classes of business are characterized by the length of run-off period and settlement pattern and the proportions of business written in each category are set by a parameter.

A3.2.3 The investment model is that given by Wilkie(1986). The initial investment mix may be varied according to the nature of the business and is specified separately for the technical provisions and asset margin. The rules for selling and buying investments may be selected. Buying is likely to occur where there is a continuing business and written premiums are growing but it also arises in the later years of a run-off where the income from the assets is large, particularly in the case of larger initial asset margins.

A3.2.4 Since the volume of written premiums affects the ratio of outstanding claims to the latest year's written premiums, premiums can be allowed to grow or diminish in real terms over the years.

A3.2.5 Corporation tax is payable by a general insurance company in the UK on its profits, which include capital gains as well as income from assets and exclude any allowance for indexation of the purchase price of securities. However, such "income" is not subject to tax if it is used to pay claims and expenses and it seems likely that with a company that is in any danger of becoming insolvent there will be past losses carried forward, as well as future claim outgo, that will probably absorb most, if not all, of the income. This will mean that the effective rate of tax on interest will be very low. Provision is made for notional rates of tax for the first five years, at rates well below the current rates of corporation tax. The "tax" is assumed also to include the payment of dividends to shareholders. This will result in an overstatement of the outcome in scenarios where the company remains solvent, but this is not the main feature of the results with which we are concerned. The tax and dividend treatment in the model could clearly be made more sophisticated.

## A3.3 The investment model

The Wilkie model has been used, notwithstanding the author's warning that it was not developed for short-term forecasting. Wilkie's own view is that its use in these simulations can be justified. We have examined the output from the model over several hundred simulations of 30 years and have satisfied ourselves that the variations in the values do not appear unreasonable in the light of experience over recent years.

## A3.4 Future statutory solvency

A3.4.1 For a continuing company it is necessary to examine the financial position at the end of each year, if not more often. Accounts and returns have to be presented and a simulation of the future development of the company for management purposes would need to have regard to how the position might appear in presentational terms at each future reporting date.

A3.4.2 For a company that is already being run off, or to test what would happen in such circumstances, the reporting constraint is less relevant and our aim has been to look at "true" solvency, rather than the position as constrained by reporting conventions. The model simply looks at the adequacy of the assets to meet the liabilities as they are simulated to arise during the run-off. It does not check the solvency position as it might be reported to shareholders or to the supervisory authority at points during the run-off. Such a factor could be introduced if a procedure for deciding on appropriate bases for the technical provisions in future years were to be defined.

## A3.5 The choice of parameters and their values

A3.5 Every parameter is allowed to have at most 9 values, but need not be given more than 1. The parameters are numbered 1 to 13 and their levels 1 to 9. The value for level 5 is the standard and a value must be inserted for this parameter in every case, even if it is not included in the list of parameters to be analysed, since the program requires a value to be assigned for every parameter. A detailed list of the parameters and the factors underlying their choice is given below:

1 Written premiums The values used are £1 million, £10 million and £100 million a year. The written premiums are taken as being net of initial expenses and commission. £10 million was taken as the standard value.

2 Claim ratio - very long This is the claim ratio for future business of a very long-tailed nature, i.e. with a run-off period of 20 years. So far no such business has been included in the simulations. Claim ratios are assumed to include the expenses of claim settlement with actual claim costs but they are related to written premiums net of commission and expenses (c.f. paragraph 4.3.2).

3 Standard deviation - very long This is the standard deviation of the above claim ratio.

4 Claim ratio - long This is the claim ratio for future business of a long-tailed nature, i.e. with a run-off period of 10 years. We have used values of 80%, 100%, 125% and 150%, with 100% as the standard.

5 Standard deviation - long We have used 5%, 10%, 15%, 20% and 25% of written premiums, with a standard value of 15%.

6 Claim ratio - short This is the claim ratio for future business of a short-tailed nature. We have used values of 80%, 100%, 125% and 150%, with a standard value of 100%.

7 Standard deviation - short We have used 5%, 10%, 15% and 20% of written premiums, with a standard value of 10%.

8 Growth rates Separate real growth rates may be assumed before and after the assessment date. Rates varying from -20% a year to +50% a year have been used and the effect of changes in the rate of growth at the date of assessment have been examined. Inflation is automatically allowed for in the program so that the growth assumptions relate to growth in real terms. The standard basis assumes no real growth before or after.

9 Proportions of business These are the proportions of written premiums represented by long-tailed business and short-tailed business, each varying from 10% to 90%, with a standard basis of 40% long-tailed and 60% short-tailed.

10 Asset mix - asset margin Different proportions of equities, gilts and cash are considered, including 100% in each and 50% in each possible pair. The standard basis is 100% in equities.

11 Asset mix - technical provisions The proportions are specified to link with the assumptions for the asset margin. The standard basis is 50% cash and 50% gilts.

12 Asset margin This is expressed as a percentage of the net written premiums in the last year before the date of assessment. The margin is allowed to range from nil to 100%. The standard value has been taken as 40%. Different reserving strength, arising from the assumptions made in calculating the outstanding claims, allowing for inflation and for discounting, can be studied by looking at different asset margins (c.f. paragraph 5.2). On the standard basis the technical provisions are established using 5% inflation and no discounting, which may be regarded as incorporating some implicit margin, in line with the practice of many companies.

13 Selling rules There are 8 alternative rules, namely:

a. Sell equities until they are exhausted, then cash and finally gilts
b. Equities, gilts, cash
c. Gilts, equities, cash
d. Gilts, cash, equities
e. Cash, equities, gilts
f. Cash, gilts, equities
g. Sell rateably (ie in proportion to the current value of holdings)
h. Sell each year whatever has performed best since the start of the run-off

Investment (where there is a surplus of income over outgo) is always done in proportion to the current value of holdings.

It is also necessary to specify:

1. The number of future years. This is limited to the range 1 to 10, but the parameter can take the values 0 or -1, meaning that we are assuming no new business written and that we have either a run-off (0) or a wind-up (-1).
2. The number of simulations
3. The number of parameters to be analysed, that is 1 or 2.
4. Which parameters are to be allowed to vary.

A3.6 The program plan

The program has been written to permit it to be run on FORTRAN IV (otherwise known as FORTRAN 66). In particular we have avoided the use of negative values in arrays. For this purpose we have assumed that the past is represented by years 1 to 20 and the future by years 21 to 46. Whilst this means that some arrays have to be larger than they would otherwise need to be, the simplification is worthwhile. The program is divided into sections:

1 Initialization This sets out the values of the parameters, dimensions the arrays and sets some initial values. The values of the parameters could be inserted by lead cards if preferred. This section also includes the values for the number of future years, the parameters to be analysed and the number of simulations. This section also contains some data manipulation and checking to avoid time-consuming operations later in the program.

2 The random number generator This generates the necessary number of random normal variates and stores them in an array for use by the later stages of the program. This ensures that the same numbers are used for every parameter combination in respect of each realization of random numbers. They are recalculated for each further realization. The random number generator of the machine has been used to generate uniform random variates in the range 0 to 2. After subtracting 1 these are used in Marsaglia's polar method to generate the corresponding random normal variates. This method requires pairs of uniform randoms and produces normal variates if, and only if, the sum of the squares of the two variates is less than 1. The program counts the number of useful pairs and stops when it has enough to fill the array.

We have tested this process and found that a distribution of 3 million variates was very closely normal, using 9-figure tables of the normal integral for the test. This however does not test that they come in a random order and we have further tested them to count the number of cases where there is a run of 1 increase, 2 increases and so on up to 7 increases. It is not difficult to calculate theoretically the expected number of such runs both upwards and downwards and their expected size. The results are within expected limits. The methods will, it is hoped, be described in detail in a paper to be written by two of the authors of this report, together with notes on the times taken to make the calculations. These seem to vary considerably from one method to another. It is perhaps worth mentioning that what we require are representative sequences rather than purely random ones. Kendall and Babington Smith noted in 1938 that a sequence of $10^{10}$ random numbers is almost certain to contain a sequence of a million zeros (or, for that matter any other sequence you care to specify). This might be a random sequence but it is not very useful in practice for simulation.

3 Investment values The program now calculates the investment values for up to 26 future years, depending on the particular run-off period involved. The values are of:

1. The retail price index
2. Equity dividends
3. Equity yield
4. Equity price
5. Irredeemable gilt yield
6. Gilt price
7. Cash yield
8. Borrowing rate
9. A net income multiplier (see below)
10. An equity price ratio over half a year
11. A gilt price ratio over half a year
12. A mean retail price index

Note: Items 10, 11 and 12 are required in order to permit calculation of sales and purchases at an assumed mid-year point.

The reason for a "cash" yield is that gilts are assumed to relate to medium or long term, whilst "cash" is assumed to be money on deposit or very short term gilts. It is assumed that the cash yield is 1% below that of irredeemable gilts and that when cash becomes negative and we have to borrow, it is at a rate 2% higher than the irredeemable gilt rate. The gilt and equity yields have a minimum of 0.5%.

The equity price ratio is the square root of the ratio of the equity price at the end of the relevant year to its value at the start of the year. Its purpose is to revalue equities from the year-end value, on which the income is based, to the mid-year value at which it is assumed that sales take place or purchases are made. The gilt price ratio performs a similar function for gilts. Cash is assumed not to vary. After the mid-year transactions the remaining values of gilts and equities are updated to the year-end by a further multiplication by the equity (or gilt) price ratio. Although interest is calculated on the values at the start of the year, allowance is made for the loss of income on selling during the year by multiplying the net outgo by a factor of 1 plus half the average yearly yield on the investments. Whilst this assumes that the values of all three classes are equal, the effect of differences is likely to be too small to be of any consequence in practice.

4 Best investment The next section is really a continuation of section 3 in that it calculates which of the three classes of investment has performed best since the start of year 21 and stores this information for use later in the program.

5 Outstanding claims The program now calculates the outstanding claims at the end of year 20. For each earlier year the program calculates the claims according to the mean claim ratios and then, using the run-off rates shown below, calculates the amounts, in real (constant money terms), which it expects to pay out in each future year.

| Duration from year of origin | Proportion of claims settled Short-tail | Long-tail |
|---|---|---|
| 0 | 61.2% | 5.6% |
| 1 | 24.1 | 25.3 |
| 2 | 5.2 | 18.7 |
| 3 | 3.7 | 13.2 |
| 4 | 2.7 | 10.4 |
| 5 | 2.2 | 7.9 |
| 6 | 0.9 | 6.4 |
| 7 | - | 4.6 |
| 8 | - | 3.8 |
| 9 | - | 3.0 |
| 10 | - | 1.1 |
| | 100.0 | 100.0 |

Notes: The settlement patterns are taken from Abbott et al(1981)

These are stored in an array by year of expected payment and the total is accumulated, allowing for 5% future inflation, in a variable TOTOS which is the total provision for claim amounts outstanding at the end of year 20. By using these run-offs we have automatically taken into account the IBNR claims. If we have a wind-up situation then TOTOS is the technical provision.

If we are considering a run-off or a continuing business, then we must add 50% of the net written premiums for year 20 into TOTOS as the unearned premium reserve. This figure for technical provisions, together with the asset margin obtained from the product of the assumed asset margin percentage and the net written premiums for year 20, enables us to calculate the initial amounts of each type of asset using the specified proportions. This is the initial investment portfolio.

6 Future premiums The program adds into the arrays of future payments the expected contribution to claim outgo arising from future written premiums and from the unearned premium reserve for the last year, to give the expected claim outgo in real (constant money) terms.

7 Emerging costs The program now has the information to enable it to calculate the expected payments in each future year. The claim outgo is adjusted for inflation according to the Wilkie model and is allowed to vary stochastically. We assume a normal distribution and a formula of $0.15x + 75\sqrt{x}$ as the standard deviation for the total claim outgo in any year. The square root factor is dominant for the smaller amounts and the smaller companies but for the larger companies the stochastic variation is negligible and it is only realistic to assume some sort of overall secular variation (see Appendix 5).

We take the values of the assets at the beginning of the year and calculate the income on each type of asset, reducing the total income for the year by the tax factor where appropriate. We then have the outgo, adjusted to allow for inflation and stochastic variation, less the income and less any written premiums for a continuing business. As mentioned in A3.6.3 we adjust for the loss of part of the year's investment income as a result of net selling during the year (or vice versa in a net buying situation). Investment or disinvestment is assumed to take place at mid-year values. If there is net investment, it is assumed to be carried out proportionately to the existing values of the three classes of investment. Where there is net outgo, the specified selling rule is applied.

8 Final assets This process continues until the last year's claim outgo has been paid. The final assets are in the currency of the final year as a result of the application of the investment model which revalues the assets, combined with the models for income and outgo in each year which allow implicitly for future inflation. In order to bring the final asset value into the currency of the start of the run-off, it is divided by the ratio of the retail price index in the final year to that at the date of assessment. The result is then expressed as a percentage of the written premiums in year 20 (the year before the date of assessment). These values from the 1000 simulations are grouped into ranges and output as a distribution, together with their mean and standard deviation.

## APPENDIX 4 RESULTS OF SIMULATION

Full details of the results of 1000 simulations on a variety of different bases are set out in Tables 7 to 10. Tables 7 and 8 show summary distributions of the simulations by the assets remaining at the end, as well as the number of insolvencies and the mean and standard deviation of the distributions. Results are given for a few additional variants not tabulated in Tables 3 and 4. Tables 9 and 10 also include a number of additional variants and Table 10 shows the additional asset margin required in the case of 2 years' new business as compared to the pure run-off with the same assumptions (in so far as these are applicable).

The tables show the standard basis at the top and also in each of the groups of alternative assumptions (marked (s)). The variants examine the effect of varying the one assumption referred to, whilst leaving all the other assumptions the same as in the standard basis.

The assumptions underlying the standard basis are as follows:

| | |
|---|---|
| Net written premiums | £10m a year |
| Proportion of long-tailed business | 40% of net written premiums |
| Past growth | In line with inflation |
| Future growth | In line with inflation |
| Mean claim ratio (short-tailed) | 100% of net written premiums |
| Standard deviation of claim ratio (short-tailed) | 10% of net written premiums |
| Mean claim ratio (long-tailed) | 100% of net written premiums |
| Standard deviation of claim ratio (long-tailed) | 15% of net written premiums |
| Initial asset distribution | Technical provisions: 50% cash; 50% gilts<br>Asset margin: 100% equities |
| Asset selling rule | Proportionate to holdings |
| Asset margin (for Tables 7 and 8) | 40% of net written premiums |

Notes: Premiums are net of commission and expenses. The mean claim ratio is the ratio of claims (including claim settlement expenses), without allowance for future inflation or for discounting, to premiums net of commission and expenses (see paragraph 4.3.2).

**Table 7**

**Summary of Results for Pure Run-off of Business (with 1000 simulations)**

| Assumptions | No of insol-vencies | No of simulations with remaining assets of: 0%-40% | 40%-80% | 80%-120% | 120%-160% | Over 160% | Mean assets remaining | Standard deviation of assets remaining |
|---|---|---|---|---|---|---|---|---|
| Standard basis | 8 | 98 | 252 | 264 | 173 | 205 | 112% | 70% |
| 1. Net written premiums: | | | | | | | | |
| £1m a year | 20 | 119 | 227 | 250 | 171 | 213 | 113 | 75 |
| £10m a year(s) | 8 | 98 | 252 | 264 | 173 | 205 | 112 | 70 |
| £100m a year | 6 | 93 | 258 | 275 | 164 | 204 | 112 | 69 |
| 2. Proportion of long-tailed business: | | | | | | | | |
| 20% of net written premiums | 3 | 126 | 321 | 293 | 153 | 104 | 94 | 55 |
| 40% of net written premiums (s) | 8 | 98 | 252 | 264 | 173 | 205 | 112 | 70 |
| 60% of net written premiums | 13 | 88 | 197 | 230 | 184 | 288 | 130 | 85 |
| 3. Initial asset distribution: Cash / Gilts / Equities | | | | | | | | |
| TP+AM / - / - | 3 | 128 | 303 | 295 | 162 | 109 | 95 | 53 |
| - / TP+AM / - | 20 | 159 | 220 | 208 | 142 | 251 | 120 | 98 |
| - / - / TP+AM | 49 | 124 | 182 | 181 | 149 | 315 | 136 | 115 |
| ½TP / ½TP / AM (s) | 8 | 98 | 252 | 264 | 173 | 205 | 112 | 70 |
| ½TP+½AM / ½TP+½AM / - | 14 | 127 | 260 | 255 | 150 | 194 | 107 | 72 |
| ½TP+½AM / - / ½TP+½AM | 12 | 85 | 222 | 278 | 184 | 219 | 118 | 72 |
| TP / - / AM | 3 | 93 | 283 | 312 | 176 | 133 | 102 | 54 |

**Table 7 (cont.)**

**Summary of Results for Pure Run-off of Business (with 1000 simulations)**

| Assumptions | No of insol-vencies | No of simulations with remaining assets of: 0%-40% | 40%-80% | 80%-120% | 120%-160% | Over 160% | Mean assets remaining | Standard deviation of assets remaining |
|---|---|---|---|---|---|---|---|---|
| 4. Initial asset margin: | | | | | | | | |
| 0% of net written premiums | 134 | 336 | 292 | 138 | 58 | 44 | 52% | 55% |
| 20% of net written premiums | 36 | 210 | 312 | 222 | 117 | 102 | 83 | 62 |
| 40% of net written premiums (s) | 8 | 98 | 252 | 264 | 173 | 205 | 112 | 70 |
| 60% of net written premiums | 2 | 34 | 149 | 244 | 212 | 360 | 147 | 80 |
| 80% of net written premiums | 0 | 12 | 74 | 184 | 211 | 519 | 180 | 90 |
| 110% of net written premiums | 0 | 4 | 34 | 117 | 186 | 659 | 212 | 100 |
| 5. Asset selling rules: | | | | | | | | |
| Equities; gilts; cash | 9 | 133 | 285 | 262 | 152 | 159 | 102 | 66 |
| Equities; cash; gilts | 16 | 142 | 233 | 241 | 143 | 225 | 113 | 81 |
| Gilts; equities; cash | 5 | 123 | 246 | 285 | 181 | 160 | 105 | 61 |
| Gilts; cash; equities | 3 | 67 | 249 | 314 | 201 | 166 | 111 | 58 |
| Cash; gilts; equities | 11 | 134 | 212 | 237 | 168 | 238 | 120 | 83 |
| Cash; equities; gilts | 7 | 78 | 245 | 244 | 185 | 241 | 123 | 79 |
| In proportion to holding(s) | 8 | 98 | 252 | 264 | 173 | 205 | 112 | 70 |
| Sell best performer first | 14 | 131 | 239 | 268 | 158 | 190 | 108 | 70 |

Notes: The assets remaining at the end of the run-off are deflated to the date of assessment and expressed as a percentage of net written premiums in the year before the date of assessment (See App 3.6.8).
Premiums are net of commission and expenses.
(s) indicates the assumption made for the standard basis.
TP = technical provisions, AM = asset margin.

**Table 8**

**Summary of Results with 2 Further Years' Business (with 1000 simulations)**

| Assumptions | No of insol-vencies | No of simulations with remaining assets of: 0%-40% | 40%-80% | 80%-120% | 120%-160% | Over 160% | Mean assets remaining | Standard deviation of assets remaining |
|---|---|---|---|---|---|---|---|---|
| Standard basis | 50 | 96 | 146 | 171 | 175 | 362 | 144% | 109% |
| 1. Net written premiums: | | | | | | | | |
| £1m a year | 61 | 106 | 144 | 155 | 161 | 373 | 144 | 117 |
| £10m a year | 50 | 96 | 146 | 171 | 175 | 362 | 144 | 109 |
| £100m a year | 43 | 96 | 144 | 181 | 172 | 364 | 144 | 107 |
| 2. Proportion of long-tailed business: | | | | | | | | |
| 10% of net written premiums | 52 | 136 | 217 | 220 | 164 | 211 | 108 | 83 |
| 20% of net written premiums | 48 | 116 | 190 | 212 | 159 | 275 | 120 | 91 |
| 40% of net written premiuns (s) | 50 | 96 | 146 | 171 | 175 | 362 | 144 | 109 |
| 60% of net written premiums | 52 | 83 | 120 | 141 | 159 | 445 | 168 | 130 |
| 80% of net written premiums | 53 | 77 | 99 | 117 | 126 | 528 | 191 | 151 |
| 90% of net written premiums | 58 | 71 | 93 | 106 | 118 | 554 | 203 | 162 |
| 3. Future real growth rate (in constant money terms): | | | | | | | | |
| -20% a year (real past growth -20% p.a.) | 53 | 78 | 118 | 143 | 144 | 464 | 171 | 134 |
| No growth (no real past growth) (s) | 50 | 96 | 146 | 171 | 175 | 362 | 144 | 109 |
| +50% a year (real past growth +50% pa) | 83 | 94 | 139 | 149 | 155 | 380 | 144 | 121 |
| +30% a year (no real past growth) | 66 | 93 | 131 | 144 | 151 | 415 | 155 | 127 |
| +50% a year (no real past growth) | 86 | 80 | 121 | 130 | 137 | 445 | 164 | 141 |

**Table 8 (cont.)**

**Summary of Results with 2 Further Years' Business (with 1000 simulations)**

| Assumptions | No of insol-vencies | No of simulations with remaining assets of: 0%-40% | 40%-80% | 80%-120% | 120%-160% | Over 160% | Mean assets remaining | Standard deviation of assets remaining |
|---|---|---|---|---|---|---|---|---|
| 4. Mean claim ratio (short-tailed) | | | | | | | | |
| 80% of net written premiums | 7 | 47 | 105 | 129 | 177 | 535 | 187% | 117% |
| 100% of net written premiums (s) | 50 | 96 | 146 | 171 | 175 | 362 | 144 | 109 |
| 125% of net written premiums | 165 | 167 | 177 | 168 | 120 | 203 | 90 | 103 |
| 150% of net written premiums | 380 | 158 | 183 | 110 | 67 | 102 | 35 | 102 |
| 5. Variability of claim ratio (short-tailed): | | | | | | | | |
| Standard deviation 5% NWP | 49 | 97 | 142 | 178 | 170 | 364 | 144 | 109 |
| Standard deviation 10% NWP (s) | 50 | 96 | 146 | 171 | 175 | 362 | 144 | 109 |
| Standard deviation 15% NWP | 48 | 96 | 148 | 168 | 173 | 367 | 144 | 111 |
| Standard deviation 20% NWP | 52 | 94 | 144 | 170 | 172 | 368 | 145 | 112 |
| 6. Mean claim ratio (long-tailed) | | | | | | | | |
| 80% of net written premiums | 17 | 62 | 136 | 161 | 195 | 429 | 163 | 106 |
| 100% of net written premiums (s) | 50 | 96 | 146 | 171 | 175 | 362 | 144 | 109 |
| 125% of net written premiums | 105 | 139 | 155 | 160 | 138 | 303 | 120 | 114 |
| 150% of net written premiums | 195 | 139 | 164 | 143 | 119 | 240 | 97 | 120 |

**Table 8 (cont.)**

**Summary of Results with 2 Further Years' Business (with 1000 simulations)**

| Assumptions | No of insol-vencies | No of simulations with remaining assets of: 0%-40% | 40%-80% | 80%-120% | 120%-160% | Over 160% | Mean assets remaining | Standard deviation of assets remaining |
|---|---|---|---|---|---|---|---|---|
| 7. Variability of claim ratio (long-tailed): | | | | | | | | |
| Standard deviation 5% NWP | 49 | 84 | 159 | 172 | 171 | 365 | 144% | 109% |
| Standard deviation 10% NWP | 50 | 89 | 156 | 172 | 168 | 365 | 144 | 109 |
| Standard deviation 15% NWP (s) | 50 | 96 | 146 | 171 | 175 | 362 | 144 | 109 |
| Standard deviation 20% NWP | 49 | 101 | 137 | 176 | 176 | 361 | 144 | 110 |
| Standard deviation 25% NWP | 50 | 104 | 135 | 174 | 172 | 365 | 144 | 110 |
| 8. Initial asset distribution: Cash / Gilts / Equities | | | | | | | | |
| TP+AM / - / - | 46 | 130 | 186 | 204 | 173 | 261 | 118 | 86 |
| - / TP+AM / - | 79 | 121 | 141 | 147 | 124 | 388 | 155 | 152 |
| - / - / TP+AM | 86 | 91 | 112 | 131 | 113 | 467 | 181 | 172 |
| $\frac{1}{2}$TP / $\frac{1}{2}$TP / AM (s) | 50 | 96 | 146 | 171 | 175 | 362 | 144 | 109 |
| $\frac{1}{2}$TP+$\frac{1}{2}$AM / $\frac{1}{2}$TP+$\frac{1}{2}$AM / - | 61 | 120 | 162 | 159 | 163 | 335 | 136 | 113 |
| $\frac{1}{2}$TP+$\frac{1}{2}$AM / - / $\frac{1}{2}$TP+$\frac{1}{2}$AM | 43 | 77 | 141 | 174 | 159 | 406 | 152 | 112 |
| TP / - / AM | 41 | 97 | 166 | 208 | 182 | 306 | 128 | 87 |
| 9. Initial asset margin: | | | | | | | | |
| 0% of net written premiums | 196 | 204 | 197 | 154 | 97 | 151 | 74 | 98 |
| 20% of net written premiums | 103 | 148 | 197 | 167 | 140 | 244 | 109 | 105 |
| 40% of net written premiums (s) | 50 | 96 | 146 | 171 | 175 | 362 | 144 | 109 |
| 60% of net written premiums | 24 | 54 | 115 | 151 | 158 | 497 | 180 | 123 |
| 80% of net written premiums | 11 | 29 | 75 | 127 | 140 | 619 | 216 | 133 |
| 90% of net written premiums | 3 | 18 | 45 | 88 | 128 | 718 | 252 | 144 |

**Table 8 (cont.)**

**Summary of Results with 2 Further Years' Business (with 1000 simulations)**

| Assumptions | No of insol-vencies | No of simulations with remaining assets of: 0%-40% | 40%-80% | 80%-120% | 120%-160% | Over 160% | Mean assets remaining | Standard deviation of assets remaining |
|---|---|---|---|---|---|---|---|---|
| 10. Asset selling rules: | | | | | | | | |
| Equities; gilts; cash | 56 | 120 | 161 | 175 | 150 | 338 | 136% | 113% |
| Equities; cash; gilts | 63 | 103 | 156 | 169 | 138 | 371 | 144 | 120 |
| Gilts; equities, cash | 51 | 106 | 154 | 165 | 181 | 343 | 137 | 103 |
| Gilts; cash; equities | 35 | 87 | 141 | 192 | 197 | 348 | 142 | 99 |
| Cash; gilts; equities | 41 | 76 | 143 | 173 | 173 | 394 | 154 | 116 |
| Cash; equities; gilts | 52 | 90 | 144 | 153 | 168 | 393 | 151 | 119 |
| In proportion to holding (s) | 50 | 96 | 146 | 171 | 175 | 362 | 144 | 109 |
| Sell best performer first | 58 | 101 | 154 | 164 | 159 | 364 | 142 | 114 |

Notes: The assets remaining at the end of the run-off are deflated to the date of assessment and expressed as a percentage of net written premiums in the year before the date of assessment (see App 3.6.8).
Premiums are net of commission and expenses.
The mean claim ratio is the ratio of claims (including settlement expenses), without allowance for future inflation or for discounting, to premiums net of commission and expenses (see paragraph 4.3.2).
(s) indicates the assumption made for the standard basis.
NWP = net written premiums, TP = technical provisions, AM = asset margin.

**Table 9**

**Asset Margins Required to Achieve 1/100 Probability of Ruin - No Future New Business**

| Assumptions | | | | Asset margin as % of NWP | Asset margin as % of technical provisions |
|---|---|---|---|---|---|
| Standard basis | | | | 40% | 15% |
| 1. Net written premiums: | | | | | |
| £1m a year | | | | 55 | 25 |
| £10m a year (s) | | | | 40 | 15 |
| £100m a year | | | | 35 | 15 |
| 2. Proportion of long-tailed business: | | | | | |
| 20% of net written premiums | | | | 30 | 15 |
| 40% of net written premiums (s) | | | | 40 | 15 |
| 60% of net written premiums | | | | 45 | 15 |
| 3. Initial asset distribution: | | | | | |
| Cash | Gilts | Equities | | | |
| TP+AM | - | - | | 30 | 10 |
| - | TP+AM | - | | 60 | 25 |
| - | - | TP+AM | | 80 | 35 |
| ½TP | ½TP | AM | (s) | 40 | 15 |
| ½TP+½AM | ½TP+½AM | - | | 50 | 20 |
| ½TP+½AM | - | ½TP+½AM | | 45 | 20 |
| TP | - | AM | | 30 | 10 |
| 4. Asset selling rules: | | | | | |
| Equities; gilts; cash | | | | 40 | 15 |
| Equities; cash; gilts | | | | 50 | 20 |
| Gilts; equities; cash | | | | 35 | 15 |
| Gilts; cash; equities | | | | 30 | 10 |
| Cash; gilts; equities | | | | 35 | 15 |
| Cash; equities; gilts | | | | 45 | 20 |
| In proportion to holdings (s) | | | | 40 | 15 |
| Sell best performer first | | | | 55 | 25 |

Notes: Premiums are net of commission and expenses.
(s) indicates the assumption made for the standard basis.
NWP = net written premiums, TP = technical provisions, AM = asset margin.

**Table 10**

**Asset Margins Required to Achieve 1/100 Probability of Ruin - Two Years' New Business**

| Assumptions<br>Standard basis | Asset margin as % of NWP<br>90% | Excess asset margin as compared to pure run-off (as % of NWP)<br>50% |
|---|---|---|
| 1. Net written premiums | | |
| £1m a year | 100 | 45 |
| £10m a year (s) | 90 | 50 |
| £100m a year | 80 | 45 |
| 2. Proportion of long-tailed business: | | |
| 10% of net written premiums | 75 | 45 |
| 20% of net written premiums | 80 | 50 |
| 40% of net written premiums (s) | 90 | 50 |
| 60% of net written premiums | 95 | 50 |
| 80% of net written premiums | 100 | 40 |
| 100% of net written premiums | 105 | 40 |
| 3. Future growth rate (in constant money terms): | | |
| -20% a year (real past growth -20% p.a. | 100 | 35 |
| No growth (no real past growth) (s) | 90 | 50 |
| +50% a year (real past growth +50% p.a.) | 115 | 85 |
| +30% a year (no real past growth) | 100 | 65 |
| +50% a year (no real growth) | 120 | 85 |
| 4. Mean claim ratio (short-tailed): | | |
| 80% of net written premiums | 30 | 0 |
| 100% of net written premiums (s) | 90 | 50 |
| 125% of net written premiums | 125 | 75 |
| 150% of net written premiums | 180 | 115 |

**Table 10 (cont.)**

**Asset Margins Required to Achieve 1/100 Probability of Ruin - Two Years' New Business**

| Assumptions | Asset margin as % of NWP | Excess asset margin as compared to pure run-off (as % of NWP) |
|---|---|---|
| 5. Variability of claim ratio (short-tailed): | | |
| Standard deviation 5% NWP | 80% | 45% |
| Standard deviation 10% NWP (s) | 90 | 50 |
| Standard deviation 15% NWP | 85 | 45 |
| Standard deviation 20% NWP | 90 | 50 |
| 6. Mean claim ratio (long-tailed) | | |
| 80% of net written premiums | 50 | 20 |
| 100% of net written premiums (s) | 90 | 50 |
| 125% of net written premiums | 115 | 60 |
| 150% of net written premiums | 150 | 85 |
| 7. Variability of claim ratio (long-tailed): | | |
| Standard deviation 5% NWP | 80 | 45 |
| Standard deviation 10% NWP | 85 | 50 |
| Standard deviation 15% NWP (s) | 90 | 50 |
| Standard deviation 20% NWP | 90 | 50 |
| Standard deviation 25% NWP | 90 | 50 |

**Table 10 (cont.)**

**Asset Margins Required to Achieve 1/100 Probability of Ruin - Two Years' New Business**

| Assumptions | | | Asset margin as % of NWP | Excess asset margin as compared to pure run-off (as % of NWP) |
|---|---|---|---|---|
| 8. Initial asset distribution: | | | | |
| Cash | Gilts | Equities | | |
| TP+AM | - | - | 85% | 55% |
| - | TP+AM | - | 110 | 50 |
| - | - | TP+AM | 135 | 55 |
| ½TP | ½TP | AM (s) | 90 | 50 |
| ½TP+½AM | ½TP+½AM | - | 90 | 55 |
| ½TP+½AM | - | ½TP+½AM | 90 | 45 |
| TP | - | AM | 75 | 45 |
| 9. Asset selling rules: | | | | |
| Equities; gilts; cash | | | 95 | 55 |
| Equities; cash; gilts | | | 95 | 45 |
| Gilts; equities; cash | | | 90 | 55 |
| Gilts; cash; equities | | | 70 | 40 |
| Cash; gilts; equities | | | 85 | 50 |
| Cash; equities; gilts | | | 95 | 50 |
| In proportion to holdings (s) | | | 90 | 50 |
| Sell best performer first | | | 95 | 40 |

Notes: Premiums are net of commission and expenses.
The mean claim ratio is the ratio of claims (including claim settlement expenses), without allowance for future inflation or for discounting, to premiums net of commission and expenses (see paragraph 4.3.2.).
(s) indicates the assumption made for the standard basis.
NWP = net written premiums, TP = technical provisions, AM = asset margin.

## APPENDIX 5 VARIABILITY OF CLAIM OUTGO

A5.1 Daykin and Bernstein (1985) assumed that the amount of the payments made in each development year for each year of origin varied log-normally. This meant that a payment amount that was to be varied stochastically was multiplied by exp( R*S + M) where R is a random normal variate, S the standard deviation and M the mean. In order that the overall mean should be correct, the value of M has to be equal to minus half the square of the standard deviation. This formula is suitable for a single payment, but in most cases the payment amounts considered were the totals of several or many individual amounts. Furthermore different values would need to be adopted for funds of different sizes if account were to be taken of the fact that variation is not the same for a small fund as for a large one.

A5.2 This was cumbersome and not entirely satisfactory, so an alternative approach was sought. The formula should reflect the number of payments involved and, if possible, the ratio of the standard deviation to the mean (the coefficient of variation). Consideration was given to the estimation of the number of claims (or claim payments) in each year's totals. We were unable to obtain any figures from actual portfolios but information from returns to the supervisory authority and from other sources suggested that for short-tailed business an average payment rising from £500 in the year of occurrence by multiples of 2 to £16,000 in the last year of development was not unreasonable. For long-tailed business the average payments rose over 10 years from £800 to £15,000.

A5.3 We assumed that coefficients of variation were in the range of 2 to 10, increasing at later durations as fewer, larger claims are settled. We were then able to estimate both the numbers of claims and their average amounts for different mixes of business by year of development. For this purpose it was assumed that claims were identical with payments and, whilst this is clearly not the case, it is not thought that it would make much difference if we were able to make more detailed assumptions. These calculations suggested that the formula for standard deviation should be a multiple of the square root of the number of claims, or its deemed equivalent, the total amount of payment. For convenience we used the amount of money, even though inflation would involve a change in the multiplier over time.

A5.4 It must be realized that precision was out of the question since we could not take into account all the possible variations in the make-up of a portfolio. It was also necessary to have regard to the fact that the bulk of the outstanding claims are paid in the first two or three years of run-off and relate primarily to the latest two or three years' business. Calculations showed that out of total outstandings of £1 million about one-half was paid in the first year and a quarter in the next year. By year 7 the payments were under £20,000, so that variation in these later years was less significant in the overall context. What is more, for many insurers the later payments, if they turn out to be large, may well be recoverable from reinsurers and so not form part of the problem for net run-off patterns. It simply moves the problem to another area. Further consideration would need to be given to the variability of the tail in the case of a company with a lot of long-tailed business and relatively high retentions.

A5.5 Experiment suggested that a multiplier of about 50 to 100 times the square root of the amount (in pounds sterling in 1986) was of the right order of magnitude. However, it was clear that whilst this gave a reasonable amount of variation for the smaller insurer it was wholly inadequate for a large one. In present conditions most of the variation for the larger fund arises from secular change and this is more likely to be proportional to the actual amount to be paid than to its square root. The problem is to choose a multiplier to give a realistic variation. Experience over recent years suggests that it must be at least 0.1, to give a variation of 20% in 95% of all cases. We finally adopted the formula

$$SD = aX + b\sqrt{X}$$

using values of 0.15 for a and 75 for b.

A5.6 This formula is similar to one which we understand was introduced by the Finnish supervisory authority in 1952. Whilst we are well aware of the approximations and assumptions involved in its derivation, we think it is adequate for the purpose. It also greatly simplifies the calculations. As indicated above, the earlier paper calculated the outgo for each future year for each year of occurrence and for each length of tail separately and applied the stochastic factor to each such amount. The main effect of this was to reduce the overall variation compared with applying the same formula to the total and this effect can be achieved by adjusting the overall level of the variation. It was decided, therefore, to calculate the total outgo in each year, including that from future business where appropriate, and apply the variability factor to the total.

A5.7 It is interesting to compare the values produced by the formula with those from the exponential basis. The comparisons, with values of R corresponding to the 5%, 25% and 50% points, are shown in Table 11. The correspondence between the two formulae, coupled with the size of variation by insurer, suggests that the new formula is in line with the old but more realistic in its relationship to the actual amounts of payments.

**Table 11**

Stochastic Multiplier (1 + RS/X) for Different Values of R and Standard Deviation (S)

| | Random normal variate (R) | | | | |
|---|---|---|---|---|---|
| | -1.96 | -.675 | 0 | .675 | 1.96 |
| Log-normal | | | | | |
| S = 0.3 | .53 | .78 | .96 | 1.17 | 1.72 |
| S = 0.5 | .33 | .63 | .88 | 1.24 | 2.35 |
| Square root formula (S = 0.15X + 75/X) | | | | | |
| X = 100,000 | .24 | .74 | 1.0 | 1.26 | 1.76 |
| X = 1,000,000 | .56 | .85 | 1.0 | 1.15 | 1.44 |
| X = 10,000,000 | .66 | .88 | 1.0 | 1.12 | 1.34 |

## Appendix 6 POSSIBLE APPROACH TO SIMULATING REINSURANCE RECOVERIES

A6.1 It is not possible to simulate reinsurance recoveries in our model in any very precise way, firstly because it is too complicated and secondly because the model simulates claims only in aggregate. It would in principle be possible to think in terms of a specified number of reinsurers, each bearing a share of the anticipated reinsurance recoveries, and find a way to model the failure of reinsurers. Rather easier, and probably no less realistic, would be to go directly to the proportion recovered. One way of approaching the problem is set out below.

A6.2 Reinsurers would be allocated to, say, three categories - strong, average and weak. For any class of business the proportion of reinsurance recoveries anticipated from each of the three categories of reinsurer would be input as data. The model would then be to apply a process, defined separately for each category, to determine the proportion not recovered in respect of any particular year's estimated gross claim payments. There remains, of course, the problem of estimating gross claim payments and simulating their outturn, so that there would be considerable practical problems in implementing an approach of this sort.

A6.3 The probability of recovery would be assumed to be related to the gross claim outturn for the ceding company. This is simply a proxy for deterioration in results generally in the market. One might take the estimate of gross claims paid in the year in question to be the mean estimate of claims paid, based on proportions expected to be settled in the year, the rate of inflation assumed in setting the technical provisions and, in the case of claims arising from future business, the mean claim ratio. There would then be a set of formulae, one for each category of reinsurer, to define the proportion of gross claims paid in the year which is assumed not to be recovered, based on the ratio of gross claim outturn to estimated gross claims for the year. For year j we might, for example, define the proportion not recovered $Y(j)$ by:

Weak

$$Y(j) = \frac{k(j)}{400} \qquad [0 < k(j) \leq 400]$$

Average

$$Y(j) = \frac{k(j) - 50}{500} \qquad [50 < k(j) \leq 550]$$

<u>Strong</u>

$$Y(_j) = \frac{k(_j) - 100}{800} \qquad [100 < k(_j) \leq 900]$$

where $1 + \frac{k(_j)}{100} = \frac{X(_j)}{\sum_{i \in j} \hat{X}(i;j)}$

$X(_j)$ = actual total gross claims paid in year j

and $\sum_{i \in j} \hat{X}(i;j)$ = expected gross claim payment in year j in respect of year of origin i on basis of mean claim ratio, assumed settlement pattern and expected inflation.

In terms of the notation of Appendix 1

$$X\ (i;j) = \sum_k s^k(_{j-1})\ R_k B'_k\ (i)(1+r)^{j-i}$$

A6.4 The formulae can obviously be adapted to reflect one's ideas of a plausible model for reinsurance recoveries. The general principle is that one would expect higher proportions not to be recovered from weaker reinsurers and lower proportions not to be recovered from stronger reinsurers. Above a certain threshold, higher claims relative to the expected level of claims imply a worsening market situation and hence a higher proportion not recovered. These formulae do not attempt to distinguish between high claims as a result of high initial loss ratios, high inflation or adverse development. In principle one could also develop some form of cumulative trigger so that failure to recover increased with a series of high claim payments rather than simply on the basis of a single year. This approach is very crude, based as it is on the experience of the business of the ceding company rather than the business as a whole that might be affecting reinsurance companies. However, it might help to give a broad indication of the potential impact of reinsurance failure on the situation.

A6.5 Consideration would also need to be given to whether to apply the formulae to all classes together or each class separately. Possibly the most realistic would be to apply it to the total claims on those classes of business where significant amounts are reinsured.

A6.6 The simple approach suggested here may not be sufficiently realistic for some companies for whom reinsurance recovery is a major issue. Further development of these ideas is clearly needed. However, it is suggested that it may be possible to obtain a useful indication of the role of reinsurance in a particular case by the use of straightforward models.

# 5

# SOME GENERAL APPROACHES TO COMPUTING TOTAL LOSS DISTRIBUTIONS AND THE PROBABILITY OF RUIN

Albert S. Paulson and R. Dixit

Abstract

This paper presents a completely general numerical approach to determination of total loss distributions. The approach makes use of two procedures, one involving numerical inversion of characteristic functions, and the other which utilizes the first four moments of the total loss in the Cornish-Fisher asymptotic expansion. A quantile based approximation is found to be useful in implementing these two procedures in a variety of difficult settings. When only severity of loss data $x_1, x_2, \ldots, x_n$ is available, the estimate of the total loss distribution is non-parametric. The numerical procedures lead directly to parametric and non-parametric solutions of the ruin problem.

## 1. Introduction

This paper summarizes two methods for determination of the total or aggregate loss distribution. The first, an exact and completely general method, is based on numerical inversion of characteristic functions. Since this method is completely general it is used to produce benchmark solutions against which the other, a simultaneously asymptotic and approximate, method is evaluated. Both methods have been found to be extremely useful in producing total loss distributions in practical settings. The methods are useful under the following sets of conditions.

(1) The frequency and severity distributions are completely specified and known.

(2) The functional forms of the frequency and severity distributions are completely specified but the parameters of one or both of the distributions are unknown and must be determined from available data.

(3) The functional form of the frequency distribution is known but the functional form of the severity distribution is not. Information concerning severity of loss is available only from loss data $x_1, x_2, \ldots, x_n$. The parameters of the frequency

distribution may or may not be known; if unknown, information concerning the frequency of loss distribution is available from loss frequencies $n_1, n_2, \ldots, n_a$.

The methods presented here are an outgrowth of the work of Paulson and Faris [1985] and Paulson, Dixit, Derrig, and Ulseth [1987] concerning the stable laws and domains of attraction. In the course of the work concerning domains of attraction it was determined that even extraordinarily powerful mathematical, statistical, and probabilistic results concerning sums of actual losses were frequently insufficient to produce a total loss distribution for practical applications. The occasional failures of the domains of attraction method, as well as other parametric methods, to produce an appropriate total loss distribution for actual loss data are due to the inability of the parametric severity densities to "match up" with realized losses. The methods for realized loss data presented here do not require the specification of a parametric severity density and are thus, in a limited sense, non-parametric methods. The methods would be fully non-parametric if the parametric form of the frequency distribution were eliminated from the construction of the total loss distribution. For lack of a better term, the method based on numerical inversion of characteristic functions will be referred to as "non-parametric". Our use of the word non-parametric is different from that found in the statistical literature.

A generally applicable non-parametric method for determining the aggregate loss distribution is especially important for the following reasons. First, many difficulties associated with determination of an appropriate severity distribution (e.g., choice of distribution, estimation, assessment of fit, etc.) can be completely avoided. The match of a fitted severity distribution with actual severity data is rarely good, in practical settings, as judged by informal graphical comparisons or formal statistical tests of fit. The generation of aggregate loss distributions from poorly fitting parametric severity distributions can lead to very serious under- or over-estimation of capital requirements in the conduct of a risk business. Second, it can be used to evaluate approximations such as the Cornish-Fisher, or normal powers method to the aggregate loss distribution. A particularly surprising finding detailed in this paper is that the four moment normal powers approximation to the compound Poisson, the negative binomial, and the binomial aggregate loss distribution nearly always coincides with the corresponding non-parametric aggregate loss distribution, even for cases in which the mathematical moments are infinite. Third, it can be used to economically produce total loss distribution inputs for more extensive analyses of a risk business. For example, our results can be employed to generate total losses as inputs to cash flow models concerning various aspects of an insurance or risk business [see Paulson and Dixit, 1988 and Pentikainen and Rantala, 1982].

The non-parametric development of the aggregate loss distribution relies on a delicate combination of Fourier and numerical methods. The method is applicable to both un-grouped and grouped data. An empirical investigation of the correctness of the non-parametric method is summarized. Some extensions are examined in detail.

## 2. A Non-Parametric Aggregate Loss Distribution

In the present setting we shall consider the loss process (a component of the underwriting side of a risk business) in isolation from all other aspects of the risk business. There are two cases of primary interest: (a) each severity of loss value is available, and (b) the loss data is either totally or partially grouped. Case (b) is of interest apart from the fact that in some cases loss data will be available only in a grouped format. When loss data is extensive and all individual severity of losses are available, it will be advantageous to group the data in a judicious way so as to minimize loss of information and facilitate the computation of the aggregate loss distributions.

We consider case (1) first. If severity of losses available are denoted by $x_1, x_2, \ldots, x_n$ then we define the sample characteristic function by

$$\phi_n(u) = n^{-1} \sum_{j=1}^{n} \exp(iux_j), \tag{1}$$

where $i^2 = -1$ and u is a real number. All information determinable from the x's is contained in the function $\phi_n(u)$. Moreoever, $\phi_n(u)$ is unbiased and consistent for $\phi(u)$, the population characteristic function. It is implicitly assumed that the severity of losses are approximately homogeneous although our methods do not seem to be adversely affected by departures from this assumption; indeed we have been able to develop the correct total loss distribution under very extreme conditions.

We begin with determining the distribution of the sum of N independent losses given $x_1, x_2, \ldots, x_n$. The distribution of the sum of (fixed) N independent losses has characteristic function

$$\psi_N(u) = [\phi(u)]^N. \tag{2}$$

The natural, and a consistent, estimate of $\psi_N(u)$ is

$$\psi_{n,N}(u) = [\phi_n(u)]^N. \tag{3}$$

Formally, an estimate for the distribution of the sum of N independent claims can be developed from the Gil-Pelaez [1951] inversion formula, namely,

$$\hat{F}_N(x) = \frac{1}{2} + \frac{1}{2\pi} \int_0^\infty \frac{e^{+iux}\psi_{n,N}(-u) - e^{-iux}\,\psi_{n,N}(u)}{iu}\, du, \tag{4}$$

which is the non-parametric estimate of

$$F_N(x) = \frac{1}{2} + \frac{1}{2\pi} \int_0^\infty \frac{e^{+iux}\psi_N(-u) - e^{-iux}\,\psi_N(u)}{iu}\, du.$$

The integral in (4) is evaluated by means of an adaptive quadrature algorithm. This result is highly surprising and remarkable because first, the integral (2.4) is divergent, and second, no smoothing of $\psi_{n,N}(u)$ is necessary to obtain estimates $F_N(x)$. The divergent integral (4) is useful in the same way that Stirling's formula, which is actually the leading term of a divergent series, is useful. Highly accurate numerical results are obtainable from divergent series and integrals [Whittaker and Watson, 1963, Chapters 8 and 12] if proper care is exercised. Numerical or mathematical smoothing of $\psi_{n,N}(u)$ is not required because the smoothing imparted by the N-fold convolution operation as embodied in $[\phi_n(u)]^N$ is sufficient to permit the numerical evaluation of the expression in (4).

An alternative to adaptive quadrature is to evaluate (4) by means of the Fast Fourier Transform (FFT). Using equally-spaced quadrature with width $\delta = \Delta u$ we have for (4)

$$F_N(x) = \frac{1}{2} + \frac{1}{2\pi}\sum_{k=0}^{\infty} \frac{e^{ik\delta x}\psi_N(-k\delta) - e^{-ik\delta x}\psi_N(k\delta)}{ik} \,. \tag{5}$$

For practical purposes, we will approximate (5) with a finite sum of L elements such that for $u=L\delta$, the real part of $\phi(u)$ is small enough such that the contribution of the summand in (4) for $k \geq L$ may be disregarded. Further, let us put $\Delta x = d = 2\pi/L\delta$ such that for the desired value $F(x)$, $x = x_m = md$. We then have the following approximation of $F(x)$ in terms of the following finite sum

$$F_N(x) = F(x_m) \simeq \frac{1}{2} + \frac{1}{2\pi}\left\{\frac{e^{iux}\psi_N(-u) - e^{-iux}\psi_N(u)}{ik}\right\}\Bigg|_{u=0}$$

$$+ \frac{1}{2\pi}\left\{\frac{e^{ik\delta md}\psi_N(-k\delta) - e^{-ik\delta md}\psi_N(k\delta)}{ik}\right\}$$

The second term in the right hand side above can be evaluated using L'Hospital's rule and shown to be equal to $(x-\mu)(\delta/2\pi)$ with $\mu = E(x)$. In order to use the FFT as formulated in (5), we thus see that technical considerations require that the severity distribution possess a finite mathematical mean. A finite mathematical mean is not a technical requirement for the adaptive quadrature formulation. Since $d = 2\pi/L\delta$ and $m = md$, we then have

$$F_N(x_m) \simeq \frac{1}{2} - \frac{\mu}{Ld} + \frac{m}{L} - \frac{1}{2\pi}\sum_{k=1}^{L-1}\left\{\frac{e^{-i2\pi km/L}\psi_N(k\delta)}{ik} + \frac{e^{i2\pi(k-L)m/L}\psi_N(k-L)\delta)}{i(i-N)}\right\}$$

Since $e^{-i2\pi(k-L)m/L} = e^{-i2\pi km/L}$ by its periodicity property, we now have

$$F_N(x_m) = \frac{1}{2} - \frac{\mu}{Ld} + \frac{m}{L} - Y_m \,, \tag{6}$$

where $Y_m$ is a discrete Fourier transform,

$$Y_m = \frac{1}{2\pi} \sum_{k=0}^{L-1} y_k \, e^{-i2\pi km/L}, \quad m = 0,1,2,\ldots, L-1, \tag{7}$$

and

$$y_k = \begin{cases} 0 & , \text{ for } k = 0 \\ \dfrac{\phi(k\delta)}{ik} + \dfrac{\phi((k-N)\delta)}{i(k-N)} & , \text{ for } k = 1,2,\ldots, L-1. \end{cases}$$

The discrete Fourier transform in (7) will be evaluated using the Fast Fourier Transform algorithm developed by Cooley and Tukey [1965]. For L quadrature points a straightforward computation of such series will require $L^2$ complex evaluations. The FFT algorithm reduces this to $L(\log_2 L)$ complex evaluations with the corresponding proportional reduction in computing time. For the simplest and fastest form of the FFT, $L = 2^M$, where M is an integer. An excellent reference concerning the FFT and its implementation is provided by Brigham [1974].

The accuracy in the approximations in (6) using the FFT depends on the fineness of the grid chosen (i.e., how small $\delta = \Delta u$ is) and how insignificant the contribution of the summand $y_k$ becomes for $k \geq L$ (i.e., how large $L\delta$ is). Obviously, for fixed L, these two criteria run counter to each other. The approach we have taken is iterative with L being increased until stabilization is obtained. In most cases, $L = 2^M$ with $M = 10$ or at most 11 has been found to be adequate.

We will mention here briefly the ingenious method suggested by Bohman [1963] to supplement any inversion method such that a numerical upper and lower bounds on F(x) is obtained. In particular, this method can be used to evaluate the accuracy of any method of approximating F(x), including any method based on numerical inversion. For F(x) such that $F(x) = 0$ for $x < 0$, the idea is to convolve F(x) with non-negative functions (possibly also distribution functions) $H_1(x)$ and $H_2(x)$ with bounded transforms such that for all $x \geq 0$

$$F_1(x) < F(x) < F_2(x) \tag{8}$$

where $F_j(x) = F(x)*H_j(x)$, j=1,2 and * signifies convolution. Bohman [1963] chose $H_j(x)$ with *"characteristic-like functions"*, i.e.,

$$C_j(u) = \int_{-\infty}^{\infty} e^{iux} \, dH_j(x),$$

$$C_j(u) = \begin{cases} C(u) + (-0.42)^j \, i \, C'(u), & |u| \leq 1 \\ 0 & , |u| > 1 \end{cases}$$

where

$$C(u) = (1-|u|)\cos\pi u + \frac{\sin|\pi u|}{\pi}$$

and

$$C'(u) = -\pi(1-|u|)\sin\pi u.$$

Then, $F_j(x)$ is obtained by inverting the "*characteristic-like functions*" of the convolutions, i.e., $\theta_j(u)=\psi_N(u)C_j(u)$ with $\psi_N(u)$ representing the characteristic function of $F(x)$. The final estimate of $F(x)$ is the simple average of $F_1(x)$ and $F_2(x)$. The main benefit resulting from this method is that $\theta_j(u)$ is a bounded function in u as a result of the convolution operation such that the truncation error from numerical integration is eliminated. The trade-off is the convolution error introduced. In our computational experience, we found that even without employing the above method, the approximations for $F(x)$ obtained using the FFT method generally lie within the limits in (8). A potential application of the method that we may find useful, however, is when $F(x)$ is a discrete distribution function or a mixture of discrete and continuous distribution functions. This type of mixture is almost always found in actual severity of loss data. Since the process of convolving a discrete function with an absolutely continuous one, such as $H_j(x)$ above, produces an absolutely continuous function, the above method is one way of controlling the errors introduced in the inversion by the discontinuities in $F(x)$.

The above portion of Section 2 assumed that the number of losses N was fixed for ease of development. If N is a random variable, then the total loss distribution is obtained in a straightforward way from the above. For example, if N is Poisson with known mean $\lambda$ then we replace $\psi_{n,N}(u)$ in (4) with

$$\psi_{n,\lambda}(u) = \exp(\lambda(\phi_n(u)-1)) \tag{9}$$

and proceed in exactly the same way to obtain $\hat{F}_\lambda(x)$, say. If $\lambda$ is not known but is estimated from sequences of loss data $x_{11}, x_{12}, \ldots, x_{1n_1}; x_{21}, x_{22}, \ldots, x_{2n_2}, \ldots; x_{a1}, x_{a2}, \ldots, x_{an_a}$, then $\lambda$ in (9) can be replaced by $\hat{\lambda}$ based on the $n_j$. The resulting estimate of the total loss distribution $\hat{F}_{\hat{\lambda}}(x)$, say, is subject to more uncertainty than is the estimate $F_\lambda(x)$; accordingly an assessment of the risk associated with the loss process requires more extensive analysis than in the case when $\lambda$ is known. A proper analysis for the Poisson frequency distribution, for example, will make use of the distribution of the maximum likelihood estimate $\hat{\lambda}$. In addition, since the coefficient of variation for the Poisson frequency of loss distribution is $\lambda^{-1/2}$, we must also assess risk in terms of the "size of the risk business". Small firms are subject to greater relative fluctuations in number of losses than are larger firms and this is true regardless of the frequency of loss distribution. A potentially very important implication of this observation is that the use of industry-wide or state-wide data to assess the risk associated with a particular line of insurance may result in a serious under-statement of the risk to operating firms.

We have developed a non-parametric total loss distribution methodology for the case where N is (1) Poisson, (2) negative binomial, (3) binomial, and (4) fixed. These compounding distributions are sufficiently varied to satisfy many of the needs of practical application.

The characteristic function for the compound negative binomial distribution is

$$\psi(u) = \left[1 - \frac{m}{N^*} (\phi(u)-1)\right]^{-N^*} \tag{10}$$

where the mean of the negative binomial frequency distribution is m and the variance is $m(1+m/N^*)$. The characteristic function for the compound binomial distribution is

$$\psi(u) = (q+p\phi(u))^{n^*}, \tag{11}$$

where the mean of the binomial distribution is $n^*p$ and the variance is $n^*pq$.

## 3. Normal Powers Procedures for Developing Total Loss Distributions

In much of our work we have found that the assumption of finite variance need not or may not be a good modeling assumption. The sample moments of any finite set of loss data are always finite even if the mathematical (populations) moments of the loss distribution are infinite. The oil spill case study considered by Paulson et al. [1987] led to the conclusion that the upper tail of the loss data was well described by a Type I Pareto with a shape parameter $\alpha = .78$, i.e., a severity distribution with infinite variance and infinite mean. The workmen's compensation case study led to the conclusion that a finite variance model could be improved upon by an infinite variance model since it would better explain the observed loss data. Indeed, such cases are not uncommon in the riskier lines of an insurance business. The apparent lack of finite mathematical moments would seem to obviate the applicability of normal powers methods to actual loss data in the computation of total loss distributions. As it turns out, surprisingly, this is not the case.

Let x denote the severity of loss which follows a severity distribution s(x), N the frequency of losses in a fixed accounting period, z the total loss, i.e.,

$$z = \sum_{j=1}^{N} x_j, \tag{12}$$

and set

$$z' = \frac{z-E(z)}{\sigma(z)}, \tag{13}$$

where $\sigma(z)$ represents the standard deviation of z. The Cornish-Fisher or normal powers approximation to the distribution of z results from the re-version (inversion) of the asymptotic Edgeworth expansion [see Beard, Pentikainen, and Pesonen, 1969, pp.

41-51; see also Abramowitz and Stegun, 1964, pp. 934-935]. The approximation may be written as

$$z'_\beta = \frac{z_\beta - E(z)}{\sigma(z)} = y_\beta + \frac{1}{6}\gamma_1(y_\beta^2 - 1) + \frac{1}{24}\gamma_2(y_\beta^3 - 3y_\beta)$$

$$- \frac{1}{36}\gamma_1^2(2y_\beta^3 - 5y_\beta), \tag{14}$$

where $0 \le \beta \le 1$. The representation (14) is interpreted as follows. The $\beta$ percentile of the distribution of z, $z_\beta$ say, is expressed in terms of the $\beta$ percentile of the standard normal (Gaussian) distribution, $y_\beta$, and the first four moments of z, the mean, the variance, and respectively the skewness $\gamma_1$ and the kurtosis $\gamma_2$,

$$\gamma_1(z) = \gamma_1 = \frac{\mu_3}{\mu_2^{3/2}}, \quad \gamma_2(z) = \gamma_2 = \frac{\mu_4}{\mu_2^2} - 3, \tag{15}$$

where

$$\mu_j = E(z - E(z))^j, \quad j = 2,3,4.$$

Note that

$$E(z) = E(N)E(x), \quad var(z) = E(N)var(x) + var(N)E^2(x),$$

and

$$\gamma_1(z') = \gamma_1(z), \quad \gamma_2(z') = \gamma_2(z).$$

We consider four cases for the random variable N in (12): (1) Poisson with mean $\lambda$, designated in short by $P(\lambda)$ or $Poisson(\lambda)$), (2) negative binomial with parameters m and N*, designated in short by NB(m,N*), and with characteristic function

$$E(\exp(iuN)) = (1 - \frac{m}{N^*}(\exp(iu) - 1))^{-N^*}. \tag{16}$$

and frequency distribution

$$p(x: m,N^*) = \binom{N^*+x-1}{x}\left(\frac{N^*}{m+N^*}\right)^{N^*}\left(\frac{m}{m+N^*}\right)^x, \quad x = 0,1,\ldots \tag{17}$$

The mean and variance of (17) are, respectively

$$E(N) = m, \quad var(N) = m(1 + m/N^*). \tag{18}$$

(3) binomial with parameters n* and p, in short B(n*,p), and (4) degenerate, i.e., P(N=constant) = 1.

For case (1), Poisson compounding,

$$E(z) = \lambda\mu_x, \quad E(z^2) = \lambda^2\mu_x^2 + \lambda\alpha_2$$

$$\gamma(z_1') = \frac{\alpha_3}{((\alpha_2)^{3/2}\lambda^{1/2})}, \quad \gamma(z_2') = \frac{\alpha_4}{\lambda\alpha_2^2}.$$

For case (2), negative binomial compounding,

$$E(z) = m\mu_x, \quad E(z^2) = \frac{N^*+1}{N^*} m^2\mu_x^2 + m\alpha_2,$$

$$\gamma_1(z') = \left[\frac{2m^3\mu_x^2}{N^{*2}} + \frac{3m^2\mu_x\alpha_2}{N^*} + m\alpha_3\right] \Big/ \left[m\alpha_2 + \frac{m^2\mu_x^2}{N^*}\right]^{3/2}$$

$$\gamma_2(z') = \frac{A}{B} - 3,$$

where

$$A = \frac{3(N^*+2)m^4\mu_x^4}{N^{*3}} + \frac{6(N^*+2)m^3\mu_x^2\alpha_2}{N^{*2}}$$

$$+ \frac{3(N^*+1)m^2\alpha_2}{N^*} + \frac{4(m^2\mu_x\,\alpha_2)}{N^*} + m\alpha_4,$$

$$B = \left(m\alpha_2 + \frac{m^2\mu_x^2}{N^*}\right)^2.$$

For case (3), binomial compounding,

$$E(z) = n^*p\mu_x, \quad E(z^2) = n^*(n^*-1)p^2\mu_x^2 + n^*p\alpha_2,$$

$$\gamma_1(z) = \frac{2n^*p^3\mu_x^3 - 3n^*p^2\mu_x\alpha_2 + n^*p\alpha_3}{(n^*\alpha_2 - n^*p^2\mu_x^2)^{3/2}},$$

$$\gamma_2(z) = \frac{A}{B} - 3,$$

where

$$A = 3(n^* - 2)n^*p^4\mu_x^4 - 6(n^* - 2)n^*p^3\mu_x^2\alpha_2$$

$$- 4n^*p^2\alpha_3\mu_x + 3n^*(n^* - 1)p^2\alpha_2^2 + n^*p\alpha_4,$$

$$B = n^*\alpha_2 p - n^*p^2\mu_x^2.$$

For case (4), fixed N,

$$E(z) = N\mu, \quad E(z^2) = N(N-1)\mu_x^2 + N\alpha_2,$$

$$\gamma_1(z) = \frac{(2N\mu_x^3 - 3N\mu_x\alpha_2 + N\alpha_3)}{(N\alpha_2 - N\mu_x^2)^{3/2}},$$

$$\gamma_2(z) = \frac{A}{B} - 3,$$

where

$$A = (3N(N-2)\mu_x^4 - 6N(N-2)\mu_x^2\alpha_2 - 4N\mu_x\alpha_3 + 3N(N-1)\alpha_2^2 + N\alpha_4),$$

$$B = (N\alpha_2 - N\mu_x^2)^2.$$

In all the above formulae

$$\alpha_j = E(x^j), \; j=2,3,4, \qquad \mu_x = E(x).$$

The normal powers method is not valid for all $\gamma_1$ and $\gamma_2$. Specifically is required that $z'_\beta$ be non-decreasing as $\beta$ increases from zero to unity. It is also required that $z'_\beta \geq 0$ for $\beta = 0$ and that $z'_\beta$ be nonnegative for nonnegative losses $x_j$. Thus the normal powers method will be applicable only for a subset R, say, of the $\gamma_1$, $\gamma_2$ half-plane $-\infty < \gamma_1 < \infty$, $\gamma_2 \geq -3$. The set of points R has been numerically determined and is given in Figure 1. If, for any of the four cases considered, $\gamma_1$ and $\gamma_2$ lie within R, then a bona fide distribution function for z will result. If $\gamma_1$ and $\gamma_2$ do not lie within R, then we shall say that the normal powers method technically fails. Non-monotone total loss profiles and the occurrence of negative total losses with positive probability are examples of technical failures.

The main use of the non-parametric and normal powers procedure is expected to be found in applications to the underwriting side of a risk business. Generally the population parameters will be known in these situations and must be estimated from available data. Given severities of loss $x_1, x_2, \ldots, x_n$ we replace the quantities $\mu_x$, $\alpha_2, \alpha_3$, $\alpha_4$ by their estimates

$$\frac{1}{n}\sum_{j=1}^{n} x_j^k ,$$

k = 1,2,3,4 respectively. If the population parameters of the frequency distribution are unknown, they also must be estimated from the available data or assigned values based on other information.

A completely non-parametric solution to the problem of determining total loss distribution can be effected through the use

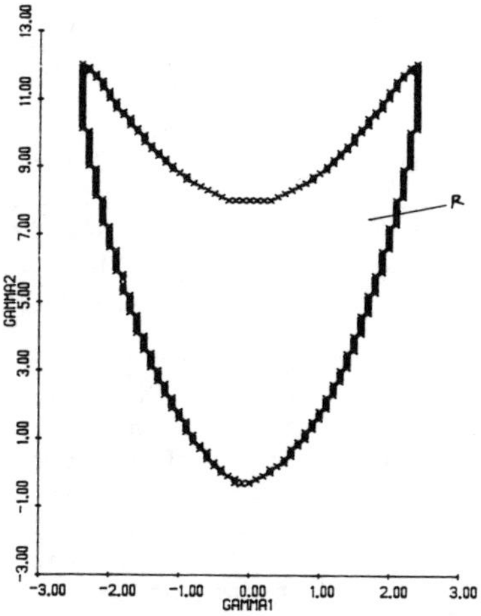


FIGURE 1: Region of applicability in $\gamma_1$ and $\gamma_2$ of four moment Normal Powers Approximation

of (4), although we have not produced the necessary algorithms at this time. If $n_1, n_2, \ldots, n_a$ represent the frequency of realized losses in accounting periods 1,2,..., a, then the sample characteristic function of the $n_j$ is defined as

$$\hat{g}(u) = a^{-1} \sum_{j=1}^{a} \exp(iun_j).$$

The estimate $\hat{g}(u)$ is consistent and unbiased for the population characteristic function g(u). The completely non-parametric and exact estimate of the total loss distribution is developed by substituting

$$\hat{g}(\phi_n(u))$$

for $\psi$ in equation (4).

## 4. Empirical Studies

The character and performance of the non-parametric and Cornish-Fisher methods were extensively investigated in order to determine the extent to which these methods may be applied in practice. The overall assessment was determined through the use of both simulated and realized severity of and frequency of loss data.

The study was designed to be as broad and as severe as we could make it. Much effort was expended in an attempt to make the algorithms fail since only then can the usefulness of the methods under study be properly delimited. The study configuration was as follows.

| Frequency Distributions | Severity Distributions |
|---|---|
| 1. Fixed N | 1. Normal |
| 2. Poisson | 2. Lognormal |
| 3. Binomial | 3. Gamma |
| 4. Negative Binomial | 4. Pareto, $\alpha \geq 0.5$ |
| | 5. Mixtures of distributions |
| | 6. Realized severity data from a variety of sources and applications |

Each frequency distribution (with a variety of parameter values) was paired with each severity distribution (over a variety of parameter values) to produce a resulting total loss distribution. The more difficult pairings were replicated at least 100 times in order to determine the extent to which the total loss distributions are reproducible and which the methods produce consistent estimates of the true total loss distribution. In every case the average over replications of the estimated total loss distribution virtually coincided with the true total loss distribution. The fluctuation in replicates of the total loss distributions depended on the potential for fluctuation in the frequency and severity distributions. For example, the fluctuations in simulated total losses for the Poisson frequency distribution with mean 100 and Pareto distribution with shape parameter 0.5 ranged over an excess of two orders of magnitude. The following are the conclusions of the empirical study.

(1) The non-parametric procedure always generates the correct total loss distribution. The FFT version of this procedure is computationally faster than the adaptive quadrature version when the mathematical mean of the severity distribution is finite. The adaptive quadrature version is generally applicable.

(2) The normal powers and the non-parametric procedures generally agree very closely. Remarkably the four term normal powers method often provides useful total loss distributions even when all the required mathematical moments are infinite. This method will sometimes generate negative losses with positive probability or non-monotone distribution functions, both technical failures. However, even under technical failure, the estimates of the total loss distribution are only slightly in error, and the nature and magnitude of the error is easily discernable.

(3) The normal powers method is computationally faster than both versions of the nonparametric procedure. We suggest that a hybrid version of the normal powers and non-parametric procedures be used in practice since the normal powers method is occasionally subject to technical failure.

Further details and graphical descriptions are available in Paulson and Dixit [1986].

## 5. Simulation of Total Loss Distributions

One of the potentially attractive applications of the non-parametric and normal powers procedures is in simulation. An explicit representation of the total loss distribution is a valuable input to more extensive analyses of an insurance or risk business. For example, many cash flow models require an input of a total loss over quarters, over years, etc. [Pentikainen and Rantala, 1982; Paulson and Dixit, 1988]. In many applications the simulation is handled as follows. Suppose the severity of loss distribution is log normal and the frequency of loss distribution is negative binomial. First a negative binomial variate is generated; second, this number of log normal variates is generated; third, the total loss is calculated and this input is made to the cash flow model and followed through time; fourth, the whole process is repeated. With the results of sections 2 and 3 the first three steps of the process can be combined into one with the potential for very substantial computational savings. Further, actual company, state-wide or industry-wide loss and frequency of loss data can be used with virtually no need to make specific distributional modeling assumptions.

The simulation of total loss distributions based on either of the non-parametric or normal powers procedures is simple. For the non-parametric procedure, an estimate of the total loss distribution $\hat{F}(x)$ is first developed over the entire range of probable x. Next, a uniform deviate is drawn, set equal to $\hat{F}(x)$, and $x = \hat{F}^{-1}(u)$ is the desired deviate from $\hat{F}(x)$.

For the normal powers procedure, a uniform deviate $\beta$ (see equation 14) is generated. Next, the standard normal quantile corresponding to $\beta$ is determined. Finally, the total loss deviate $z_\beta$ is computed. The non-parametric procedure should be used as a check to verify that the normal powers procedure produces the correct total loss profile.

A strong note of warning concerning simulation must be made at this point. The data available for computing total loss profiles will often consist of one year's experience. In this case both $\phi_n(u)$ and

$$S_n(x) = \frac{1}{n} \text{ (number of } x_i \leq x)$$

contain all the information in the loss data. Bounds can be given for $S_n(x)$. But there is only one realization of the total loss and it is not possible to make an assessment of the repeatability of the total loss. The non-parametric and normal powers procedures do not give in this setting an estimate of the variability of $\hat{F}(x)$. While we can say that

$$S_n(x) \pm 2\left(\frac{S_n(x)(1-S_n(x))}{n}\right)$$

is an approximate 95% confidence interval for S(x), nothing similar can be said about F(x) because the requisite information which would be derived from replicates is not available. This same statement is also true in the parametric setting.

If there are r stationary replicates of total losses for r consecutive years, we compute $F_1(x)$, $F_2(x), \ldots,$ $F_r(x)$ for the r years. In order to specify the variability of the total loss profile we can use the envelope generated by the profiles themselves, i.e., the profile $F_u(x)$ forms an upper bound if, for all x, $F_u(x)$ is greater than all other $F_j(x)$, while the profile $F_L(x)$ is the lower bound if, for all x, $F_L(x)$ is less than all other $F_j(x)$. Single profiles $F_L(x)$ and $F_u(x)$ need not exist. Alternatively, for $F_j(x) = p$, say, we determine the corresponding quantiles $x_{1p}$, $x_{2p}, \ldots,$ $x_{rp}$ and compute their mean and standard deviations. From this information we construct approximate probabilistic envelopes which are effectively constructed of confidence intervals for each fixed p, $0<p<1$. (Amusingly, the distribution around the resulting mean profile need not be symmetric so that the development of the probabilistic envelopes around the mean profile based on standard normal theory can be improved by an application of the normal powers procedure. We have found the normal powers approximation in these circumstances to be useful for a as small as 8.)

The frequency of loss distribution is implicitly involved in the above arguments since a frequency of loss distribution has been utilized in the computation of the total loss distribution. If $n_1, n_2, \ldots,$ $n_r$ represents the loss frequencies, then the mean and standard deviation of the $n_j$ should be used to determine the choice of compounding distribution. In particular, the coefficient of variation of the binomial and Poisson frequency distributions must always be small. For example, if the mean of a Poisson frequency distribution is 10,000 losses, then we would normally expect 10,000 $\pm$ 2(100) about 95% of the time since the coefficient of variation is 1%. For a mean frequency of 10000, the coefficient of variation for the binomial frequency distribution can be at most 1%. The coefficient of variation for the negative binomial distribution must be at least 1%.

## 6. A Quantile-Based Approximation to the Exact Total Loss Profile

In many parametric situations the characteristic function of a particular severity of loss distribution is extremely difficult to compute while certain other characteristics of the severity distribution are relatively easy to obtain. For example, for the Pareto severity distribution with distribution function

$$S(x) = 1 - (x_0/x)^{\alpha}, \ \alpha > 0, \ x > x_0, \tag{19}$$

the characteristic function is not convenient to compute numerically for small values of $\alpha$. However, the quantiles $x_p$ defined by

$$p = S(x_p) \tag{20}$$

are immediately found to be

$$x_p = \frac{x_0}{(1-p)^{1/\alpha}} . \tag{21}$$

Set for some large integer value of m

$$p = \frac{j}{m+1} , \ j=1,2,\ldots, m,$$

so that we obtain m values of x

$$x_j = \left(\frac{m+1}{m+1-j}\right)^{1/\alpha} x_0, \ j=1,2,\ldots, m. \tag{22}$$

These values $x_j$ are approximately the expected order statistics of a set of m losses from the Pareto severity distribution. The characteristic function $\phi(u)$ of the Pareto severity distribution is

$$\phi(u) = \int_o^\infty \exp(iux)s(x)dx = \int_o^\infty \exp(iux)dS(x)$$

where $s(x)=S'(x)$. The Riemann-Stieltjes integral may be approximated as

$$\phi(u) = \sum_{j=1}^{m} \exp(iux_j)(S(x_j)-S(x_{j-1})$$

$$\phi(u) \simeq \frac{1}{m} \sum_{j=1}^{m} \exp(iux_j). \tag{23}$$

since $S(x_j)-S(x_{j-1})=1/(m+1)$. We may now use the representation (23) in (4) to get an approximate total loss distribution. Alternatively, the sample moments (not the mathematical moments!) of $x_j$ may be computed in the usual fashion and the normal powers used to develop the approximation to the total loss distribution. Both approximations work very well, but some exploration and iteration will generally be necessary before an appropriate value of m is settled upon. For example, for the Pareto distribution with $x_0 = 1000$ and $\alpha = 2$, we have used m=1000 and m=2000 to compute the total loss distribution when the frequency of loss distribution is negative binomial NB(100,5.26). The total loss distributions computed by the normal powers method with m=2000 quantiles and by the non-parametric method with m=1000 and 2000 are virtually identical; we therefore conclude that this total loss profile is an excellent approximation to the exact total loss distribution. Even though the first through fourth mathematical moments of the severity and total loss distribution are infinite, the total loss distribution based on the first four moments of the quantiles in the normal powers method produces a virtually exact result. The first four (sample-like) moments of the quantiles are finite for any m but, as m increases, the resulting normal powers representation should be interpreted as an asymptotic representation in the same way that Stirling's approximation is an asymptotic representation of the gamma function.

As $\alpha$ of the Type I Pareto severity distribution decreases, the normal powers procedure technically fails whereas the nonparametric methods continue to be applicable. However, even under failure, the normal powers method still provides useful information over most of the total loss profile.

This approximation to the total loss distribution has been investigated for a variety of cases which are generally difficult to deal with in practice. For example, the agreement of this approximation with the exact (as developed numerically) to the total loss distribution is excellent when among others, the severity distribution is lognormal, log-gamma, gamma, and Weibull and the compounding distribution is Poisson, negative binomial, binomial, or fixed. The details in these other cases follow along the lines developed for the Pareto.

Approximations based on quantiles are useful in a variety of other contexts. In particular, this procedure may be used in cases of parametric estimation cases. Suppose that $x_1, x_2, \ldots, x_n$ represents a set of loss severities with an extremely long tail, as might be the case in fire insurance. In this case a transformation of the data is a reasonable tack to consider. For example, often the transformed variate $y_j = \log x_j$ may be successfully modeled as normal, gamma, or Weibull. Suppose specifically that the logarithm of the losses are gamma distributed, the parameters are estimated by maximum likelihood, and the agreement between expected and observed is found to be good. How does one develop the total loss distribution? If $G(y;\hat{\alpha},\hat{\beta})$ represents the distribution function of the fitted gamma density

$$g(y;\alpha,\beta) = \frac{y^{\alpha-1}\exp(-y/\beta)}{\Gamma(\alpha)\beta^{\alpha}}, \quad \alpha > 0,\ \beta > 0,\ y > 0,$$

then the y quantiles are given by solving numerically for

$$p = G(y_p;\ \hat{\alpha},\hat{\beta}).$$

The x-quantiles are determined from those of the y-quantiles by the inverse transformation

$$x_p = \exp(y_p).$$

We now proceed exactly as in the Type I Pareto case. Considerable care must be exercised in the parametric framework because the degree of fit in the tail can have substantial influence on the resulting total loss profile. If the fitted severity distribution function is longer-tailed than the empirical severity distribution function, the total loss profile will indicate greater riskiness than the actual loss data may warrant. On the other hand, if the fitted severity distribution function is not as long-tailed as its empirical counterpart, then the total loss profile can substantially understate the riskiness of the line being studied. It is our experience that two or three parameter summaries of loss severity data are rarely adequate.

## 7. Probability of Ruin

The methods discussed in Section 2 and 3 can be applied directly to obtain estimates of probabilty of ruin. We shall consider only the usual case described by the equation

$$Y(t) = R + pt - \sum_{j=1}^{N(t)} x_j \tag{24}$$

where R is an initial reserve which has been put in place at time 0, Y(t) represents the asset amount at the end of a period of length t, pt represents the amount of income (premium) to the asset amount over the time interval of length t, N(t) represents the number of claims against the assets at the end of time t, and $x_j$ represents the jth claim against the asset amount. If N(t) is Poisson with mean $\lambda t$ for example, then the characteristic function of $\sum_{j=1}^{N(t)} x_j$ is

$$\omega(u) = \exp(\lambda t(\phi(u)-1)), \tag{25}$$

if the loss claims $x_j$ have common characteristic function $\phi(u)$.

The non-parametric procedure of Section 2 in possible combination with the results of Section 6 allows us to compute immediately the probability

$$G(R+pt) = \Pr\left\{ \sum_{j=1}^{N(t)} x_j \le R+pt \right\} \tag{26}$$

for fixed t, p, and R. An estimate of the probability of ruin is therefore 1-G(R+pt). Note that we can get nonparametric estimates of the probability of ruin by replacing $\phi(u)$ by $\phi_n(u)$ when only the data $x_1, x_2, \ldots, x_n$ are given and if $\lambda$ is known. If $\lambda$ is not known we can replace $\lambda$ by $\hat{\lambda}$, the maximum likelihood estimate of $\lambda$, to get an estimate of the probability of ruin. In these latter cases the probability of ruin estimate has its own probability distribution.

In terms of the normal powers approximation, we numerically determine that value of $\beta$ in (14) for which

$$z_\beta = R+pt; \tag{27}$$

an estimate of the probability of ruin is $1-\beta$. Again, if the severity of loss distribution is not known, we replace the moments $\mu$, $\alpha_2$, $\alpha_3$, $\alpha_4$ by their data-based estimates.

These methods should not be used for long-term estimates of the probability of ruin unless the severity distribution and the frequency of loss distribution are completely specified. If, for example, the severity of loss distribution is not specified then its characteristic function $\phi(u)$ is estimated by $\phi_n(u)$. Over the long term, $E(N(t)) \gg n$, the number of claims upon which $\phi_n(u)$ is based, so that we would be effectively extrapolating to the long term from a short record. Even though there are reasons to be skeptical of estimates for the long term based on short records, this method often works quite well for stationary environments. Of course, in practice stationarity is a rare or non-existent exception.

We have developed the numerical methods to produce estimates of the probability of ruin for the cases in which (1) the frequency and severity distributions of N and $x_j$, respectively, are completely specified, (2) the frequency distribution of N is completely specified and the severity of loss distribution of the $x_j$ is estimated from a set of loss data. Based on a few cases, these algorithms appear to produce excellent results.

## 8. Acknowledgement

We are pleased to acknowledge our considerable indebtedness to the Massachusetts Rating Bureaus and the U.S. Army Research office (under contract DAAG29-81-K-0110) for the support under which this research was undertaken and completed.

## 9. References

1. Abramowitz, M. and Stegun, I.A. [1964]. *Handbook of Mathematical Functions*. Washington: National Bureau of Standards.

2. Beard, R.E., Pentikainen, T. and Pesonen, E. [1977]. *Risk Theory*. London: Chapman and Hall.

3. Bohman, H. [1963]. To Compute the Distribution Function When the Characteristic Function is Known. *Skandinavisk Aktuarietidskrift*, pp. 41-46.

4. Brigham, E.D. [1974]. *The Fast Fourier Transform*. Englewood Cliffs: Prentice Hall.

5. Cooley, J.W. and Tukey, J.W. [1965]. An Algorithm for the Machine Calculation of Complex Fourier Series. *Mathematics of Computation*, 19, pp. 207-301.

6. Gil-Pelaez, J. [1951]. Note on the Inversion Theorem. *Biometrika*, 38, pp. 481-482.

7. Paulson, A.S., Dixit, R., Derrig, R.A. and Ulseth, G.W. [1987]. The Applicability of the Stable Laws in Collective Risk Theory and Practice. *The Journal of Risk and Insurance*. To appear.

8. Paulson, A.S. and Dixit, R. [1986]. Some General Approaches to Computing Total Loss Distributions and the Probability of Ruin. Troy, New York: School of Management, Rensselaer Polytechnic Institute.

9. Paulson, A.S. and Dixit, R. [1988]. Flow Models for Premium and Surplus Analysis. Troy, New York: School of Management, Rensselaer Polytechnic Institute.

10. Paulson, A.S. and Faris, N.J. [1985]. Practical Approach to Measuring the Distribution of Total Annual Claims. *Strategic Planning and Modeling in Property-Liability Insurance*. Edited by J.D. Cummins. Boston: Kluwer-Nijhoff.

11. Pentikainen, T. and Rantala, J. [1982]. *Solvency of Insurers and Equalization Reserves*, Vol. I-II. Helsinki: Insurance Publishing Company.

12. Whittaker, E.T. and Watson, G.N. [1963]. *A Course of Modern Analysis*. Cambridge: Cambridge University Press.

# 6

# METHODS FOR ANALYZING THE EFFECTS OF UNDERWRITING RISK ON THE INSURER'S LONG-TERM SOLVENCY

Jukka Rantala

Abstract

The aim of this paper is to develop further the ideas put forward in the Finnish solvency report (Pentikäinen-Rantala [1982]), and to provide a coherent framework for analyzing of how the insurer's solvency is affected by the underwriting risk. The focus is primarily on long-term relations and properties. The insurer is viewed as a filter transforming the claims process the most important outputs being claims reserve, accumulated profit and the future premium rates. Main points of interest are the variability of both premiums and accumulated profit and the long-term need for the safety loading when stochastic structure of the claims process is varying and different rating rules are applied. The methods of time series theory and stochastic control theory are utilized. Also a practical example is considered.

## 1. The Filter Presentation of the Insurer

The traditional way to model the insurer is to assume that a solvency reserve is established and the premiums are charged before the corresponding claim payments. An essential feature is that the rating of premiums is based on estimation of future claims and evaluation of the need to support the solvency reserve, to pay dividends and to meet all other commitments. Another way which may prove useful is to reverse the order of considerations, i.e. to interpret the insurer as a "filter" transforming the claims process $X_0(t)$ (= input) to some new processes (= outputs) such as claims reserves, future premium rates and solvency reserves (=accumulated profits). This mode of approach can be derived from the fact that the rating is based on past experience. Therefore, the calculation of premiums, reserves etc. can also described as a process which transforms the available actual data into relevant rates to be applied among other things in control of continuing future business. A merit of this approach is that the ideas and also the techniques well developed in engineering control theory can be utilized also in the insurance environment. The diagram of Figure 1 illustrates the idea.

The original claims process $X_0(t)$ goes first to the reserving filter, where an estimate of the unpaid and unreported claims is made and a corresponding claims reserve is established. The resulting process $\hat{X}_0(t)$, which is an estimate for the unknown $X_0(t)$, is then passed through the reinsurance filter, the output being the retained part of the claims incurred = $X(t)$. The difference between revenues (= the retained part of risk premiums + investment income) and $X(t)$ is transferred to the solvency reserve $U(t)$. In addition, the future premiums $P(t+d)$ are (possibly also regarding some external factors such as inflation, the market situation etc.) adjusted on the

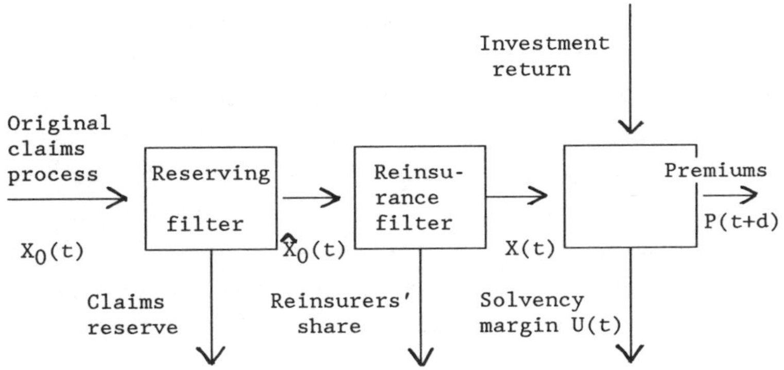


Fig.1. The most important input and output processes of the insurer.

basis of the observed X(t) and U(t), d denoting the time delay which is needed to implement the changes in premium rates. The filter model is much used in engineering sciences and to some extent also in economics. Actuarial works along these lines include Balzer-Benjamin [1980], [1982], who consider deterministic claims processes, Ryder [1977], Bohman [1979], Martin-Löf [1983] and Rantala [1984], [1986], who allow the claims process to be stochastic.

The filter model may be used to describe the actual functioning of the insurer. However, equally important is to seek a means for a sensible control and management of insurer's risk business, that is, to investigate what kind of filters give tolerable outputs and react in an appropriate way to both expected and unexpected fluctuations in the input process. This is especially important in cases where some automatic loss/profit sharing systems are applied.

In the following the considerations are mainly restricted to linear filters (i.e. the outputs are linear combinations of past X(t):s) in order to preserve the easy possibility of extracting some analytic results.

Of course, the above filter model does not in itself suffice to describe properly the whole complexity of the long-term solvency conditions. The main omission in the following considerations is the absence of the asset risk. However, for the analysis of the pure underwriting risk the model may prove useful.

## 2. Assumptions

In order to achieve exact results from the above formulation we have to specify:

(1) the stochastic structure of $X_0(t)$ and the claims development pattern

(2) the reserving rule

(3) the reinsurance scheme

(4) the rating rule .

### (1) The stochastic structure of $X_0(t)$

The conventional assumption is that the claims in a particular year t occur according to a homogeneous Poisson process and the individual claim amounts are independent of each other and of the number of the claims. Thus the total claims amount follows so called compound Poisson distribution (see Beard-Pentikäinen-Pesonen [1984]). It is assumed that, in addition to real growth and inflation trends, the basic level of the claims process changes from year to year according to economic, weather and other conditions. Using the terminology of Pentikäinen-Rantala [1982], the fluctuations of the basic level may be divided into two components: short- and long-term fluctuations. The latter is mainly due to economic conditions and the former to more rapidly changing circumstances such as the weather. It is often assumed that these components are included in a random variable q(t) operating on the expected number of claims. The scale of q(t) is so chosen that Eq(t)=1. Moreover, it is assumed that q(t) is a weakly stationary (i.e. the moments up to second order are independent of time) random process with variance $\sigma_q^2$ and that for given values of q(s) and q(t), $X_0(s)$ and $X_0(t)$ are independent ($s \neq t$). The claims size distribution is assumed to be only rescaled by inflation.

In what follows we take process X(t) as the starting point so that we need not specify the assumptions concerning $X_0(t)$.

(2) The reserving rule and the development pattern

The delay in claims settlement has of course been a central aspect in reserve calculation theory and practice, and numerous valuable works have been published on these topics in recent years. However the effects of the development pattern and the different reserving rules on the run-off risk and the solvency conditions are little discussed in actuarial model building. One of the early attempts to build up such a "run-off theory" was that of Philipson [1965]. This issue was recently discussed in two papers (Daykin-Bernstein [1985], Pentikäinen-Rantala [1986]) presented at the ASTIN Colloquium in Biarritz in 1985. In order to prevent the present paper from expanding too much, this part of the above model is not considered further, but the interested reader is asked to consult the papers referred to and also Rantala [1984].

(3) The reinsurance scheme

Neither is the reinsurance scheme elaborated further in this paper. We simply restrict our considerations to the residual variance coming through the reinsurance scheme. As noted in Pentikäinen-Rantala [1982] the solvency properties are not very heavily dependent on the reinsurance form provided that equivalent retention levels are assume. Ibid., Vol II, Chapter VI, contains a tentative analysis of the optimal long-term choice of the retention level. We also refer to the vast existing literature on reinsurances which are optimal under some specific criterions. However, the time horizons assumed there are usually shorter (e.g. one year) than needed in the long-term solvency model.

(4) The rating rule

This paper concentrates on an analysis of the interrelations between incurred claims X(t), solvency reserve U(t) and premiums P(t+d). We are especially interested in how the rating rule and the stochastic structure of X(t) influence the variability of the premiums and the solvency reserve and the need for the safety loading in the long run. The rating rule may be given or it may be a result of optimality considerations.

## 3. The Questions to be Answered

We measure all the quantities by some volume measure V(t) and denote the corresponding accumulated profit (for which we use also the name solvency capital), premiums and claims by small letters u(t), p(t) and x(t) and call them <u>rates</u>. The basic equation is

$$u(t) = r(t)u(t-1) + p(t) - x(t) \quad (3.1)$$

where relative interest coefficient r(t) = (1 + interest rate(t)) divided by (1 + growth rate(t) of V(t)). In order to facilitate the mathematical treatment of the model r(t) is taken as a constant r and x(t) is assumed to be weakly stationary; i.e. the marginal distribution of x(t) has a constant and a finite mean Ex and variance $\sigma_x^2$ (see also Section 2).

Note 1. Note that the volume and inflation trends have been removed from x(t), since x(t) is proportional to the volume measure V(t). Thus the assumption of weak stationarity is not very restrictive. As a limiting case x(t) is allowed to be a random walk process which is viewed as "the most dangerous case". For cases where only the d-th difference of x(t) is assumed to be weakly stationary Rantala [1986] is referred to.

Note 2. The stochastic properties of x(t) can, at least in principle, be calculated from the stochastic properties of $x_0(t)$, when the claims development, reserve calculation rule and the reinsurance scheme are given. For example, by the traditional assumptions made in Section 2 process $x_0(t)$ is weakly stationary apart from a possible slight decrease or increase in $Var(x_0(t))$ due to the Poisson component if the real growth is non-zero. It can be shown (see Pentikäinen-Rantala [1986]) that with a linear reserve calculation rule (based on the combination of the claims paid and premiums) and with an inflation immune reinsurance scheme also x(t) is a weakly stationary process, whose covariance structure is a transformation of the covariance structure of $x_0(t)$.

A natural demand for any mathematical rating rule is that u(t) has (at least asymptotically) a marginal distribution with a finite mean Eu and variance $\sigma_u^2$, i.e. process u(t) is also weakly stationary. Let $R_u$ be a suitable multiple of $\sigma_u$ (perhaps taking into account the skewness of u(t)) which is aimed to describe the "variation range"

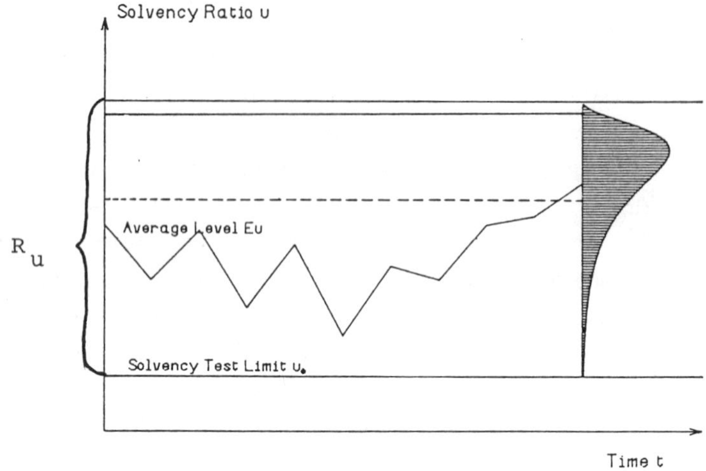


Fig. 2. The marginal distribution of the solvency rate u(t).

of the equilibrium distribution of u(t) (see Fig.2).

Let $R_x$, $R_p$ and $R_{\Delta p}$ be the corresponding variation ranges for x(t), p(t) and $\Delta p(t) = p(t)-p(t-1)$. We should be able to solve among other things the following problems:

(1) For a given rating rule, compute $R_u$, $R_p$ and $R_{\Delta p}$ as a function of the correlation structure of x(t).

(2) For a given rating rule find $\max R_u$, $\max R_p$ and $\max R_{\Delta p}$, independent of the correlation structure of x(t), as a function of $R_x$.

(3) For a given correlation structure of x(t) find rating rule minimizing $R_u$ when $R_p$ or $R_{\Delta p}$ is fixed.

Observe that criteria (2)-(3) differ those from traditionally used in experience rating or credibility theories. There the interest is usually in maximum accuracy; i.e. premiums p(t) should be a best estimate of x(t), usually in the LSE sense. No weight is placed on the time stability of premiums or insurer's solvency rate. In experience rating theory some attention has been paid to the limited fluctuation criterion, where variance in premiums has to be restricted. However, the starting-point is generally a fixed formula whose optimality properties are usually not investigated and the link between the rating formula and the insurer's solvency rate is not considered.

If the correlation structure of x(t) is known (or estimated) then obviously the "best" rating rule is given by an answer to problem (3). Which combination of $R_u$ and $R_p$ or $R_{\Delta p}$ should be used depends on specific circumstances in each situation e.g. how strong smoothing of the claims process the policy holders desire. It is probable that in most cases $R_{\Delta p}$ and $R_p$ should be clearly smaller than $R_x$. On the other hand, since we cannot be sure that the correlation structure chosen is the correct one, we should also answer question (2) by using the rating rule derived from question (3).

The total variation in x(t) places limits on available combinations of $R_p$ and $R_u$; the "energy" of x(t) cannot be reduced by the system; the energy can only be conducted to either solvency rate or premium rates (see Fig.3). The smaller the variations in premiums, the greater these will be in the solvency rate.

For every rating rule and correlation structure of x(t) the necessary long-term safety loading can be calculated by demanding that equilibrium distribution of

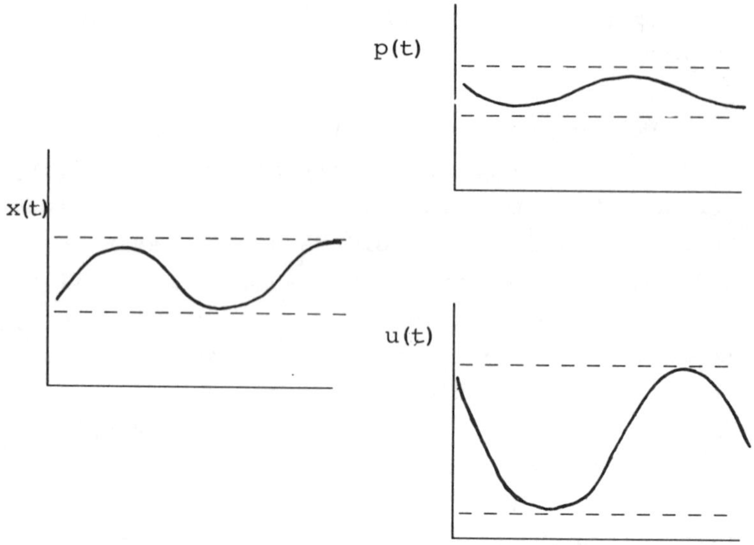


Fig.3. The channels for the variat on "energy" of claims process x(t).

u(t) is well above a ruin barrier $u_B$. This condition can be approximated by requirement

$$Eu \geq kR_u + u_B \qquad (3.2)$$

where k is close to 0.5 ( for a symmetric distribution of u(t) exactly 0.5). An appropriate statutory upper limit for u(t) (e.g. for taxation purposes) is $R_u+u_B$, since it is the smallest upper limit which allows fluctuations of u(t) to remain above the ruin barrier $u_B$.

Requirement (3.2) can be fulfilled for every rating rule by adding a suitable safety loading to the premiums. The expectation of u is

$$Eu = E(p-x)/(1-r) = \lambda_1/(1-r) \qquad (3.3)$$

(excluding for brevity the case r=1). Addition of $\lambda_2$ into p(t) means that Eu changes accordingly (see formulae (5.4.1) -(5.4.2)). Note that the necessary minimum long-term safety loading is positive if $r<1$ and negative if $r>1$; i.e. the sign of the safety loading depends on whether the interest rate is sufficient to compensate the inflation effect of the growth rate of the basic volume measure V(t) on the solvency reserve.

## 4. Which Methods Can Be Used ?

One way to try to find solutions to problems (1) - (3) posed in the preceding section is to utilize the methods of time series and stochastic control theories. Among other things the following techniques can be employed.

(1) Time response functions of the filters show how e.g. an impulse or a step is passed through the system. We may inquire e.g. for what kinds of inputs the system is stable, whether the system generates cyclical or other oscillations etc.

(2) Frequency response functions show among other things how the sine-waves with different wave-lengths are amplified in the system. By this technique it is also possible to answer question (2) of Section 3.

(3) Kalman filter technique and other methods of stochastic control theory can be used to solve problem (3) of Section 3.

## 4.1. Impulse and Step Response Functions

The impulse at time 0 in the claims rate is defined by

$$x(t) = \begin{cases} 1 , & \text{for } t=0 \\ 0 , & \text{otherwise} \end{cases} \tag{4.1.1}$$

and the step at time 0 is defined by

$$x(t) = \begin{cases} 1 , & \text{for } t\geq 0 \\ 0 , & \text{for } t<0 \end{cases} , \tag{4.1.2}$$

or equivalently

$$x(t) = \begin{cases} 1 , & \text{for } t=0 \\ 0 , & \text{otherwise} \end{cases} . \tag{4.1.3}$$

The impulse response function of a filter tells how an isolated disturbance reflects in the system. For example, in the present context the response of the premium rate to an impulse in the claims rate indicates how the claims incurred in a particular year are "paid" by the policyholders in later years. The impulse response function tells whether the premiums and solvency rate react appropriately to an unexpected claims year; i.e. whether they return to their original levels and if so, how fast. Thus it may be a useful measure of performance e.g. with very skew claims distributions where the variance is an inadequate measure.

The step response function of a filter describes the reactions of the filter to a permanent change in the level of the input process. The step response function reveals whether the premiums reach the right level and whether the solvency rate reverts to its original level

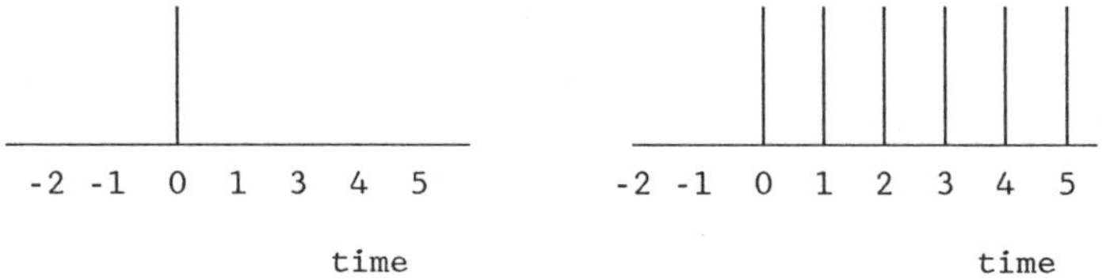


Fig.4. Impulse and step in the claims rate.

after a sudden permanent unexpected change in the level of the claims rate.

The step from time-response to simulation is short: in fact simulation essentially means that deterministic impulses and steps are replaced by stochastic ones and the responses due to separate origin years are combined.

## 4.2. Frequency Response Functions

According to the famous spectral representation theorem of weakly stationary processes every weakly stationary process x(t) can be expressed in integral form, called spectral representation:

$$x(t) = \int_{-\pi}^{\pi} e^{iwt} dz(w) \tag{4.2.1}$$

where i is the imaginary unit and dz(w):s ($-\pi < w \leq \pi$) are complex valued random variables uncorrelated with each other. For a real valued process x(t) representation (4.2.1) can be transformed to the real spectral representation

$$x(t) = \int_{-\pi}^{\pi} [\cos(wt)dz_1(w) + \sin(wt)dz_2(w)] \qquad (4.2.2)$$

where $dz_1(w)$ and $dz_2(w)$ $(0<w\leq\pi)$ are real valued random variables with properties

$$\begin{aligned} &\mathrm{Cov}(dz_1(w_1), dz_2(w_2)) = 0 \quad \text{for all } w_1, w_2 \\ &\mathrm{Cov}(dz_1(w_1), dz_1(w_2)) = \mathrm{Cov}(dz_2(w_1), dz_2(w_2)) = 0 \\ &\qquad\qquad \text{for } w_1 \neq w_2 \end{aligned} \qquad (4.2.3)$$

(see Koopmans [1974], Sections 2.8 and 6.2 and Priestley [1981], Section 4.11).

It can be seen from (4.2.2) that, intuitively speaking, every weakly stationary stochastic process can be thought to be composed of an infinite number of sine waves with independent random amplitudes and random phases.

Consider next a linear filter transforming $x(t)$ to $y(t)$ according to

$$y(t) = \sum_{j=0}^{\infty} a_j x(t-j) \qquad (4.2.4)$$

with $\sum_{j=0}^{\infty} a_j^2$ convergent.

If we replace $x(t)$ in (4.2.4) by its spectral representation and change the order of summation and integration we obtain

$$\begin{aligned} y(t) &= \int_{-\pi}^{\pi} \Big(\sum_{j=0}^{\infty} a_j e^{-iwj}\Big) e^{iwt} dz(w) \\ &= \int_{-\pi}^{\pi} A(w) e^{iwt} dz(w) \end{aligned} \qquad (4.2.5)$$

where

$$A(w) = \sum_{j=0}^{\infty} a_j e^{-iwj} \qquad (-\pi < w \leq \pi) \qquad (4.2.6)$$

is called the <u>transfer function</u> or the <u>frequency response function</u> of filter (4.2.4). By expressing A(w) in (4.2.5) as $|A(w)|^{i}e^{\gamma(w)}$ where A(w) is the modulus and $\gamma(w)$ the phase angle of A(w), it easy to see that the physical interpretation of the transfer function of a linear system is : when the input to the system is a sine wave at frequency w then the output will be a sine wave at the same frequency w, with an amplitude which is the original amplitude multiplied by the modulus (called the <u>gain function</u> of the filter) of the transfer function and with a phase shift given by the phase angle of the transfer function. This interpretation is especially important in view of the spectral representation (4.2.1).

The inversion formula for (4.2.6) is given through equation

$$a_j = (2\pi)^{-1}\int_{-\pi}^{\pi} e^{iwj}A(w)\,dw \qquad (j=0,1,2,...) \qquad (4.2.7)$$

The so-called Parseval's relation states that

$$\sum_{j=0}^{\infty} a_j^2 = (2\pi)^{-1}\int_{-\pi}^{\pi} |A(w)|^2\,dw \qquad (4.2.8)$$

i.e. if x(t) is a white noise process then the variance of y(t) is given by Var(x(t)) times integral in (4.2.8).

<u>Note 1.</u> The principle for evaluating frequency response functions is simple: apply the filter to the input $x(t) = e^{iwt}$ (t=0,1,2,...). then the output will be $y(t) = A(w)e^{iwt}$, where A(w) is the transfer function of the filter. For example, the transfer function of the

difference filter $y(t) = x(t) - x(t-1)$ is $A(w) = 1-e^{-iw}$, as can easily be seen by applying this method.

Note 2. From the above considerations it is clear that if another filter $z(t) = \Sigma b_k y(t-k)$ with transfer function $A_1(w)$ is applied to series $y(t)$ given by (4.2.4) then the transfer function of the compound filter transforming $x(t)$ into $z(t)$ is simply $A(w)A_1(w)$.

More details on the transfer functions of linear filters can be found e.g. in the monographs of Koopmans [1974] and Priestley [1981].

Upper limits for $\sigma_u/\sigma_x$, $\sigma_p/\sigma_x$ and $\sigma_{\Delta p}/\sigma_x$ in the case of a weakly stationary claims rate are easily derived from the transfer functions. Let the $x(t)$ process be given by

$$x(t) = \sum_{j=0}^{\infty} a_j \varepsilon(t-j) \tag{4.2.9}$$

where $\varepsilon(t)$:s are uncorrelated with expectation zero and with variance $\sigma_\varepsilon^2$. Let the frequency response function corresponding to (4.2.9) be $A(w)$. Then the variance of $x(t)$ can be obtained from equation

$$\sigma_x^2 = \sigma_\varepsilon^2 (2\pi)^{-1} \int_{-\pi}^{\pi} |A(w)|^2 dw \tag{4.2.10}$$

On the other hand, the variance of the solvency rate on the basis of Remark 2 and equation (3.1) can be computed from

$$\sigma_u^2 = \sigma_\varepsilon^2 (2\pi)^{-1} \int_{-\pi}^{\pi} |A_u(w)A(w)|^2 dw \tag{4.2.11}$$

where $A_u(w)$ is the transfer function of the filter (3.1). Thus we have from (4.2.10) and (4.2.11)

$$\sigma_u/\sigma_x \le M_u = \max_w |A_u(w)| \tag{4.2.12}$$

for arbitrary stationary x(t). In fact, the upper limit is arrived at by a sine wave of random amplitude corresponding to frequency w, giving the maximum of $|A_u(w)|$. In a similar way we obtain the upper limit for

$$\sigma_p/\sigma_x \leq M_p = \max_w |A_p(w)| \tag{4.2.13}$$

and for

$$\sigma_{\Delta p}/\sigma_x \leq M_{\Delta p} = \max_w |A_{\Delta p}(w)| \tag{4.2.14}$$

where $A_p(w)$ and $A_{\Delta p}(w)$ are the transfer functions of p(t) and $\Delta p(t)$ respectively. The idea is illustrated by Fig.5.

We may note that the above upper limits are good approximations if the spectrum $|A(w)|$ of x(t) concentrates in the same area as $M_u$ or $|A(w)|$ does not vary much at w-values of interest. The upper limits cannot be improved since there always exists a process for which the limits are exact; namely a sine wave with frequency $M_u$ and with a stochastic amplitude.

The upper limits $M_u$ etc. are useful since they are independent of the correlation structure of x(t). In practice that structure is often unknown and difficult to estimate but usually the range $R_x$ of x(t) is available at least as an approximation. If there is more information as to the correlation structure (or equivalently the spectrum $|A(w)|$ of x(t)) it can give somewhat more exact approximations for $\sigma_u$ etc. than the absolute upper limits. The information available may for example be, that the cycles in x(t) have a wave-length around 7 years (meaning a peak in A(w) around frequency 1.1) or that the claims rates of consecutive years are "almost" i.i.d. (meaning an "almost" constant spectrum A(w) of x(t)).

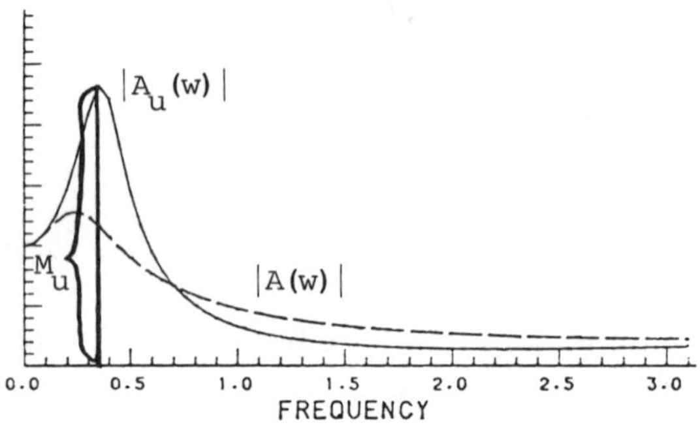


Fig.5. The idea of determining the maximum possible value of $\sigma_u$.

## 4.3. Feedforward and Feedback Control

According to Fig.1 the insurer steers the premium level on the basis of the past claims and the level of the solvency rate. This control method may be viewed as feedback control, since there the steering is based on earlier values of one of the variables to be controlled. It is known from general control theory that feedback control is in general very effective and it is robust against the model specification: i.e. it works well even if the model used is not the correct one or there are unidentified sources of extra noises.

However, it is also known that the introduction of feedforward control (in addition to feedback) may often improve the characteristics of the control program especially if the time-lag in the feedback is long (see e.g. Box-Jenkins [1976] p.451).

In feedforward control one tries to predict the future values of the main variables on the basis of some exogenous factors and then uses the estimated values as "extra" information in addition to pure feedback control. In the present context the main feedforward control action might be the prediction of future aggregate claim amounts on the basis of some external factors such as inflation, economic cycles etc. In order to improve the feedback rule the forecasts of future claims amount x(t) should not be based merely on past x(t):s, since then the resulting control scheme would again be a feedback rule. In fact, it is then the combined performance of the feedback rule and the forecast rule which is the most crucial criterion from the control theoretical point of view.

In the literature much attention has been paid to the experience rating and credibility theories. These theories also deal with premium determination solely on the basis of the observed claims rates. However, their scope might be somewhat more limited than that of the control theory: prediction is more strongly stressed than the control aspects. If some credibility rating is applied, its effects on the system must be regarded when the control is designed. Also the effects of possible adaptive estimation procedures for the relevant parameters of the credibility formula have to be considered.

Perhaps the most famous method in the control theory for optimization is the Kalman filter technique. We are not going to describe that technique in this paper; we refer to the vast existing literature. An insurance application along the lines developed in this paper is Rantala [1986].

Another useful method for some low-order processes (i.i.d., AR(1), AR(2), random walk) can after modifications be derived from the technique presented in Box-Jenkins [1976], Chapter 13 (see Rantala [1984]). The formulae to be presented in Section 5 have been derived by this technique.

## 5. Examples

In this section the following specific rating rules are investigated using the techniques of Section 4:

(1) Premium rate is a constant.

(2) Premiums are experience rated by exponential smoothing

(3) Rating rule minimizing $R_u$ for given $R_p$ when $x(t)$:s are i.i.d.

(4) Rating rule minimizing $R_u$ for given $R_p$ or $R_{\Delta p}$ when $x(t)$ is an autoregressive process of order one or a random walk ("the most dangerous alternative").

### 5.1. A Constant Premium Rate

The simplest possible rating rule is to apply a constant premium rate p irrespective of fluctuations in the claims rate and solvency rate. The formula (3.1) then reduces to

$$u(t) = ru(t-1) + p - x(t) \qquad (5.1.1)$$

In this case the demand of stable marginal distribution for the solvency rate $u(t)$ cannot be satisfied , unless the relative interest coefficient $r<1$. Thus a constant premium rate is not applicable if the interest rate is greater than the growth rate of the basic volume measure $V(t)$.

It can be shown that if r<1 then

$$Eu(t) = \frac{p - Ex(t)}{1 - r} \tag{5.1.2}$$

$$\sigma_u^2 = \frac{1 + 2 \sum_{j=1}^{\infty} \rho_x(j) r^j}{1 - r^2} \sigma_x^2 \tag{5.1.3}$$

where $\rho_x(j)$ is the j-th order autocorrelation of x(t).

Note that the constant rate rule gives the smallest possible value = 0 for $\sigma_p$ and $\sigma_{\Delta p}$.

Since $|\rho_x(j)| \leq 1$, an absolute upper limit for the standard deviation $\sigma_u$ of the solvency rate u(t) is obtained if all $\rho_x(j)$:s are put equal to 1 in (5.1.3). Then

$$\sigma_u^2 \leq \sigma_x^2/(1-r)^2 \tag{5.1.4}$$

which does not contain the correlation structure of x(t), only the standard deviation $\sigma_x$ of the claims rate process. Condition $\rho_x(j) \equiv 1$ means that all x(t):s are equal with probability one, which can be interpreted as a case where the claims rate suddenly changes its level, on which it thereafter stabilizes. We shall return to this case in Section 5.2.

## 5.2. Rating by Exponential Smoothing

The constant premium rate is applicable only if the relative interest coefficient r is less than one. In addition, that rule's proper functioning requires that the expectation and the range of the claims rate process x(t) are known closely enough as can be seen from equations (5.1.2) and (5.1.3). These demands can be relaxed by letting the premium rate vary according to fluctuations in the claims rate and solvency rate. A very natural way to do this is to let the premium rate be in proportion to the accumulated profit/loss; i.e. the premium rate is proportional function of the solvency rate u(t): if the solvency rate is above (below) a certain target level $u_0$, premiums are reduced (enhanced) by an amount $b(u(t)-u_0)$. This means that the premium rate p(t) is given by

$$p(t) = p_0 + bu(t-1) \tag{5.2.1}$$

where $p_0$ is the basic premium rate.

Note 1. "Bonus" bu(t-1) can also be interpreted as dividends paid to solvency capital. Then the premiums would have a constant rate $p_0$.The considerations below apply equally to this interpretation; i.e. the variations in the premium rate should then be regarded as variations in the dividend rate.

Note 2. It is easy to show that the rating formula (5.2.1) is equivalent to formula

$$p(t) = (r-b)p(t-1) + bx(t-1) + p_0(1-r) \tag{5.2.2}$$

This is the famous formula of experience rating. It is extensively studied both in actuarial (cf. Whitney [1917], Simberg [1964], Bühlmann [1970]) and in other scientific literature (cf. Brown [1962], Box-Jenkins [1976]).

If p(t) in (3.1) is substituted by (5.2.1) we obtain

$$u(t) = (r-b)u(t-1) + p_0 - x(t) \tag{5.2.3}$$

Thus we have the same formula as in Section 5.1 but with r replaced by r-b. This implies that $|r-b|$ should be less than one. Formulae (5.1.2) and (5.1.3) are then valid with r replaced by r-b. In addition

$$Ep(t) = p_0 - bEu(t)$$

$$= \frac{bEx(t) + p_0(1-r)}{1 - (r-b)} \qquad (5.2.4)$$

$$\sigma_p^2 = b^2\sigma_u^2 \le \frac{b^2\sigma_x^2}{(1 - (r-b))^2} \qquad (5.2.5)$$

$$\sigma_{\Delta p}^2 = b^2 \frac{1 + 2\sum_{j=1}^{\infty}(r-b)^j\rho_{\Delta x}(j)}{1 - (r-b)^2}\sigma_{\Delta x}^2 \le \frac{b^2\sigma_{\Delta x}^2}{(1-(r-b))^2} \qquad (5.2.6)$$

with obvious notations.

It can also be shown that exponential smoothing is the solution to the problem: minimize $\sigma_u$ for given $\sigma_p$ when x(t):s are i.i.d. random variables.

The behavior of the exponential smoothing rating formula (5.2.2) is essentially the same as that of constant premium rates for r<1. Hence the case $\rho_x(j) \equiv 1$ gives again the highest value for $\sigma_u/\sigma_x$. This upper value can also be seen from the frequency response functions in Fig.12 since they have the maximums at frequency value w=0. The corresponding time response can be seen in Figs.9 and 11.

We see that also the exponential smoothing is incapable of coping with permanent change in the claims rate. The premium rate adopts asymptotically to the "right" level but the solvency rate does not recover. In the following section we look for a rating procedure which would react properly to this kind of situation.

## 5.3. The Optimal Rating Rule For a Random Walk Claims Rate

1. AR(1) and ARIMA(0,1,1) processes. In this section we generalize the deterministic claims process arrived at in Section 5.2 and introduce a rating rule suitable for such processes.

The deterministic process above can be viewed as a limiting case of an autoregressive process

$$x(t) = \phi x(t-1) + \varepsilon(t) \tag{5.3.1}$$

when $\phi$ tends to 1 and simultaneously $\sigma_\varepsilon^2 = \mathrm{Var}(\varepsilon(t))$ tends to zero. Here $\varepsilon(t)$ is a sequence of uncorrelated random variables. A more general process results if $\phi=1$ but $\sigma_\varepsilon{}^2 > 0$; i.e. x(t) is a random walk process.

The autoregressive process (5.3.1) provides a useful means of producing a variety of processes ranging from the white noise case to the random walk, these respective extremes being in practice perhaps the safest and most dangerous alternatives among the possible candidates for a claims process.

Another set of processes ranging from white noise to random walk is the class of ARIMA(0,1,1) models. In an ARIMA(0,1,1) model $x(t)-x(t-1) = \varepsilon(t) - \theta\varepsilon(t-1)$, where $\varepsilon(t)$:s are uncorrelated random variables with zero mean. This assumption has the following interpretation (see Box-Jenkins [1976], Chapter 4). Equation $\Delta x(t) = \varepsilon(t)-\theta\varepsilon(t-1)$ may be rewritten in the form

$$\begin{aligned} x(t) &= x_0(t-1) + \varepsilon(t) \\ x_0(t) &= x_0(t-1) + (1-\theta)\varepsilon(t) \end{aligned} \tag{5.3.2}$$

where $x_0(t)$ is the basic "level" of the claims rate in the year t. The first equation shows how, with the "level" of the claims rate at $x_0(t-1)$, a shock $\varepsilon(t)$ is added in the year t and produces a value x(t). However, the second equation shows that only a proportion $1-\theta$ of the shock is actually absorbed into the level and has lasting influence, the remaining proportion being dissipated. Now a level $x_0(t)$ having been established by the absorption of $\varepsilon(t)$, a new shock enters the system at time t+1. The equations (5.3.2) with arguments increased by unity, will then show how this shock produces x(t+1) and how a proportion $1-\theta$ of it is absorbed into system to produce a new level $x_0(t+1)$, and so on.

In practice perhaps not every new shock changes the level and the claims process may be "stationary" over short time intervals. Then (5.3.2) may be regarded as a cautious approximation. Equations (5.3.2) may also be interpreted to approximate the case when the basic level of the claims process is unknown and continuously changing. When $\theta=0$ we obtain a random walk process; i.e.every new shock is totally absorbed into the level. Another extreme case is $\theta=1$ giving the white noise process.

Since the variance of x(t) is now infinite we cannot demand that the variances of both premiums p(t) and solvency rate u(t) be finite.

Fig.6 gives two realizations of the processes generated by (5.3.2).

2. A further requirement for the control program. Obviously good protection against permanent changes in the claims rate is important enough to be added to the characteristics of the optimal rating rules:

A permanent change in the claims rate must not cause a persisting deviation of the solvency rate from the target level.

According to this requirement we should look for procedures minimizing the variance of changes in premium rate when the

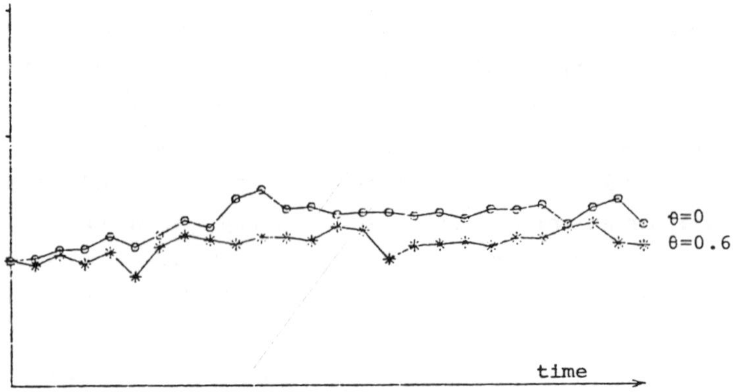


Fig. 6. Two time series generated from an ARIMA(0,1,1) processes.

variance of the solvency rate has fixed value and when the claims rate is an ARIMA(0,1,1) process.

Note. Balzer-Benjamin [1982] have also considered the deterministic x(t)-case arrived at in Sections 5.1 and 5.2 (their "persisting unpredicted claims" corresponding to our "most dangerous" x(t)). Thus the procedures below are generalizations of their "integral control action" for a more general case (see also Box-Jenkins [1976], Section 12.2.2).

3. Description of the problem. In this and in the following sections we consider only the deviations of the variables from their expected values, so that the basic level of the claims process is taken as zero. The rating procedures are assumed to be based on past solvency rates, but this is no restriction, since knowledge of past

solvency rates is equivalent to knowledge of past claims rates. This also means that the introduction of both past solvency rates and claims rates into the formulae would not produce any improvement in the procedures.

Our assumption is

$$x(t) = x(t-1) + \varepsilon(t) - \theta\varepsilon(t-1) \qquad (5.3.3)$$

where $\varepsilon(t)$:s are uncorrelated with $E\varepsilon(t)=0$ and $\sigma_\varepsilon^2=Var(\varepsilon(t))$. Assume again that the solvency rate u(t) is governed by equation

$$u(t) = ru(t-1) + p(t) - x(t) \qquad (5.3.4)$$

We here place no restriction on r than its positivity; i.e. r may also be $\geq 1$.

Obviously the minimum possible value of the variance of the solvency rate is $\sigma_\varepsilon^2$, which results if we use rating procedure

$$p(t) = -ru(t-1) + x(t-1) - \theta\varepsilon(t-1) \qquad (5.3.5)$$

In this case $u(t)=-\varepsilon(t)$, and then the premiums will include the compensation $-ru(t-1)$ for the deviation of the solvency rate from the target level and the best prediction $x(t-1)-\theta\varepsilon(t-1)$ for the claims rate in the following year. This might be seen as a variant of "pay as you go" system. Now the change in premiums is given by

$$\Delta p(t) = (r+1-\theta)\varepsilon(t-1) - r\varepsilon(t-2) \qquad (5.3.6)$$

so that

$$\sigma_{\Delta p}^2 = [(1+r-\theta)^2 + r^2]\sigma_\varepsilon^2 \qquad (5.3.7)$$

Hence the variance of the changes $\Delta p$ will be considerably larger than that of the changes in the claims rate.

According to the above considerations let us state the problem in the following form:
Given that the variance of the solvency rate is fixed at a value $(1+\delta)\sigma_{\varepsilon}^{2}$ $(\delta>0)$, find a rating procedure giving the minimum possible variance to the changes in premiums, when the claims rate is an ARIMA(0,1,1) process.

4. Solution. The optimal rating scheme can be shown to be (see Rantala [1984])

$$\Delta p(t) = (\theta k_1/r)\Delta p(t-1) - [\theta(k_1-r)/r+r-k_0+1]u(t-1)$$

$$+ [r-k_1 -\theta(k_0-k_1-k_1/r)]u(t-2) \qquad (5.3.8)$$

Coefficients $k_0$ and $k_1$ can be found by the following simple procedure:

(1) Compute $M = (1+r)^2/r$ and $N = [(1+r)^2+(1+r^2)+v]/r$ for a series of values of v chosen to provide a suitable range for $\sigma_u$ and $\sigma_{\Delta p}$.

(2) Compute $u_1 = 0.5(N-2) + [(\frac{N-2}{2})^2 + 2N - M^2]^{\frac{1}{2}}$

and $u_2 = 0.5(N-2) - [(\frac{N-2}{2})^2 + 2N - M^2]^{\frac{1}{2}}$

(3) Compute $k_1 = 0.5u_1- [(0.5u_1)^2- 1]^{\frac{1}{2}}$

and $k_2 = [k_1(u_2+2)]^{\frac{1}{2}}$

Note that the same rating procedures would result if instead of the variance of the solvency rate we restricted the variance of the changes in premiums and looked for a control scheme providing minimum variance for the solvency rate.

The corresponding variances are obtained from equations

$$\sigma_u^2 = \frac{(1+k_1)[1+(\theta k_1/r)^2) - 2\theta k_0 k_1/r}{(1-k_1)[(1+k_1)^2 - k_0^2]}\sigma_\varepsilon^2 \qquad (5.3.9)$$

and

$$\sigma_{\Delta p}^2 = \frac{(1+k_1)(w_0^2+w_1^2) - 2k_0 w_0 w_1}{(1-k_1)[(1+k_1)^2 - k_0^2]}\sigma_\varepsilon^2 \qquad (5.3.10)$$

where $w_0=(r-k_0+1)+\theta(k_1-r)/r$ and $w_1=(r-k_1)-\theta(k_0-k_1-k_1/r)$.

Of course these variance formulae hold only for an ARIMA(0,1,1) process as the claims process. The corresponding variances etc. for other cases can also be calculated, if needed.

In what follows the properties of the rating rule (5.3.8) are studied when $\theta=0$.

It is easy to see that then (5.3.8) can also be written in an equivalent form involving previous x(t):s:

$$p(t) = k_0 p(t-1)+k_1 p(t-2)+(r-k_0+1)x(t-1) + (r-k_1)x(t-2) \qquad (5.3.11)$$

In fact formulae (5.3.8) with $\theta=0$ and (5.3.11) lead to identical rating rules irrespective of the structure of the claims process. In the following this control rule is called the random walk rating.

5. Which variance combinations are possible? By computing (5.3.8) and (5.3.10) for different values of v a set of possible combinations of $\sigma_{\Delta p}$ and $\sigma_u$ can be produced. This is done in Fig.7 for r=0.9, 1.0 and 1.1.

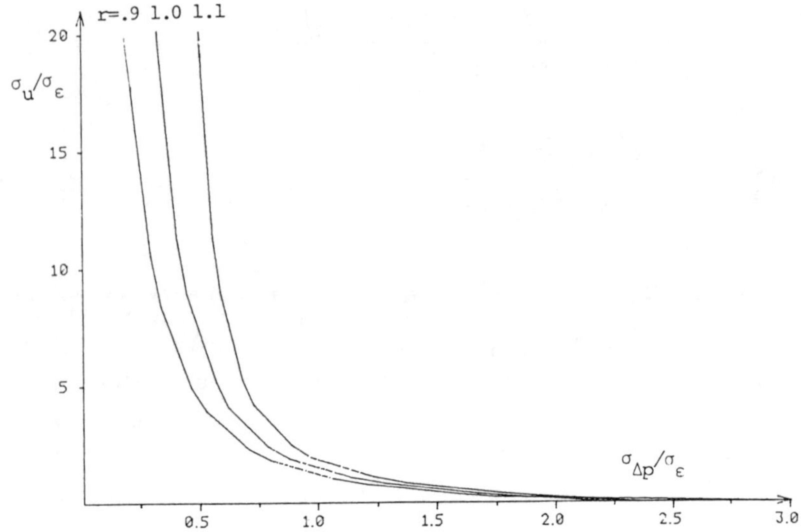


Fig. 7. Different optimum combinations of $\sigma_u$ and $\sigma_{\Delta p}$, when r=0.9, 1.0 and 1.1.

It can be seen from Fig.7 that the possible variances increase with increasing r. The dependence on r is not very strong , so that the procedure does not demand particularly exact estimates for r.

It can also be seen that reduction of the standard deviation $\sigma_{\Delta p}$ below $0.5\sigma_\varepsilon$ entails a rapid increase in the standard deviation $\sigma_u$ of the solvency rate. Formally a suitable combination could be found by defining a loss function involving $\sigma_u$ and $\sigma_{\Delta p}$ and by computing its minimum.

Note also the superiority of the above optimal scheme over the "naive" strategy p(t)=x(t-1); i.e. the claims of the preceding year are paid in the next year (this is here also the "pure" credibility rating rule; i.e.the premiums are set equal to the best predictor of the total claims amount of the following year without regard for the amount of the accumulated surplus). For example, if r=0.9, by this policy the standard deviation of the solvency rate would be $\sigma_\varepsilon/\sqrt{1-r^2} = 2.3\sigma_\varepsilon$ and the standard deviation of the change in the premium rate would be $\sigma_\varepsilon$. However, using the above optimal scheme this latter variance can be achieved with standard deviation $\sigma_u$ at only $1.44\sigma_\varepsilon$.

In view of considerations in the beginning of this section the cases x(t):s are i.i.d vs. x(t) is a random walk process can in a way be regarded as the extremes among the possible claims rate alternatives. Thus it may be instructive to study the properties of the rating procedures which are optimal in these cases, by means of methods mentioned in Section 4. This is done in Figures 8-12. Before doing this we also introduce the rating rule which is the solution to for the problem: minimize $\sigma_{\Delta p}$ for given $\sigma_u$ when x(t):s are i.i.d. That rule is given by

$$p(t) = r^{-1}k_1 p(t-1) - (r+r^{-1}k_1-k_0)u(t-1) \qquad (5.3.12)$$

where $k_0$ and $k_1$ are again given by the procedure in paragraph 4.

All the procedures manage the impulses in the claims rate fairly well although there are differences in performances. The differences between procedures can be clearly seen in the step responses. Neither the exponential smoothing nor procedure (5.3.12) can properly cope with a permanent change in the level of the claims rate; the solvency rate does not recover from its downswing. Also for the random walk rating (5.3.11) the recovery is slow. However, to make it faster would also mean greater oscillations in the premium rate.

The corresponding frequency responses are plotted in Figs.12- 14.

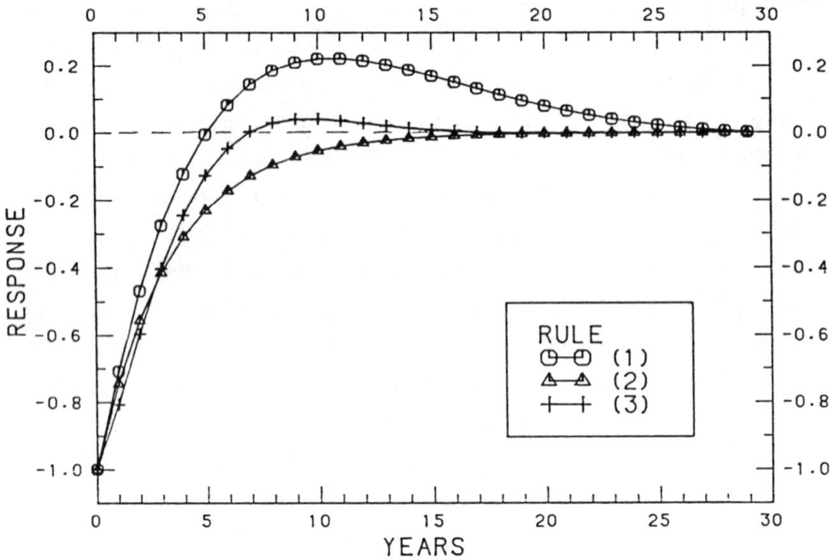


Fig.8. Impulse responses of the solvency rate when r=0.9 and with rating formulae
(1) (5.3.11) with $k_0$=1.71 and $k_1$=0.74
(2) (5.2.2) with b=0.155
(3) (5.3.12) with $k_0$=1.41 and $k_1$=0.54

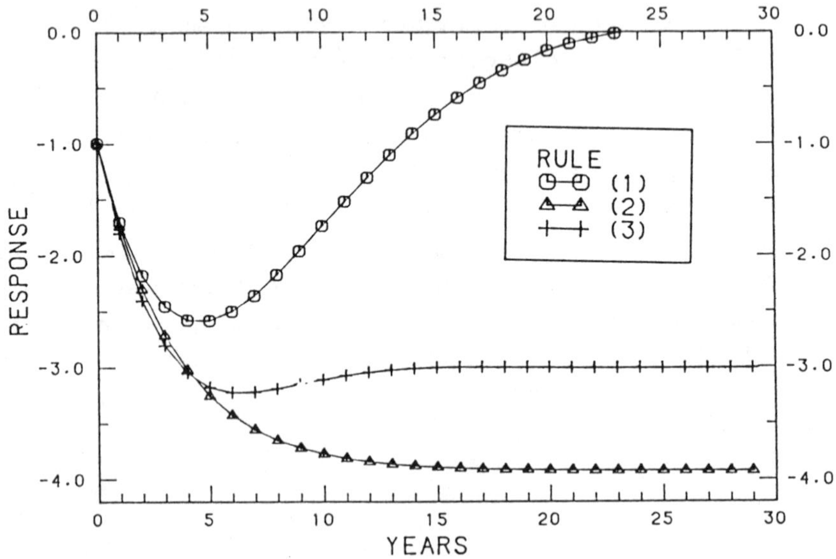


Fig.9. Step responses of the solvency rate when the rating formulae are as in Fig.8.

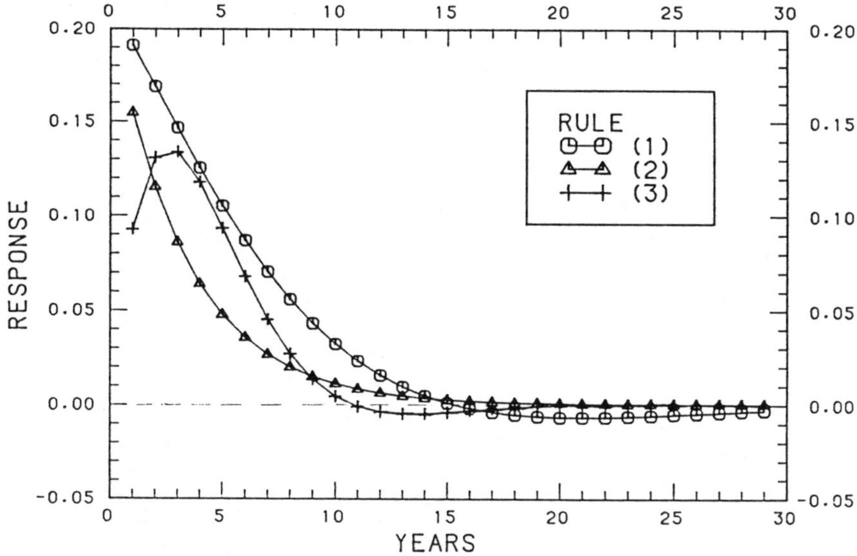


**Fig.10.** Impulse responses of the premium rate when the rating formulae are as in Fig.8.

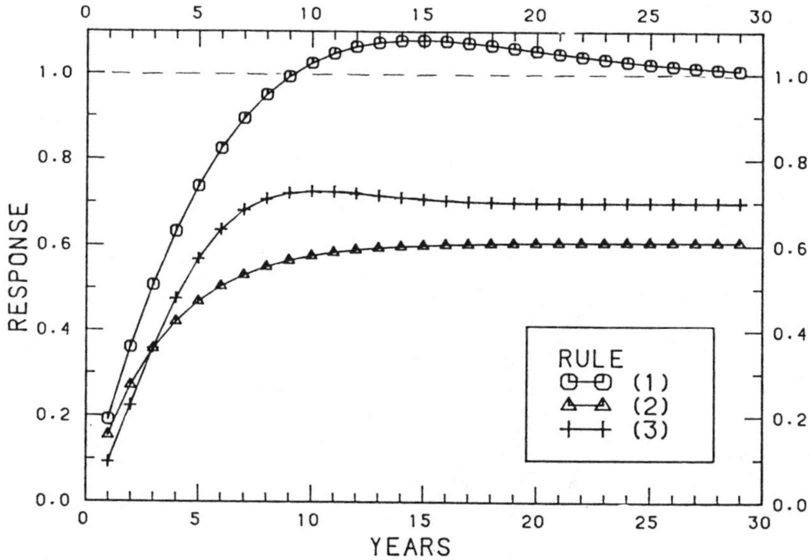


**Fig.11.** Step responses of the premium rate when the rating formulae are as in Fig.8.

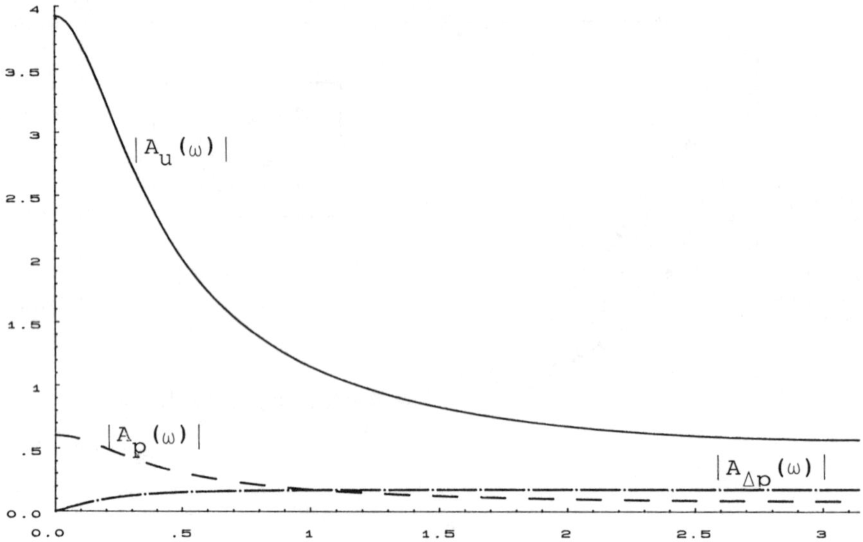


<u>Fig.12.</u> Frequency response functions of procedure (5.2.2) when r=0.9 and b=0.155

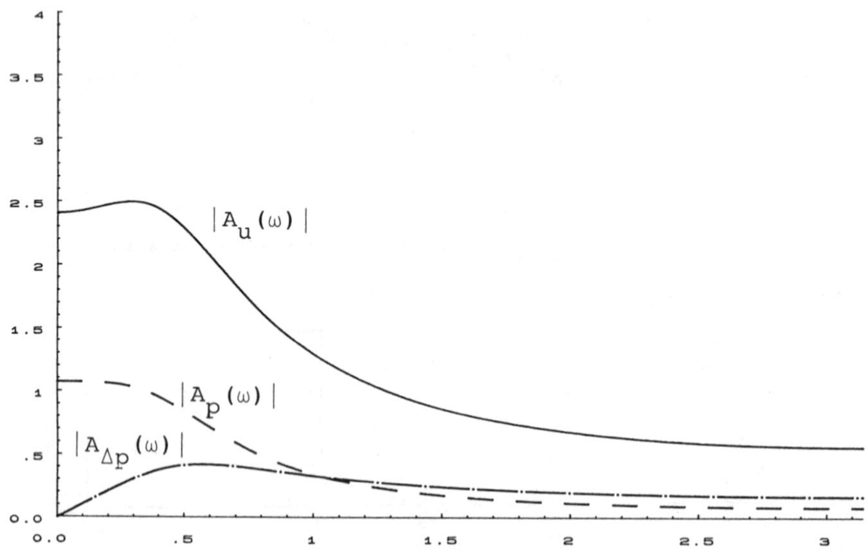


<u>Fig.13.</u> Frequency response functions of procedure (5.3.12) when r=0.9, $k_0$=1.23 and $k_1$=0.44

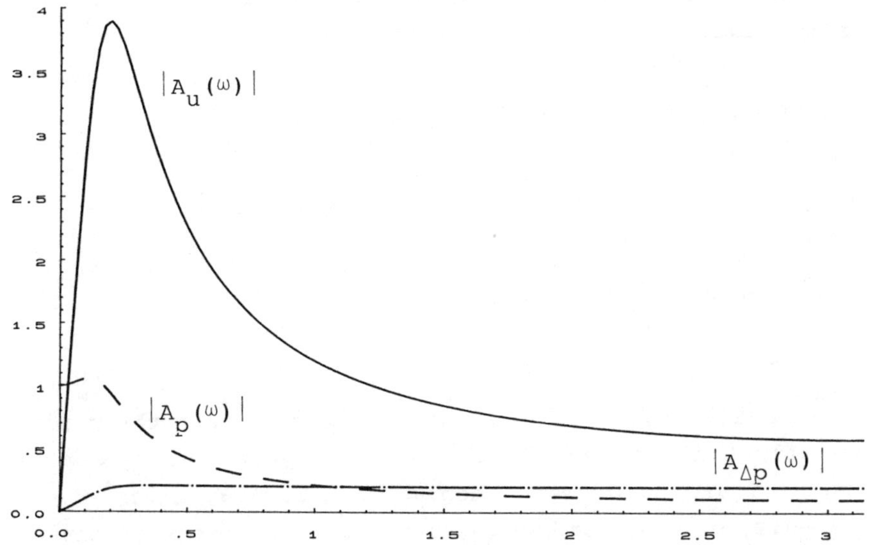


Fig.14. Frequency response functions of procedure (5.3.11) when r=0.9 and $k_0$=1.71 and $k_1$=0.74

It can be concluded from the frequency response functions that for the parameter values used and for any weakly stationary claims rate process

(1) for exponential smoothing $\sigma_u/\sigma_x \leq 4$, $\sigma_p/\sigma_x \leq 0.6$ and $\sigma_{\Delta p}/\sigma_x \leq 0.2$

(2) for procedure (5.3.12) $\sigma_u/\sigma_x \leq 2.5$ , $\sigma_p/\sigma_x \leq 0.75$ and $\sigma_{\Delta p}/\sigma_x \leq 0.3$

(3) for random walk rating $\sigma_u/\sigma_x \leq 3.9$, $\sigma_p/\sigma_x \leq 1.0$ and $\sigma_{\Delta p}/\sigma_x \leq 0.2$.

In addition, if it is known for example that the claims rate fluctuations are dominated by cycles with a wave length of around 6 years then $\sigma_u/\sigma_x \approx 1.2, 1.3, 1.2$; $\sigma_p/\sigma_x \approx 0.2, 0.3, 0.2$ and $\sigma_{\Delta p}/\sigma_x \approx 0.2, 0.2, 0.2$ for procedures (5.2.2), (5.3.11) and (5.3.12) respectively with parameters values shown.

## 5.4. Summary

As a summary the optimal rating procedures are collected for the cases, where x(t):s are i.i.d., x(t) is an AR(1) process and x(t) is a random walk.

I. Claims rates are i.i.d.

IA. Minimize $\sigma_p$ for given $\sigma_u$:

$p(t) = -bu(t-1)$ or equivalently

$p(t) = (r-b)p(t-1) + bx(t-1)$ .

IB. Minimize $\sigma_{\Delta p}$ for given $\sigma_u$:

$p(t) = r^{-1}k_1p(t-1) - (r+r^{-1}k_1-k_0)u(t-1)$ ,

where $k_0$ and $k_1$ are given by the procedure in paragraph 5.3.4

II. Claims rate $x(t)$ is an AR(1) process: $x(t) = \phi x(t-1) + \varepsilon(t)$ with $|\phi|<1$ and $\varepsilon(t)$:s i.i.d.

IIa. Minimize $\sigma_p$ for given $\sigma_u$:

$$p(t) = ap(t-1) - (r+a-z_0)u(t-1) + rau(t-2) \quad ,$$

where

$$a = (1-A)z_0 + A$$

$$A = 1 - \frac{(r\phi-1)\phi}{r^{2} - (1+r^2+v) + r}$$

$$rz_0^2 - (1+r^2+v)z_0 + r = 0 \text{ with } |z_0|< 1$$

and v is the parameter determining $\sigma_u/\sigma_x$.

IIB. Minimize $\sigma_{\Delta p}$ for given $\sigma_u$:

$$p(t) = \alpha p(t-1)-(r+\alpha-k_0)u(t-1)+(r\alpha-k_1)u(t-2) \quad ,$$

where

$$\alpha = (1-D)\phi + Dk_0 - Dk_1/\phi$$

$$D/\phi = D'/[r\phi^4-(r+1)^2\phi^3+c\phi^2-(r+1)^2\phi+r]$$

$$D' = r\phi^3-(2r+1)\phi^2+(r+2)\phi-1 = r(\phi-1)^2(\phi-r^{-1})$$

$$c = 2(1+r+r^2) + v$$

and $k_0$ and $k_1$ are given the procedure in paragraph 5.3.4.

III. $x(t)$ is an ARIMA(0,1,1) process: $x(t)=x(t-1)+\varepsilon(t)-\theta\varepsilon(t-1)$.

IIIA. Minimize $\sigma_{\Delta p}$ for given $\sigma_u$:

$$\Delta p(t) = (\theta k_1/r)\Delta p(t-1) - [\theta(k_1-r)/r+r-k_0+1]u(t-1)$$

$$+ [r-k_1 -\theta(k_0-k_1-k_1/r)]u(t-2) \quad .$$

In the formulae above we have assumed that $Ex(t)=0$ (except in case III where $Ex(t)$ does not exist) so that also $Ep(t)=0$ (except in case III). Since the premiums do not contain a safety loading also $Eu(t)=0$. In a straightforward manner the formulae may be generalized for the case where the target level of the solvency rate is taken as positive. In fact, $u(t)$ of the preceding sections may be interpreted to mean deviation from a target level, which here will be denoted $u_0$ and which will also be the expected value of $u(t)$. Since the basic equation of the solvency rate can be modified to

$$u(t)-u_0 = r(u(t-1)-u_0)+p(t)+(r-1)u_0-x(t) \qquad (5.4.1)$$

it can be seen that $p(t)-(1-r)u_0$ may be treated as equivalent to $p(t)$ of the preceding sections and $u(t)$ is replaced by $u(t)-u_0$.Then, if $x(t)$ is a weakly stationary process, the expectation of the premium rate is

$$Ep(t) = Ex(t) + (1-r)u_0 \qquad (5.4.2)$$

where the latter term is due to maintenance of the level $u_0$ of the solvency rate in the long run. It indicates a positive safety loading if $r<1$ and a negative safety loading if $r>1$; i.e. then a part of the interest yield of the solvency reserve may be used to cover claim payments.

In the random walk case neither $Ex(t)$ nor $Ep(t)$ exists, but it still makes sense to talk about $Eu(t)$.

## 6. A Practical Application

This section contains a practical application of the above results to the experience rating of worker's compensation insurance. The worker's compensation insurance in Finland in the years 1959-1981 is considered. In Fig. 15 the incurred claims in this class are given as per milles of the total payroll. The curve shows clear changes in level, so that the assumption of a random walk might not be very far-fetched in this case. Also the actual premium rate is given. The actual rate has been so adjusted that the averages of premium rates and claims rates are equal. Thus the safety loading in the premiums is set at zero. The third curve shows the hypothetical premium rate which would have resulted if the random walk rating with r=1 (i.e. the interest rate equals the growth rate of the payroll), $k_0$=1.63 , $k_1$=0.69, $u_0$=0 and with initial values p(1958)=9.112 and u(1957)=u(1958)=0 were applied. With this scheme and by the random walk assumption we have from (3.3.11) and (3.3.12) $\sigma_u/\sigma_\varepsilon$=5.16 and $\sigma_{\Delta p}/\sigma_\varepsilon$=0.566.

Fig.16 gives the corresponding accumulated profits, when the initial value is set zero.

Of course, comparison of the actual and random walk rates is not straightforward, since the actual rate is an aggregate of many minor rating schemes concerning specific classes of policies ranging from collectively rated policies to policies where the claims are totally paid by the policy-holder himself, the insurer in fact taking care of administrative routines only. In any case, it can be seen that the actual rate and the rate emerging from the random walk rating are fairly close to each other, as are also the accumulated profits. The greatest accumulated loss ,in the random walk rating (in 1973) is somewhat smaller than that really observed. In both cases the range of the accumulated profit is of about the same magnitude as the annual premium income.

In Fig.17 the yearly actual and random walk rating changes in the premium rate are plotted. The random walk rating would have produced somewhat smaller fluctuations, the maximum changes being +1.02 and -1.18 per mille units. The corresponding actual figures are +1.48 and -1.18 per mille units.

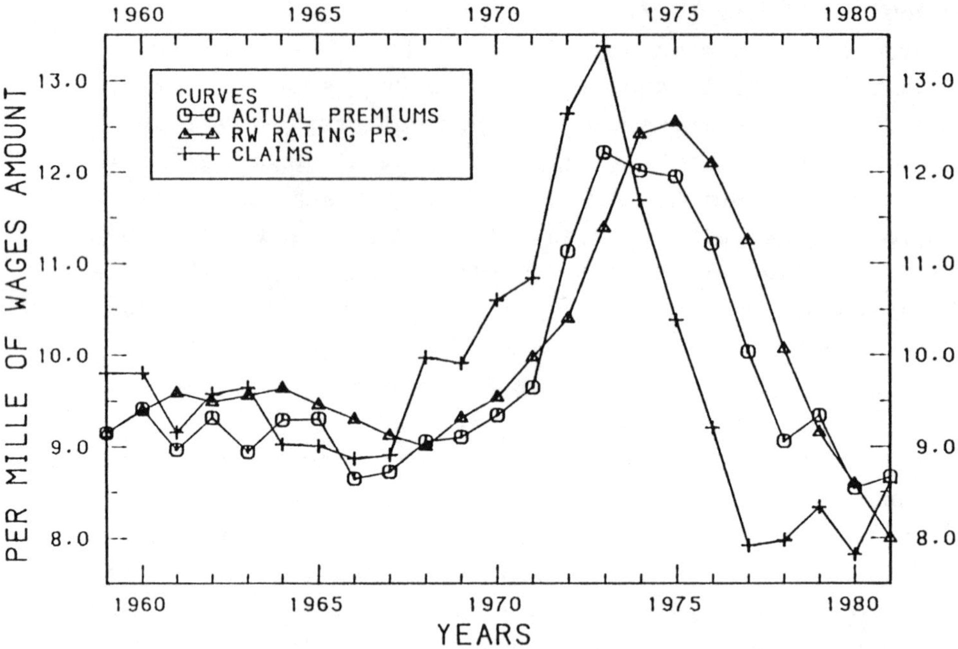


Fig.15. Worker's compensation insurance in Finland 1958-81. Claims rate, actual premium rate and random walk rating with $k_0$=1.62 and $k_1$=0.69

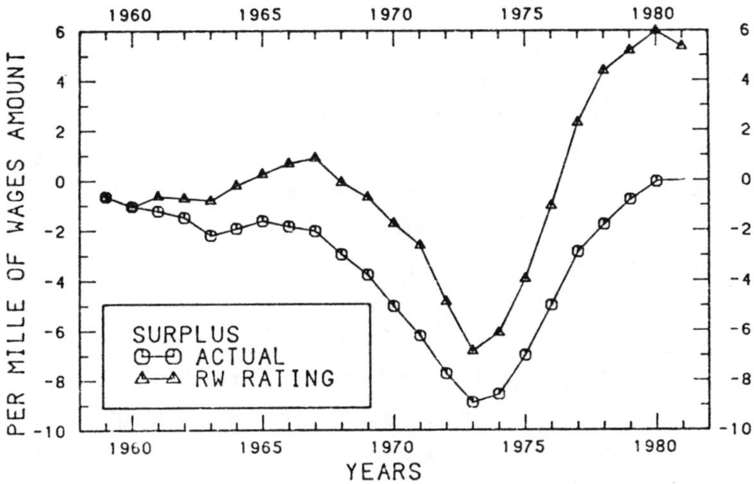


Fig.16. Accumulated profit computed from Fig.15 with r=1

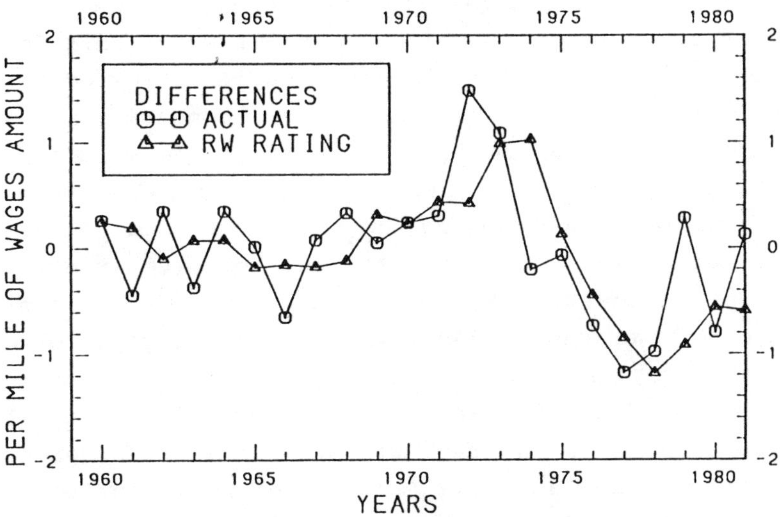


Fig.17. Difference of premium rates computed from Fig.15

## 7. Discussion

1. The potential applicability area of the results. In many important cases premiums cannot be totally controlled by the insurer but are determined e.g. market competition. Since in this study we have assumed that the controller is able to set the premiums at the level he desires, the results should be interpreted to concern mainly those insurance classes where the rates are subject to public control or e.g. long-term reinsurance agreements or individually rated policies. But also for other cases the results may be of some interest e.g. when the appropriate solvency margins are dimensioned or joint tariffs, based on the outcomes of the whole market, are used.

Some of the technical details such as the need of positive safety loading vary according to specific circumstances: e.g. whether a company level or a single insurance line is considered.

2. Technical details need further research. There are many technical details in the above model which call for a further elaboration: for example, the linearity of the formulae, the effects of the market competition, a stochastic volume measure V(t), changes in the portfolio composition etc. Many of these can be approximated by adding suitable noise terms to the model (see e.g. Rantala [1984]). More difficult is to make the relative interest coefficient stochastic (which in fact includes the consideration of the asset risk) and simultaneously preserve the manageability of the analytic formulae. However, it is not possible without such an elaboration to make the model better correspond to the real world. Another enlargement needed for arriving at a realistic model is to introduce the time delay d into the model, which is necessary in realizing the premium rate changes after the observations on the claims rate process (see Section 1). However, this is technically not a difficult task. It is especially easy

in the Kalman filter framework (cf. Rantala [1984] and [1986]).

3. Other research on the stochastic control theory in insurance. The idea of using (stochastic) control theory in premium setting is not new. A rich branch of literature has concentrated on optimal dividend policy of the insurer. The goal may be e.g. to maximize expected total dividend payments of the insurer. This branch of study was initiated by DeFinetti [1957]. Bühlmann [1970] and Gerber [1980] contain some results of these studies and lists of important references. But, as noted above, the problem setting in this study is somewhat different: we concentrate on the fluctuation properties of premium and solvency reserve processes, especially on the variances related to them. Actuarial works along this line include Balzer-Benjamin [1980], [1982], Ryder [1977], Bohman [1979] and Martin-Löf [1983]. However, in these works the evaluation of the goodness of the procedures is based on other properties than variances. Tapiero [1982] has investigated optimal extra payment and refunding strategies of a mutual insurance firm, the optimal solution for the cost function chosen resembling those arrived at in the search for optimal dividend policies.

Also the papers of Banasinski [1971], [1980], outlining a cybernetic theory of insurance, and those of Frisque [1974], Pentikäinen [1975], [1976], [1978] and Veit [1976] utilizing stochastic-dynamic programming are related to these matters.

4. The main emphasis in the study has been on demonstrating the usefulness of the control-theoretical approach to the underwriting risk problem. The methods of the paper should not be seen as suggestions for explicit solutions to the problems but rather as a suggestion to a coherent way to approach the problems. The methods are very powerful and they may help us to make a more profound analysis of the insurance business and the rating procedures. The stochastic control theory is surprisingly little used in

actuarial applications. It is my firm opinion that it has much to give to the actuarial profession and should be more used in both theory and practice.

References

Bailey, A.L. 1917. Credibility Procedures, LaPlaces's Generalization of Bayes rule, and the Combination of Collateral Knowledge with the Observed Data. Proceedings of the Casualty Actuarial Society 37: 7-23.

Balzer, L.A. and Benjamin, S. 1980. Dynamic response of insurance with delayed profit/loss sharing feedback to isolated unpredicted claims. Journal of Institute of Actuaries 107: 513-529.

Balzer, L.A. and Benjamin, S. 1982. Control of insurance systems with delayed profit/loss sharing feedback and persisting unpredicted claims. Journal of Institute of Actuaries 109: 285-316.

Banasinski, A. 1971. Insurance as a cybernetic institution of self-regulation of the national economy. Astin Bulletin 5: 393-401.

Banasinski, A. 1980. Generalized Model of Insurance Business in Poland. Transactions, 21st International Congress of Actuaries. Zürich-Lausanne.

Beard, R.E., Pentikäinen, T. and Pesonen, E. 1984. Risk Theory. London: Chapman & Hall.

Bohman, H. 1979. Insurance economics. Scandinavian Actuarial Journal No 2 : 57-74.

Box, G.P.E.-Jenkins,G.M. 1976. Time series analysis. New York: Holden Day.

Brown, R.G. 1962. Smoothing, forecasting and prediction of discrete time series. London: Prentice Hall.

Bühlmann, H. 1970. Mathematical methods in risk theory. New York: Springer Verlag.

Daykin, C.D. and Bernstein, G.D. 1985. A simulation model to examine questions of solvency in the light of asset and asset risks. A paper presented at the ASTIN Colloquium in Biarritz.

DeFinetti, B. 1957. Su un impostazione alternativa della teoria colletiva del rischio. Transactions, 15th International Congress of Actuaries. New York.

Frisque,A. 1974. Dynamic model of insurance company's management. Astin Bulletin 8: 57-65.

Gerber, H. 1980. An Introduction to Mathematical Risk Theory. Philadelphia: S.S.Huebner Foundation.

Koopmans, L.H. 1974. The spectral theory of time series. New York: Academic Press.

Martin-Löf, A. 1983. Premium Control in an Insurance System, an Approach using Linear Control Theory. Scandinavian Actuarial Journal No 1: 1-28.

Pentikäinen, T. 1975. A Model of Stochastic-Dynamic Prognosis. Scandinavian Actuarial Journal.

Pentikäinen, T. 1976. Stochastic-Dynamic Prognosis. Transactions, 20th International Congress of Actuaries. Tokyo.

Pentikäinen, T. 1978. A Solvency Testing Model Building Approach for Business Planning. Scandinavian Actuarial Journal.

Pentikäinen, T. and Rantala, J. 1982. Solvency of Insurers and Equalization Reserves, I-II. Helsinki: Insurance Publishing Company Ltd.

Pentikäinen, T. and Rantala, J. 1986. Run-off risk as a part of claims fluctuation. Astin Bulletin 16: 113-147.

Philipson, C. 1965. A Generalized Model for the Risk process and its Application to a Tentative Evaluation of the Outstanding Liabilities. Astin Bulletin 3: 215-239.

Priestley, M.B. 1981. Spectral Analysis and Time-series. New york: Academic Press.

Rantala, J. 1984. An application of stochastic control theory to insurance business (Ph.D. thesis). Tampere: University of Tampere.

Rantala, J. 1986. Experience rating of ARIMA claims

#202 16-02-2009 4:03PM
Item(s) checked out to PATTNI, AMRITA HI

TITLE: Insurance regulation in Europe.
BARCODE: 3 8008 02032 8935
DUE DATE: 09-03-09

TITLE: Life insurance
BARCODE: 38008002662897
DUE DATE: 09-03-09

TITLE: Reserving and solvency in insuran
BARCODE: 3 8008 02032 0452
DUE DATE: 09-03-09

TITLE: Financial models of insurance sol
BARCODE: 38008020459987
DUE DATE: 23-02-09

TITLE: Financial management of life insu
BARCODE: 38008020459995
DUE DATE: 23-02-09

processes using Kalman filter. Astin Bulletin 16: 19-32.

Ryder, J.M. 1977. Predicting future premiums - theory and practice. General Insurance Bulletin.

Simberg, H. 1964. Individuell Prämienregelung, eine Art des "Experience rating". Transactions, 17th International Congress of Actuaries. London - Edinburgh.

Tapiero, C.S. 1982. The optimal Control of a Jump Mutual Insurance process. Astin Bulletin 13: 13-21.

Veit, K. 1976. The Use of System Dynamics Simulation Models for Corporate Long Range Strategic Planning. Transactions, 20th International Congress of Actuaries. Tokyo.

Whitney, A.W. 1918. The theory of experience rating. Proceedings of the Casualty Actuarial Society.

# 7

# CONCEPTS AND TRENDS IN THE STUDY OF INSURER'S SOLVENCY

Yehuda Kahane, Charles S. Tapiero, and Laurent Jacques

## 1. Introduction

### 1.1. On the Definition of Solvency

Insolvency, a fundamental term in the insurance literature, is not clearly defined. Basically a firm is "solvent" within a single period model if its terminal value is higher than the total obligations to its creditors. For the more realistic case of a going concern, another definition is needed: an insurer will be regarded "ruined" (bankrupt) if its liabilities exceed the value of its assets, i.e., equity is zero (negative equity cannot occur in a stock company due to the limited liability!). In this situation the value of all future income streams is lower than the value of all debts (Stiglitz [1972]).

Others define solvency in terms of "liquidity" - the firm is "solvent" as long as it is able to meet its **current** obligations as they fall due. Although "ruin" and "illiquidity" seem to contain two distinct concepts they are actually quite similar: if the value of the future income streams exceeds the debts, the firm may still be able to borrow in the capital market to pay its current obligations and, thereby, to overcome temporary illiquidity. The equivalence of "ruin", "illiquidity" (and "insolvency") thus depends on the perfection of the capital market.

Illiquidity and ruin may often be considered synonymous, though in an imperfect market a firm may be liquid (able to meet its current obligations by using its current cash flows) while being ruined in the long term sense (liabilities exceeding assets). In other cases, the firm may be illiquid (unable to meet current liabilities due to inability to borrow), despite not being ruined (having assets exceeding liabilities)!

There are several points of view - actuarial, financial, legal, accounting, etc. - from which the insurance firm may be seen as solvent or insolvent. Lacking a clear definition of solvency, its measurement is of course difficult too (Pesonen [1964]). There is a whole array of variables which may be used for the measurement of solvency, reflecting the need and the perspectives used by accountants, economists, financial experts and regulators.

Typically the measurement of solvency is associated with accounting ratios describing the capitalization of the company, and the leverage - premium/equity or liabilities/equity ratios (Kenney [1967]). Other measures of financial strength consider future developments of the firm rather than snapshots taken at specific dates. There is, however, no agreement in the literature (and practice) concerning the inclusion of possible future developments in analysis of solvency, (i.e., whether solvency should be analyzed on the basis of existing business only, or, the possible effects of new and future business should be considered as well - a "going concern" approach). These approaches are similar only in perfect markets (see below).

There is an important volume of literature which examines the accounting aspects of solvency and sets standards for insurers and examiners. Among these are methods such as those used by A.M. Best Co. and the early warning systems used by insurance commissioners around the world (see NAIC [1970] Bar-Niv [1983]).

Although we shall emphasize insolvency from micro-economic and financial points of view, some comments must be made concerning the accountants' approach. A major problem with the accounting approach is that it is deterministic, ignoring the stochastic nature of the problem, despite the fact that the uncertainty effects of future transactions are crucial to the determination of solvency in insurance. Another drawback is that accounting measurements are often biased in practice, and may, therefore, be misleading; although a firm can perfectly balance its asset and liability portfolios in the accounting sense it may still be practically insolvent. This may happen since in practice reserves and solvency margins are often set as a function of the premium volume. Thus, an inappropriate insurance pricing, or inappropriate treatment of the interest rate in the valuation of the assets and liabilities, may generate a misleading picture of solvency.

### 1.2. Financial Aspects of Solvency

The insurance literature emphasizes the relationships between the capital, the insurance leverage (premium/equity ratio), and the insurer's solvency. Due to the similarity between the insurance leverage and the financial leverage (debt/equity ratio) of a non-insurance firm (Kahane [JRI 1978]), it seems that the insurance solvency literature could benefit from the relevant literature on the financial leverage and the optimal capital structure of corporations.

The insurance literature has apparently evolved in isolation from the finance (and banking) literature insofar as financial solidity is concerned. For the last three decades financial theory has studied the issue of the optimal capital structure of a firm - and concluded that there is no optimal leverage for a firm, except for the case of imperfections - like taxes, or costly bankruptcies. Only in such cases does the value of the firm depend on its leverage, thus leading to the optimal capital structure-solvency level (see, for example, the seminal works of Modigliani and Miller [1958], Stiglitz [1972], and the survey by Chen [1979]). We shall suggest that the same analysis and conclusions should be applied to the area of insurance solvency. This perspective is explained later.

### 1.3. The Scope of the Present Paper

The purpose of this study is to review the voluminous literature on solvency, while emphasizing certain perspectives which, in our view, have not received sufficient attention. Insurance solvency has often been studied with an emphasise on the mathematical and actuarial concepts, less attention being paid to micro-economic and financial aspects. It is our intention to focus on these latter aspects.

Although this study was in an advanced stage when we became aware of a recent comprehensive survey of solvency (Kastelijn and Remmerswaal [May 1986]), it could be regarded as an extension of this survey, with the addition of changes in the focus.

Our review purports to focus on the increased relevance (and irrelevance) of insolvency to insurance. In the following section, the classical approach to ruin, relating to claims and premium (as well as investment) return processes, is reviewed to provide a continuous state stochastic approach to valuation of the assets/liabilities paradgigm. In section 3, solvency is analyzed in analogy to the financial leverage problem, while in section 4 a micro-economic approach, viewing solvency as a problem of information exchange and incentives in a "game", is discussed.

Finally, several outstanding issues and problems for future solvency research are outlined in the concluding remarks.

## 2. Solvency: Claims and Investment Processes

Claims and investment processes induce several types of risks in terms of which solvency is defined. These include essentially underwriting risks, investment risks, a combination of both investment and underwriting results and the integration of solvency considerations within general corporate performance. These are briefly discussed below.

### 2.1. Solvency and Underwriting Risk

Earlier models focused on the underwriting process and evaluated the probability for the claims to exceed the premium income, creating a "ruin". This so-called "ruin theory" reached a high degree of mathematical sophistication - starting from simple collective normal processes, and ending with complicated skewed claim processes, and in some cases with "knotty" mathematical properties. Popular processes used include compound processes made up of two distributions: the distribution of the number of claims (frequency), and the distribution of claim size (severity) (see Beard et al. [1972], Bohman [1974], Buhlmann [1970], Gerber [1979], Seal [1979], Wooddy [1975] and others.)

It is noteworthy that some recent models still regard the underwriting risk as the major parameter controlling solvency. This way of thinking still affects the setting of reserves in practice (see Norberg and Sundt [1985]). Some recent papers seem to continue this stream of thought, using computers to simulate complex processes and seek numerical results where analytical tools fail to provide explicit answers (e.g. Pentikainen et al. [1975], [1982]). Recent extensions include continuous time claim (underwriting) jump processes as in Tapiero [1986a] and Tapiero, Zuckerman and Kahane [1978].

### 2.2. Solvency and Investment Risks

More than thirty years ago, some researchers felt that insurers' solvency depends more on the performance of insurers' investment portfolios than on the underwriting portfolio. Much attention was, therefore, given to the investment risk, and the ways in which it may be controlled. The theory of finance has come up with a plethora of ideas, including, among others, the seminal works of Markowitz [1952] concerning the investment portfolio model, and the Sharpe-Lintner-Mossin [1964-1966] models, known as the Capital Assets Pricing Model (CAPM). It was only natural that similar instruments penetrated the actuarial literature (e.g., see the portfolio approach used in the optimization of underwriting portfolios (Hofflander & Duvall [1967], Ferrari [1968]) and the direct application to solvency by Hammond, Shapiro and Shilling [1978]).

The exclusive focus on underwriting activities resulted from the belief that "...any attempt to analyze insurer investment and underwriting interaction is greatly complicated by the fact that it is extremely difficult to generate accurate estimates of investment returns associated with each line of insurance..." (Hammond et al. [1978], p. 18). In other words, concentrating on underwriting results did not mean that the investment risk had been overlooked, but rather that it was difficult to include it in the same framework.

### 2.3. Solvency and Both Investment and Underwriting Results

In parallel to these basic trends, there have been several studies in which the insurer's solvency was (justifiably) thought to depend on both underwriting and investment activities, rather than investment or underwriting separately. These include immunization of the overall portfolios by matching assets and liabilities (see

Redington [1952] - where portfolios were matched according to the duration.

Other models, balancing the profitability and riskiness of assets and liabilities of financial intermediaries, were developed with the tools of portfolio theory. (See Michaelsen and Goshay [1967], Pyle [1971], Krause [1970], Cummins and Nye [1973], Quirin et al. [1974], Kahane and Nye [1975], Kahane [1977c], and others. McCabe and Witt [1977] used a somewhat different approach to get similar results.) The concept turned out to be useful for the analysis of the solvency of financial intermediaries (Kahane [1977b], [1978a]).

The analysis is based on the proposition that capital requirement must be related to the overall performance of the insurance company. The overall performance is a function of both underwriting and investment incomes and their risks. A simplified model (Kahane [1978a]) examined the case where the insurer has only one insurance and one investment activity and analyzed the role of insurance leverage. A more extensive model examines the complex case where the company is operating in several insurance and investment activities (Kahane [1977b]). This model adds a new dimension to the regulatory problem by bringing out the effects of diversification of the insurer's business. It makes possible the study of the simultaneous effects of both the leverage and the portfolio composition on the probability of ruin. Both models were used to demonstrate that the existing forms of regulation do not necessarily reach their stated goals of mitigating the probability of ruin.

The insurer, as with other firms, faces the choice among various business strategies which can be summarized as a choice between profitability and risk. The finance literature recommends the use of the expected return as a measure of profitability and the standard deviation as a risk measure (Markowitz [1952]). The "efficient" strategies are those which have the minimal standard deviation for any level of expected value.[1] The locus of these startegies may be found analytically and can be described graphically by the curve EF' in Figure 1 (the "Efficiency Frontier").

For general non-life insurance firms, ruin is examined under relatively simple conditions. When the firm is limited to a single type of insurance activity and one investment, its profitability and risk may be controlled (i.e., the firm may move along the efficiency frontier) only by changing the amount of premiums it sells with a given capital - i.e., by changing the "leverage".

When profitability (of the insurance firm) and solvency are examined, "ruin" is defined then in terms of the rate of return on the equity - random variable - falling below a certain level h.[2] Setting regulatory solvency standard is equivalent then to determining the level of h and an upper bound on the probability of ruin. This, in turn, determines the risk-return combinations that should not be employed by the company. Actually it defines a half-plane bounded by a straight line such as line HH' in Figure 1 (see Kahane [1977]).

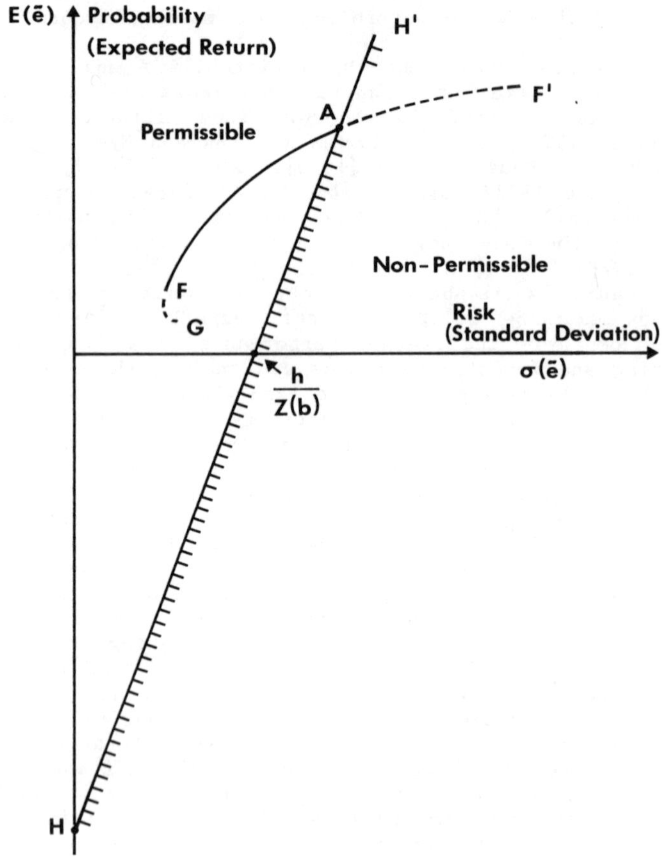


**Figure 1 - The Ruin Constraint**

This figure shows that the ruin constraint may intersect with the efficiency frontier, which defines the permissible and non-permissible strategies. For example, the firm would be permitted to operate only in section FA of the efficiency frontier. Under the assumed case there is a direct relationship between the degree of leverage and the expected return. Thus the ruin constraint clearly defines a range of permissible leverage. As a result, the probabilistic ruin constraint can be translated directly into a more practical constraint, such as a constraint on the insurer's leverage.[3]

## 2.4. Solvency with Investment and Underwriting Portfolios

In realistic situations - the insurer has a multiple-line activity, and its efficiency frontier can be derived with the aid of portfolio theory (see Haugen and Kroncke [1971], Hart and Jaffee [1974], Kahane and Nye [1975], Krouse [1970], Parkin (1970], Quirin et al. [1974] Bachman [1978] and others). In other words, the rate of return on equity and its distribution is affected by the stochastic processes of both underwriting and investment activites, and by their correlation. Analysis of solvency remains essentially as in Figure 1, except that the efficiency frontier is constructed in a more complicated manner.

Portfolio models are used to solve for the optimal size of each insurance and investment line in the portfolio expressed in relation to the capital of the firm (which is the scale factor of the system). (See Kahane and Nye [1975].) The size of each underwriting activity is expressed by either the premium volume, or the size of the reserves held for this line. Therefore, a by-product of the model is a specific solvency level for each insurance line - besides the determination of the overall solvency level - as measured by the insurance leverage (total premiums/equity). In other words, the specific solvency for each line results automatically from the overall level of leverage. This result has been recently used by Derrig [1986].

Under the multiline analysis, a distinct efficiency frontier could be formed for each level of leverage (premium/capital ratio). Each frontier is formed by solving the optimal portfolio problems under the constraint that the leverage ratio is given (see Figure 2). When the problem is solved without the leverage constraint an envelope frontier - which is tangent to these curves - is obtained (Kahane and Nye [1975], Quirin et al. [1974]). A movement along the envelope curve (curve FCF') means a change in the degree of leverage in addition to changes in the composition of insurance and investment portfolios.

Once again, the ruin constraint is superimposed (see line HH' in Figure 2). However, the ruin constraint cannot now be directly translated into a constraint on the leverage. Constraining the leverage turns out to be an ineffective means for bounding the probability of ruin. Assume that point C in Figure 2 - which is the intercept of the unconstrained frontier, FCF', with the ruin constaint - corresponds to a leverage k*. Using k* as the regulatory constraint means that the new (constrained) frontier is the one described by the curve FCD in Figure 2. This frontier is a combination of section FC of the unconstrained frontier, plus section CD - where the new constraint is binding.

The insurer is able to reach an excessive risk level despite the regulation. The insurer may, for example, hold a portfolio D which complies with the leverage constraint but clearly does not comply with the ruin constraint (Portfolio D lies below the ruin constraint HH'). Moreover, the regulation encourages the insurer to hold an inefficient portfolio: without regulation the insurer may hold a portfolio with the same expected profit but a lower risk (e.g., portfolio L).

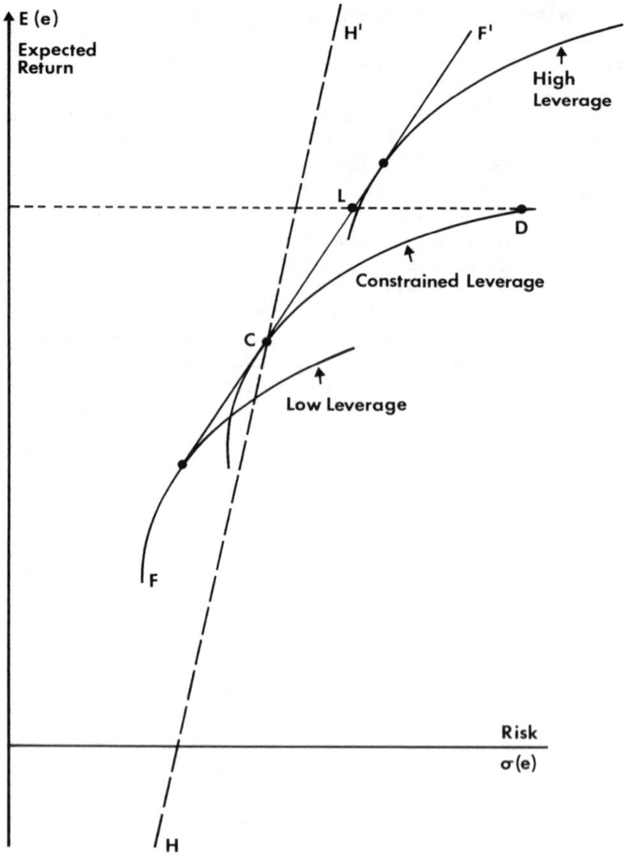


Figure 2 – The Envelope Frontier and The Ruin Constraint

Constraining the portfolio composition turns out to be ineffective, too. Under such constraints, the efficiency frontier at each level of leverage is truncated and shifts downward and to the right. For example, for a given leverage ratio, k, the constrained frontier ABC in Figure 3 is shifted to the lower level DEF. As long as the insurer is free to set the degree of leverage, the relevant shift is from the envelope IBJ to GEL. The insurer may indefinitely increase the expected return on equity and its standard deviation by simply increasing the leverage. Thus, the regulatory goal is not reached since the insurer may hold a portfolio with excessive probability of ruin (e.g., point 1 in Figure 3).

It becomes clear that minimum capital requirements or constraints on the portfolio composition, per se, cannot be regarded as effective means of bounding the probability of ruin. This goal can be reached only by simultaneously using the two instruments.

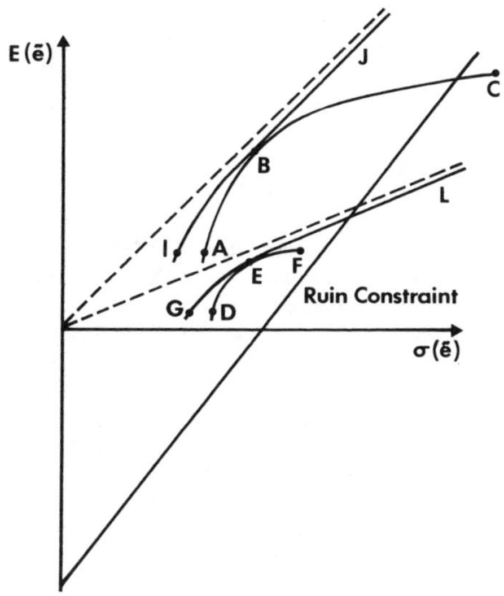


Figure 3 – Constraints On The Portfolio Composition

The portfolio approach to the analysis of insurer solvency can take a different direction as well: the portfolio model could be applied in order to obtain a specific solvency margin for each line of insurance according to the risk associated with this line (and the investments associated with it). For that purpose the analysis of the risk element in each line (Kahane [1977a], [1979], Biger and Kahane [1978], and later developments by Fairly [1979] and Hill [1979]) could be applied. This route of thinking is suggested by Derrig [1986] and Cummins [1986].

As an interim summary at this point it is essential to remember that solvency may not be studied in isolation from the capital market requirements. If regulators impose too stringent controls on the required capital and on the portfolio composition, they may create a situation where insurers cannot compete in the capital markets and cannot raise the required capital (see Joskow [1973] and Kahane and Sarnat [1978]).

## 2.5. Solvency and Corporate Activity

Recently, it has been recognized that solvency depends on the entire operation of the firm and not only on its underwriting and investment activites. It may depend for example on pricing, on managerial expenses, reinsurance, dividend policy, external conditions such as inflation, regulation, economic growth, cycles, etc., and it may depend also on the techniques used by the firm - use of data bases, and the development and use of knowhow, etc. As a result, integrated models have been formed to simulate the operation of the entire firms. Most of these ("corporate") models were developed, of course, in a continuous time framework. Due to the complexity of the models, numerical methods and simulations are often used [see, for example, Bohman [1976], Pentikainen [1975], Pentikainen and Rantala [1982], Coutts et al. [1983] Daykin et al. [1985] and others). Exceptions are the papers of Tapiero [1985] [1986] and Tapiero et al. [1978] [1982], which provide an optimal control approach.

The analysis of solvency within a continuous time framework helps to capture the dynamic nature of the issue. The models falling within this area are more commonly known as "ruin theory", and they focus on the measurement of the probability of ruin within a certain (usually long) period of time, or on the measurement of the life expectancy of the insurer. These models emphasize the stochastic nature of solvency and often use complex claims and investment processes. Dealing with problems of such complexity leads to complex mathematical analyses, simplified to some extent by abandoning a multiline framework and returning to that of a single activity. (See Buhlmann [1971], Borch [1974], Hallin [1977] Gerber [1979] and the references mentioned therein - especially Borch, De Finetti, Tapiero et al. [1978], [1982], [1983], [1985]).

## 3. Solvency and the Theory of Financial Leverage

### 3.1. Irrelevance of Financial Leverage?

From a financial point of view, the problem of insurer's solvency is similar to problems of optimal capital structure. Increasing the premium to equity ratio (or, alternatively, lowering the minimum capital requirements for a given volume of insurance business) could be used by the shareholders to increase the expected return on investment in the shares of the insurance company - similarly to the effects of using a higher financial leverage (debt/equity ratio).

Financial literature shows that in the absence of taxes and bankruptcy risk, the value of the firm is invariant to its capital structure, and the level of leverage is irrelevant (i.e., the higher return obtained by the shareholders is offset by their increased risk). This was shown in the late fifties by Modigliani and Miller [1958] following Durand. The well known proof of this argument by Modigliani and Miller, is based on an "arbitrage" argument: If the market value of the firm could be increased by changing the capital structure, people could benefit from the same effect by employing "homemade leverage" (borrowing on their personal account) - without having to operate through a corporation. Similarly if the value of a firm with a lower leverage is higher, people would be able to benefit from "undoing" the leverage of a levered firm (by lending). The MM results were later obtained also under more general conditions (see Stiglitz [1974]).

There are three major reasons which may still justify an optimal capital structure for a corporation despite the arbitrage argument.

a) The market is imperfect so that arbitrage possibilities (creating homemade leverage or undoing corporate leverage) are impossible.
b) Corporate taxes create an advantage to the firms employing a higher leverage: taxation leads to a corner solution - where 100% debt financing is optimal.[4]
c) There are costs associated with financial distress and bankruptices - so that corporate leverage and homemade leverage are imperfect substitutes.[5] Where both corporate tax and bankruptcy costs are present, debt will be utilized up to the point where the gain from tax savings on the debt is offset by the costs of financial distress (Miller [1977]).

The same type of reasoning may be applied to the question of optimal solvency standards (optimal insurance leverage). Further research is, however, needed to show that optimal solvency (leverage) may result from the factors listed below (and their interaction).

a) Due to licencing of insurance companies, the possiblity of arbitrage (through "homemade" insurance leverage) is limited, and, therefore, there could be an optimal insurance leverage.
b) Insurers enjoy certain tax advantages that could not be obtained by individuals. These tax advantages result from the special accounting techniques (reserving) used in this field (tax deferral effect). Therefore, a higher insurance leverage (premiums/ equity ratio) is beneficial.
c) The potential costs of financial distress create a motive for avoiding excessive insurance leverage. We shall elaborate upon this point, below.

### 3.2. Insurance Leverage: The Cost of Financial Distress

Insurance leverage could be viewed quite similarly to financial leverage of a non-insurance firm. Both borrowing and employing insurance leverage may increase the probability (and costs) associated with financial distress. This may affect the market value of the securities of a levered firm, and serve as a force which offsets the wish to increase borrowing infinitly (e.g., due to the tax shelter of debt). Therefore, we have a trade-off between the tax effect versus the cost of financial distress associated with financial leverage.

Corporate bankruptcy means that shareholders exercise their legal right to benefit from the limited liability principle - i.e., they decide to cut their losses (lose all they had) and to shift all potential losses to the company creditors. This is a valuable option for the shareholders of a corporation - because under unlimited liability the shareholders are **personally** liable for the firm's debts. The shareholders' option is the bondholders' worry! Similarly bankruptcy of an insurance firm may shift the risk back to the insureds. The **total** value of the firm's securities (stock and bonds) should remain unaffected by leverage - if no costs are associated with the process. However, in reality there are costs involved, and, therefore, the total value of a levered firm is lower (reflecting the higher probability of ruin).

The possibility of bankruptcy may emphasize the difference between a stock company and a mutual insurer: under a stock company, there is a risk that shareholders may exercise their limited liability option and shift the burden of losses to insureds (the "lenders" of the insurance company). Under a mutual arrangement the shareholders and the insureds are the same entities - therefore the potential conflict between the shareholders and insureds is avoided.

## 4. Integrating Solvency in Insurance Management

An integrated viewpoint is expounded in Tapiero [1985], [1986], highlighting the interdependency of solvency with a large number of parameters in and outside the firm. Thus, solvency is determined by a balancing of conflicting interests - of the various participants - insureds, insurers, regulators, shareholders, potential insured, insurers and investors, etc. Focusing on such a viewpoint may lead to useful and practical results for the study of solvency.

Several attempts have been made in the literature. In this section we summarize two studies:

a) The Tapiero, Zuckerman and Kahane paper [1978] (hereafter TZK), which shows that solvency could result from a trade-off between a regulated minimium capital requirement and some sort of a penalty system for violating a barrier policy.
b) The Tapiero, Kahane and Jacque paper [1986], which shows that solvency could be detemined by balancing the insureds' conflicting goals: the wish to pay low premiums, and the wish to be insured by a solvent insurer.

### 4.1. Solvency as a Trade-Off Between Capital Requirement and Penalties

The TZK paper uses a continuous time framework, which borrows some ideas from ruin theory. The novelty in the TZK approach, however, is in the use of a definition of "ruin" whereby (unlike previous models), once a firms violates the regulatory standards it is regarded as "ruined", and is forced to go out of business. In the TZK analysis such a situation is expressed by payment of a "penalty", which enables the firms to resume operation. The penalty may take various forms: a fine, extra cost of reorganization, etc. Such a model provides a better description of reality since insurers, after being practically ruined, often resume operation, by the way of merger, purchase, or reinsurance. This solution may also be regarded as more reasonable since ruin can result from the random nature of the claims and reserves processes, and continuing operation after practically being ruined may enable the firm to recover in the long run. Finally, the TZK model integrates the penalty costs considered by management when selecting an optimal strategy.

The basics of the TZK model are as follows: the firm's reserve process is affected by incoming premiums and by the payment of claims. Premiums are assumed to occur at a constant rate which is equal to the expected claims rate plus a proportional loading factor.[6] Claims are assumed to occur at a Poisson rate $\lambda$ with successive claims assumed positive, independent and identically distributed random variables (with a mean $\zeta$). The net reserve of the firm at any point in time is composed of the initial reserve plus the difference between the premiums and the claims.

The reserve process is subject to certain constraints which provide the constraint set in an optimization problem. On the one hand, there is a minimum reserve level, K, required by the regulator. Violating this capital requirement involves a penalty against the firm. The penalty may be a combination of several elements: for example, it may consist of a fixed cost element for the downcrossing, and a variable cost proportional to the size of the jump below K. The variable cost may be regarded as the cost of a "loan" given to a failing firm so that it returns immediately to the reserve level K. Alternatively, this may represent the cost of converting other assets into the form of cash. The model can easily be extended to handle additional costs: for instance, the costs associated with situations of negative reserves.

The firm wishes to hold net reserves greater than K to avoid the case of incidental downcrossing of the regulatory standard. However, it refrains from holding an infinite reserve, since holding such cash reserves involves an opportunity cost (in the form of an interest rate, r).[7]

A decision variable (a barrier policy), A - denoting the initial level of reserves - must therefore be introduced. Any reserve above this level incurs a cost r. If the reserve falls below A the firm retains all net accumulation of premiums and keeps it in the form of cash. If the reserves fall below the minimum capital requirement, K, there is a penalty and the firm automatically returns to reserve level K. (See Figure 4 for a graphical description of the process.)

The long-run profit of the firm is a function of the minimum reserve, K, the cost elements, and the barrier strategy A. Using the tools of renewal theory this function can be specified and studied. With it, quantities of interest such as the expected time between the events of downcrossing the regulatory standards, etc. are derived. Further, the expected long-run profit can be specified, and the optimal strategy A can be found. The formula is developed and reported in TZK (equation 2-4). Due to mathematical complications, it is often necessary to rely on numerical methods to find the optimal strategy.

The penalties serve as the means for internalizing the external cost of bankruptcy. If the cost of ruin considered by the management is lower than the cost from a societal point of view, the firm may be prepared to take "excessive" risk. The regulator's problem should, therefore, be aimed toward equating the external and internal costs, affecting thereby the reserve level, A. It appears that this relationship is often disregarded by regulators since the penalty system is determined in an arbitrary way. The model can be used to assist the regulator in determining the "optimal" penalty (the lowest penalty for a given probability of ruin).

Regulators set both the minimum capital requirement, K, and the penalty for downcrossing this requirement. These parameters would

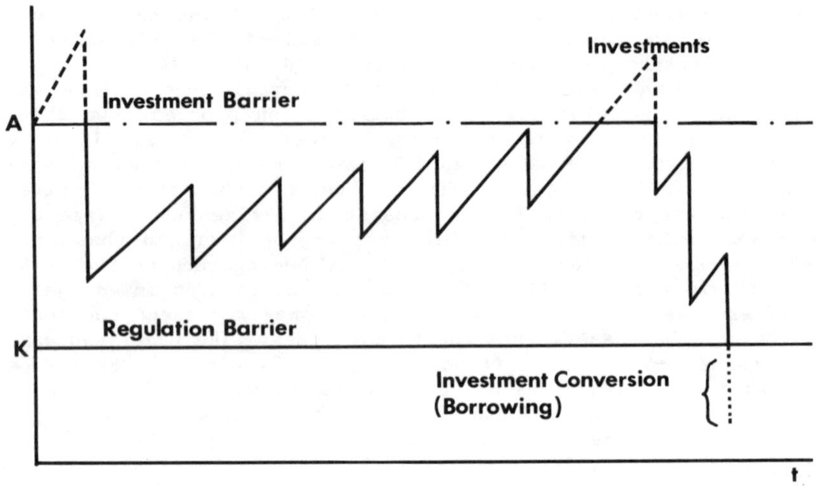


Figure 4 – Ruin as a Band Strategy Problem

typically motivate the firm to hold a reserve, A, larger than the required minimum (A > K). Thus, if the regulator prefers to have a certain reserve level, he should determine a lower minimum capital requirement.

There is a certain trade-off between the minimum capital requirement and the size of the penalty, in the sense that different policies may lead to the same reserve level, A, and thus to the same probability of ruin. Regulators may prefer to have higher penalties rather than a higher minimum capital requirement because of political considerations (a high minimum capital requirement may force the companies to take immediate steps and increase their capital, which may be unpopular).

Viewing the firm's decision under this model provides much insight into the problem of solvency regulation: it is the purpose of regulation to prevent deliberately caused ruin, and this can be achieved by introducing a potential penalty (i.e., a "threat") into the system. Management would take this penalty into consideration in their decision making. Note, also, that empirical studies show that one of the major reasons for the failure of banks and financial intermediaries is fraud. The common regulatory techniques, including the leverage constraints, are ineffective in preventing this type of ruin. A penalty system, which weakens the protection given to management by "limited liability", may serve as a better deterrent against ruin caused by fraud.

### 4.2. Solvency and Insurance Rates

The theory relating to insurance pricing often regards insurance contracts as transactions where insureds exchange uncertain "prospects" with certain ones at the cost of a premium paid to the insurer (e.g., see Beard et al. [1972], Buhlman [1970], Borch [1974]). In this context, the insured faces no risk once he has taken out and paid for the insurance contract. Practically, however, insurers are subject to default risk, and this risk (or its perception) may affect the policy-holders' response to a particular premium (or loading factor) policy which is proposed by the insurer. This is particularly the case in collective risk sharing schemes (e.g., mutual insurance, Tapiero [1982], [1984] where the loss distributions have large tails, leading to appreciable probabilities of failure). In such cases, the default risk becomes dependent on the premiums, in addition to the factors which have been discussed earlier - such as the insurer's capitalization, the returns on investments, and the distributional properties of the loss severity and frequency. Therefore, a premium or loading factor policy must necessarily be a function of the insured's reaction towards the probability of insurer's default (Tapiero et al. [1983]). In other words, the optimal premium rate depends on the default risk - which, in turn, depends on the premium rate itself.

The case of a mutual insurer is emphasized since it introduces two notions of solvency and default, namely, the probability of the insurer's ruin, and the "perceived" probability of default from the insured's point of view (see Tapiero, Kahane and Jacque [1986]). The objective probability of ruin - the probability that the insurer will be unable to meet its obligations - is not always the relevant parameters in the insured's decision making. Rather, the insured's decision may be guided by his/her perception of the probability of being affected by the ruin of the insurer. Tapiero et al. [1986] defined and measured this perceived probability of ruin and assessed its effects on the premium policy.

It is shown that the premium that each insured is willing to pay depends of the payments of the other insureds as well as their claim distributions, reflecting thereby the simultaneity, and mutual dependence, of insureds. This, of course, is noticeable only for mutuals having a relatively small number of members, where the contribution of each individual member on the pool is noticeable.

Both the Tapiero, Kahane and Jacque model, and the TZK model discussed earlier, draw attention to the rich research opportunities which open up once researchers begin investigating the relationships among insurers and regulators or among the insureds and insurers. An additional promising line of research is to analyze the interactions and motivations of the many "participants" engaged in insurance; insureds, insurers, regulators, potential insureds and insurers, tax authorities, etc., rather than focus on one or two concerned parties, as has been done in previous studies. In such studies a focus on the role of information transfers, signaling, moral hazard, and principal-agent relationships are essential. In addition, it should be remembered that insurers often consider the problem of solvency as a tax issue. Being allowed to set aside large solvency margins will help to reduce the tax burden of the firm.

The insureds are subject to conflicting interests: while they are interested in the stability of their insurer, they are less happy about the higher loading factor and higher premiums that this stability implies. This trade-off has been discussed in the previous section. Similarly, insurance regulators are also torn between conflicting goals: it is unclear which goal they serve - are they supposed to protect the insureds or the insurers? Are they supposed to prevent bankruptcies at all costs? Should they let insurers go under - so that the awareness of such possibilities should increase, and so that insureds and insurers be more cautious? In some cases, letting the insurer go bankrupt is the least expensive and most effective solution. The insurance commissioner, discovering that an insurer is exposed to a more risky situation than is regarded as acceptable thus faces the uneasy decision whether to make the information public and to take any steps or not. Taking steps, in itself, may turn a risky situation into a certain bankruptcy. Should the regulator conceal his actions, or avoid taking action, merely because of fear of such an undesirable development? Tools which handle solvency in such a way that the regulator receives warning early enough to prevent the treatment from turning the situation into a one-way route towards bankruptcy are, therefore, needed.

The above discussion indicates that solvency relates to the sharing of information, and may be analyzed within the theory of agency: the insurer signals to the potential insureds that he is selling coverage at the lowest possible premiums, while still maintaining an appropriate level of safety (solvency). That is, the insurer signals to the insureds that he will still be there at the time when claims have to be paid. The insured is looking for guarantees that this signalling is not false. The role of the insurance commissioner may then be seen as supplying further evidence and approval for the validity and credibility of the signalling by the insurer. In this respect, the role of the insurance commissioner is essentially informative. He should perform the research and tests that are needed for the approval of the solvency. Such an agency may fulfill a useful and important function only if it is capable of handling information in the most efficient, reliable and least expensive way in comparison to the efficiency of each individual doing the same job. From this perspective, the role of the insurance regulatory authority is mainly in the collection, analysis and distribution of information. The insurance commissioner should then make public any information concerning the financial conditions of the regulated insurers.

We have not yet devised a general theoretical framework which incorporates all parties, within a unified model. We believe that future studies of solvency will take the above-mentioned directions emphasizing, however, the concepts of information, signalling and agency theory.

**5. Concluding Remarks**

Although this article was in an advanced stage of preparation when we became aware of the comprehensive recent surveys of solvency by Kastelijn and Remmerswaal [May 1986], and Derrig [1986], it may nevertheless be regarded as complementary to these surveys.

The essential conclusions of the present study may be summarized as follows:

(a) The term "solvency" should be redefined in a more explicit and precise way. In particular, a distinction between the concept of "liquidity" and "bankruptcy" should be made, and a decision has to be made whether solvency should reflect merely existing (past) business, or, rather, the going concern approach should be adopted, whereby the effect of new business (and expected - future - business) is considered. The two approaches are identical in a perfect market, where the firm may rely on borrowing against future income to cover temporary illiquidity. However, this is not necessarily the case under prevalent imperfect conditions.

(b) The drawbacks of the accounting approach to solvency were emphasized: it is deterministic, and does not relate to the stochastic nature of solvency. Moreover, since most ratios and reserves are related to the premium income - they may be biased when insurance is sold against inappropriate premiums.

(c) The solvency literature is at present isolated from the financial literature concerning the optimal "leverage" (debt-equity ratio) of firms, but the two should be integrated. The latter emphasizes the market considerations and uses the valuation of the shares of the insurer as the benchmark for determining his optimal policy. When solvency is determined in isolation from market considerations, the insurer may face situations where he cannot compete in the capital market and cannot raise required capital.

(d) Solvency is a function of the overall performance of the firm, and depends on a large number of parameters: the underwriting and investment risks (and their interaction), pricing methods in use, managerial expenses, reinsurance, etc. In addition it depends on conditions which are external to the firm - economic growth, inflation, regulation, taxes, capital markets, etc. Solvency should, therefore, be studied within an integrated model of the firm.

(e) Solvency could be regulated by setting "penalties" for downcrossing the minimum capital requirements - rather than bringing about immediate ruin. This enables recovery from unfavorable developments (going concern approach).

(f) The major role of the regulators is to make information public and provide signals in order to enable insureds to express their preferences concerning the trade-off between lower premiums and higher solvency standards.

(g) Solvency could and should be analyzed as a special case of information theory, where the roles of the insurers, insureds and regulators are expressed in terms of signals, an exchange of information and the selling and buying of options. This avenue of research seems to have greater potential (see Cummins [1986], Derrig [1986]).

**Notes**

1. The mean-variance approach is acceptable under the assumption that the relevant distributions are normal. The normality assumption is often used in the insurance context, since although the return on each policy or investment activity may have a skewed distribution, the distribution of the return on highly diversified portfolios is approximately normal.

2. Such a definition is adopted by Borch [1974], Hofflander and Duvall [1967] (implicit in their equation (8)) and Hammond et al. [1978].

3. Due to the quadratic shape of the efficiency frontier and its concave nature there may be no intercept, or at most two intercepts, with the ruin constraint. When only one intercept exists the use of leverage above the level at the point of intercept should be prohibited. A more peculiar case is when the expected return decreases when the leverage is increased. (This may happen when the underwriting and/or investment activities are quite unprofitable.) The regulator should then prohibit the use of leverage below a certain level. When the ruin constraint has two intercepts with the efficiency frontier, the regulator should set both an upper and a lower bound on insurance leverage.

4. This tax benefit was refuted later by Miller [1977], who showed that when both corporate and personal taxes are considered, financial managers should disregard taxes in determining the optimal capital structure.

5. The cost of financial distress is composed of legal costs related to actual bankruptcy, administrative costs (the costs of running the business while going through bankruptcy), and costs associated with "near bankruptcy" situations - where the conflicting interests of the various stakeholders disturb the operation of the firm.

6. Administrative expenses are included together with claims. The loading factor represents only an expected underwriting profit. A possible extension of the model, not repeated here, may include the loading factor among the decision variables of the firm.

7. In another model by TKZ it is assumed that the surplus is distributed as dividends and drawn out of the system. Holding cash reserves incurs the opportunity cost of non-payment of dividend.

**References**


Bachman, J. [1978). *Capitalization Requirements for Multiple Line Property-Liability Insurance Companies,* Huebner Foundation Monographic 6.

Bar-Niv, R. [1983]. "Insolvency prediction for P-L insurers: new statistical measures and the effects of accounting practices", presented at the ARIA meetings, Philadelphia, August.

Beard, R.E., T. Pentikainen and E. Pesonen [1969]. *Risk Theory. Methuen (and later extended editions).*

*Beckman, R.W. and R.N. Tremeling 1972 . "The relationship between net premium written and policyholders surplus", Proceedings of Casualty Actuarial Society* 59: 203-220.

Biger, N. and Y. Kahane [1978]. "Risk considerations in insurance ratemaking", *The Journal of Risk and Insurance* 45(1) (March) 121-132.

Bohman, H. [1974]. "Solvency and profitability standards", *Scandinavian Actuarial Journal,* 111-113.

Bohman, H. [1974]. "Rule of thumb for the determination of a sufficient risk reserve", *Scandinavia Actuarial Journal,* 237-240.

Borch, K. [1974]. "Markets and the supervision of insurance companies", *The Journal of Risk and Insurance* 41: 397-406.

Borch, K. [1974]. *The Mathematical Theory of Insurance,* Lexington Books, Lexington, Mass.

Buhlmann, H. [1970]. *Mathematical Methods in Risk Theory,* Grundlehren der Mathematischen Wissenschaften in Einzeldarstellung, Band 172, 1.

Chen, A.H. [1979]. "A theory of corporate bankruptcy and optimal capital structure" in L.A. Bicksler (ed.) *Handbook of Financial Economies,* North Holland, pp. 275-291.

Coutts S.M., E.R.F. Devitt and G.A.F. Ross [1983]. "A practical probabilistic approach to solvency", presentation at the Institute of Actuaries, London, December.

Cummins, J.D. and J.D. Nye [1980]. "The stochastic characteristics of property-liability insurance profits", *Journal of Risk and Insurance* 47: 61-80.

Cummins, J.D. [1986]. "Risk based premiums for guarantee funds", International Conference on Insurance Solvency, Wharton School, June.

Daykin, C.D. and G.D. Bernstein [1985]. "A simulation model to examine questions of solvency in the light of assets and run-off risk", paper presented at *ASTIN* meetings, Biarritz, September.

De Wit, G.W. and W.M. Kastelijn [1980]. "The solvency margin in non life insurance companies", *ASTIN-Bulletin*.

Derrig, R.A. [1986]. "Solvency levels and risk loadings appropriate for fully guaranteed property-liability insurance contracts: a financial view", unpublished mansucript, June.

Ferrari, J.R. [1968]. "The relationship of underwriting investment, leverage, and exposure to total return on owners' equity", Proceedings of the Casualty Actuarial Society 55: 295-302; discussion by R.J. Balcarek and R.A. Bailey, 56 [1969]: 58-62.

Gerber, H. [1979]. *An Introduction to Mathematical Risk Theory*. Huebner Foundation Monograph Series, 8.

Gordon, M.J. [1971]. "Towards the theory of financial distress", *Journal of Finance* 26 (May): 347-356.

Hallin, M. [1977]. "Band strategies: The random walk of reserves",Working Paper 3, Universite Libre de Bruxelles, Institute of Statistics, December 1977.

Hammond, J.D., A. Shapiro and N. Shilling [1978]. "The regulation of insurer solidity through capital and surplus requirements," Technical Report, NSF GRANT -16550 A01, March 1978.

Hammond J.D. and N. Shilling [1978]. "Some relationships of portfolio theory to the regulation of insurance solidity", *Journal of Risk and Insurance* 45.

Hart, O.D. and D.M. Jaffee [1974]. "On the application of portfolio theory to depository financial intermediaries", *Review of Economic Studies* 41, No.1.

Haugen, R.A. and C.O. Kroncke [1970]. "Optimizing the structure of capital claims and assets of a stock insurance company", Journal of Risk and Insurance 37: 41-49; and "Reply", 39 [1972]: 305-316.

Hofflander, A.E. and R.M. Duvall [1967]. "The ruin problem in multiple line insurance: A simplified model", *Journal of Financial and Quantitative Analysis* 2: 150-165.

Joskow, P.L. [1973]. "Cartels, competition and regulation in the property-liability insurance industry", *The Bell Journal of Economics and Management Science* 4: 375-427.

Kahane, Y. [1977a]. "Ratemaking and regulation in property-liability insurance", *The Quarterly Review of Economics and Business* 17(2): 97.112.

Kahane, Y. [1977b]. "Capital adequacy and the regulation of financial intermediaries", *Journal of Banking and Finance*, 207-218.

Kahane, Y. [1977c]. "Determining the product mix and the business policy of an insurance company - a portfolio approach", *Management Science* 23(10) (June): 1060-1069.

Kahane, Y. [1978a]. "Solidity, leverage and the regulation of insurance companies", *The Geneva Papers on Risk and Insurance* (December): 3-19.

Kahane, Y. [1978b]. "Generation of investable funds and the portfolio behavior of non-life insurance companies", *The Journal of Risk and Insurance* 45(1) (March): 65-77.

Kahane, Y. [1979]. "The theory of insurance risk premiums - a re-examination in light of recent development in capital market theory", *The ASTIN Bulletin* 10(2) (March): 223-239.

Kahane, Y., and D. Nye [1975]. "A portfolio approach to the property-liability insurance industry", *The Journal of Risk and Insurance* 42: 579-598.

Kahane, Y. and M. Sarnat [1978]. "Alternative approaches to the evaluation of the profitability of property-liability insurance industry", *CPU Journal* 31(4): 215-218.

Kastelijn, W.M. and J.C.M. Remmerswaal [1986]. *Solvency: Surveys of Acturial Studies* No. 3, the National Nederlanden N.V. (May).

Kenney, R. [1967]. *Fundamentals of Fire and Casualty Studies,* The Kennedy Insurance Studies, Dedham (Mass.).

Krouse, C.G. [1970]. "Portfolio balancing corporate assets and liablities with special application to insurance management", Journal of Financial and Quantitative Analysis 5: 77-105.

Markowitz, H.M. [1952]. "Portfolio selection", *Journal of Finance,* (March).

McCabe G.M. and R.C. Witt [1977]. "The insurer under solvency regulation: a non-linear chance constrained programming formulation", Working Paper 77-84, University of Texas at Austin, October.

Michaelsen, J.B. and R.C. Goshay [1967]. "Portfolio selection in financial intermediaries: a new approach", *Journal of Financial and Quantitative Analysis* 2: 166-199.

Miller, M.H. [1977]. "Debt and taxes", *Journal of Finance* 32 (May): 261-276.

Modigliani, F. and M.H. Miller [1958]. "The Cost of capital, corporation finance and the theory of investment", *American Economic Review* 48: pp. 261-297.

National Association of Insurance Commissioners [1970]. Measurement of Profitability and Treatment of Investment

Norberg R. and B. Sundt [1985]. "Draft of a system for solvency control in non-life insurance", *ASTIN Bulletin* 15: 149-169.

Parkin, M. [1970]. "Discount house portfolio and debt selection", *Review of Economic Studies* 37, No. 4.

Pardo Vivero, A. [1984]. "Reinsurance, reserves and solvency", Proceedings International Congress of Actuaries, 22 Vol. 3, pp. 527- 539.

Pentikainen, T. [1975]. "A model of stochastic-dynamic prognosis", *Scandinavian Actuarial Journal,* pp. 29-53.

Pentikainen, T. and J. Rantala [1982]. *Solvency of Insurers and Equalization Reserves,* Insurance Publishing Co., Helsinki, Finland.

Pesonen, E. [1964]. "Solvency measurement", *Transactions of the International Congress of Actuaries.*

Pyle, D.H. [1971]. "On the theory of financial intermediation", *Journal of Finance,* 737-747.

Quirin, D., P. Halpern, B. Kalymon, J. Mathewson and W. Waters [1974]. *Competition, Economic Efficiency and Profitability in the Canadian Property and Casualty Insurance Industry,* prepared for the Insurance Bureau of Canada, Toronto.

Redington, F.M. [1952]. "Review of the principles of life-office valuations", *Journal of the Institute of Actuaries* 3.

Ryan, J.P. [1980]. "Application of model office techniques to the solvency questions", *Proceedings, International Congress of Actuaries,* 21, Vol. 1, pp. 403-410.

Seal H. [1979]. *Survival Probabilities: The Goal of Risk Theory,* Springer Verlag.

Stilitz J.E. [1972]. "Some aspects of the pure theory of corporate finance: bankruptcies and take-overs", *Bell Journal of Economics* 3(2) (Autumn).

Tapiero, C.S. [1982]. "The optimal control of a mutual insurance process, *ASTIN Bulletin* 13: 13-21.

Tapiero, C.S. [1985]. "A dynamic stock insurance firm model and dividend optimization", *Journal of Large Scale Systems.*

Tapiero, C.S. [1986]. "The systems approach to insurance company management", in C. Carraro, and D. Sartore, Dordrecht, Nighoff (eds.), *Developments of Control Theory for Economic Analysis* (forthcoming).

Tapiero, C.S., Y. Kahane and L. Jacque [1986]. "Insurance premiums and default risk in mutual insurance", *Scandinavian Actuarial Journal.*

Tapiero, C.S., D. Zuckerman and Y. Kahane Y. [1978]. "Regulation of an insurance firm with a compound poisson claim process", in Y. Kahane (ed.), *New Frontiers in Insurance,* Papirus press, Tel Aviv.

Tapiero, C.S., D. Zuckerman and Y. Kahane [1983]. "Optimal investment-dividend policy of an insurance firm under regulation, *Scandinavian Actuarial Journal,* 65-78.

Wooddy, J. [1973]. *Risk Theory,* Society of Actuaries, Part 5 Study Notes, Chicago.

# 8

# ON THE APPLICATION OF FINANCE THEORY TO THE INSURANCE FIRM

James R. Garven

"The focal point in the theory of risk . . . has for almost a century been the probability of ruin. It has been assumed that at least a partial objective of the insurance company is to make certain that the probability of ruin does not exceed a given number, say $\alpha$. The theory is usually vague, or completely silent about how the number should be determined. The model seems to make most sense if a value of $\alpha$ is imposed from outside, for instance, by a government inspector."

Karl Borch, *The Mathematical Theory of Insurance*, 1974
(Lexington Books, p. 107)

## I. Introduction

Traditional risk theory has tended to view the insurance firm too much from within. Although the insurance firm exists in an economic environment within which it must compete with other insurance firms as well as institutions which provide close substitutes to insurance services, this fact of life appears to have largely escaped the attention of risk theorists. While the implications of default risk for insurance company decision making and regulatory policy are widely discussed in the insurance solvency literature, this literature does not provide an internally consistent theoretical framework within which an acceptable ruin probability can be determined. As noted in the above quotation from Karl Borch's well-known and highly regarded book, the literature treats the determination of the appropriate ruin probability as exogenous to the firm. One can only hope that Borch's government inspector is endowed with King Solomon's wisdom.

Unfortunately, the insurance literature in general and the solvency literature in particular have grown in isolation of a plethora of useful studies in the financial economics literature which provide a powerful analytic framework for the study of the firm. Similarly, the finance profession has until recently all but ignored the insurance firm.[1] However, a resurgence of interest has occurred within the past decade in the finance literature regarding the general theory of organizations and its implications for optimal contract structure in a firm. Since there is probably no other industry in existence which features such a diverse set of organizational forms, the insurance industry has provided a nearly ideal laboratory setting for the development of this theory (e.g., see Fama and Jensen [1983a, 1983b, 1985] and Mayers and Smith [1981, 1982a, 1982b, 1987]).

The primary argument set forth in this paper is that the theory of finance can and should be rigorously applied to the study of the insurance firm. In order to illustrate this point, we apply financial theory to the question of insurance solvency. Rather than treat the probability of ruin as an exogenous constraint that is arbitrarily imposed by regulators, the approach taken here is to endogenize the probability of ruin with respect to a complex contracting process undertaken by a variety of self-interested claimholders. This treatment enables us to meaningfully evaluate regulatory constraints such as minimum capital requirements within a rigorous theoretical framework.

In what follows, we analyze optimal capital decisions in the context of an unregulated insurance market. The next section of the paper provides a relatively general characterization of the traditional theory of the insurance firm, our purpose being to demonstrate what we believe to be some major methodological shortcomings which are substantively resolved by adopting the agency theoretic view of the firm that is prevalent in the financial economics literature. The third section of the paper considers the determination of the insurer's optimal capital decision when the writing and enforcement of the various contracts that comprise the insurance firm is costless (costly). Under costless contracting and no taxation, the choice of capital is shown to be an irrelevant consideration. With taxes, the rational insurer will employ as little capital as possible. Only when we explicitly recognize the existence of phenomena such as redundant tax shields, bankruptcy costs, and agency costs are we able to arrive at an optimal capital decision which involves the employment of positive levels of capital. Section IV of the paper provides a brief summary of the results and suggestions for future research.

While the methodology followed in this paper represents a fundamental departure from more traditional approaches to the theory of the insurance firm, various results are shown which are not attainable with the traditional theories. Specifically, our analysis suggests that, even in an unregulated market, insurers would voluntarily limit their premium-capital ratios in an effort to economize on contracting costs. Furthermore, mutual insurers are likely, *ceteris paribus*, to be less highly levered than insurers organized as stock corporations.

## II. The Objectives of the Insurance Firm

### A. *Collective Risk Theory and the Expected Utility Hypothesis*

Historically, solvency has been emphasized as one of the primary goals of insurance regulation. Munch and Smallwood [1981] attribute this emphasis on solvency regulation to the difficulty allegedly faced by policyholders in establishing the financial soundness of alternative firms.[2] Boyle and Butterworth [1982] note that the trend toward solvency regulation was accelerated by insurance company failures, so that by the beginning of the 20th century, many western countries had enacted legislation which heavily emphasized the solvency of insurance companies. Finsinger and Pauly [1984] note that virtually all western countries regulate the reserves of insurance firms, even when they do not directly regulate the premiums charged.

Given this regulatory emphasis on insurance company solvency, actuaries sought to build quantitative models which would enable insurance company managements to incorporate ruin probabilities into their decision making. The body of theory that resulted is known as the collective theory of risk. Some of the contributions of the collective risk theorists parallel highly regarded work in the option pricing area of the financial economics literature. For example, Lundberg [1909] used continuous time processes to model the evolution of an insurance company's liabilities. As Borch [1974] points out, it is natural to compare Lundberg's contribution with that of Bachelier [1900], the only significant difference being that Bachelier's work dealt with a stochastic model for assets rather than liabilities.

In spite of the mathematical elegance and rigor of the collective theory of risk,[3] we believe that it fails to provide an economically meaningful framework for the evaluation of managerial and regulatory policies. Although it is never explicitly stated as such, risk theory essentially treats survival as the goal of the firm.[4] While attempts have been made to reconcile risk theory with paradigms such as the expected utility hypothesis, a number of problems remain:

1. Behavioral models which are based upon survival objectives (e.g., expected utility models that are constrained by ruin probabilities or models which make use of safety-first decision criteria) are likely to yield lower utility rankings than unconstrained models.[5]

2. Most insurance firms are not owned and operated by individual entrepreneurs; rather, they are comprised of a complex set of contracts among policyholders, stockholders, and managers. Furthermore, substantive disagreements are likely to exist across and even among these classes of claimholders with respect to rates of time preference, risk preferences, and opinions concerning what constitute the "best" corporate policies for the firm to follow. Therefore, even if one can demonstrate that the objections raised in the first point are not generally valid, these considerations cast serious

doubt upon the use of the expected utility hypothesis *per se*, since a collective utility function is likely to be impossible to construct due to the problem of intransitivity (e.g., see Arrow [1950]).

3. As we suggested earlier, the risk theory approach to the evaluation of managerial and regulatory policies is deficient because it cannot provide any insight into how "acceptable" ruin probabilities are determined. As we shall see in the next section of the paper, a more dynamic theory of the insurance firm is required before this issue can be adequately addressed.

*B. Agency Theory and the Market Value Rule*

We believe that the objections we have raised above can be largely resolved by a careful reconsideration of the nature of the insurance firm. Jensen and Meckling [1976, p. 310] note that most organizations, including firms, mutual organizations, non-profit institutions, and even governmental bodies, are simply "*legal fictions which serve as a nexus for a set of contracting relationships among individuals*." The definition of contracts here is in fact rather broad, including both written and unwritten contracts. These contracts define a set of agency relationships under which principal(s) engage agent(s) to perform some service on their behalf, a decision which invariably involves delegating some decision making authority to the agent. Agency problems and their attendant costs arise when both parties to the agency relationship are self-interested and it is costly to write and enforce the contracts which define this relationship. As Fama and Jensen [1983b] have noted, to the extent that contracting is costly, the set of agency relationships which make up the firm is not a trivial consideration, since the resulting contract structure combines with available production technologies and external legal constraints to determine the firm's cost function. The organizational form which delivers output demanded by consumers at the lowest price, while covering costs, survives.[6]

Given our agency theoretic definition of the firm, it is appropriate to give further consideration to the identification of just who the principals and agents are in the context of an insurance operation. Mayers and Smith [1987] note that, regardless of whether the firm is organized as a stock or mutual company, it is characterized by three major functions which are allocated across various claimholders: the managerial function, the ownership/riskbearing function, and the customer/policyholder function. The owner, being the claimant to the *residual* cash flows of the firm,[7] is characterized as the riskbearer, since he/she essentially guarantees the payoffs promised under the firm's contracts with its managers and customers. The manner in which mutual and stock organizations differ is primarily characterized by the way these functions are allocated across claimholders. In the stock company, the three functions are vested in three distinct claimants: managers, stockholders, and policyholders. The manner in which the literature has treated these three claimants is to view the managers as the agents of the stockholders, while the stockholders are typically viewed as the agents of the policyholders (e.g., see Mayers and Smith [1981]). In the case of the mutual company, the ownership/riskbearing function and the customer/policyholder function are carried out by policyholders. Therefore, the principal/agent relationship that is of interest is that which exists between policyholders and managers.

Regardless of whether the writing and enforcing of contracts is costly or costless, the agency theoretic perspective of the firm gives rise to a set of logically consistent decision rules. In a recent paper, Fama and Jensen [1985] analyze investment decision rules for different types of business organizations that are distinguished by the characteristics of their residual claims. While their analysis focuses on investment decisions, the rules that are implied are applicable to all decisions. Their analysis indicates that decision rules for publicly traded stock corporations and financial mutuals are most logically modeled by the market value, or maximum wealth rule. For the stock corporation whose residual claimholder is the stockholder, and the financial mutual whose residual claimholder is the customer, this implies that these claimants are best served by decisions which maximize the current market value of their wealth. The proof given by Fama and Jensen for stock corporations is rather simple and intuitively appealing: when prices reflect available information and stocks are traded without transactions costs in a perfectly competitive market, the consumption streams that can be realized in future periods are only constrained by current wealth. In this situation, it is fairly easy to show that stockholders will agree that all decisions, including investments with payoffs in future periods, should be evaluated according to their contribution to the current market value of their residual claims, defined as including all costs, even agency costs and bankruptcy costs. When the stream of payoffs implied by the market value rule does not correspond to any given investor's optimal consumption stream, the capital market can be used to exchange residual claims of one firm for those of another with the same market value but with a stream of payoffs which better match the investor's desired consumption stream.[8] Similarly, Fama and Jensen's analysis demonstrates that since financial mutuals repackage already available securities, the residual claimants of these organizations will also agree that the market value rule best serves their interests.

One can quarrel with the perfect market assumptions that are needed to show that residual claimants of both stock and mutual insurance companies prefer the market value rule as the criterion upon which investment, underwriting, and dividend decisions are to be judged.[9] However, at least the market value rule is logically consistent with the underlying economic relationships which make up the firm. This cannot, for the reasons cited earlier, be claimed for the types of decision rules we often see used in the insurance solvency literature.

## III. The Optimal Capital Decision for an Insurance Firm

### A. Case 1: *Perfect Markets, No Risk of Default*

Next, we formalize the arguments advanced in the previous section of the paper, our purpose being to demonstrate the determinants of the insurer's capital decision in an unregulated market. To do this, we employ a two-date model in which the activities of the insurance firm can be characterized as follows.[10] At the beginning of the period, the firm is formed for the purpose of maximizing the value of its shares. For simplicity, we assume that the firm underwrites only one line of insurance for which it receives premium income $P_o$.[11] Paid-in equity capital ($S_o$) and premium income are allocated to an investment portfolio comprised of financial assets. At the end of the period, the firm's cash flows from its investment and underwriting activities are realized.

Initially, we consider the case of perfect insurance and capital markets in the absence of default risk and taxes. Under the same set of assumptions, Hill [1979], Fairley [1979], and Kraus and Ross [1982] show that the supply curve for insurance is perfectly elastic. Consequently, stockholders receive fair returns on their invested capital, which implies that the market value of equity subsequent to the formation of the firm ($V_e$) will be the same as its initial paid-in capital; i.e., $V_e = S_o$.

In order to derive an expression for premium income, we must first value the equity of the firm. To do this, we employ the certainty-equivalent formulation of the Sharpe [1964]-Lintner [1965]-Mossin [1966] Capital Asset Pricing Model (CAPM). This allows us to express equity value as simply the discounted value of the certainty-equivalent terminal cash flow:

$$V_e = R_f^{-1}\int_{-\infty}^{\infty} Y_e f'(Y_e)dY_e$$

$$= R_f^{-1}E(Y_e), \tag{1}$$

where

$Y_e$ = cash flow accruing to stockholders at the end of the period;
$R_f$ = $1+r_f$, where $r_f$ is the riskless interest rate;
$f'(Y_e)$ = "risk neutral" normal density function;[12]
$E'(Y_e)$ = the certainty-equivalent expectation of $Y_e$
$= E(Y_e) - \lambda COV(Y_e, r_m)$;
$\lambda$ = the market price of risk
$= [E(r_m) - r_f]/\sigma^2_m$;
$E(r_m)$ = the expected return on the market portfolio;
$\sigma^2_m$ = the variance of returns on the market portfolio;
$COV(\cdot)$ = the covariance operator.

The certainty-equivalent expectation of terminal cash flow accruing to stockholders is given by equation (2):

$$E'(Y_e) = (S_o + P_o)(1 + E'(r_i)) - E'(L), \tag{2}$$

where

$E'(r_i)$ = the certainty-equivalent expectation of the rate of return on the insurer's investment portfolio
$= E(r_i) - \lambda COV(r_i, r_m) = r_f$;
$E'(L)$ = certainty-equivalent expectation of total claims costs
$= E(L) - \lambda COV(L, r_m)$.

By substituting the right-hand side of equation (2) into equation (1), setting $S_o$ equal to $V_e$, and simplifying, we derive the following analytic expressions for premium income and the rate of return on underwriting:

$$P_o = \frac{E(L)}{(1 - E(r_u))}, \tag{3}$$

where

$$E(r_u) = [P_o - E(L)]/P_o$$
$$= -r_f + \lambda COV(r_u, r_m). \tag{3a}$$

Equation (3) demonstrates that competitively priced insurance policies resemble pure discount bonds with a terminal value of E(L) and rate of return of $-E(r_u)$. This rate of return is the same as the so-called "fair" underwriting profit rate derived by Hill and Fairley. Furthermore, competitive insurance premiums are independent of the amount of equity capital employed by the insurer. This result is obvious since the value of equity does not enter anywhere into the formula. Consequently, the insurer's premium-capital ratio is a matter of indifference to both the firm's policyholders and stockholders, since both pay fair, competitively determined prices for their claims. This result is analogous to Modigliani and Miller's [1958] capital structure irrelevance theorem which states that the total market value of the firm is independent of the manner in which its claims are "packaged".

*B. Case 2: The Effect of Corporate Taxation*

Next, we extend our analysis to a consideration of the effect of corporate taxation. The tax treatment of underwriting income (losses) is fairly straightforward; for every dollar of income (losses), a tax liability (shield) of $\$\tau$ is realized, where $\tau$ is the statutory corporate income tax rate. The tax treatment of investment income is more complicated due to the fact that the effective tax rate depends critically upon the composition of the investment portfolio. For simplicity, we assume that every dollar of investment income (loss) generates a tax liability (shield) of $\$\theta\tau$.[13] Furthermore, we assume initially that all tax shields generated by investment or underwriting losses are fully utilized. Under these assumptions concerning taxation, the certainty-equivalent expectation of terminal cash flow is given as follows:

$$E'(Y_e) = S_o + (1-\theta\tau)E'(r_i)(S_o + P_o) + (1-\tau)(P_o - E'(L)). \quad (4)$$

By substituting the right-hand side of equation (4) into equation (1), setting $S_o$ equal to $V_e$, and simplifying, we derive the following analytic expressions for premium income and the rate of return on underwriting:

$$P_o = \frac{E(L)}{(1 - E(r_u))}, \quad (5)$$

where

$$\begin{aligned} E(r_u) &= [P_o - E(L)]/P_o \\ &= -\frac{(1-\theta\tau)}{(1-\tau)}r_f + (V_e/P_o)\frac{\theta\tau}{(1-\tau)}r_f + \lambda COV(r_u, r_m). \end{aligned} \quad (5a)$$

The rate of return on underwriting given in equation (5a) is comparable to the expression derived by Hill and Modigliani [1986]. This equation demonstrates that corporate taxation has two opposite effects on the underwriting rate of return: 1) to the extent that $\theta$ is less than unity, tax shield benefits from the firm's investment and underwriting activities flow through to policyholders in the guise of a higher rate of return on their default-free "loans"; i.e., $[(1-\theta\tau)/(1-\tau)]r_f > r_f$ if $\theta < 1.0$, and 2) corporate taxation simultaneously imposes an expected tax burden on stockholders of $(V_e/P_o)[\theta\tau/(1-\tau)]r_f$ per dollar of premiums written which results in a lowering of the overall rate of return. Although equation (5) implies a price for insurance that is greater than its price in a tax-free setting, firms could lower the prices they charge and hence expand their underwritings by employing near zero equity capital. Furthermore, assuming that the tax authorities do not offer rebates for unused tax shields, insurance firms face incentives to invest strictly in fully taxable securities so as to ensure that tax shields due to underwriting losses are fully utilized.[14] Hence the equilibrium which would obtain in this setting would feature an effectively tax-exempt insurance industry offering policies at underwriting rates of return that are consistent with equation (3a). However, the analysis also implies that the insurance firm should seek a nearly "all-debt" capital structure by employing a minimal amount of capital. Not surprisingly, this result is analogous to Modigliani and Miller's [1963] "correction" of their original irrelevance theorem, which holds that taxable corporations should adopt nearly all-debt capital structures due to tax incentives.

The propositions derived above have considerable appeal as logical corollaries of the Modigliani and Miller capital structure theorems. Next, we shall consider how robust these results are with respect to changes in the underlying assumptions; i.e., what are the likely effects of phenomena such as redundant tax shields, default risk, bankruptcy costs, and agency costs?

### C. *Case 3: Redundant Tax Shields*

It is well known that insurance firms are typically constrained by regulation to hold minimum levels of capital relative to premiums written, the main justification being that the probability of ruin is thereby decreased, *ceteris paribus*. However, our model demonstrates a cost associated with minimum capital requirements that is not well known; viz., minimum capital requirements increase the firm's expected tax liability and consequently the premiums it must charge so as to generate a fair return for stockholders. Competitive forces in the insurance market are therefore likely to induce firms to 1) shelter investment income by allocating greater proportions of their portfolios to the purchase of tax-exempt securities,[15] and/or 2) lower prices so as to generate underwriting losses that can be used to shelter taxable investment income. However, such strategies increase the probability that tax shields derived from the firm's investment and underwriting activities will be wasted. There exist a number of private market mechanisms which may provide solutions to the problem of redundant tax shields. One solution would be a merger with a firm that has a higher marginal tax rate. Another solution may possibly involve the purchase of reinsurance; i.e., reinsurance could conceivably be used to allocate tax shields to firms which have the greatest capacity for using them, in much the same manner as leasing companies share tax shield benefits with lessees.[16] In view of the existence of private market mechanisms such as these, tax shield redundancy *per se* does not constitute a necessary or sufficient condition for rejecting these corollaries to the Modigliani-Miller capital structure theorems.

### D. *Case 4: Default Risk and Bankruptcy Costs*

Doherty [1986] has shown that if the insurance market is competitive and information concerning default risk is impounded in insurance prices, then the Modigliani-Miller capital structure theorems hold even when default risk is present, so long as bankruptcy is costless. This result is consistent with results obtained by Stiglitz [1974] and Galai and Masulis [1976] for nonfinancial firms, and is implicit in the comparative statics of Doherty and Garven's [1986] contingent claims model for pricing property-liability insurance. However, numerous scholars have demonstrated that costly bankruptcy invalidates these theorems. In the insurance literature, Munch and Smallwood and Finsinger and Pauly discuss the impact of bankruptcy-type costs upon capital structure decisions of limited liability insurers. Although not without merit, their results are largely driven by the assumption that insurance prices do not impound information about default risk. In view of the fact that the industry is characterized by a substantial amount of investment in information production activities (e.g., agents and brokers provide consumers with price and quality information, while A. M. Best rates the financial condition of insurance companies) it would be surprising if prices did not impound such information.

To date, there does not exist a complete treatment of insurer capital structure decision making in a world in which premiums are sensitive to default risk and bankruptcy is costly. However, this is not the case in the capital structure literature for nonfinancial firms and banks. A number of studies (e.g., see Kraus and Litzenberger [1973]; Scott [1976]; Kim [1978]; Turnbull [1979]; DeAngelo and Masulis [1980]) conclude that limited liability nonfinancial firms will employ positive levels of equity so as to balance the marginal benefits of debt-related tax shields against the marginal costs of explicit bankruptcy penalties (e.g., administrative expenses that must be paid to third parties such as lawyers and accountants). Similarly, Buser, Chen and Kane [1981] show that limited liability banking firms would, in the absence of deposit insurance, select capital structures which match the marginal value of debt (deposit) related tax shields with the marginal value of bankruptcy costs. Although we would expect similar results to obtain in a unregulated insurance market in which prices are default risk sensitive, we believe that this tax-shield/bankruptcy cost trade-off theory is largely invalidated in the case of the insurance industry due to the wide-spread existence of post-insolvency assessment insurance guaranty funds.[17] The existence of these funds eliminates or greatly reduces the risk that claims will not be paid.[18] Furthermore, the funding arrangements upon which these guarantee funds are based ensure that bankruptcy costs are largely borne *ex post* by surviving firms. Since insurers do not have to bear these costs *ex ante*, our analysis predicts that firms will employ as much leverage as possible.[19]

Interestingly, casual empirical evidence does not provide very strong support for these predictions. In view of the 3:1 premium-capital ratio standard used by the National Association of Insurance Commissioners (NAIC), we would expect to observe a clustering of premium-capital ratios around this standard. Table 1 records frequency distributions of premium-capital ratios for all A.M. Best rated stock insurance firms and groups having U. S. property-casualty income and complete data on premium-capital ratios during the five year period beginning in 1981 and ending in 1985.

It appears from these data that, while the NAIC 3:1 guideline in fact represents an industry standard for maximum leverage, it is nowhere close to being a binding constraint for most firms. Indeed, with transaction costs we would expect firms to operate within the constraint so as to enable them to absorb fluctuations in premium-capital ratios without violating the constraint and thereby necessitating the frequent issuance of new equity, purchase of reinsurance, or scaling back of the volume of new business. However, since 1) both frequency distributions are so significantly skewed toward very low (less than unity) premium-capital ratios, and 2) only a small minority of firms have had premium-capital ratios which exceed the NAIC standard, the facts seem to suggest that there are yet other important factors which need to be taken into account. We believe that a very important missing piece to this puzzle is agency costs.

*E. Case 5: Agency Costs*

As we stated earlier, agency costs arise when both parties to the agency relationship are self-interested and it is costly to write and

**Table 1**

**Premium-Capital Ratios of U.S. Stock Insurance Firms and Groups**

| $P_0/S_0$ Range | *Percentage of Sample having $P_0/S_0$ Ratio Within Range* 1985 | 1981-1985 |
|---|---|---|
| Less than unity | 31.0% | 33.2% |
| 1.0 to 1.5 | 15.0 | 17.3 |
| 1.5 to 2.0 | 15.8 | 18.4 |
| 2.0 to 2.5 | 13.7 | 13.5 |
| 2.5 to 3.0 | 13.1 | 9.6 |
| Exceeding 3.0 | 11.4 | 8.0 |
| **Mean** | 1.82 | 1.62 |
| **Standard Deviation** | 1.63 | 1.42 |

Sample: All A.M. Best rated stock insurance firms and groups having 1) U.S. property-casualty income, and 2) complete data on premium-capital ratios. Sample size 1040 (1985), 888 (1981-1985).
Source: A.M. Best Key Rating Guide, 1981-1985.

enforce the contracts which define this relationship. The preceding analysis assumed contracting to be costless; we now relax this assumption and assume that contracting is in fact costly. Enforcement costs include the costs borne by principals to monitor contract compliance and costs borne by agents to bond their behavior. Although principal and agent have divergent interests, they will seek to write and enforce contracts which minimize agency costs, since one or both can thereby be made better off. However, this also implies that it will generally be unlikely that contracts will be perfectly enforced, since the monitoring and bonding expenditures required to ensure perfect compliance may exceed the benefits. Jensen and Meckling [1976] define the opportunity loss that remains when contracts are optimally but imperfectly enforced as the residual loss.

Fama and Jensen [1983b] argue that if contracting is costly, then the firm's contract structure will have an important effect on its cost function. Therefore, the organizational form adopted by any given insurer will be determined endogenously, along with its investment, underwriting, and dividend policies. Indeed, this is the basic theme of the series of papers by Mayers and Smith [1981, 1982b, 1987] which seek to produce an internally consistent, interrelated set of potentially testable hypotheses regarding organizational forms and contractual practices in the insurance industry. Their work suggests that there are incentive conflicts between policyholders and stockholders over investment, underwriting, and dividend decisions and between owners and managers over investment policy. Next, we will summarize their results and attempt to relate these considerations to the relationship between solvency and the choice of an optimal capital structure.

*1. Stockholder/Policyholder Conflicts*

Incentive conflicts exist between principals and agents whenever agents do not bear the full wealth effects of their actions. Furthermore, the mere existence of default risk exacerbates incentive conflicts. This can be easily seen by considering the stockholder/policyholder relationship for a riskless insurer. If the claims held by policyholders are free of default risk, there will be no incentive conflict, since the value of these claims will not change as a result of investment, underwriting, and dividend decisions made on behalf of stockholders. Next, consider the stockholder/policyholder relationship for a risky insurer. Like lenders in the bond market, the risky insurer's policyholders will experience incentive conflicts with stockholders because stockholders may be able to effect wealth transfers from policyholders by altering the insurer's investment, underwriting or dividend policies after issuing insurance.[20] However, since policyholders recognize the incentives faced by stockholders, the prices they are willing to pay for the policies will reflect unbiased estimates of the expected behavior of stockholders. Furthermore, the greater the premium-capital ratio employed by the firm, the greater will be the magnitude of agency costs borne by stockholders in the guise of lower premiums.[21] It is therefore in the self-interest of the stockholders to provide policyholders with guarantees against expropriative behavior if such guarantees are less costly than the agency problems. Several mechanisms exist for providing guarantees, such as purchasing reinsurance, employing positive levels of equity, or contractually limiting dividend and investment policies. The use of equity as a bonding mechanism has been suggested by Easterbrook and Fischel [1985], while the use of contractual limitations of dividend and investment policy as bonding mechanisms has been suggested by Mayers and Smith [1981].

Besides the risk incentive effect described above, other explanations exist for why insurers may choose to employ positive levels of capital and/or purchase reinsurance contracts. To see this, consider Mayers and Smith's [1982b] explanations for both the individual and corporate demands for insurance. In the case of the individual demand for insurance, they contend that the most fundamental reason why insurance services are produced is because an unfilled demand for risk reduction would otherwise exist. A sufficient, although not necessary condition for the need for further risk reduction is the existence of nonmarketable assets such as human capital. Another important reason for the existence of insurance services which is relevant to both individual and corporate demands relates to the manner in which insurance contracts help to bring about socially efficient levels of investment in monitoring and bonding activities. Finally, they note that insurance contracts are likely to be valuable to both individuals and corporations because insurance companies provide real service efficiencies in the production of claims administration activities. Therefore, to the extent that the bankruptcy of an insurer would impose additional costs upon policyholders due to the cessation of these services, then it would be reasonable to view mechanisms such as the employment of positive levels of capital and/or purchase of reinsurance as rational responses to policyholders' demands for "safe" policies. Following Titman [1984], such mechanisms may provide methods by which insurers can bond, or precommit itself from imposing costs of this nature upon policyholders. Interestingly, these results obtain even in a world where policyholders are otherwise well diversified.

The introduction of insurance guaranty funds eliminates or at least greatly reduces the risk that claims will not be paid and therefore mitigates the incentive conflicts between stockholders and policyholders. Hence consumers will not penalize risky firms by paying lower prices; neither will it be in their interest to produce information regarding the financial viability of the insurer, since they no longer bear the wealth effects associated with failing to engage in such behavior. Furthermore, the decision to guarantee payoffs on insurance policies makes regulatory supervision of insurance firms inevitable. In the case of insurance regulation, the protections which actually exist resemble the kinds of protections that we described above.[22] While the above analysis applies to insurance firms whose liabilities are insured by a guaranty fund, many of the same notions are also applicable to insured banks and thrift institutions.

2. *Owner/Manager Conflicts*

An alternative mechanism for resolving stockholder/policyholder incentive conflicts involves merging the two functions; viz., by imposing a mutual ownership structure. Mayers and Smith's analysis suggests that this advantage of the mutual ownership structure is offset by a worsened incentive problem between owners and managers. While stockholders can rely upon the threat of an unfriendly takeover to discipline managers, the policyholders of the mutual insurer must rely upon a less effective and more expensive mechanism, the proxy fight. Since it is more costly to control managerial behavior in a mutual than it is in a stock firm, the Mayers/Smith and Fama/Jensen analyses predict that the investment and underwriting activities of mutual insurers will be characterized by the placement of substantial limitations upon discretionary managerial behavior. Specifically, mutual insurers will tend to underwrite fewer lines of insurance than stock insurers, and they will tend to be more prevalent than stock companies in lines of insurance for which "good" actuarial tables exist, since this will give managers less discretion in the rate-setting process. Furthermore, mutual insurers' investments will tend to be more concentrated than stock insurers' investments in assets for which accurate indices of value are available; i.e., mutuals will hold larger proportions of their investment portfolios in financial assets and smaller proportions in nonfinancial assets than will stock insurers. Casual empirical evidence provided by Fama and Jensen [1983a] bear this latter prediction out.

While the introduction of insurance guaranty funds is likely to mitigate stockholder/policyholder incentive conflicts, these funds do not provide managers with any contractual guarantees. In fact, depending upon the manner in which management is compensated, the guaranty funds may provide managers with a rather perverse set of incentives. Consider the case of a stock insurer which weights its managerial compensation schedule rather heavily toward stock options. Since the value of management's claims will increase the greater the premium-capital ratio, we can expect that such a firm will tend to be highly levered, everything else the same. On the other hand, if the compensation schedule is tilted more toward a fixed salary, we would expect managers to select lower premium-capital ratios so as to provide themselves with greater employment security. Since mutual insurers are precluded by virtue of their ownership structure from compensating their executives with stock options, we might expect mutual insurers to employ lower premium-capital ratios than stock insurers, *ceteris paribus*.[23] However, even if the managers of stock insurance firms receive a substantial proportion of their compensation via stock options, it is not clear whether this prediction would hold either in the absence of a guaranty fund or in the presence of a guaranty fund which charges risk-based premiums.

## IV. Conclusion

This paper has set forth the argument that the theory of finance can and should be rigorously applied to the study of the insurance firm. In order to illustrate this point, we turned our attention to the insurance solvency literature. Perhaps the most important insight provided in this paper is the prediction that, even in an unregulated market, insurers would voluntarily limit their premium-capital ratios in an effort to economize on contracting costs. Our analysis also suggests that mutual insurers are likely to be less highly levered, *ceteris paribus*, than insurers organized as stock corporations.

The issue of solvency and how the insurer's capital decision relates to it constitutes a fertile area for future research. Definitive answers are needed for a number of questions. We list some of the more obvious unresolved issues that are related to this topic:

1. Our analysis primarily considered the capital decisions of stock and mutual insurers. Given the diverse set of organizational forms that we observe in the insurance industry, it would be useful to not only sharpen the focus of the present analysis, but also to extend it to the cases of reciprocal associations and Lloyd's associations. Also, empirical work investigating the relationship between capital structure choices and organizational form is very much in order.[24]

2. How managers of insurance firms are compensated is obviously an empirical issue worth investigating. In particular, it would be interesting to investigate 1) whether any cross-sectional regularities exist in managerial compensation contract design across organizational forms, 2) how effective compensation contracts are in controlling owner-manager incentive conflicts, and 3) the extent to which compensation

contracts influence insurers' capital decisions.[25]

3. Another important area for further research concerns optimal guaranty fund design. Since most funds are operated on a post-insolvency assessment basis, firms have incentives under the current system to pursue more risky underwriting and investment strategies than they would otherwise undertake in the absence of such a guaranty fund.[26]

The reader may have noticed that once we strayed from the perfect market models in the third section of the paper, the remainder of the analysis was largely non-mathematical. The financial theory of agency constitutes such a radical departure from the perfect market models that a great deal of work remains to be done in terms of defining the dimensionality of the issues discussed here before mathematics can be fruitfully applied.[27] A more robust theory of market equilibrium is clearly needed in which interactions between markets in which the firm competes can be adequately modeled.[28] We believe that the more integrated view of the insurer provided by such a theory would very likely produce sharper insights than the collective risk and expected utility models since it would provide the basis for analyzing insurance company behavior in the context of a much richer economic environment.

## Notes

1. Mayers and Smith [1982a, p. 253] note that the topic of insurance is nowhere to be found in virtually all finance textbooks.

2. Stigler [1975, pp. 109-110] goes as far as to suggest that the historical rationale for the regulation of insurance companies was rooted in the belief that consumers of insurance needed protection because they would not, of their own volition, acquire a proper amount of information, even if it were available for sale at its cost of production. According to this view, the problem faced by consumers in making their insurance decisions is not necessarily costly or imperfect information; rather, it is one of irrationality manifested in the form of an underinvestment in information. Of course, such a belief about consumer behavior begs the obvious question: if consumers are so irrational, why do they purchase insurance in the first place?

3. In fact, risk theory is perhaps most noted for its important contributions to theoretical statistics. Borch [1974, p. 73] suggests that "These by-products are probably of greater value than the theory itself, which has found few applications in practice."

4. This emphasis on survival pervades the insurance literature. For example, in his critique of the risk management literature, Doherty [1983] notes that the traditional risk management structure is based in part upon the notion that survival is a major corporate objective. As we shall soon see, survival as a corporate objective is dominated by the market value rule, which treats the probability of ruin as endogenous to the more general problem of maximizing the value of the claims held by the firm's residual claimholders.

5. For examples of such approaches, see Cummins and Nye [1981, pp. 418-419].

6. Of course, all of this is a moot point in a world in which the writing and enforcing of contracts is not costly. In such a world, the firm's contract structure would have no effect on its cost function. Therefore, there would be no reason for one organizational form to dominate any other in the production of goods and services. This result obtains as a logical corollary of Coase's [1960] theorem, which asserts that there can be no misallocation of resources in the absence of transaction costs.

7. Following Fama and Jensen [1983b, p. 302], we define residual claims as claims to the net difference between stochastic inflows of resources and promised payments to agents.

8. For a more detailed elaboration of this proof, see Fama [1978].

9. The assumption of a perfect markets framework does raise an interesting conundrum. Borrowing from Miller [1977, p. 273], if markets are perfect, then financial firms can best be described as "neutral

mutations"; viz., while they serve no unique economic function, neither do they do any harm. Therefore, a major challenge facing researchers in the field of financial intermediation relates to producing models of market equilibrium in which the existence of intermediaries is endogenous. An excellent example of this type of research which relates to depository financial intermediaries is the recent paper by Sealey [1983]. In the spirit of Sealey's work, Doherty [1986] argues that the issue of insurance policies by an insurance firm is simultaneously an operating and a financing decision. This inherent simultaneity of operating and financing decisions consequently raises questions concerning the applicability of capital structure theories that are based upon perfect market assumptions. Doherty contends that such theories cannot apply to insurance firms unless the insurance market is competitive and information concerning default risk is impounded in insurance prices.

10. The analysis that follows is largely adapted from Doherty and Garven [1986] and Garven [1987]. We analyze optimal capital structure decisions of insurance firms in a world characterized by the existence of perfectly competitive markets for the equity and liability claims they issue. As we suggested in footnote 7, there is no *a priori* reason to believe that the same basic results would not also generalize to an insurer that is organized as a mutual company, given the nature of the assumed economic environment (i.e., no transaction costs or information costs). If the reader finds such a statement to be rather unsettling, the fact that we observe both stock and mutual firms competing successfully with each other in common insurance lines would seem to suggest that this is a reasonable assertion, even in the presence of transaction costs and information costs.

11. For simplicity of notation, we assume that either there are no transaction costs associated with writing policies, or that premium income $P_0$ is defined net of such expenses.

12. A "risk neutral" density function is a density function whose location parameter is chosen so that the mean of the distribution is its certainty-equivalent.

13. The parameter $\theta$ is a factor of proportionality defined over the interval [0,1]. This parameter is functionally related to the composition of the insurer's investment portfolio. For example, if the investment portfolio is comprised of strictly tax-exempt securities, then $\theta = 0$. Conversely, if only fully taxable claims such as corporate bonds and U.S. Treasury securities are chosen, then $\theta = 1$. If some combination of tax-exempt and taxable claims are chosen, then $0 < \theta < 1$.

14. The above assertions are easily supported. First, we divide equation (5) through by E(L) to obtain a price of

$$P_0/E(L) = \left[1 + \frac{(1-\theta\tau)}{(1-\tau)} r_f - (V_e/P_0)\frac{\theta\tau}{(1-\tau)} r_f - \lambda COV(r_u, r_m)\right]^{-1}$$

per dollar of coverage. Taking the limit of this expression as the market value of equity tends toward zero, we obtain

$$\lim_{V_e \to 0} P_0/E(L) = \left[1 + \frac{(1-\theta\tau)}{(1-\tau)} r_f - \lambda COV(r_u, r_m)\right]^{-1}.$$

However, in the absence of tax rebates from the government or a market for unused tax shields, insurers choose $\theta = 1$; therefore, the insurance price which obtains in a competitive equilibrium is the same as in the no-tax case; viz.,

$$P_o/E(L) = \left[1 + r_f - \lambda COV(r_u, r_m)\right]^{-1}.$$

15. It is well known that, apart from households, the principal investors in the market for tax-exempt bonds are commercial banks and property-liability insurance companies. As noted by Hill [p. 181], the fact that tax-exempt bonds typically constitute anywhere from 15 percent to 50 percent of the portfolios of large stock insurers suggests that the tax burden associated with minimum capital requirements is non-trivial.

16. Although reinsurance is not commonly viewed as a leasing arrangement as we have suggested here, Main [1983] has used the leasing analogy to analyze insurance purchases by nonfinancial corporations. Also, a number of other potentially testable hypotheses exist for explaining reinsurance purchases by insurance firms. For example, Doherty and Tinic [1981] note that reinsurance can also be used to release reserve funds which can provide a basis for further premium expansion without violating minimum capital requirements. This may be especially important to mutual insurers who lack direct access to the capital markets. Mayers and Smith [1981] motivate the demand for reinsurance largely on the basis of the so-called costly contracting hypothesis; viz., policyholders may prefer to contract for insurance with one carrier and have the insurer reinsure through established channels rather than hold a diversified portfolio of insurance contracts without reinsurance for the simple reason that such an arrangement economizes on contracting costs.

17. For a comprehensive appraisal of post-insolvency assessment guaranty funds, see the recent paper by Duncan [1984].

18. As Cummins [1986, p. 2, fn. 2] points out, guarantee funds may not in fact accomplish this in practice. For example, the actual payment of claims may be delayed while the liabilities of the insolvent insurer are transferred to the guarantor. Furthermore, most guaranty funds impose maximum limits upon payments per claim; hence policyholders with large claims may not be fully compensated. Similar caveats would also apply to guaranty arrangements such as those found in the banking industry. For example, the FDIC and FSLIC limit guarantees to deposits of $100,000 and less.

19. Although there has (justifiably) been considerable criticism in the banking literature of the flat premium system used by both the FDIC and FSLIC (e.g., see Kane [1986]), at least banks and thrift institutions are required to bear *some* of the cost of the insurance *ex ante*. For example, the FDIC currently charges a flat, up front premium of 1/12 percent of the dollar amount of the deposits of insured banks. However, the FDIC guaranty arrangement is not without its similarities to the post-insolvency assessment insurance guaranty arrangements. The similarity comes into play by virtue of the FDIC's *ex post* rebate policy in which 60% of the difference between the FDIC's revenue and expenses is subsequently rebated to member banks.

20. The logic underlying these propositions can be formally demonstrated by invoking the comparative statics of the option pricing model. Black and Scholes [1973] suggest that the equity of a levered firm can be valued as a call option on the terminal value of its assets, with an

exercise price equal to the face value of its debt. Galai and Masulis [1976] make use of this insight in order to show how the value of the equity of a nonfinancial firm varies with respect to changes in its asset and liability structures. By analogy, Doherty and Garven [1986] show that the equity of a stock insurance firm can be characterized as a call option on the terminal value of its assets, with an exercise price equal to its terminal claims costs. The value of this call option will increase (accompanied by a corresponding decrease in the value of policyholders' claims) with 1) increases in the riskiness of the insurer's assets, 2) increases in its dividend payments, and 3) increases (decreases) in the riskiness of its liabilities, assuming that the insurer's claims costs and investment income are positively (negatively) correlated.

21. As Jensen and Meckling [1976] show, the agency costs of debt (and by analogy, insurance policies) are a monotonically increasing function of the firm's leverage (premium-capital) ratio. The reason for this is quite simple; as the total amount of debt financing (premium volume) increases relative to equity financing, it becomes progressively easier for stockholders to expropriate larger amounts of wealth from bondholders (policyholders) by altering the firm's policies after issuing the bonds (insurance policies). The logic of this proposition can also be shown via comparative static relationships derived from the option pricing model.

22. However, we have no guarantee that the regulator will engage in an socially optimal level of monitoring, since as an employee of the state the regulator does not bear the full wealth effects of his or her edicts. Quoting Stigler [1975, p. 113], "We may tell the society to jump out of the market frying pan, but we have no basis for predicting whether it will land in the fire or a luxurious bed."

23. Since mutual insurers lack direct access to the capital markets, we may also expect mutual insurers to hold more surplus as a way to ensure that they don't violate the NAIC standard. However, like stock companies, mutuals can use other mechanisms such as reinsurance to accomplish the same objective.

24. Given the diversity of organizational forms within the insurance industry, it may provide empirical researchers as well as theorists with a laboratory setting for testing some fundamental results in capital structure theory. For example, Jensen and Meckling [1976, p. 347] contend that optimal capital structure decisions involve trading off the agency costs of debt against the agency costs associated with outside equity. The fact that Lloyds associations preclude themselves by virtue of their organizational form from issuing outside equity is certain to have significant capital structure implications.

25. A substantial literature has developed in the accounting and finance journals over the three to four years concerning the relationship between managerial compensation contracts and decision making. Lambert and Larcker [1985] review this literature and conclude that compensation schemes really do "matter" in the sense that executives respond predictably to the incentives built into their compensation contracts. Furthermore, they note that changes in contract design affect executive decision-making in ways consistent with agency theory. Given the diversity of organizational forms within the insurance

industry, the use of insurance data may be very helpful in producing useful contributions to this literature as well as the capital structure literature. Obviously, such results may also have potentially important regulatory policy implications.

26. Cummins [1986] has developed a promising approach based upon risk-based premiums. He argues that the likely effects of risk-based premiums would be to 1) eliminate the incentive for insurers to pursue risky strategies by charging them the full market value of the risk they place on the guaranty fund, and 2) reduce regulatory monitoring costs since firms would be less likely to adopt high risk strategies. Similar results are obtained for banking firms by Merton [1977], Kane [1986], and others.

27. Unfortunately, the lack of integration of capital market theory and principal-agent theory makes it difficult to provide formal mathematical analysis of the solvency issue in an equilibrium setting. Instead, one must rely upon intuitive descriptive analysis, since the dimensionality of the problem is so ill-defined. Given the current state of the financial theory of agency, Jensen [1983] suggests that the extensive use of mathematics may even be counterproductive.

28. Some noteworthy examples of this type of research include the papers by Arnott and Gersovitz [1980], Diamond and Verrechia [1982], Ramakrishnan and Thakor [1984], and Titman [1984].

## References


Arnott, R. J. and M. Gersovitz. 1980. Corporate Financial Structure and the Funding of Private Pension Plans. *Journal of Public Economics* 13(April):231-247.

Arrow, K. J. 1950. A Difficulty in the Concept of Social Welfare. *Journal of Political Economy* 58 (August):328-346.

Bachelier, M. L. 1900. *Theorie de la Speculation*. Paris: Guthier-Villars.

Borch, K. 1974. *The Mathematical Theory of Insurance*. Lexington, Massachusetts: Lexington Books.

Boyle, P. P. and J. E. Butterworth. 1982. Links Between Modern Finance and Insurance. Paper presented at the *Second Symposium on Money, Banking, and Insurance* in Karlsruhe, Germany.

Black, F. and M. Scholes. 1973. The Pricing of Options and Corporate Liabilities. *Journal of Political Economy* 81(May/June):637-659.

Buser, S. A., Chen, A. H. and E. J. Kane. 1981. Federal Deposit Insurance, Regulatory Policy, and Optimal Bank Capital. *Journal of Finance* 35(March):51-60.

Coase, R. H.. 1960. The Problem of Social Cost. *Journal of Law and Economics* 3(October):1-44.

Cummins, J. D. 1986. Risk Based Premiums for Insurance Guaranty Funds. Paper presented at the *First International Conference of Insurance Solvency*.

Cummins, J. D. and D. J. Nye. 1981. Portfolio Optimization Models for Property-Liability Insurance Companies: An Analysis and Some Extensions. *Management Science* 27(April):414-430.

DeAngelo, H. and R. W. Masulis. 1980. Optimal Capital Structure under Corporate and Personal Taxation. *Journal of Financial Economics* 8(March):3-29.

Diamond, D. and R. Verrechia. 1982. Optimal Managerial Contracts and Equilibrium Security Prices. *Journal of Finance* 37(May):275-288.

Doherty, N. A. 1986. On the Capital Structure of Insurance Firms. Paper presented at the *First International Conference of Insurance Solvency*.

Doherty, N. A. 1983. Risk Management - A Financial Critique and an Alternative Structure. Discussion Paper for the *Geneva Association*.

Doherty, N. A., and J. R. Garven. 1986. Price Regulation in Property-Liability Insurance: A Contingent Claims Approach. *Journal of Finance* 41(December):1031-1050.

Doherty, N. A. and S. M. Tinic. 1981. Reinsurance under Conditions of Capital Market Equilibrium: A Note. *Journal of Finance* 36(September): 949-953.

Duncan, M. 1984. An Appraisal of Property and Casualty Post-Assessment Guaranty Funds. *Journal of Insurance Regulation* 2(March):289-303.

Easterbrook, F. H. and D. R. Fischel. 1985. Limited Liability and the Corporation. *The University of Chicago Law Review* 52(Winter):89-117.

Fairley, W. 1979. Investment Income and Profit Margins in Property-Liability Insurance: Theory and Empirical Results. *Bell Journal of Economics* 10(Spring):172-191.

Fama, E. F. 1978. The Effects of a Firm's Investment and Financing Decisions on the Welfare of its Security Holders. *American Economic Review* 68(June):272-284.

Fama, E. F. and M. C. Jensen. 1983a. Agency Problems and Residual Claims. *Journal of Law and Economics* 26(June):327-349.

Fama, E. F. and M. C. Jensen. 1985. Organizational Forms and Investment Decisions. *Journal of Financial Economics* 14(March):101-119.

Fama, E. F. and M. C. Jensen. 1983b. Separation of Ownership and Control. *Journal of Law and Economics* 26(June):301-325.

Finsinger, J. and M. Pauly. 1984. Reserve Levels and the Reserve Requirements for Profit Maximizing Insurance Firms. *Risk and Capital* (G. Bamberg and K. Spremann, editors). Berlin-Heidelberg: Springer-Verlag.

Galai, D. and R. W. Masulis. 1976. The Option Pricing Model and the Risk Factor of Stock. *Journal of Financial Economics* 3(January/March):53-81.

Garven, J. R. 1987. Capital Structure and Financial Intermediation: The Case of Reinsurance. Working Paper, The Pennsylvania State University, University Park, PA, U.S.A.

Hill, R. 1979. Profit Regulation in Property-Liability Insurance. *Bell Journal of Economics* 10(Spring):172-191.

Hill, R. and F. Modigliani. 1986. The Massachusetts Model of Profit Regulation in Non-Life Insurance: An Appraisal and Extensions. *Fair Rate of Return in Property-Liability Insurance* (Cummins, D. and S. Harrington, editors). Higham, MA: Kluwer-Nijhoff.

Jensen, M. C. 1983. Organization Theory and Methodology. *The Accounting Review* 58(April):319-339.

Jensen, M. C. and W. H. Meckling. 1976. Theory of the Firm: Managerial Behavior, Agency Costs, and Ownership Structure. *Journal of Financial Economics* 3(October):305-360.

Kane, E. J. 1986. Appearance and Reality in Deposit Insurance. *Journal of Banking and Finance* 10(June):175-188.

Kim, E. H. 1978. A Mean-Variance Theory of Optimal Capital Structure and Corporate Debt Capacity. *Journal of Finance* 33(March):45-63.

Kraus, A. and R. Litzenberger. 1973. A State-Preference Model of Optimal Financial Leverage," *Journal of Finance* 28(September):911-922.

Kraus, A. and S. Ross. 1982. The Determination of Fair Profits for the Property-Liability Insurance Firm. *Journal of Finance* 37(September): 1015-1028.

Lambert, R. A. and D. F. Larcker. 1985. Executive Compensation, Corporate Decision-Making, and Shareholder Wealth: A Review of the Evidence. *Midland Corporate Finance Journal* 2(Winter):6-22.

Lintner, J. 1965. The Valuation of Risk Assets and the Selection of Risky Investments in Stock Portfolios and Capital Budgets. *Review of Economics and Statistics* 47(February):13-37.

Lundberg, F. 1909. Uber die Theorie der Ruckversicherung. *Transactions VI International Congress of Actuaries* 1:877-955.

Main, B. G. M. 1983. Corporate Insurance Purchases and Taxes. *Journal of Risk and Insurance* 50 (June):197-223.

Mayers, D. and C. W. Smith. 1981. Contractual Provisions, Organizational Structure, and Conflict Control in Insurance Markets. *Journal of Business* 54(July):407-434.

Mayers, D. and C. W. Smith. 1982a. On the Corporate Demand for Insurance. *Journal of Business* 55(April):281-296.

Mayers, D. and C. W. Smith. 1982b. Toward a Positive Theory of Insurance. Monograph 1982-1. New York: *Salomon Brothers Center for the Study of Financial Institutions*.

Mayers, D. and C. W. Smith. 1987. Ownership Structure Across Lines of Insurance. *Journal of Law and Economics* (forthcoming).

Merton, R. C. 1977. An Analytic Derivation of the Cost of Deposit Insurance and Loan Guarantees. *Journal of Banking and Finance* 1 (June):3-11.

Miller, M. H. 1977. Debt and Taxes. *Journal of Finance* 32 (May):261-275.

Modigliani, F. and M. H. Miller. 1958. The Cost of Capital, Corporation Finance and the Theory of Investment. *American Economic Review* 48(June):261-297.

Modigliani, F. and M. H. Miller. 1963. Corporate Income Taxes and the Cost of Capital: A Correction. *American Economic Review* 53(June): 433-443.

Mossin, J. 1966. Equilibrium in a Capital Asset Market. *Econometrica* 34(October):768-783.

Munch, P. and D. Smallwood. 1981. Theory of Solvency Regulation. *Studies in Public Regulation* (Gary Fromm, Editor). Cambridge, Massachusetts: MIT Press.

Ramakrishnan, R. T. S. and A. V. Thakor. 1984. The Valuation of Assets Under Moral Hazard. *Journal of Finance* 39(March):229-238.

Scott, J. 1976. A Theory of Optimal Capital Structure. *Bell Journal of Economics and Management Science* 7(Spring):33-54.

Sealey, C. W. 1983. Valuation, Capital Structure, and Shareholder Unanimity for Depository Financial Intermediaries. *Journal of Finance* 38(June):1139-1154.

Sharpe, W. F. 1964. Capital Asset Prices: A Theory of Market Equilibrium Under Conditions of Risk. *Journal of Finance* 19 (September):425-442.

Stigler, G. J. 1975. *The Citizen and the State*. Chicago: University of Chicago Press.

Stiglitz, J. 1974. On the Irrelevance of Corporate Financial Policy. *American Economic Review* 64(December):851-866.

Titman, S. 1984. The Effect of Capital Structure on a Firm's Liquidation Decision. *Journal of Financial Economics* 13(March):137-144.

Turnbull, S. M. 1979. Debt Capacity. *Journal of Finance* 34(September): 931-940.

# 9

# ON THE CAPITAL STRUCTURE OF INSURANCE FIRMS

Neil Doherty

## 1. Introduction

Following Modigliani and Miller [1958], it has been customary to address the capital structure issue on the assumption that the firm's operating decisions are predetermined and separable from its financing decisions. This convenient separation of operating and financing decisions is inappropriate for financial intermediaries. For example, Sealey [1982] points out that, for banks, the issue of deposits is simultaneously an operating and a financing decision. Similar issues arise for insurance firms. The sale of insurance policies generates the operating revenue of the insurance firm. But, although these "debt like" instruments are sold in the insurance product market (rather than in the capital market), they afford the firm a source of capital. The insurance "debt" and the equity issued by the insurer are used to construct a portfolio consisting of mostly of financial assets.

The simultaneity of operating and financing decisions for insurance firms raises questions about the relevance of standard capital structure results. As an illustration, consider the M and M irrelevance (no taxes) proposition. This result is conditioned first by the separation of the operating and financing decisions and, second, by a set of assumptions concerning the competitiveness of the capital market in which the firm's financial claims are traded. To embrace insurance firms under the theorem, further restrictive assumptions are required. Unlike non-financial firms, the insurance firms' "debt" instrument are not traded on the conventional capital markets but on the insurance product market.[1] Consequently, it is necessary to impose the same restrictions on the insurance product market as upon the capital market. To apply M and M to insurance, we must assume perfect product markets as well as perfect capital markets.

While capital structure irrelevancy can be forced upon insurance firms in this way, the additional assumptions beg too many questions. Aggressive and informationally efficient markets serve as a convenient approximation when describing capital markets. But is the same true of insurance product markets? In fact, insurance markets all too often are characterized by their informational asymmetries, which give rise to adverse selection (e.g., Ackerloff [1970], Rothschild and Stiglitz [1976] and moral hazard (e.g., Marshall [1976]). Moreover, insurance markets typically are heavily regulated though there is divergence of opinion over whether this fosters or hinders competition (see a recent survey by Harrington [1984]). These considerations indicate that the competitive structure of the insurance product market may have a big role to play in the determination of the insurance firm's capital structure.

We will examine the capital structure decision of the insurance firm and show how this is affected by the product market conditions in which the firm operates. For exposition, we focus on the property liability stock insurer. First, it is assumed that customers are unable to monitor the financial condition of the insurance firm. Subsequently, we examine the capital structure with financial monitoring showing the effects of product demand elasticities and cost functions. When time inconsistent incentives are considered, a zero surplus corner solution is shown to be opitmal.

The zero surplus capital structure leaves an open question on the existence of an insurance market. However, we then show that existing regulations may promote constrained interior optimal solutions thereby providing an explanation for the presence of insurance carriers. Finally, our model predicts that the distribution of capital structures chosen by firms will be clustered within the constraint. Cross section evidence is compatible with this prediction.

## 2. Assumptions and Basic Relationships

The required assumptions are:

(1) Capital markets are complete and in a state of competitive equilibrium. This permits use of the value maximization objective.

(2) Taxes are not considered.

(3) There are no transaction costs associated with the "ruin" of the insurance firm.

(4) There are no agency costs arising from the relationship between the owners of the insurance firm (as principals) and its managers (as agents).

(5) Contracts are presented in a simple single period framework in which all cash flows arise at the beginning or end of the contract. The firm is sold at the end of the period for its terminal market value.

(6) The insurer is a stock, rather than a mutual, firm.

(7) The terminal value of the insurer's asset portfolio is non-negative.

The insurer will be considered to be a leveraged financial intermediary. At the beginning of the period, the firm issues new equity (or inherits equity from a previous period) and insurance policies. The proceeds are used to construct an asset portfolio. At the end of the period, the value of the asset portfolio is used to discharge policyholder claims, the residual value accruing to equityholders. The opening cash flow is

$$Y_0 = E + P - X \tag{1}$$

Where E is paid in equity (or surplus in insurance terminology), P is premium income and X is the insurer's production and marketing expenses which are assumed to be incurred up front. The proceeds, net of expenses, are invested. However, the firm is subject to a regulatory constraint that, in effect, forces it to invest a certain proportion c of its opening value in assets of low risk yielding a return $r_c$. The residual proportion (1-c) may be invested without constraint yielding a risky return $r_i$. Thus the terminal value of the portfolio is

$$Y_1 = (E+P-X)\,(1+r_i) - c(P-X)(r_i-r_c) \tag{2}$$

The policyholders will receive the assessed value of losses L if $Y_1$ is sufficiently large, otherwise they will receive $Y_1$ (if positive) leaving nothing for equityholders. Thus the terminal value of the policyholders' claim may be written

$$H_1 = MIN(L,Y_1) \tag{3}$$

This payoff structure has the characteristics of a European option and we may write its present value as

$$H_0 = V(Y_1) - c(Y_1,L) \equiv V(H_1) \tag{4}$$

where $V(\cdot)$ is the present value operator and $c(Y_1,L)$ is a European call option written on $Y_1$ with striking price L. In fact, the striking price here, L, is stochastic, but this should not cause great problems.

Since we ignore taxes, the residual value of the asset portfolio accrues to equityholders. Consequently, the present value of the equity claim is

$$\begin{aligned} V(E) &= V(Y_1) - H_0 \\ &= c(Y_1,L) \end{aligned} \tag{5}$$

### 3. Capital Structure and Solvency Regulation in the Absence Monitoring

Consider that consumers cannot monitor the financial condition of the insurer. The prices consumers are willing to pay for the policies offered by different companies are insensitive to their respective choices of leverage. In this situation, it is easily shown that the optimal level of surplus E, to be held for any given premium income P, is zero. The assumed objective is that the insurer wishes to maximize the value added to its equity (surplus) contribution. i.e.,

$$\max_{E}\; V(E) - E \tag{6}$$

Since, by assumption, the capital market yields equilibrium expected returns on financial assets, it follows that

$$V(Y_1) = Y_0 = E + P - X \quad \text{since } V(1+r_i) = V(1+r_c) = 1 \tag{7}$$

Now, $dV(Y_1)/dE$ must equal unity since P is insensitive to choice of surplus by the information assumption. Any change in E will increase the value of the equity call (equation 5), since it increases the value of the underlying asset $Y_1$ on which the call is written. But with any nonzero probability that the option will expire worthless (a nonzero probability of ruin) the call cannot increase by greater value than the underlying asset.[2] Consequently

$$0 < d[c(Y_1,L)]/dE < 1$$

Using these properties and returning to the objective function (6)

$$\underset{E}{MAX}[V(E)-E] = \underset{E}{MAX}[c(Y_1,L)-E] \quad (6)$$

The derivative is negative

$$\frac{d[c(Y_1,L) - E]}{dE} < 0 \quad (8)$$

(expect in the limiting case where the probability of ruin is zero). Since the insurer cannot provide negative surplus, the value maximizing choice of E is zero. Notice also that reductions in E imply a wealth transfer from policyholders to equityholders since

$$\frac{dH_0}{dE} = \frac{dV(Y_1)}{dE} - \frac{dc(Y_1,L)}{dE} > 0 \quad (9)$$

A similar result has been derived elsewhere using a long term profit maximization objective (cf. Munch and Smallwood [1981] and Finsinger and Pauly [1984]). In fact, they also examine possible positive capital structures by postulating costs to insolvency in the form of "re-entry" cost.[3] Nevertheless, the case does illustrate the possibility for wealth expropriation by equityholders, thereby fueling the argument for leverage regulation in the interests of consumer protection.

The examination of capital structure here rests upon the absence of monitoring such that the financial condition of the insurer is not reflected in its contract prices. Given the nature of insurance markets, it would be somewhat surprising if prices did not impound some information on default probabilities. Consumers make extensive use of professional intermediaries, independent agents and brokers, who make available price/quality information. Furthermore, the market is serviced by a rating agency (A.M. best and Company) that produces ratings of financial condition, analogous to bond ratings. We now address capital structure and solvency regulation in the face of complete monitoring.

## 4. Capital Structure and Solvency with Monitorintg

### 4.1 Capital Structure When thy Firm is a Price Taker

In the presence cf perfect monitoring, the insurance premium P reflects the value of the insurance portfolio $H_0$ (equation 4) but includes a markup $p = (1-k)^{-1}$ for expenses and profit.

$$P = pH_0 = [V(Y_1) - c(Y_1,L)](1-k)^{-1} \quad (11)$$

Expenses X will be assumed to be functionally related to the market value $H_0$. Accordingly, if average costs $x = X/P$ are equal to k, the firm will not earn any excess profit, i.e., it will earn a competitive expected rate of return on equity. Such a premium would prevail in a competitive insurance market. The case of a "price taker" is defined such that the demand for insurance is perfectly elastic at the exogenously determined k. Such a value may be set either by competitive process or by regulation. The latter case permits k to diverge from x.

In examining capital structure, it is noted that leverage depends both on the choice of output and the choice of surplus. The market value of liabilities $H_0$ will be used as the output measure and, as before, the choice of surplus is E. The firm again maximizes the increase in its value of equity.

$$\underset{H_0E}{MAX}[V(E) - E] = \underset{H_0E}{MAX}[c(Y_1,L) - E] \tag{12}$$

Substituting (7) into (11) yields

$$c(Y_1,L) - E = H_0[\frac{k-x}{1-k}] \tag{13}$$

The first order conditions are

$$\frac{\partial[c(Y_1,L) - E]}{\partial H_0} = (1-k)^{-1}[k - x - H_0\frac{dx}{dH_0}] = 0 \tag{14a}$$

$$\frac{\partial[c(Y_1,L) - E]}{\partial E} = (1-k)^{-1}[k - x - H_0\frac{dx}{dH_0}] \frac{\partial H_0}{\partial E} = 0 \tag{14b}$$

Several solutions may be noted.

(a) A long run competitive solution may be attained if $k = x$ and the firm chooses output at the minimum point on the average cost curve, $dx/dH_0 = 0$. At this level of output, both conditions (14a) and (14b) are satisfied whatever the level of surplus E, since the common square bracket is zero. Thus, in a perfectly competitive market with firms producing at their least cost level of output, capital structure is irrelevant.

(b) The firm may capture rent (e.g., through regulated prices) if $k > x$. In this case, satisfaction of (14a) requires that the firm produce at an output level reflecting diseconomies of scale, $dx/dH_0 > 0$. This may be possible with a "U" shaped average cost curve. At such an output level, the square bracket in (14a) may be equated to zero which will also ensure satisfaction of (14b) whatever the choice of surplus E. In this case also, the capital structure is irrelevant if the firm selects its value maximizing level of output.

(c) Now suppose $k > x$ but the firm does not exhibit increasing returns at any output level, i.e., $dx/dH_0 \leq 0$ for all $H_0$. Conditions (14a) and (14b) cannot be satisfied (except in the trivial cases where $k = 1$ or $\partial H_0/\partial E = 0$). Thus (14a) and (14b) will both be positive since $\partial H_0/\partial E$ is positive (equation 9). The optimal output and optimal surplus both are infinite.

(d) For completeness, it should be added that if $k < x$, a zero level of surplus may be optimal. This case is not too interesting since the expected return on equity is insufficient to maintain capital to the industry and, presumably, the supply of insurance service would dry up.

### 4.2 The Choice of Capital Structure When Demand is Price Sensitive

The firm may now choose either price or output since its demand function is assumed to be downwards sloping. We will further generalize the discussion by permitting demand to be sensitive to the choice of surplus. The rationale for the latter relationship rests on the default probability. If an insurance policy is risky in the sense that it carries a non zero probability of default, it is not efficient in reducing the dispersion of wealth across states of nature. Consequently, such a policy would be less attractive to risk averse consumers than a non risky policy even if both were actuarially priced. The structure of the firms's demand function under these circumstances is examined by Doherty and Schlesinger [1986]. To formalize these relationships, we break down output $H_0$ into nominal and valuation factors

$$H_0 = m\bar{L} \tag{15}$$

where $\bar{L}$ is the face value of the insurance policies,. i.e., the expected value of claim payments in the absence of default. The term m is the average present market value of each dollar of promised expected liability undertaken by the insurer taking account of default risk. Collecting these pieces together

$$\frac{dm}{dE} > 0; \frac{\partial \bar{L}}{\partial E} > 0; \frac{\partial \bar{L}}{\partial k} < 0. \tag{16}$$

We now choose the leverage structure that maximizes the value added to the equityholders' contributed surplus. Given the demand schedule, $\bar{L} = \bar{L}(E,K)$, we an select either output or price as a decision variable. It is convenient here to choose the latter.

$$\underset{k,E}{\mathrm{MAX}}[c(Y_1,E) - E] \tag{17}$$

The first order conditions are

$$\frac{\partial[c(Y_1,E) - E]}{\partial k} = m(1-k)^{-1}[k - x - H_0\frac{dx}{dH_0}]\frac{\partial \bar{L}}{\partial k} + H_0\{\frac{1-x}{(1-k)^2}\} = 0 \tag{18a}$$

$$\frac{\partial[c(Y_1,E) - E]}{\partial E} = (1-k)^{-1}\{m\frac{\partial \bar{L}}{\partial E} + \bar{L}\frac{dm}{dE}\}[k - x - H_0\frac{dx}{dH_0}] = 0 \tag{18b}$$

The problem now arises that a simultaneous solution of (18a) and (18b) may not be found. For example, the effect of price sensitivity will be to induce the firm to restrict its output (or equivalently increase its price), such that the square bracketted term in (18a) is positive. This follows since $\partial\bar{L}/\partial k < 0$. But this condition precludes an interior solution to (18b) which requires the same square bracketted term to be zero. Thus, a possible corner solution to the capital structure problem arises with the following sequence. First, output is selected by condition (18a). This implies that (18b) will be positive. Thus, the firm selects the maximum possible (theoretically infinite) level of surplus to complement this output choice. Other possible solutions may exist; e.g., by reversing the decision sequence.

The possible capital structures described so far are illustrated in Figure 1. Depending upon whether the firm is a price taker or price maker and upon the shape of its cost function, the optimal leverage may be irrelevant (line AA) or infinite (line BB). We have ignored negative equity optimal solutions as trivial.

Now consider the implications of imposing regulatory constraints on the insurance firm's leverage. Most jurisdictions do concern themselves with the solvency of insurance firms and leverage is a major focus of regulatory attention. For the time being, we consider a very simple form of regulation; by fiat, the ratio of surplus to premiums is constrained to fall at or above a prescribed level. The constraint is shown as $E_c$ in Figure 1. Given the capital structures illustrated, it would

Figure 1
Possible capital structures with Perfect Monitoring

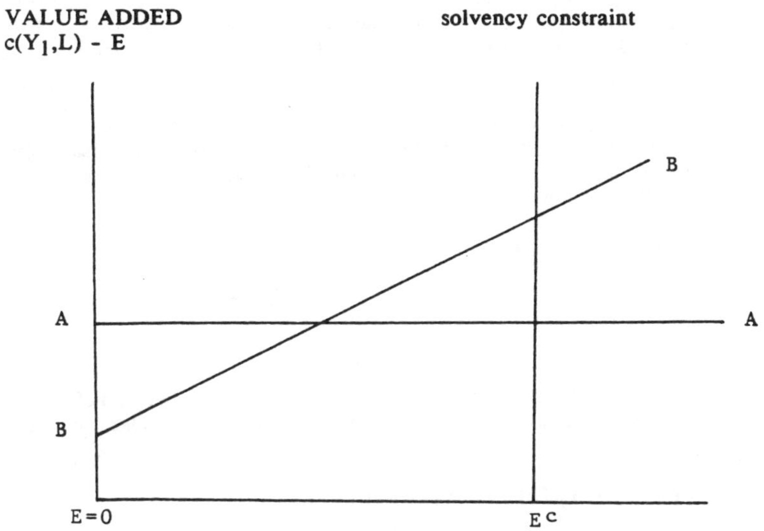


Key AA- irrelevance structures may arise for the price taking firm (a) if $k = x$ and $dx/dH_0 = 0$; or (b) if $k > x$ and $dx/dH_0$ is positive

BB- positive (infinite) leverage may arise (a) for the price taking if $dx/dH_0 \leq 0$ or (b) for the firm facing downwards sloping demand.

appear that solvency regulation is irrelevant or redundant to the insurer. With value line AA, constraints on capital structure cannot affect value since value is independent of E. With line BB, constraints on leverage are redundant since the equityholders would rationally choose levels of surplus in excess of any finite constraint such as $E_c$. Nor can we argue that consumers would have much interest in solvency regulation since they are able to monitor the financial condition of insurers and default risk is properly priced. We now turn to the issue of time inconsistent incentives.

### 4.3 Time Inconsistent Incentives and Wealth Expropriation

Consider the following sequence, (i) the insurer makes a set of financial decisions [A] relevant to the default probability; (ii) the insurer then issues policies to customers who may costlessly monitor [A]; (iii) the insurer the substitutes a new set of decisions [A'] which imply a greater default cost to be borne by the policyholders. Such time inconsistent incentives have been analyzed for non insurance firms. For example, the equityholders of a firm may be able to confiscate wealth of bondholders by changing operating decisions or capital structure after the bonds have been issued (cf. Myers [1977]; Titman [1984]). No doubt bondholders, or in our case policyholders, will anticipate such pernicious behavior in negotiating their original contracts. This will be addressed presently. First, we illustrate possible forms of time inconsistent incentives and show the value that may be expropriated.

Example 1 Payment of premature dividend to equityholders. Premature, in this case, means after policies are issued but before policy liabilities have been discharged by the payment of claims. At the time of policy issue, the value of the equityholders' and policyholders' claims are shown by the earlier equations;

$$V(Y_1) - c(Y_1,L) \tag{4}$$

and

$$c(Y_1,L) \tag{5}$$

Now consider that equityholders pay themselves a dividend, K, immediately before the losses L are known and discharged. The present value of the policyholders' claim is reduced by

$$[V(Y_1)-c(Y_1,L)] - [V(Y_1-K)-c(Y_1-K,L)] \tag{19}$$

Equityholders benefit by an equivalent value.

Example 2 An increase in the size of the liability portfolio without a corresponding increase in surplus. For simplicity we assume that having issued a set of policies yielding $P_0$ in premiums and having an expected liability E(L), the insurer now issues another set of policies having the same expected liability E(L) but now priced at $P_N$. Presumably, the original policies were priced on the assumption that the leverage ratio was $P_0/E$. The new policies are now sold to customers who monitor the leverage ratio as $(P_0+P_N)/E$. If all policies have equal priority, we may identify the loss in value to the old policyholders as (for simplicity, the investment constraint and expenses are ignored, i.e., c=X=0)

$$\{V[(E+P_0)(1+r_i)] - c[(E+P_0)(1+r_i);L]\} \tag{20}$$

$$- \{V[(\frac{E + P_0 + P_N}{2})(1+r_i)] - c[(\frac{E + P_0 + P_N}{2})(1+r_i);L]\}$$

Since new policyholders are aware of the increased default probability, $P_N < P_0$. This implies that old policyholders do indeed lose wealth and equityholders correspondingly benefit. There is no expropriation from the new policyholders.

Example 3 Increase in the risk structure of the insurer's asset portfolio. The policyholders have a short position in a call option written on $Y_1$ with a stochastic, striking price L. Equityholders have a long position in the same call. Now, the value of a rationally priced call will be positively related to the variance of the underlying asset (see Merton [1973]). Our example is a little more complex since the striking price, L, also is stochastic and its correlation with $Y_1$ is important (see Stapleton and Subrahmanyan [1984], p. 224). For simplicity, the correlation between $Y_1$ and L is assumed to be zero. This ensures the positive relationship between the variance of

$Y_1$ and the value of the call is maintained. Consequently, an increase in the variance of the asset portfolio will enhance the value of the equityholders' long position in the call and correspondingly reduce the value of the policyholders' short position. Notice that the value of the policyholders' claim also depends upon $V(Y_1)$. But if the new, more risky, assets also are priced at equilibrium, this value will not change with the change in asset composition.

Other examples of such wealth expropriation may be envisioned such as a change in the reinsurance arrangements selected by the insurer.

**4.5 Capital Structure with Monitoring and Time Inconsistent Incentives**

Consider that equityholders expropriate wealth as shown in example 1 in the previous section; i.e., by paying a dividend K after the issue of policies but before the payment of claims. The value of wealth expropriated shown in equation (19) is positive monotonic in K. Thus, equityholders would pay the largest dividend permissible. In the absence of other regulations, we assume this to be the entire surplus E. Thus outstanding insurance policies will run off without any surplus; E = 0.

Such post contract wealth expropriation would be anticipated by aware and rational consumers and would be priced into the insurance contract. Thus the monitoring price would be

$$P_{E=0} = [V(Y_1)_{E=0} - c(Y_1,L)_{E=0}](1-k)^{-1} \tag{21}$$

Given that the contract price already impounds the wealth expropriation, insurers would use this price in determining their initial capital structure. In fact, the use of such a price does not change the general characteristics of the output decision (or price decision), (i.e., equations (14a) and (18a)), but it does affect the choice of surplus E; (equations (14b) and 18b)). Since zero surplus is assumed in the pricing decision, then dP/dE is zero. This is similar to the no monitoring case (equation 8) and, for identical reasons, the effect is that

$$\frac{\partial[c(Y_1,E) - E]}{\partial E} < 0 \tag{22}$$

which implies a zero precontract choice of surplus, E = 0. There is no advantage to insurers in providing positive surplus since it will not change the price paid by consumers for their policies. These contracts are priced on the assumption of zero surplus and that is what would be provided by equityholders. There is no longer any incentive to switch from a pre contract level of surplus to a different post contract level since the wealth expropriation already has been anticipated.

Now consider the effects on leverage regulation. The possible capital structures shown in Figure 1 are reproduced in Figure 2. These were constructed in the absence of time inconsistent incentives. The effects of time inconsistent incentives are shown by the dashed lines AA′ and BB′. Also shown is a leverage constraint. Since output is given, a fixed level of E, i.e., $E^c$, corresponds to a fixed ratio of surplus to policy liabilities. Insurers cannot fall below this level.

Figure 2

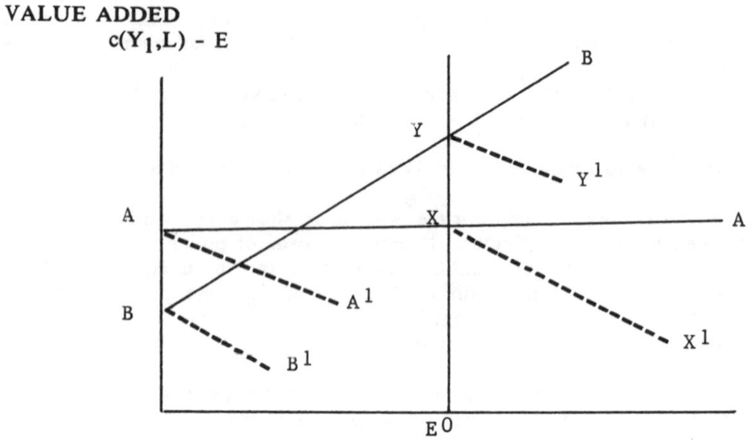


First, we address the case in which choice of surplus was irrelevant as show by line AA. The introduction of time inconsistent incentives leads to the alternative AA' as indicated by inequality (22). Now, zero surplus creates most value for shareholders. However, the wealth of equityholders has not been diminished since the zero surplus solution was one of an infinite number of solutions derived on AA that all yield the same value added for equityholders. The introduction of the leverage constraints leaves equityholders no better off or no worse off as shown by position X. If surplus is increased beyond X, the value of equity will fall as shown by the line XX'. This follows since the condition (22) is negative at any fixed price. Thus producers would tend to cluster at the constrained leverage ratio, i.e. at position X.

The second case in Figure 3 arises with line BB. In the absence of time inconsistent incentives, the level of surplus that maximizes value added is infinite. But time inconsistent incentives reduce the optimal surplus to zero as indicated by BB'. There is a clear wealth loss to equityholders. Regulation permits some of this wealth loss to be recaptured by moving surplus to the constraint $E^c$. Now, consumers will anticipate the post contract choice of $E^c$ surplus and this will be priced into the contract. Consequently, this level is chosen by equityholders. This is shown by position Y. Increase in surplus beyond $E^c$ would not be chosen as value added still is negative in E as shown by the Line YY'.

It is also possible that consumers benefit from such regulation. The effect of regulation is that consumers are offered policies with a higher level of surplus and therefore a lower probability of default. If the demand function is positive in E as indicated, then by reaping the "consumer surplus" (not to be confused with the insurance surplus or "paid in" equity) the consumers secure a welfare gain. The high surplus policies are more efficient at equalizing wealth across states of nature thus leading to a richer (more complete) market in contingent claims, (see Lynch [1981] and Doherty and Schlesinger [1986]).

## 5. Some Observations

With some exceptions (e.g., Wisconsin) the main regulatory vehicles for controlling capital structure in the United States are somewhat softer than an absolute constraint. The National Association of Insurance Commissioners operates an "Early Warning System" to identify insurers in financial distress. This system focusses on key financial ratios including the leverage ratio. The guideline used for leverage is a ratio of three dollars of premiums to one dollar of surplus. Given adverse performance against this and and other ratios, the regulator will normally intervene to attempt corrective action. Details of such action will vary according to the State in question and according to the circumstances of the case. While exceptions do arise, the effect of this form of control is probably to constrain the leverage ratios roughly at a maximum of three dollars premiums to one dollar surplus.

Given this form of constraint, our model suggest that insurers would cluster at the constraint. This prediction follows both from the "no monitoring" model and from the "monitoring " model with the time inconsistent incentives. This prediction may be modified slightly if allowance is made for the stochastic nature of leverage ratio and for adjustment cost. We suppose that the firm aims at some long run optimal capital structure. Short run variations from this level will be observed as the vagaries of the capital market affect the value of the firm's asset portfolio and thereby affect the value of its equity. With zero transaction costs, the firm rationally would continuously adjust to its optimal capital structure. But with transaction costs, a realistic strategy would be to aim at a capital structure distinctly within the constraint. Thus, the firm could absorb some degree of fluctuation in the value of its equity without offending the constraint and without need for new equity issue. The optimal safety margin would balance the expected present value of adjustment costs with the cost of excessive capitalization. Thus, we predict that the observed capital structures of insurance firms should be clustered at leverage rates at some reasonable margin with the 3:1 ratio. What is a "reasonable " safety margin rests somewhat on the risk preferences of the contracting parties and we are unable to put a value on this margin.

Table 1 records the distribution of premium to surplus ratios for stock property casualty insurers operating within the U.S. Small firms were excluded merely for convenience and company results were aggregated into group figures where appropriate. To smooth out the effects of short run fluctuations in equity values, the mean ratios for the three-year period 1982-84 are reported, (1984 results are also reported and these do exhibit a greater dispersion). The Table reveals the following features. Of the fifty-five sample firms, all but three lay within the NAIC 3:1 guideline when considering the three year averages. In any one year, several more firms exceeded the 3:1 ratio but these were usually temporary "violations." It does appear that the NAIC guideline represents a standard for the industry, though it clearly is not binding. Second, the distribution of leverage ratios does show some evidence of clustering. Almost 40 percent of firms have ratios between 2.0 and 2.5 and three quarters of firms have ratios within 1.5 and 3.0.

Table 1

Premium/Surplus (P/S) Ratios of U.S. Stock Insurance Firms and Groups

| P/S Range | Percentage of Sample Having P/S Within Range; 1984 | 1982/1984 |
|---|---|---|
| Less than unity | 3.7 | 1.9 |
| 1.0 to 1.5 | 11.1 | 16.7 |
| 1.5 to 2.0 | 20.4 | 20.0 |
| 2.0 to 2.5 | 33.3 | 38.8 |
| 2.5 to 3.0 | 18.5 | 16.7 |
| Exceeding 3.0 | 13.0 | 5.5 |
| Mean | 2.30 | 2.07 |
| Standard deviation | 0.78 | 0.56 |

Sample: Stock firms and groups having U.S. property-casualty premium income in excess of $200 million in 1984. Sample size 55. Source. A.M. Best "Aggregates and Averages" 1982 to 1985.

**Conclusion**

1) Modigliani and Miller's capital structure irrelevancy proposition does not necessarily prevail in insurance markets given the strong capital market assumptions they propose. This exception arises from the inseparability of financing and operating decisions. We identify exceptions to M and M. Necessary, but not sufficient, conditions for irrelevancy include costless financial monitoring and that the firm be a price taker in the insurance product market. In general, capital structure results generated for non- insurance firms do not transfer to insurance firms without imposing restrictions on the product market.

2) Examples of post contract wealth expropriation arising from time inconsistent incentives are given. These include premature dividends, expansion of the insurance liability portfolio and restructuring of the firm's reinsurance portfolio.

3) Given time inconsistent incentives and a regulatory constraint on the maximum leverage, our model predicts that the distribution of observed capital structure should cluster at the constraint. This prediction is independent of the monitoring assumptions chosen. When allowance is made for transaction costs, the optimal capital structure is established at some reasonable safety margin with the constraint.

4) Insurance markets do indeed face regulatory constraint, though the leverage ratio constraint is "softer" than a binding constraint. The distribution of observed leverage ratios clusters within this suggested constraint. Although this is not a strong test of our model, this result is entirely consistent with the predictions discussed.

5) In the absence of leverage regulation, the insurance market would consist trade in very risky insurance policies. This follows from the lack of incentive forinsurers to invest positive surplus in the insurance market. This result is conditioned by the absence of financial monitoring and/or by time inconsistent incentives. The effect of regulation is to restore incentive for positive equity investment, by implicitly transmitting financial information and by restricting post contract wealth expropriation. Leverage regulation thereby conveys economic benefit both to customer and to those investing equity capital in the insurance product market.

   The analytic framework used consisted of an option valuation model applied in a single period no tax world. Factors known to be relevant to capital structure have been assumed away. The virtues of this simplified approach are its tractability and that it facilities comparison of the capital structure issue of the insurance and non-insurance firms. In particular, it highlights the effects of interdependent financing and operating decisions for the insurance firm. A more complete approach will require, inter alia, that corporate and personal taxes be addressed; that time inconsistent incentives be considered in a multi-period context: and that bankruptcy cost and other types of agency costs be considered.

**Notes**

1. Insurance firms typically do not use conventional sources of debt. At December 1983, non-insurance debt of U.S. property-casualty firms comprised about three-tenths of one percent of total liabilities (Best's Aggregates and Averages). Thus non-insurance debt is ignored.

2. The proof that a call option cannot increase by a value greater than the increase in value of the underlying asset is as follows. Consider the call c(Y,L) and then increase the value Y by some arbitrary positive K. The call c(Y,L) and the call c(Y+K,L) have the following payoffs at maturity.

Payoff in states where:

| | 1. $Y \leq L-K$ | 2. $L-K \leq Y < L$ | 3. $L < Y$ |
|---|---|---|---|
| c(Y,L) | 0 | 0 | Y-L |
| c(Y+K,L) | 0 | Y+K-L | Y+K-L |
| additional payoff on second call | 0 | $Y+K-L < K$ | K |

Notice that additional payoffs only arise in the second and third columns. But additional payoff in the second column Y+K-L must be less than K since $Y < L$. Therefore a payoff of K, or strictly less than K, arises in all states of nature.

Now consider the increase in value of the underlying asset. The payoff increases by K (from Y to Y+K) in <u>all</u> states of nature. Consequently, the increase in value of the call option cannot exceed the increase in the value of the underlying asset in equilibrium.

3. See Borch [1981] for a discussion of related issues.

**References**

Ackerloff, A. [1970], "The Market for Lemons: Quality Uncertainty and the Market Mechanism," Quarterly Journal of Eonomics, Vol. 74, pp.488-50.

Borch, K. [1981],"Is Regulation and Supervision of Insurance Companies Necessary?" Scandinavian Acturarial Journal, pp. 179-190.

Doherty, N.A. and H. Schlesinger [1983], "Optimal Insurance in Incomplete Markets," Journal of Political Economy, Vol. 91, pp. 1045-1054.

Finsinger, J.and M. Pauly [1984], "Reserve Levels and Reserve Requirements for Profit Maximizing Insurance Firms." in Risk and Capital (eds. G. Bamberg and K.Spremann), Springer-Vering, Berlin-Heidelberg.

Harrington, S. [1984], "The Impact of Rate Regulation on Prices and Underwriting Results in the Property Liability Insurance Industry." Journal of Risk and Insurance, Vol. 51, pp. 577-623.

Lynch, M.P. [1981], "Comment on Munch and Smallwood," in Studies in Public Regulation, ibid.

Marshall, J.M. [1976], "Moral Hazard." American Economic Review, Vol. 66, pp. 882-890.

Merton, R.C. [1973], "Theory of Rational Option Pricing," Bell Journal of Economics and Management Science, Vol. 4, pp. 141-183.

Modigliani, F. and M. Miller [1958], "The Cost of Capital, Corporation Finance and the Theory of Investment," American Economic Review, Vol. 48, pp. 261- 297.

Munch, P. and D. Smallwood [1981], "Theory of Solvency Regulation in the property and Casualty Insurance Industry," in Studies in Public Relation (ed. G. Fromm), M.I.T Press, Cambridge, Mass.

Myers, S. [1977], "The Determinants of Corporate Borrowing," Journal of Financial Economics, Vol. 5, pp. 147-175.

Rothschild, M. and J. Stiglitz [1976], "Equilibrium in Competitive Insurance Markets: "An Essay in the Economics of Imperfect Information," Quarterly Journal of Economics, Vol. 90, pp. 629-649.

Stapelton, R.G. and M. Subrahmanyam [1984], "The Valuation of Multivariate Contingent Claims in Discrete Time Models." Journal of Finance, Vol. 37, pp. 207-228.

Titman, S. [1984], "The Effect of Capital Structure on a Firm's Liquidation Decision," Journal of Financial Economics, Vol. 13, pp. 137-151.

# 10

# RISK BASED PREMIUMS FOR INSURANCE GUARANTY FUNDS

J. David Cummins

Property-liability insurance companies currently are subject to extensive solvency regulation. Insurers must satisfy minimum capital and surplus requirements and invest their assets within constraints imposed by state laws. Rates are regulated in most states with a principal objective being protection against "rate wars" and inadequate rates.

Insurer compliance with solvency regulations is monitored by an extensive auditing system. Detailed financial reports must be submitted annually to the insurance commissioner of every state in which a company does business. The reports must conform to statutory accounting principles, which adopt a liquidation rather than going concern view of the firm (Troxel and Breslin [1983]). Insurer financial statements are subjected to computerized audits each year by the National Association of Insurance Commissioners (NAIC). Companies failing four or more of eleven audit ratio tests are singled out for special regulatory scrutiny. Each company is thoroughly audited by a team of state examiners every three to five years.

Policyholders are protected against the consequences of insolvencies by state insurance guaranty funds. Property-liability insolvency funds exist in all United States jurisdictions. Nearly all funds operate on a post-assessment basis, i.e., solvent companies are assessed after an insolvency has occurred to pay losses that cannot be paid from the remaining assets of the insolvent firm. Assessments are a flat percentage of premium volume for all solvent companies (Duncan [1984]).

An alternative to the regulatory regime of solvency surveillance and guaranty funds would be a substantially deregulated environment in which weak companies were allowed to fail. Such a system would have some desirable economic consequences. In theory, policyholders would be able to choose insurers along a continuum ranging from high premium, low risk firms to low premium, high risk firms. Inefficient firms would no longer be protected, and the friction costs of risk sharing would be reduced.

In spite of the potential benefits of deregulation, solvency surveillance is likely to continue in insurance markets for the foreseeable future. The following are among the major reasons: (1) As in banking, government regulation may produce significant savings in information and surveillance costs, especially for the small policyholder Merton [1977]). And, (2) many types of insurance (e.g., automobile liability insurance and workers' compensation) are purchased in whole or in part for the protection of third parties. Thus, insurance insolvencies impose costs upon individuals who have no role in the selection of the insurance company.

If the solvency surveillance system is to be retained, it should be designed to avoid any potential adverse effects. One such effect arises due to the flat premiums charged by insurance guaranty funds. Insurance companies can be viewed as levered firms in which the debt capital is supplied by policyholders in the form of premiums paid in advance of loss payments (Quirin an Waters [1975]).[1] In a competitive market with perfect information and no regulation, the cost of debt capital (the underwriting loss (profit)) would vary directly with the risk of the firm (i.e., the uncertainty regarding the firm's ability to pay policyholder claims). Hence, a more risky firm would be forced to charge lower premiums in order to attract policyholders.

With the introduction of guaranty funds, the risk that claims will not be paid is eliminated or greatly reduced.[2] Hence, the product market will no longer penalize risky firms. If guaranty fund premiums do not reflect insurer risk, the immediate effect of introducing the fund is a gain in the market value of equity for more risky firms. In addition, an incentive is created for firms to adopt more risky strategies.

The adverse effects of guaranty funds can be mitigated by the adoption of risk based premiums. Such premiums eliminate the incentive for firms to pursue more risky strategies by charging each insurer the full market value of the risk it places on the guaranty fund. Since firms would be less likely to adopt high risk strategies, regulatory monitoring costs would be reduced (Pennacchi [1984]).

The purpose of this paper is to develop a methodology for estimating risk-based premiums for insurance guaranty funds. The methodology draws upon and extends work on deposit insurance premiums by Merton [1977] and [1978] and Pennacchi [1984]. The approach is to model the assets and liabilities of the firm as diffusion processes.[3] The resulting premium equations depend upon only a few parameters which are relatively easy to estimate. This represents an improvement over prior insurance pricing models (e.g., Fairley [1976], Hill [1976], and Kraus and Ross [1982]), which require the estimation of systematic risk coefficients for underwriting profits or losses. Such coefficients are extremely difficult to estimate due to data limitations (Hill and Modigliani [1982]) and appear to be highly unstable (Cummins and Harrington [1985]).

This article develops premium equations for three cases: (1) an ongoing insurer with stochastic assets and liabilities but no additional sources of risk, (2) an insurer with stochastic assets, stochastic liabilities, and randomly occurring, lognormally distributed jumps in liabilities (catastrophes), and (3) a policy cohort, where the insurer's liability is gradually reduced as claims are paid. The first two models provide risk based guaranty fund premiums for ongoing insurers, while the latter provides the fair market value of the guarantor's promise to discharge the obligations of a bankrupt insurer.

The article extends the work of Merton [1977] and [1978] and Pennacchi [1984] in several important ways. First, the models specifically reflect the characteristics of insurance companies rather than banks. Among other things, this entails a respecification of the drift terms and boundary conditions of the relevant diffusions. Second, allowance is made for discrete jumps in liabilities (catastrophes), a major problem faced by insurers. Finally, the policy cohort model is developed and guaranty fund premiums are calculated based on realistic parameter estimates. The premiums implied by the model are compared to actual insolvency assessment rates for the period 1969-1981.

## 1. Premiums for Ongoing Insurers

### 1.1. Stochastic Assets and Liabilities

Assume that the insurer enters into a contractual arrangement with the guaranty fund at the beginning of a specified contract period. The contract period is of fixed length (e.g., one year). The guaranty fund premium is determined and a premium charge is made at the beginning of the period. At the end of the period, an audit occurs. If assets (A) exceed liabilities (L) at the audit date, the company is permitted to continue operating. A new premium is calculated, applying to the next contract period. If liabilities exceed assets, the regulator takes over the assets of the company and discharges its liabilities. The costs to the guaranty fund are L - A. The guaranty fund is assumed to be certain to pay its obligations.

Except for the prepayment of the guaranty fund premium, the above assumptions are consistent with current regulatory practices in insurance. Audits are non-random and conducted annually, with more extensive audits conducted at three to five year intervals. Audit costs are charged to insurers and thus can be considered part of the expense charge in the guaranty fund premium.

The following additional assumptions are made:

1. Trading in securities takes place continuously in time. Borrowing and lending takes place at a known rate of interest r, which is assumed to be constant over time. Securities are assumed to be priced so as to satisfy the security market line equation in the continuous time version of the capital asset pricing model (CAPM).

2. Insurer assets consist of marketable securities. The value of these assets is determined according to the following continuous time diffusion process:

$$dA = (\mu_A A + \rho N - \theta L)\, dt + A\, \sigma_A\, dz_A \tag{1}$$

where $A$ = assets,
$L$ = liabilities,
$N$ = the number of policies,
$\mu_A$ = the instantaneous expected rate of return on assets per unit time,
$\rho$ = the instantaneous rate of premium inflow per policy insured,
$\theta$ = the instantaneous rate of claims payment per dollar of liabilities,
$\sigma_A$ = the instantaneous standard deviation of return on insurer assets, and
$z_A(t)$ = a standard Brownian motion process for assets.

Assets thus are assumed to grow due to investment income and premium payments and to be reduced as claims are paid. Note that the model applies to the entire company rather than to any given entry year class of policies.

3. Premiums are collected in advance and held until claims are paid. Liabilities are assumed to be determined according to the following diffusion process:

$$dL = (r_L L + \eta N - \theta L)\, dt + L\, \sigma_L\, dz_L \tag{2}$$

where $r_L$ = the instantaneous expected inflation rate of insurance claims,
$\eta$ = the instantaneous rate of occurrence of new claims,
$\sigma_L$ = the instantaneous standard deviation of liabilities per unit time, and
$z_L(t)$ = a standard Brownian motion process for liabilities.

Liabilities are assumed to grow due to inflation and the occurrence of new claims and to be drawn down due to the payment of claims.[4] Insurance inflation is initially assumed to be equal to general inflation and the Fisher equation is assumed to apply so that, approximately, $r_L + r^* = r$,
where $r^*$ = the real rate of interest, and
$r$ = the risk free nominal rate of interest.

The real rate is assumed to remain constant through time, and insurance pricing is assumed to allow for expected claims inflation.

Assets and liabilities are assumed to be uncorrelated, and liabilities are assumed to have no systematic risk. Fairley [1979], Hill and Modigliani [1983], and Cummins and Harrington [1985] all found very low systematic risk for insurer liabilities. Consequently, this assumption is reasonable as a first approximation. The analysis can easily be generalized to take into account systematic risk of liabilities.

The value of guaranty fund insurance can be written as follows: $P(A,L,\tau)$, where $\tau$ = the time remaining until the next audit. The premium is similar to a put option since its value at the audit date is Max(0, L-A). Assets and liabilities both are assumed to drift through time, and the guaranty fund is required to assume the insurer's obligations if liabilities have drifted above assets by the audit date.

Applying the Ito transformation formula (Karlin and Taylor [1981]), the following differential equation for the value of the guaranty fund premium is obtained:

$$dP = P_A\,dA + P_L\,dL - P_\tau\,dt + (1/2)\,P_{AA}\,(dA)^2 + (1/2)\,P_{LL}\,(dL)^2 \tag{3}$$

Substituting from (1) and (2), one obtains:

$$\begin{aligned} dP = {} & [(\mu_A A + \rho N - \theta L)\,P_A + (r_L L + \eta N - \theta L)\,P_L - P_\tau \\ & + (1/2)\,A^2\,\sigma_A^2\,P_{AA} + (1/2)\,L^2\,\sigma_L^2\,P_{LL}]\,dt + P_A\,A\,\sigma_A\,dz_A \\ & + P_L\,L\,\sigma_L\,dz_L \end{aligned} \tag{4}$$

The guaranty fund premium is assumed to be priced according to the continuous time CAPM. (A similar assumption is employed by Merton [1978] in the deposit insurance case.) This implies that $E(dP/P) = r + (A\,P_A\,/\,P)\,(\mu_A - r)$. Substituting the CAPM pricing relation for dP in (4) and taking expectations yields:

$$\begin{aligned} 0 = {} & -\,rP + (rA + \rho N - \theta L)\,P_A + (r_L L + \eta N - \theta L)\,P_L - P_\tau \\ & + (1/2)\,A^2\,\sigma_A^2\,P_{AA} + (1/2)\,L^2\,\sigma_L^2\,P_{LL} \end{aligned} \tag{5}$$

This equation can be solved numerically to obtain the value of the guaranty fund premium.

In order to facilitate the discussion, it is helpful to simplify equation (5) by making the following additional assumption: $\rho N = \theta L = \eta N$, i.e., premium inflow, claims outflow, and the incidence of new claims are assumed to be equal. With this assumption, the model represents an insurer that has achieved a steady-state position. It is important to stress that this assumption is merely an expositional convenience and is not necessary in order to obtain premium rates.

Making the change of variables $x = A/L$ and $p(x) = p = P(A,L,\tau)/L$ in equation (5), the following equation is obtained:

$$(r - r_L)\,x\,p + (1/2)\,x^2\,(\sigma_A^2 + \sigma_L^2)\,p_{xx} - (r - r_L)\,p = p_\tau \tag{6}$$

The boundary conditions for equation (6) are the following:

$$p(0,\tau) = \exp(-r^*\tau) \tag{7}$$

$$p(x,0) = \mathrm{Max}(0,\ 1-x) \tag{8}$$

The guaranty fund premium thus is the value of a put option with interest rate $(r - r_L)$ and diffusion parameter $\sigma^2 = \sigma_A^2 + \sigma_L^2$. If claims inflation is the same as general inflation, as assumed above, this is equivalent to valuing the option at the real rate of interest, $r^*$. Policies thus are priced to credit policyholders with the real rate.[5]

The model can be used to analyze the impact of guaranty fund insurance on firm value. Assume initially that no guaranty fund exists. The value of insurance to policyholders then can be considered analogous to the value of risky corporate debt, i.e., the value of insurance liabilities would be:

$$V(L) = L\,[\exp(-r^*\tau) - p(x,\tau)] \tag{9}$$

where V(L) = value of liabilities.

Liabilities will be worth less than their discounted present value because of the probability that the insurer will default. The value of insurance company equity will be equal to the value of a call option, which is valued according to a differential equation exactly analogous to equation (6), with the following boundary conditions: $c(0,\tau) = 0$ and $c(x,0) = \mathrm{Max}(0, x-1)$. Insurer assets satisfy the following equality:

$$A = E + L\,[\exp(-r^*\tau) - p(x,\tau)] \tag{10}$$

where E = insurance company equity. Recalling that insurer assets are marketable securities, it is clear from equation (10) that the assets are obtained from two sources: stockholder funds (E) and premiums (discounted claims less the value of the put).[6]

There is, of course, an interaction between the funds initially put up by stockholders and the value of the put, i.e., the put value is affected by firm capital structure. We assume that insurance market equilibrium results in insurers being arrayed along a continuum of capital structures, to serve policyholders with different levels of risk aversion. Policyholders are assumed to have complete information about the premium rates and default risk of competing insurers and to choose a company with a premium/default probability combination consistent with their tastes.

Suppose that guaranty fund insurance is introduced, with a flat premium payment, k, expressed as a proportion of liabilities. Assume that all existing policies are cancelled and replaced by new policies reflecting the existence of the guaranty fund. All insurers will now receive a premium of $\exp(-r^*\tau)$ per dollar of liabilities from policyholders and pay the guaranty fund a premium of kL. The value of the firm's assets becomes:

$$A' = E + L\,[\exp(-r^*\tau) - k\,] \tag{11}$$

The change in the assets of any given insurer due to the introduction of the guaranty fund will be:

$$A' - A = L\,[p(x,\tau) - k] \tag{12}$$

The flat premium charge k will be a pooled value based upon the insurer's share of the insolvency costs of all insurers in the market. Since assets represent marketable securities which are priced according to the CAPM, the introduction of the guaranty fund will penalize the equity holders of better than average firms and reward equity holders of worse than average firms.

The existence of a guaranty fund with flat premiums also gives insurers an incentive to assume greater risk since they are no longer penalized individually by the product market and are penalized by the guaranty fund only as a group (through increases in k as average risk increases). Hence, the introduction of guaranty funds may actually increase the rate of insolvency in the insurance market.

Charging a risk-based premium solves the problem by reinstating equation (10). Thus, insurers will collect a premium equal to L $\exp(-r^*\tau)$ from policyholders and pay L $p(x,\tau)$ to the guaranty fund. Each firm's equity value will be the same as it was prior to the introduction of the guaranty fund. However, policyholders will pay higher premiums, reflecting the reduction in default probabilities.[7]

## 1.2 Liability Jumps (Catastrophes)

The lognormal diffusion process hypothesized above implies a continuous sample path for liabilities. However, many types of insurance subject the insurer to large potential jumps in liabilities. Examples include chemical catastrophes, airline disasters, hurricanes, and changing judicial interpretations of contract provisions. Although reinsurance is used to cushion the impact of some of the events, it is impossible to perfectly insulate insurers from this type of claim. This section develops a pricing model for guaranty fund insurance when insurers are subject to discontinuous changes in liabilities.

Assets are assumed to be governed by equation (1), while liabilities now develop according to the following equation:

$$dL = (r_L L + \eta N - \theta L - \lambda k L)\, dt + \sigma_L\, L\, dz_L + dq \tag{13}$$

where $q(t)$= a Poisson process with parameter $\lambda$,
$k$ = $E(Y - 1)$, and
$Y$ = the random variable representing the magnitude of the jump, $Y > 0$.
The model assumes that jumps occur according to a Poisson process, i.e., the intervals between jumps are exponentially distributed. When a jump occurs, liabilities change from L to LY. Successive values of Y are assumed to be independent and identically distributed. The expected impact of the jump process in any small interval is $\lambda k L\, dt$. A similar model has been applied to stock prices by Merton [1976] and other authors.

The Poisson model is the premier model of insurance claim arrivals, having been applied to automobile insurance, fire insurance, and liability insurance, among others. (See Beard, Pentikainen, and Pesonen [1984].) Distributions applied to claim severity (Y) include the gamma, the lognormal, the Burr, and the Pareto. (See Hogg and Klugman [1984].)

Representing the guaranty fund premium by $P(A,L,\tau)$ and applying the Ito transformation formula and a corresponding formula for Poisson processes (See Merton [1971]) yields the following differential equation:

$$\begin{aligned} dP = {} & [\mu_A' \, A \, P_A + (\mu_L - \lambda k)\, L\, P_L - P_\tau + (1/2)\, P_{AA}\, A^2\, \sigma_A^2 \\ & + (1/2)\, P_{LL}\, L^2\, \sigma_L^2 - \lambda P\, k_P]\, dt + P_A\, A\, \sigma_A\, dz_A \\ & + P_L\, L\, \sigma_L\, dz_L + P\, dq_P + \lambda E[P(A,YL,\tau) - P(A,L,\tau)]\, dt \end{aligned} \tag{14}$$

where $\mu_A' = \mu_A + \rho\,(N/A) - \theta\,(L/A)$,
$\mu_L = r_L + \eta\,(N/L) - \theta$,
$q_P$ = an independent Poisson process with parameter $\lambda$,
$k_P = E(Y_P - 1)$, and
$Y_P$= the random variable representing the impact of the jump on the guaranty fund premium.

In order to eliminate risk from equation (14), two assumptions are made: (1) the guaranty fund premium is priced according to the continuous time version of the CAPM, and (2) jump risk is nonsystematic. The former assumption is retained from the preceding case, while the latter is necessary because no hedge portfolio can be constructed that will eliminate the jump risk (see Merton [1976, p. 131]). In order to simplify the following discussion, the assumption that $\rho N = \eta N = \theta L$ also is retained from above.

Assuming that the jump risk is nonsystematic is probably more reasonable for insurance liabilities than for stock prices. While certain "catastrophes" (e.g., liberalization of tort rules) undoubtedly have a systematic effect, most such events are unsystematic by definition, i.e., they occur randomly and independently through time. Nevertheless, to the extent that jump risk has a systematic component, the resulting guaranty fund premium will be underestimated.

Introducing the above assumptions and taking expectations in equation (14), one obtains:

$$P_\tau = -rP + A\,P_A\,r + L\,P_L\,(r_L - \lambda k) + (1/2)\,P_{AA}\,A^2\,\sigma_A^2 + (1/2)\,P_{LL}\,L^2\,\sigma_L^2 + \lambda E[P(A,YL,\tau) - P(A,L,\tau)] \tag{15}$$

The solution to this equation is:

$$P(A,L,\tau) = \sum_{N=0}^{\infty} p(N)\,E_N[W(A,\,X_N L e^{-k\lambda\tau},\,\tau\,;\,r,\,r_L - \lambda k,\,\sigma_A^2,\,\sigma_L^2)] \tag{16}$$

where $p(N) = e^{-\lambda\tau}(\lambda\tau)^N/N!$,

$W(\cdot)$ = the value of a put option with stochastic exercise price $X_N L e^{-k\lambda\tau}$, on an asset with current value A, time to expiration $\tau$, drift parameters (for the asset and exercise values) r and $r_L - \lambda k$, and diffusion parameters $\sigma_A^2$ and $\sigma_L^2$,

$X_N$ = the product of N independent random variables, each distribute identically to Y, and

$E_N$ = the expectation operator over the distribution of $X_N$.

Making the transformations $x = A/L$ and $p(x,\tau) = P/L$, yields the following simpler differential equation for the value of the guaranty fund premium:

$$p_\tau = -p(r - r_L + \lambda k) + x\,p_x\,(r - r_L + \lambda k) + (1/2)\,x^2\,p_{xx}\,\sigma^2 + \lambda\,E_Y[p(x/Y,\,\tau) - p(x,\tau)] \tag{17}$$

where $\sigma^2 = \sigma_A^2 + \sigma_L^2$.

The solution to this equation is given below:

$$p(x,\tau) = \sum_{N=0}^{\infty} p(N)\,E_N[W(x/X_N,\,\tau\,;\,1,\,\sigma^2,\,r - r_L + \lambda k)] \tag{18}$$

where $W(x/X_N,\,\tau\,;\,1,\,\sigma^2,\,r - r_L + \lambda k)$ = the value of a put option on an asset with value $x/X_N$, time to expiration $\tau$, exercise price 1, interest rate $r - r_L + \lambda k$, and diffusion parameter $\sigma^2$.

Equation (18) is the weighted average of guaranty fund premiums with asset to liability ratio $x/X_N$ and exercise price 1. In effect, the occurrence of catastrophes has a multiplicative effect on liabilities and hence affects the denominator of the asset-to-liability ratio.

No distributional assumption has been made with regard to the random variable Y. However, if Y is lognormal, then a closed form expression can be derived for the value of the guaranty fund premium. This expression is equation (18) with the following substituted for $E_N[W(\cdot)]$ :

$$E_N[W(\cdot)] = e^{-(r - r_L + \lambda k)\tau}\,\Phi[(-\ln x - \mu^*\tau)/\sigma^*\sqrt{\tau}]$$

$$- x\, e^{N\gamma}\,\Phi[(-\ln x - \mu^*\tau - \sigma^{*2}\tau)/\sigma^*\sqrt{\tau}] \quad (19)$$

where $\mu^* = r - r_L + \lambda k - (\sigma^2/2) - (N\alpha/\tau)$,
$\sigma^{*2} = \sigma^2 + (N\delta^2/2)$,
$\Phi(\cdot)$ = the standard normal distribution function,
$\alpha,\delta^2$ = the mean and variance parameters of ln(Y), and
$\gamma = -\alpha + \delta^2/2$.

The derivation of this equation utilizes the property that the product of lognormally distributed random variables is lognormally distributed.[8] The expected value of the jump, E(Y) is $(\alpha + \delta^2/2)$ and $\ln(1 + k) = \alpha + \delta^2/2$. The expected impact of the jump on the asset-to-liability ratio is $E(1/Y) = \exp(-\alpha + \delta^2/2)$.

If the Poisson intensity parameter and the liability jump parameters are set equal to zero, the jump model reverts to the no jump case. However, if the expected value of the jump is zero (i.e., $\alpha = -\delta^2/2$) but jumps can occur ($\lambda \neq 0$), the premium implied by equations (18) and (19) tends to be higher than in the no jump case when $x > 1$. This occurs primarily because of the effect of the jump variance parameter on $\theta^{*2}$. When x is sufficiently less than 1, the premium implied by the jump model when E(Y) = 1 tends to be less than the premium in the no jump case. This is attributable to the fact that the expected impact of the jump on x, i.e., E(1/Y) is positive when $\alpha = -\delta^2/2$.

## 2. A Cohort of Policies

The models developed above apply to an ongoing insurer that purchases guaranty fund insurance covering a fixed period of time. Although such models are useful, it is also important to be able to price the guaranty involved in a policy cohort. This guaranty would have no expiration date. Essentially, the guarantor would be responsible for paying all claims arising from a set of policies regardless of when the claim payments are made.

More specifically, consider a situation in which the insurer agrees to pay all claims arising from a group of policies in return for a fixed premium, G, to be paid at the inception of the contract. Initially, assume that the present value of liabilities under the set of policies is a known value, L. The funds represented by G are invested in marketable securities. G and L are governed by the following differential equations:

$$dG = (\mu_A G - \theta L)\,dt + \sigma_A G\,dz_A \quad (20a)$$

$$dL = (r_L L - \theta L)\,dt + \sigma_L L\,dz_L \quad (20b)$$

The loss account, represented by L, increases due to claims inflation and is drawn down as claims are paid. The premium account grows due to investment income and is depleted as claims are paid. If the accumulated value of G is eventually exhausted by claim payments, the insurer is still liable for the unpaid component of L. It is assumed that the insurer is certain to pay this obligation. The value of the insurer's obligation is denoted by $\Pi(G,L)$.

The value of $\Pi(G,L)$ is derived conditional on the initial values of G and L being known. This model would be appropriate for a number of insurance pricing problems that arise in the real world. For example, if the guaranty fund were to assume control of an insolvent insurer, it would obtain the remaining assets and be responsible for paying the remaining liabilities. Both assets and liabilities would have known or estimable market values at the time of the takeover and would be subject to stochastic variation thereafter. This is precisely the situation defined above with assets and liabilities represented by G and L, respectively. The model would also be appropriate for pricing transfers of blocks of loss reserves among insurers (so-called loss portfolio transfers).

Differentiating $\Pi$, one obtains:

$$d\Pi = \Pi_G \, dG + \Pi_L \, dL + (1/2) \, \Pi_{GG} \, (dG)^2 + (1/2) \, \Pi_{LL} \, (dL)^2 \tag{21}$$

Substituting for dG and dL from equations (20a) and (20b) and simplifying the resulting expression yields:

$$d\Pi = [\Pi_G \, (\mu_A G - \theta L) + \Pi_L \, (r_L L - \theta L) + (1/2) \, (\Pi_{GG} \, G^2 \, \sigma_A^2 + \Pi_{LL} \, L^2 \, \sigma_L^2)] \, dt + \Pi_G \, \sigma_A \, dz_A + \Pi_L \, \sigma_L \, dz_L \tag{22}$$

If the value of the guaranty reflects only systematic risk, equation (22) can be simplified. The procedure is similar to that utilized above. Specifically, retaining the assumption that liabilities do not have systematic risk, we note that:

$$E \left( \frac{d\Pi}{\Pi} \right) = r + \frac{G\Pi_G}{\Pi} (\mu A - r) \tag{23}$$

This permits the elimination of $\mu_A$ from (22) yielding:

$$\Pi r = \Pi_G \, (rG - \theta L) + \Pi_L \, (r_L L - \theta L) + (1/2) \, (\Pi_{GG} \, G^2 \, \sigma_A^2 + \Pi_{LL} \, L^2 \, \sigma_L^2 ) \tag{24}$$

Finally, making the change of variables $x = G/L$ and $\pi = \Pi/L$, one obtains the following differential equation for the value of the guaranty:

$$\pi(r - r_L + \theta) = \pi_x \, [x(r - r_L + \theta) - \theta] + (1/2) \, x^2 \, \pi_{xx} \, (\sigma_A^2 + \sigma_L^2) \tag{25}$$

The boundary conditions are:

$$\lim_{x \to 0} \pi(x) = 1 \tag{26a}$$

$$\lim_{x \to \infty} \pi(x) = 0 \tag{26b}$$

The conditions imply that the value of the guaranty approaches zero as the asset to liability ratio becomes large and approaches the value of liabilities as the asset to liability ratio goes to zero. Thus, if the premium account is exhausted, the value of the guarantor's promise is equal to the value of liabilities.

The solution of equation (24) subject to boundary condition (26a) and (26b) is the following:

$$\pi(x) = \frac{\Gamma(a)}{\Gamma(b)} (2\theta/Q)^{b-a} \, x^{r_{12}} \, e^{-2\theta/Q} \, M(a,b,2\theta/Qx) \tag{27}$$

where $a = 2$,
$b = 2 \, [1 + (r + \theta)/Q]$,
$r_{12} = -(2/Q)(r + \theta)$,
$Q = \sigma_A^2 + \sigma_L^2$, and
$M(.,.,.)$ = Kummer's function.

An appendix available from the author discusses the derivation of equation (27).

The derivative of $\Pi(x)$ with respect to x is unambiguously negative, i.e., the value of the guaranty is less when the premium account is larger relative to the loss account. For reasonable parameter values (see below), the premium varies inversely with the risk free rate and directly with the variance parameter (Q).

The effect of the payout parameter $\theta$ on the value of the guaranty is ambiguous. For large values of x (e.g., $x > 1$), $\Pi(x)$ tends to be inversely related to $\theta$. Intuitively, this occurs because a faster payout reduces the risk that adverse loss fluctuations will exhaust the premium fund. For values of x sufficiently less than 1, on the other hand, the value of the guaranty tends to be directly related to the payout parameter. In this case, a significant proportion of the liabilities are likely to be paid out of the guarantor's funds (rather than the premium account). Thus, it is best to delay payment as long as possible. Numerical examples are utilized in the next section to illustrate these and other effects.

The above results rest on the assumption that both G and L are known. However, in some instances, only L is known. For example, in a transaction involving the "sale" or transfer of loss obligations between two companies, L would be known but G would be subject to negotiation. The buyer would receive $G + \Pi$ from the seller in return for assuming the obligation to pay L.

Under competition, the price for assuming a given block of loss obligations would be the minimum value of $x + \Pi(x)$. Competing buyers would have an incentive to undercut a higher price. This is the case since for fixed x, $\Pi(x)$ is the fair price for the guaranty.

For small values of x, $d(x + \Pi)/dx < 0$, while for large values, $d(x + \Pi) > 0$. Since the second derivative is always positive, a unique minimum value exists for $x + \Pi(x)$.

## 3. Numerical Examples

This section provides numerical examples of guaranty fund premia. The goal is to develop premium estimates that are realistic in order of magnitude. These estimates are compared with the actual assessment rates of insurance guaranty funds. The results should be indicative both of the size of the premiums and the realism of the model.

The most basic guaranty fund model for an ongoing firm depends upon only five parameters: the risk free rate (r), the liability inflation rate ($r_L$), the variance parameters for assets and liabilities $\sigma_A^2$ and $\sigma_L^2$), and the correlation coefficient between the asset and liability random shock terms ($\rho$).

Initially, it is assumed that insurance liability inflation is substantially the same as inflation in the economy as a whole. Thus, the difference between r and $r_L$ is approximately the real rate of return. This is assumed to be .025. In fact, claims inflation in many lines of insurance probably is higher than general inflation. Thus, $r - r_L$ may be less than the real rate and the guaranty fund premiums should be higher than the premiums implied by the real rate assumption. Sensitivity of the premiums to the difference between r and $r_L$ is tested below.

Property-liability insurers hold four major classes of assets; stocks, long-term bonds, short-term securities, and non-invested assets. The latter consist of accounts such as balances due from agents and reinsures. This category amounts to about 15 percent of total industry assets. (See A.M. Best Co. [1985].)

For purposes of obtaining premium estimates, it is assumed that insurers' asset portfolios can be represented by two asset categories -- corporate equities and long-term bonds. This probably slightly overstates the risk parameter of insurers' short-term securities since treasury bills, for example, have a lower variance than long-term bonds (Ibbotson, Sinquefield, and Siegel [1982]). However, over the period covered by the study (1926-1980), insurers held only small amounts of short-term investments (2 to 4 percent of assets). The assumption that the risk of non-invested assets is similar to that of long-term bonds has been used by other researchers (e.g., Hill and Modigliani [1985]). The sensitivity of the premiums to the risk parameters is tested below.

To estimate the diffusion parameters of corporate equities and long-term bonds, the data presented in Ibbotson, Sinquefield, and Siegel [1982] are used. The lognormal diffusion assumption implies that the logs of value relatives are normally distributed. Hence, the appropriate estimate of the diffusion parameter is the variance of the log of the value relative. This parameter was estimated for stocks, long-term corporate bonds, and long-term government bonds for the period 1926-1980. The results are shown in Table 1. The correlation matrix of the logs of the relevant value relatives also are presented in this table.

Since corporate and government bonds are highly correlated and have approximately the same diffusion parameter, the assumption was made that the parameter for the bond and non-invested asset segment of the portfolio is .003, which represents both the long corporate and long government parameter rounded to three decimal places. For equities, the parameter was assumed to be .044. The correlation coefficient between the stock and bond segments of the portfolio was assumed to be .15, which is the correlation coefficient between stocks and corporate bonds over the study period.

The asset variance parameter for use in the models was estimated using the 1980 portfolio proportions of stock property-liability insurers as weights. The proportion of equities to total assets in that year was about .25.

The risk parameter for stock insurance company liabilities was estimated as the variance of the log of (L/L-1), where L = aggregate stock company liabilities.[9] The correlation coefficient between liabilities and assets was assumed to be zero.

To estimate premiums using the jump diffusion (catastrophe) model, three additional parameter estimates are needed, i.e., the Poisson arrival rate and the parameters of the lognormal distribution of catastrophe magnitudes. Since virtually no data of this type are available publicly, the arrival rate was arbitrarily assumed to be .2, i.e., on the average one catastrophe was assumed to occur every five years.

For catastrophe severity, the location parameter was assumed to be -.005 and the dispersion parameter .01. This implies that the expected impact of a catastrophe on liabilities is zero. "Catastrophes" can either increase or decrease insurer liabilities. This is probably realistic since the arrival of new information could imply that claims are being settled either for more or less than the original estimates. The assumed dispersion parameter implies that the standard deviation of catastrophe severity is 10 percent of insurer liabilities. This is likely to be reasonable since reinsurance cushions the impact of very large catastrophes.

The final parameter estimate needed to test the premium models is the claims settlement parameter ($\theta$) which appears in the policy cohort model. The set-up of the model implies that the claims runoff follows an exponential distribution, i.e., with no random shock or drift, the proportion of claims remaining to be paid at time t is $\exp(-\theta t)$. The average claim payoff date occurs $(1/\theta)$ periods after the starting date (time zero).

The exponential assumption also was used by Kraus and Ross [1982]. In order to test the validity of the assumption and obtain a realistic estimate of $\theta$, data on automobile liability insurance claims in Massachusetts were analyzed. The results indicated that the exponential distribution provided a very good fit to the claims runoff, with a runoff parameter ($\theta$) of .4. This may slightly overestimate the runoff parameter for the industry as a whole because insurers write both short-tail (e.g., fire, auto physical damage) and long-tail (e.g., auto liability, workers' compensation) lines. Sensitivity is tested below. The parameter estimates are summarized in Table 2.

TABLE 1

**Summary Statistics for Security Returns (Monthly Observations)**

| Variable | Variances 1926-80 | Variances 1959-80 |
|---|---|---|
| S & P 500 | 0.043700 | 0.02530 |
| Long-term Corporate Bonds | 0.002840 | 0.00477 |
| Long-term Government Bonds | 0.002987 | 0.00410 |
| Stock Co. Liabilities | 0.004780 | 0.00160 |

| | Correlation Matrix: 1926-80 | | | |
|---|---|---|---|---|
| | S & P 500 | Corp. | Govt. | Stock Cos. |
| S & P 500 | 1 | 0.153 | 0.045 | -0.052 |
| Long-term Corporate Bonds | 0.153 | 1 | 0.842 | -0.222 |
| Long-term Government Bonds | 0.045 | 0.842 | 1 | -0.0934 |
| Stock Co. Liabilities | -0.052 | -0.222 | -0.0934 | 1 |

| | Correlation Matrix: 1959-80 | | | |
|---|---|---|---|---|
| | S & P 500 | Corp. | Govt. | Stock Cos. |
| S & P 500 | 1 | 0.263 | 0.0054 | 0.023 |
| Long-term Corporate Bonds | 0.263 | 1 | 0.883 | 0.185 |
| Long-term Government Bonds | 0.0054 | 0.883 | 1 | 0.112 |
| Stock Co. Liabilities | 0.023 | 0.185 | 0.112 | 1 |

Note: All statistics are calculated from natural logs of value relatives.
Source: Data on security returns were obtained from Ibbotson, Sinquefield, and Siegel [1982].

TABLE 2

**Parameter Estimates for Guaranty Fund Calculations**

| Parameter | Sample Period 1926-80 | Sample Period 1959-80 |
|---|---|---|
| Corporate equity risk | .044 | .025 |
| Other asset risk | .003 | .0048 |
| Stock/other asset correlations | .150 | .150 |
| Asset portfolio risk ($\sigma_A^2$) | .0051 | .0047 |
| Liability risk ($\sigma_L^2$) | .0048 | .0016 |
| $r - r_L$ | .025 | .025 |
| Poisson arrival rate | .2 | .2 |
| Catastrophe location parameter ($\alpha$) | -.005 | -.005 |
| Catastrophe risk parameter ($\delta^2$) | .01 | .01 |
| Payout parameter ($\theta$) | .4 | .4 |

The premium estimates for the basic and catastrophe models are shown in Table 3. Estimates are presented both for the period 1926-1980 and for an alternative sample period, 1959-1980. The latter was chosen because of the possibility that the probability distribution of insurance liabilities has been non-stationary due to changes in the regulatory environment and market conditions. The use of the latter period tends to give uniformly lower premium estimates.

The actual asset-liability ratio for the insurance industry over the past ten years has been about 1.4. However, this is probably overstated due to the fact that bonds are reported at book rather than market values (Troxel and Breslin [1983]). In addition, the ratio is not uniform across companies. Hence, the premiums were estimated using asset-to-liability ratios ranging from 1.2 to 1.4.

The premium estimates for the basic model over the period 1926-1980 with ($r-r_L$) set at .025 range from .000718 (or about .07 of 1 percent) of liabilities when (A/L) = 1.2 to .000003 for (A/L) = 1.4. The premiums are increased by about 30 percent when a higher liability inflation rate is used (i.e., $r - r_L = .015$).

The introduction of catastrophes leads to significantly larger premium estimates. The catastrophe estimates are presented for three arrival rates, .33, .2, and .1, corresponding to expected arrivals every three, five, and ten years, respectively. The premiums for the five-year arrival assumption with parameter estimates over the period 1926-1980 are .001405 for (A/L) = 1.2 and .000057 for (A/L) = 1.4.

To test the realism of the results, the actual guaranty fund assessment rate over the period 1969-1981 was computed. The rate is defined as aggregate assessments by all state guaranty funds in the U.S. during the period 1969-1981 divided by aggregate property-liability insurance liabilities for the same period.[10] The assessments for this period amounted to .000307 or about .03 of 1 percent of industry liabilities. This rate is of the same order of magnitude as the premium estimates in Table 2. For example, it is about the same as the estimates for the basic model (no catastrophes) if ($r - r_L$) = .025 and (A/L) = 1.24 with parameter estimates based on the period 1926-1980. In the catastrophe case, the actual assessment rate is close to the rate implied by (A/L) = 1.29 and $\lambda$ = .2 with parameters estimated over 1926-1980. These results are encouraging and indicate that the models may provide accurate estimates of guaranty fund premiums for individual companies.

The premium estimates for the policy cohort model are shown in Table 4. These results indicate the premium that would be required to compensate the guarantor for the risk inherent in assuming responsibility for a block of policies with a known initial asset-to-liability ratio. This model would be appropriate in pricing the guaranty fund's obligation to discharge the liabilities of an insolvent insurer or the sale or transfer of a block of existing policies between two insurers.

As expected, the premiums vary inversely with the asset-to-liability ratio and the interest rate differential ($r - r_L$) and directly with the variance parameter. The effect of the runoff parameter ($\theta$) depends upon the initial asset-to-liability ratio.

If the initial value of (A/L) is greater than 1, reducing the runoff parameter (i.e., lengthening the payout period) tends to increase the premium. This occurs because a longer payout period increases the risk that adverse developments will cause liabilities to drift above remaining assets, placing the guarantor in a deficit position. When (A/L) is sufficiently less than 1, on the other hand, a lower runoff parameter implies a lower premium. If the insurer is initially in a deficit position, it is best to postpone the loss payments as long as possible.

As explained above, the sum of (A/L) = x and the premium has a unique minimum for any given set of parameter values. The minima are shown in Table 4 for each parameter set tested. The accompanying minimum values of x also are shown. An increase in the risk parameter Q reduces the value of x at which the minimum is attained but increases the sum of x and the guaranty premium.

TABLE 3

**Guaranty Fund Premiums**

Case 1: Jump Process

Constant Parameters: $\alpha = -0.005$
$\delta^2 = 0.01$
$\tau = 1$
$r - r_L = 0.025$

| A/L Ratio | $\lambda = .33$ | | $\lambda = .2$ | | $\lambda = .1$ | |
|---|---|---|---|---|---|---|
| | 1926-80 | 1959-80 | 1926-80 | 1959-80 | 1926-80 | 1959-80 |
| 1.2 | 0.001879 | 0.001001 | 0.001405 | 0.000631 | 0.001058 | 0.000369 |
| 1.3 | 0.000428 | 0.000222 | 0.000269 | 0.000121 | 0.000160 | 0.000056 |
| 1.4 | 0.000104 | 0.000051 | 0.000057 | 0.000024 | 0.000027 | 0.000010 |

Case 2: No Jumps

Constant Parameters: $\alpha = 0$
$\delta^2 = 0$
$\tau = 1$

| A/L Ratio | | $r - r_L = .025$ | | $r - r_L = .015$ | |
|---|---|---|---|---|---|
| | | 1926-80 | 1959-80 | 1926-80 | 1959-80 |
| 1.2 | Does not vary with $\lambda$ | 0.000718 | 0.000121 | 0.000948 | 0.000184 |
| 1.3 | | 0.000061 | 0.000003 | 0.000087 | 0.000005 |
| 1.4 | | 0.000003 | <.000000 | 0.000005 | <.000000 |

$\sigma^2$ for 1926-80 = .009862.
$\sigma^2$ for 1959-80 = .006312.

Key: $\alpha$ = location parameter for jumps, $\delta$ = dispersion parameter for jumps, $\tau$ = time to expiration of guaranty, r = risk free rate, $r_L$ = liability inflation rate, $\lambda$ = Poisson arrival rate, A = assets, L = liabilities, and $\sigma^2$ = the sum of the asset and liability risk parameters.

TABLE 4

**Policy Cohort Premiums**

| | | | | | |
|---|---|---|---|---|---|
| Q = | 0.009862 | 0.006312 | 0.009862 | 0.006312 | 0.006312 |
| $r - r_L$ = | 0.025 | 0.025 | 0.015 | 0.015 | 0.015 |
| $\theta$ = | 0.4 | 0.4 | 0.4 | 0.4 | 0.2 |
| x | Premiums = $\pi$ | | | | |
| 1.4 | 9.58E-06 | 1.81E-07 | 2.34E-05 | 6.93E-07 | 3.38E-05 |
| 1.2 | 0.000674 | 0.000104 | 0.001250 | 0.000254 | 0.001160 |
| 1.0 | 0.020200 | 0.012900 | 0.028300 | 0.020000 | 0.021800 |
| 0.8 | 0.153000 | 0.151000 | 0.171000 | 0.170000 | 0.145000 |
| MIN x | 0.7935 | 0.8215 | 0.7923 | 0.8225 | 0.7750 |
| MIN (x+$\pi$) | 0.9525 | 0.9504 | 0.9715 | 0.9701 | 0.9446 |

Key: Q = sum of the asset and liability risk parameters, r = risk free rate, $r_L$ = liability inflation rate, $\theta$ = claims payout rate, x = asset-to-liability ratio, and $\pi$ = guaranty fund premium.

## 4. Summary and Conclusions

This paper develops premium calculation models for insurance guaranty funds. Three models are developed: (1) a basic model for a one-year guaranty applicable to an ongoing company, (2) a one-year premium model with allowance for catastrophes, again for an ongoing company, and (3) a policy cohort model for a block of policies where liabilities will eventually run off to zero.

The models are based on the assumption that the paths of assets and liabilities over time can be described by diffusion processes. They also assume that the value of the guaranty fund itself reflects only systematic risk. The guaranty fund is assumed to pay its obligations with probability 1.

The premium models account for asset risk, liability risk, and the risk of catastrophes. Unlike previous pricing models for insurance risk (e.g., Fairley [1979]), the models developed in this paper recognize the value of the guarantor's promise to pay losses even if the premium account has been exhausted. Thus, they provide a link between capital market theory and traditional actuarial ruin models.

Additional empirical research is needed to provide parameter estimates which take into account the asset and liability portfolio characteristics of individual companies. Further analysis on the liability runoff parameter and the clams inflation rate also would be helpful. Theoretical research into the effects of stochastic interest and other types of jump processes also would be useful. If this research can be conducted successfully, the models developed in this paper have the potential to yield significant improvements in pricing techniques utilized in insurance.

## Notes

1. State regulations prevent most insurance companies from issuing significant amounts of conventional debt securities.

2. Insolvency funds may not totally eliminate the costs of insolvencies from the policyholders' perspective. For example, payment of claims may be delayed if the insurer becomes insolvent and the liabilities are transferred to the guarantor. In addition, guaranty funds usually impose a maximum payment per claim. See Duncan [1984]. Hence, policyholders with very large claims will not receive full payment.

3. An alternative approach based on stable processes rather than diffusion processes is suggested by McCulloch [1981] and [1985]. Another potential methodology is actuarial ruin theory, which is the traditional approach for computing the probability and costs of insurer insolvencies. See, for example, Buhlmann [1971], Gerber [1979], and Beard, Pentikainen, and Pesonen [1984]. Actuarial ruin theory was not adopted in this study for the following reasons: (1) it is mathematically intractable for all but the simplest cases, (2) most of the literature ignores investment risk and focuses exclusively on underwriting risk, and (3) it is essentially a supply-side approach which assumes that risk premia are set by insurers independently of the operation of the insurance market.

4. If N can be expressed as a constant percentage of liabilities, equation (2) asserts that insurer liabilities follow a lognormal diffusion process. Cummins and Nye [1980] have provided evidence that the lognormal distribution is a reasonable model for insurer liabilities.

5. Kraus and Ross [1982] also found that the real rate is appropriate for valuing insurance contracts.

6. Actual premiums would include an expense loading and thus would exceed $L\,[\exp(-r^{*}\tau) - p(x,\tau)]$.

7. This may reduce overall consumer welfare because policyholders who prefer to take some default risk will not have this option available in insurance markets. However, they could create "homemade" default risk by purchasing incomplete coverage.

8. Equations (18) and (19) do not simplify into a weighted sum of Black-Scholes option values with new Poisson parameter $\lambda' = \lambda(1+k)$ as in Merton [1976, p. 135]. The reason is that $\ln(1+k) = \alpha + \delta^2/2$, while $\ln E(1/X_N) = -N\alpha + N\delta^2/2$. The difference is that the jump affects the denominator rather than the numerator, as in Merton's jump model for stocks.

9. The estimate is almost identical to the variance of ln(L/L-1) about its least squares trend line. The estimation procedure probably understates the parameter which would be obtained for individual firms, because a pooling effect occurs when aggregating across companies to obtain the industry total. However, since underwriting results of insurers are highly correlated (Cummins and Nye [1980]), the understatement is not likely to be significant.

10. Property-liability insurance guaranty funds did not exist prior to 1969. The data on assessments is obtained from National Association on Insurance Guaranty Funds [1984].

**References**

A.M. Best Co. (1985). Best's Aggregates and Averages. Oldwick, N.J.

Beard, R.E.; T. Pentikainen; and E. Pesonen (1984). Risk Theory, 3d ed. New York: Chapman and Hall.

Buhlmann, Hans (1970). Mathematical Methods in Risk Theory. New York: Springer-Verlag.

Cummins, J. David and David J. Nye (1980). "The Stochastic Characteristics of Property-Liability Insurance Profits." Journal of Risk and Insurance 47: 61-80.

Cummins J.David and Scott Harrington (1985). "Property-Liability Insurance Rate Regulation: Estimation of Underwriting Betas Using Quarterly Profit Data, Journal of Risk and Insurance 52: 16-43.

Duncan, M. (1984). "An Appraisal of Property and Casualty Post-Assessment Guaranty Funds." Journal of Insurance Regulation 2: 289-303.

Fairley, William B. (1979). "Investment Income and Profit Margins in Property-Liability Insurance: Theory and Empirical Tests." Bell Journal 10: 192-210.

Gerber, Hans U. (1979). An Introduction to Mathematical Risk Theory. Philadelphia: S.S. Huebner Foundation, University of Pennsylvania.

Harrington, Scott E. and Jack Nelson (1984). "A Regression Based Methodology for Predicting Property-Liability Insurance Company Insolvency." Center for Research on Risk and Insurance Working Paper, University of Pennsylvania, Philadelphia.

Hill, Raymond D. (1979). "Profit Regulation in Property-Liability Insurance." Bell Journal 10: 172-191.

____________ and Franco Modigliani (1986). "The Massachusetts Model of Profit Regulation in Non-Life Insurance: An Appraisal and Extensions." In J.D. Cummins and S.E. Harrington, eds., Fair Rate of Return in Property-Liability Insurance. Hingham, MA: Kluwer-Nijhoff Publishing Co.

Hogg, Robert V. and Stuart A. Klugman (1984). Loss Distributions. New York: John Wiley & Sons.

Ibbotson, Robert; Rex Sinquefield; and Laurence Siegel (1982). "Historical Returns on Principal Types of Investments." Center for Research in Security Prices Working Paper No. 71, University of Chicago, Chicago.

Jarrow, Robert A. and Andrew Rudd (1983). Option Pricing. Homewood, IL: Richard D. Irwin.

Karlin, Samuel and Howard Taylor (1981). A Second Course in Stochastic Processes. New York: Academic Press.

Kraus, Alan and Stephen A. Ross (1982). "The Determination of Fair Profits for the Property-Liability Insurance Firm." Journal of Finance 37: 1015-1028.

McCulloch, J. Huston (1981). "Interest Rate Risk and Capital Adequacy for Traditional Banks and Financial Intermediaries." In Sherman J. Maisel, ed., Risk and Capital Adequacy in Commercial Banks. Chicago: University of Chicago Press.

____________ (1985). "Interest-Risk Sensitive Deposit Insurance Premia:Stable ACH Estimates." Journal of Banking and Finance 9: 137-156.

Merton, Robert C. (1971). "Optimum Consumption and Portfolio Rules in a Continuous-Time Model." Journal of Economic Theory 3: 373-413.

____________ (1976). "Option Pricing When Underlying Stock Returns Are Discontinuous." Journal of Financial Economics 3: 125-144.

____________ (1977). "An Analytic Derivation of the Cost of Deposit Insurance and Loan Guarantees: An Application of Modern Option Pricing Theory." Journal of Banking and Finance 1: 3-11.

____________ (1978). "On the Cost of Deposit Insurance When There Are Surveillance Costs." Journal of Business 51: 439-452.

Myers, Stewart and Richard Cohn (1986). "Insurance Rate Regulation and the Capital Asset Pricing Model." In J.D. Cummins and S.E. Harrington, eds., Fair Rate of Return in Property-Liability Insurance. Hingham, MA: Kluwer-Nijhoff Publishing Co.

National Committee on Insurance Guaranty Funds (1984). "Special NCIGF Report: State Insurance Guaranty Funds and Insurance Company Insolvency Assessment Information." Schaumburg, Ill.

Pennacchi, George G. (1984). "Valuing Alternative Forms of Deposit Insurance for Intermediaries Subject to Interest Rate Risk." Working Paper, Rodney White Center for Financial Research, Wharton School, University of Pennsylvania, Philadelphia.

Pinches, George and James Trieschmann (1974). "The Efficiency of Alternative Models for Solvency Surveillance in the Insurance Industry." Journal of Risk and Insurance 41: 563-577.

Quirin, David G. and Waters, William R. (1975). "Market Efficiency and the Cost of Capital: The Strange Case of Fire and Casualty Insurance Companies." Journal of Finance 30: 427-450.

Smith, Clifford W., Jr. (1976). "Option Pricing: A Review." Journal of Financial Economics 3: 3-51.

Troxel, Terrie E. and Cormick Breslin (1983). Property-Liability Insurance Accounting and Finance. 2d ed. Malvern, PA: The American Institute.

# 11

# SOLVENCY LEVELS AND RISK LOADINGS APPROPRIATE FOR FULLY GUARANTEED PROPERTY-LIABILITY INSURANCE CONTRACTS: A FINANCIAL VIEW

Richard A. Derrig

## I. Introduction

In the past, the determination of appropriate solvency levels for U.S. companies writing major property-liability insurance lines took a decidedly non-analytic approach. Verbal persuasion, reinforced by continual empirical observation, allowed for the dominance of the so-called Kenney Rules for the determination of an appropriate level of financial assets, relative to premiums written, as the required solvency level. For example, it would be assumed for regulatory purposes that if the ratio of assets to written premiums were normally 3/2 then policyholders could be assured of the payments of all their contractual claims.[1]

According to Hofflander, the major difficulty in the way of prescribing precise solvency levels was the lack of an appropriate analytic setting for the solvency problem ([17][2], p. 67). Houston [18] provided the American actuarial literature with qualitative properties that required solvency levels should possess. In particular, the surplus of assets over current outstanding liabilities should be sufficiently large enough at all times to absorb future random fluctuations in market returns on the invested financial assets and in the final realized values of the current outstanding claims. Surplus might also serve to absorb "unexpected" future liabilities due to misfeasance or malfeasance on the part of insurer management.

Structures for solvency margins have been sought since that time by various researchers. During the 70's, Stone's Theory of Capacity [22] and the investigation of simple variances of loss ratios by line of insurance by Hammond, Shilling and Shapiro [14] were two of the endeavors that (1) showed the numerical importance of the variations in liabilities and (2) pointed toward the complex interrelationship of assets and liabilities. Increasingly complex techniques were developed, mostly in Europe, under the rubic of "Ruin Theory", which sometimes seemed to show that surprisingly low levels of surplus were needed to keep the probability that liabilities would exceed assets ("ruin") at low levels. Cummins [8] suggests:

> In spite of its mathematical sophistication, actuarial ruin theory has been of limited practicality applicability. The principal problems are (1) the mathematical intractability of most of the results, (2) the nearly universal tendency to ignore investment risk, and (3) the failure to recognize that insurance companies operate in a market economy where insurance premiums and asset prices are determined by the interaction of supply and demand.

In most of the analytic endeavors, risk loadings were assumed to be simple proportions of liabilities determined either exogenously (1921 Profit Formula) or as some function of the variation of liabilities. Financial risk loadings, derived from asset pricing models such as CAPM or APT, have been introduced by Fairley [13], Hill [15], Hill and Modigliani [16] and Kraus and Ross [20] since the late 70's. These developments all ignored, or assumed away, <u>any</u> dependence of the appropriate risk loading on required solvency levels, except possibly for the important effect of taxation of income on supporting surplus (Derrig [10]). More importantly, surplus levels were not required by the analytic structure and could, therefore, be set exogenously and/or by regulatory fiat.

In 1981, Myers and Cohn [22] introduced a general financial present value model to calculate a fair market premium for an insurance contract. Their notion was simply that the economically fair premium was equal to the present risk-adjusted value of the loss and expense payment cash flows plus the present value of the income tax liability on all underwriting and investment income, including the income on required surplus. Although their model required risk-adjusted discount rates appropriate to each type of flow and each time period, the current practice in Massachusetts of using a single discount rate adjustment appropriate for all lines, for all time periods, and for all uncertain flows was accepted for their present purposes. Overall surplus requirements would be exogenous to the model but by-line allocations of that surplus by line would then be determined by the constant risk-adjustment assumption. Section II reviews the argument that a constant per-period risk adjustment <u>requires</u> that supporting surplus be allocated approximately in proportion to outstanding liabilities (reserves) by using the Fairley one period premium model calculation and the financial principle that equal rates of return are required for accepting equal (systematic) risks. Section III sets forth a proposed criterion for determining required solvency margins in terms of options pricing concepts. The proposal replaces the usual probability level criterion for solvency by a financial value criterion: the value of the premium to reinsure the liability portfolio given the current level of assets. Section IV discusses Cummins' newly developed guaranty fund premium model in order to provide for some examples of the required solvency margins as defined in Section III. Section V applies the notions of Sections III and IV to obtain the appropriate solvency margins for a fully guaranteed insurance contract using Massachusetts data. Section VI proposes to interpret the Cummins' risk premium to reinsure a policy cohort having an asset/liability ratio of 1 as a (first approximation to) quantification of the proper risk loading in a fully guaranteed insurance contract. Section VII offers a summary and some concluding remarks.

## II. Surplus Allocation by Line

An area of central importance in the application of fair premium models for pricing insurance contracts has been the amount of surplus supporting each line of insurance. The determination of the proper amount of surplus is important because, as Myers and Cohn [22] showed, the fair premium must include the present value of the taxes on the investment income attributable to the surplus supporting the policy. As more or less surplus is allocated to the line of insurance, higher or lower tax burdens will be inferred with resultant higher or lower underwriting profit margins. Modelling the insurance contract as a multi-period flow process demands that surplus requirements be treated in each period during the life of the contract. This is the so-called "flow" model for surplus.

Both conventional accounting wisdom and the early Stone-Fairley models related surplus needs to premium. The so-called "Kenney Rule" was used by Stone in 1976 to estimate surplus needs at one-half of the premium value. Although this seemed like the proper course to take for overall regulatory purposes, the economics-based cash flow methodologies required an allocation scheme by line of insurance.[3]

Other regulators have reached similar conclusions about the need to allocate surplus or net worth to lines of insurance. In the mid-1970's the New York Insurance Department developed, in response to a statutory requirement, a methodology for measuring the profitability of property and liability insurance by line and by state. As part of its methodology the New York Department was required to allocate surplus by line. The Department published the "appropriate" premium-to-surplus ratio for each line of business in New York Insurance Department Regulation 70. Table II-1 reproduces the original New York premium to surplus ratios calculated by the Department. These ratios show allocations roughly in proportion to statutory reserves.[4]

More recently in a study prepared for the New York Insurance Department, Williams [25] considered the problem of how to allocate investment income and net worth to the various automobile insurance lines. He noted that there was no standard approach to such allocation, that net worth (or surplus) might in theory be allocated among lines by premium, by reserves, or by the relative risk of the various lines. He concluded that it was not necessary to resolve the issue in his case, because whatever method of allocation was chosen, the amount of net worth allocated to the combined

Table II - I

Excerpt from New York Regulation 70

| Line of Insurance | Premium Earned-to-Surplus Ratio |
|---|---|
| Fire | 1.8 |
| Allied Lines | 2.2 |
| Homeowners multiple peril | 2.2 |
| Commercial multiple peril | 1.6 |
| Inland marine | 2.3 |
| Workmen's compensation | 1.0 |
| Liability other than auto (BI) | .6 |
| Liability other than auto (PD) | 1.0 |
| Auto no-fault and liability (BI) | 1.0 |
| Auto liability (PD) | 2.7 |
| Auto collision | 5.5 |
| Auto fire, theft and comprehensive | 4.9 |
| Aircraft (all perils) | 1.8 |
| Fidelity | .8 |
| Surety | 1.6 |
| Glass | 4.5 |
| Burglary and theft | 2.3 |
| Boiler and machinery | 1.4 |
| Credit | 3.7 |

These ratios were derived on the basis of the experience of all companies for the years 1969 through 1973 in accordance with the allocation method described in Section 165.2(d) of Regulation No. 70, Insurance Department of the State of New York 11NYCRR 165 Methodologies for Measuring the Profitability of Property and Liability Insurance Lines Written in New York State, January 1975.

automobile lines would be about the same. Williams expressly noted, however, that the same conclusion would not apply to other lines.

During the hearing on the 1981 Massachusetts Workers' Compensation rates, it was shown that Fairley's accounting-like model treatment of surplus would not produce equal rates of return for equally risky amounts of surplus committed over the same period of time.[5] Fairley's model would yield equal rates of return for equally risky commitments of surplus only if the variable ks, roughly total reserves to surplus, were held constant. This meant that the overall surplus level should be related to reserves, not premium and that the allocation by line should also be by reserves rather than premium.

Briefly, if $r_f$, $\bar{r}_m$, $\bar{r}_E$ and $\bar{r}_A$ are expected returns on risk-free investments, the market, shareholders equity and the insurer's invested assets, then for $\beta_A$ and $\beta_L$ the asset and liability "betas", premium to surplus ratio s and reserves to premium ratio k, Fairley derived the expected shareholders rate of return equation

$$\bar{r}_E = \bar{r}_A + (\beta_A - \beta_L)(\bar{r}_m - r_f)ks$$

under the assumption that equal amounts of surplus underly the line of insurance regardless of the size of reserves (k). This, of course, produces expected rates of return which differ by line, since k differs by line, despite the fact that the risk coefficients, $\beta_A$ and $\beta_L$, are assumed constant.

As a practical matter, and for ease of understanding, this requirement could be restated in terms of the accounting premium-to-surplus ratio used in the Fairley model. Using Fairley's estimate of k for the automobile and worker's compensation lines of insurance (see [13], p. 197) and his estimate of a constant premium-to-surplus ratio by line, we have the following target rates of return on shareholders equity by line:

| Line | Fairley k | Premium Surplus Ratio | Return on Equity |
|---|---|---|---|
| Auto BI | 1.60 | 2 | 30.00 |
| Auto PD | .31 | 2 | 13.88 |
| Workers Comp. | 1.60 | 2 | 30.00 |

Alternatively, using a surplus provision proportional to the "reserves" k of each line, would yield the following:

| Line | Fairley k | Premium Surplus Ratio | Return on Equity |
|---|---|---|---|
| Auto BI | 1.60 | 1.25 | 22.50 |
| Auto PD | .31 | 6.45 | 22.50 |
| Workers Comp. | 1.60 | 1.25 | 22.50 |

The upshot of the analysis was that there had to be a per-period relationship between the amount of surplus (equity) committed in that period and the relative magnitude of the risk (beta) in that period. Further, in the event that the per-period risk adjustment was constant by period and line, as in all applications to date in Massachusetts, then the commitment of surplus per-period must be in proportion to the outstanding reserves. Thus it followed that more surplus should be committed to the long-tailed, large-reserve, Schedule P lines then to the short-term, small-reserve, Schedule O lines of insurance. Recent results show that workable equivalent accounting premium-to-surplus ratios are about 1 to 1 for automobile bodily injury and workers' compensation, 2 to 1 for automobile property damage liability, and 3 to 1 for automobile physical damage.

The multiperiod Myers-Cohn model, on the other hand, explicitly models the flow of surplus based on the assumption that companies hold surplus for a longer period of time on long-tailed lines. Since surplus is exposed to underwriting risk for a longer period of time, companies require more cumulative compensation on long-tailed lines -- just as in the Fairley model -- but the per-period rate of return on surplus is constant among lines when the per-period measure of risk is assumed to be constant.

The notion of allocating surplus in proportion to reserves can be seen to be an attractive position by the following heuristic argument. It is reasonable to assume a priori that surplus exists because the policyholder (and the regulator) wants evidence that all claim payment obligations can be met. It follows that surplus should be a function of expected liabilities, time, and perhaps other variables which we disregard for this exercise. Symbolically,

$$\text{Surplus} = S(\overline{\text{Liabilities}}, \text{Time}) \tag{1}$$

where the bar represents market values. Assume S is smooth enough for a Taylor Series expansion in expected liabilities $\bar{L}$ with center at time $\tau$ equal zero; i.e.,

$$S\ (\bar{L}, \tau) = a_o(\tau) + a_1(\tau)\bar{L}(\tau) + \ldots \tag{2}$$

Then for each time period $\tau$, the linear approximation to S is:

$$S\ (\bar{L}, \tau) = a_1(\tau)\bar{L}(\tau) \tag{3}$$

because $S = 0$ if $\bar{L} = 0$ would imply that $a_0(\tau) = 0$ for all $\tau$.

The special case envisioned by Myers and Cohn, in the presence of constant per-period risk and constant per period rates of return, would be the requirement that

$$a_1(\tau) = a(o) = a,\ \text{Surplus/Liabilities, for all } \tau. \tag{4}$$

or

$$S\ (\bar{L}, \tau) = a\bar{L}(\tau) \quad \text{for all } \tau \tag{5}$$

Committing surplus in the same constant proportion to outstanding liabilities at each point in time leads to the same situation in which surplus is allocated across all lines in proportion to outstanding reserves for liabilities. Since we are using market values of liabilities, it is the case that surplus is allocated to line by written premium (market value of new policy liabilities) plus the market value of outstanding reserves on the run-off of prior policies.

None of the above arguments reveal the proper overall amount of surplus to be held by a company and then allocated to each line in proportion to reserves. Indeed, to the extent that the risk loading induced by the liability beta is not constant per period[6], the above allocation technique will not be in proportion to reserves but only in proportion to the relative riskiness of reserves. We next turn to a general model of insurance pricing from which we may be able to estimate required surplus, or solvency margin, based upon financial principles other than equal rates of return for equal risk.

## III. A Criterion for Solvency Margins

According to standard ruin theory concepts, a company can be called solvent if there is a high degree of probability that all of its liabilities will be covered by the assets it now holds. Stated formally, between the present ($\tau = 0$) and some future time ($\tau = T$), if at each time $\tau$, $0 \leq \tau \leq T$, we denote the value of the liabilities by $L(\tau)$ and the value of the assets by $A(\tau)$ then we call a company solvent at T with probability $1 - \varepsilon$ if

$$\text{Prob}\,\{\, A(T) < L(T) \,\} < \varepsilon. \tag{6}$$

Typically, $\varepsilon$ is taken to be at the same numerical levels used for statistical hypothesis testing with confidence intervals; i.e., $\varepsilon$ = 10%, 5%, 1% or, perhaps, even smaller.

The solvency margin $S(\tau)$ can then be defined at each time $\tau$ to be the difference between the assets and liabilities; i.e.,

$$S(\tau) = A(\tau) - L(\tau) \tag{7}$$

The solvency margin defined in this manner corresponds to the economic concept of net worth when $A(\tau)$ and $L(\tau)$ are denominated in market values; whereas, $S(\tau)$ corresponds to the accounting concept of policyholders surplus when $A(\tau)$ and $L(\tau)$ are denominated in statutory accounting (book) values.

One undesirable feature of the criterion in equation (6) is that, although the ingredients $A(\tau)$ and $L(\tau)$ are financial concepts the criterion itself, "probability less than $\varepsilon$", is not. It would seem that a more appropriate and consistent criterion should involve the **economic** value of this probabilistic statement rather than its **statistical** value.

To set the stage for the appropriate financial criteria, let us consider an analogy with ordinary bond pricing. Both insurance contracts and coupon bonds involve the promise to pay prespecified amounts (claim payment, coupon and face amounts) at prespecified times (presentation of claim, scheduled coupon and maturity payment dates). The difference, of course, is that bonds promise to pay certain amounts at certain times[7] while insurance contracts promise to pay uncertain amounts at uncertain times. The commonality is that in either case the promise may not be realized; debtor firms may not be able to pay their bondholders and insurance companies may not be able to make their claim payments. The risk that bondholders may not receive their promised payments is known as default risk and is commonly understood to demand a risk premium within the price, and therefore yield, of the bond. One standard measurement of the mean default premium of U.S. corporate bonds over the assumed default-free U.S. Government bonds is an investment yield of 0.6% based upon data from 1926-1985 (Ibbotson [19], Exhibit 10, p.44). The point to be made here is that, although there no doubt is a non-trivial time-dependent probability distribution of default lurking behind any bond which is not fully guaranteed to be default-free, that distribution is not itself generally observable but its economic valuation is observable in the market price of the bond. In a sense then, the probability of default is irrelevant given the operation of a reasonably efficient financial market.

We propose to state a solvency criterion for the insurance contract in a manner that is analogous to the default premium on bonds. In verbal form, we shall call a company solvent at time T at level $\epsilon$ if the premium required to fully reinsure the companies liabilities L(0) against default is less than $\epsilon L(0)$. The formal setting for this criterion will be within financial options or contingent claims theory. The theory of options pricing has only recently been applied in the context of insurance pricing (Cummins [8], [9], Doherty and Garven [12]) and this author borrows liberally from their approach. It may be useful to set these notions down in a formal manner for a simple case.

Let $L(\tau)$ = Liabilities $0 \le \tau \le T$
$A(\tau)$ = Assets $0 \le \tau \le T$
T = Time of a Single Liability Payment

Assume T is fixed at $\tau = 0$ and L and A each follow a stochastic process. Now at time T (or anytime $\tau$ for that matter)

$$0 = A(T) - L(T) - MAX(0,A(T)-L(T)) + MAX(0,L(T)-A(T)) \quad (8)$$

So under certain conditions (absence of arbitrage, efficient market, or valuation is a martingale) the present value must be zero. So if $PV_0$ (•) is the present-value-at-time-0 operator, then

$$PV_0 (A(T)) - PV_0 (MAX(0, L(T) - A(T))) \quad (9)$$

$$= PV_0 (L(T)) - PV_0 (MAX(0, A(T) - L(T)))$$

Now, assuming market values for assets and liabilities, we have

$$PV_0 (A(T)) = A(0) \text{ and } PV_0 (L(T)) = L(0)$$

i.e., total assets at time T have a present value equal to the current value and L(0) is known. In case L(T) is known with certainty then $PV_0$ (L(T)) = exp(-rT) L(T), with r the risk-free rate of interest. Now if we define functions c and p by

$$PV_0\ (MAX(0,\ A(T) - L(T))) = c(A,\ L,\ T) \text{ and} \tag{10}$$

$$PV_0\ (MAX(0,\ L(T) - A(T))) = p(A,\ L,\ T) \tag{11}$$

then c is the value of a (European) call to buy A(T) at a price L(T) at time T and p is the value of a (European) put to sell A(T) at a price L(T) at time T.

Thus we have the usual equilibrium equation (e.g., Cox & Ross, [7] Eq. 2)

$$A(0) = [-p(A,\ L,\ T) + PV_0\ (L(T))] + c(A,\ L,\ T) \tag{12}$$

Viewing the current assets A(0) of the insurance company we have (ignoring taxes)[8]

$$\text{Assets} = \text{Policyholder Claims} + \text{Shareholders Claims} \tag{13}$$

For a cohort of policies with all liabilities payable at time T and (fair) premium P, invested equity (equivalently net worth or surplus) S = S(0), we have

$$A(0) = P + S \tag{14}$$

Under a fair premium standard (invested equity must equal value of equity, Myers & Cohn [22])

$$P = PV_0\ (L(T)) - p(A,\ L,\ T) + [c(A,\ L,\ T) - S] \tag{15}$$

In words, the fair premium is equal to the present value of the liabilities less the value of the (default) put option on the assets for the value of the liabilities at time T plus the "in the money" portion of a call option on those same assets. Unless liability payments[9] are fully guaranteed to be paid at time T, the fair premium must be reduced by the cost of such a guarantee, p(A,L,T), given the value of the invested equity S(0) and the processes $A(\tau)$, $L(\tau)$.

Consider two cases: one where the policyholder self-insures with his premium as his assets and one where the policyholder insures with a company. So, for $0 \leq \tau \leq T$, if $P(\tau)$ = value of the fair premium P at time $\tau$,

<u>Case I</u>

$$\begin{aligned} P_I(\tau) &- c(P_I(T),\ L(T),\ T - \tau) \\ &= PV_\tau\ [L(T)] - p(P_I(T),\ L(T),\ T - \tau) \end{aligned} \tag{16a}$$

Case II

$$P_{II}(\tau) + S(\tau) - c(P_{II}(T) + S(T), L(T), T - \tau) \tag{16b}$$

$$= PV_{\tau} [(L(T)] - p(P_{II}(T) + S(T), L(T), T - \tau)$$

In each case the fair premium consists of the present value of the expected losses L(T) plus the value of call options on the underlying assets (Case I premiums, Case II premiums and surplus) less the put option valuing the price of default given those underlying assets. Within this framework we can provide our formal definition of solvency margin.

We can interpret the value of the put option in either case as the premium the insured would pay to guarantee (reinsure) that his claim payments are default free. Now at $\tau = 0$, if S*(0) is chosen so that the value of the put option in Case II is (approximately) zero, then (16b) gives:

$$P(0) \simeq PV_0 [L(T)] + [c(P(T) + S^*(T), L(T), T) - S^*(0)] \tag{17}$$

when $p(P(T) + S^*(T), L(T), T) \simeq 0$.

But P + S* is invested in a portfolio with returns $1 + r_A$ so

$$P(T) + S^*(T) = (P(0) + S^*(0))(1 + r_A)^T \tag{18}$$

so $p((P(0) + S^*(0))(1 + r_A)^T, L(T), T) \simeq 0$

or $p(P(0)(1 + \text{Surplus/Premium})(1 + r_A)^T, L(T), T) \simeq 0$

If the put option P is also homogeneous[10] then we have

$$p(P(0)/L(0)(1+\text{Surplus/Premium})(1+r_A)^T, L(T)/L(0), T)\ L(0) \simeq 0 \tag{19}$$

Equation (19) can, in theory, be solved for the number Surplus/Premium = S*(0)/P(0) knowing the investment process with returns $(1 + r_A)$, the relative loss process L(T)/L(0) and the asset process (in terms of the relative asset/liability ratio (P(0) + S*(0))/L(0)). This value of S*(0)/P(0) provides the appropriate surplus requirement for a fully guaranteed insurance contract on the liabilities L(0).

More formally, we say that a company with premiums P(0), Surplus S(0) and Liabilities L(0) is solvent at time T at level $\varepsilon$ if the value of the relative put option p is less than $\varepsilon$, i.e.

$$p([(P(0) + S(0))/(L(0)](1 - r_A)^T, L(T)/L(0), T) < \varepsilon \tag{20}$$

Depending on how the premium and liability processes are viewed; i.e. as an on-going firm or as a policy cohort ("break-up value"), this criterion can play the role of required solvency margins for solidity or required solvency margin for pricing the policy cohort insurance contracts. We turn next to the implementation of Cummins's application of options pricing in order to obtain some examples of this viewpoint.

## IV. Cummins Guaranty Fund Model

Recently, both[11] Cummins [8] and Doherty and Garven [12], have proposed that option pricing theory can be used to determine risk loadings appropriate for insurance contracts. Those studies provide somewhat differing views of the insurance process but each eventually adapts some rather sophisticated notions underlying the financial theory of contingent claims to provide a natural setting for the pricing of insurance and reinsurance contracts. Doherty and Garven prefer to work with a discrete model while Cummins chooses to adapt a continuous model. Both employ normality assumptions for tractability. At bottom, however, their common central view is that the insurance contract provides policyholders with a priority claim on the insurance company's assets (premiums and surplus) in return for a "fair" premium. Intuitively, it then follows that the more assets the company has to satisfy the policyholders claim (the more surplus contributed by shareholders), the more valuable the policyholders claim becomes and the larger the "fair" premium should be. The contingent claims view may provide, therefore, the essential analytic and structural dependence of the premium upon the surplus provided by the company rather than a mere tangential dependency on surplus for including the tax liability in the fair premium.

The early work by Hill [15] and Fairley [13] did not employ any structural dependence on the amount of surplus provided by the company other than for the purpose of calculating a tax liability. Hill [p. 180] remarked that "the insurance contract has no 'return to capital' dimension .... the firm is indifferent to the premium-capital ratio. (This irrelevance of the premium-capital ratio also depends on the assumption that policies have no default risk.)." Hill also suggested that "if there is some risk that the firm will become insolvent, and thus unable to reimburse losses, fair premiums would be below those (calculated by his CAPM model)." Under the general framework in Section III, this diminution in fair premium[12] is measured by the value of the put option p(A(T), L(T), T).

Likewise, under the financial solvency criterion (III-17) the insurance contract is effectively default-free precisely when there is enough surplus $S^*(0)$ committed to the insurance contract to make this reinsurance premium (the put option) virtually zero. We will use Cummins's guaranty fund model for a policy cohort to obtain some examples of appropriate values for $S^*$ using data obtained for the Massachusetts lines of private passenger automobile, both liability and physical damage coverages, and workers' compensation for the period 1976-1985.

In Cummins's policy cohort model ([8], p.15) the asset/liability process is assumed to be generated by two simultaneous geometric Brownian motion processes with drift.

$$dA = (r_A A - \theta L)dt + \sigma_A A\, dZ_A \qquad (21)$$

$$dL = (r_L L - \theta L)dt + \sigma_L L\, dZ_L$$

where assets A, invested in marketable securities, continually change according to the returns on those invested assets $r_A$, less the claims payment $\Theta L$, subject to a random disturbance term with variance parameter $\sigma^2_A$. Liabilities, at some point $\tau = \tau_o$ in the process, also continually change at some rate $r_L$, less the claim payment $\Theta L$, subject to its random disturbance term with variance parameters $\sigma_L^2$. Further, it is assumed that all liabilities (claim payments) are paid through a claim on the assets A, available to the policy cohort, plus other assets (not included in A) for which a premium $\Pi(A,L)$ must be paid.[13]

Cummins derives a tractable solution by using the Ito calculus together with the assumptions that:

$\Pi$ reflects only systematic risk. (22a)

systematic risk of liabilities is zero, and (22b)

$\Pi(A,L) = \pi(x)\, L$, with $x = A/L$. (22c)

These assumptions allow the reduction of equation (21) to an ordinary 2nd order linear differential equation in x, the asset/-liability ratio,

$$\pi(r-r_L+\Theta) = \pi_x[x\,(r-r_L+\Theta) - \Theta] + \tfrac{1}{2}\, x^2\, \pi_{xx}\,(\sigma_A^2 + \sigma_L^2) \qquad (23)$$

where $r$ = risk-free rate, assumed constant
$r_L$ = rate of return on liabilities, assumed constant
$\Theta$ = rate of payment of liabilities, assumed constant
$\sigma_A^2$ = variance of returns on assets, assumed constant
$\sigma_L^2$ = variance of returns on liabilities, assumed constant

For notational convenience, we set new constants a and b as

$$a = (r - r_L + \Theta)/(\sigma_A^2 + \sigma_L^2)/2$$

$$b = \Theta/(\sigma_A^2 + \sigma_L^2)/2$$

and obtain

$$x^2\, \pi_{xx} + [ax - b]\, \pi_x - a\pi = 0 \qquad (24)$$

Cummins provides for 2 boundary conditions in order to generate a unique solution; namely,

$$\lim_{x\to\infty} \pi(x) = 0 \qquad (25a)$$

$$\lim_{x\to 0+} \pi(x) = \pi(0+) = 1 \qquad (25b)$$

It can then be shown[14] that equation (24) can be solved for $\pi(x)$ using the method of Frobenius (Spiegal [25], p.292) to obtain a solution satisfying boundary condition (25a).

The solution is

$$\pi(x) = c\, x^{-a}\, M(a,\ a + 2,\ -b/x), \text{ for some constant } c. \qquad (26)$$

where M(a,b,Z) is the general Kummer[15] function

$$M(a,b,Z) = {}_1F_1\,(a,b,Z) = \sum_{i=0}^{\infty} \frac{(a)_i}{(b)_i}\ \frac{Z^i}{i!}$$

with $(a)_i = a(a+1)\ \ldots\ (a+i-1)$, a product of i terms

The constant c in (26) can then be expressed in terms of the 2nd boundary condition (25b) constant $\pi(0+)$ giving[16]

$$\pi(x) = \frac{\pi(0+)}{\Gamma(a + 2)}\ (b/x)^a\ e^{-b/x}\ M(2,\ a + 2,\ b/x) \qquad (27)$$

Given the general form of the solution (27) then with any $\pi(0+) > 0$ it can also be shown that

$$\pi_x < 0 \quad \text{and } \pi_{xx} > 0 \quad \text{for all } x > 0. \qquad (28)$$

Thus we have the shape of $\pi$ as:

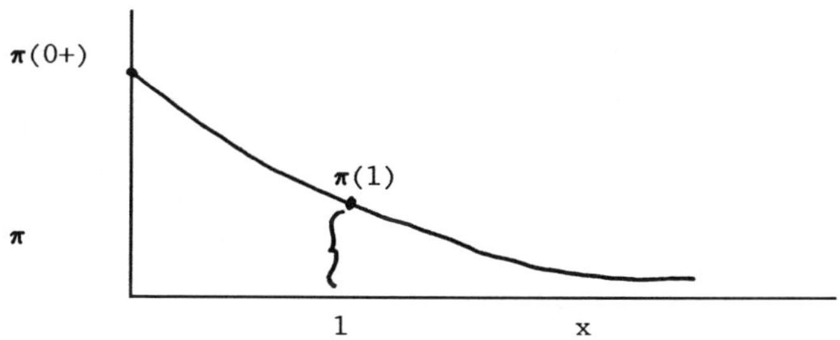


Now in the terminology of Cummins's model, we can restate our financial solvency criterion of III-20 in a way more consistent with the verbal definition of a company solvent at time T at level $\varepsilon$. With assets A(0) = P(0) + S(0), the premium and the surplus in support of the policy cohort, and liabilities L(0), at present value, then the policy cohort is solvent at level $\varepsilon$ if

$$\pi(x) < \varepsilon \quad \text{for} \quad x = A(0)/L(0). \qquad (29)$$

In the case of interest here, we wish to use the Cummins's framework to deduce the amount of surplus necessary to fully guarantee the policyholders' contract. Quite literally, only an infinite amount of surplus can completely guarantee that all payments will be made, but under our assumption in Section III-17, that the policyholders default put option is **virtually** 0, we can choose some small $\varepsilon$ and define that the policy cohort contracts are (virtually) fully guaranteed by surplus S*(0) if, when A*(0) = P(0) + S*(0) and x* = A*/L,

$$\pi(x^*) < \varepsilon \quad \text{for sufficiently small } \varepsilon > 0. \tag{30}$$

In our calculations we will assume, somewhat arbitrarily, that $\varepsilon$ = 1E(-5); i.e., the cohort has fully guaranteed contracts for liabilities L(0) if the premium to reinsure liabilities L(0), having assets A*(0), is less than 1/1000% of the liabilities L(0). We now turn to those examples using data from the Massachusetts automobile and workers' compensation markets for 1976-1985.

## V. Some Examples of Required Solvency Margins For Fully Guaranteed Insurances Contracts Using Massachusetts Data 1976 - 1985

Cummins' model requires the estimation of a number of parameters in order to calculate the guaranty fund premium. They include interest rates r and $r_L$, variance parameters $\sigma_A^2$ and $\sigma_L^2$, and the payout parameter $\theta$. We discuss each choice in turn.

A. Interest Rates

Although two interest rates are shown in the defining process equations, IV-21 above, the parameter that affects the solution guaranty fund premiums is the rate r* equal to the difference between the risk-free rate r and the expected liability growth rate $r_L$.

$$r^* = r - r_L \tag{31}$$

For our examples, we show calculations for three alternatives.

r* = .025, Cummins' Table 2 parameter for the "real" rate ([8], p.24) (32a)

r* = .014 = (.16)(.09), the systematic risk adjustment assumed in Massachusetts in recent years to discount the risky liabilities.[17] (32b)

r* = .000. This case provides for perhaps a more reasonable interpretation of the general Cummins model in terms of a policy cohort. Presumably, the initial value of the liabilities L(0) will be the nominal loss payments discounted at the appropriate risk-adjusted rate $r_L$. If, indeed, we are talking about default-free loss payments, (32c)

$L(\tau_i)$, L = 1,...N and we assume both systematic risk pricing (IV-22a) and systematic liability risk of zero (IV-22b) then the market value of the $L(\tau_i)$ payments would be the discounted value at the risk-free rate. Thus consistency may demand that $r_L = r$ or $r^* = 0$ if we assume, as we should, that the market value of the liabilities are priced in accordance with the assumptions of the model (22a,b,c).

B. Variance Parameters

For the examples presented here, we will accept the Cummins' calculations for the variance of the log relative returns for assets typical of insurers portfolios for 1980 based upon U.S. capital market returns for 1959-1980. That sets $\sigma_A^2 = .0048$. However, we modify the variance for liability from the small all industry inflation value, .0016 which may be appropriate for the non-cohort cases of a one-year on-going company and the one-year on-going company with allowances for catastrophes, by adding[18] a more realistic estimate of the variance of the original estimated market value of L.

The nominal value of L, expected in the premium charges P(0), and hence in the market value L(0), can differ from the realized value of L for many reasons. Among those reasons are several which are commonly recognized as affecting the variation in L faced by real companies, but missing from the pure industrywide inflation estimate made by Cummins. They include

Size of company; (33a)

The line and/or mix of lines written by the company; (33b)

The regulatory restrictions on the premiums allowed to be charged (regulatory delay). (33c)

The Massachusetts lines of private passenger and workers' compensation during the last ten years provide the opportunity to affect a measurement of those deviations from expected results due to the three influences (33a,b,c).

Table V-1 displays the results of calculating the variances of the log loss ratios from Annual Statements for workers' compensation and private passenger automobile for 1976-1985 for all company groups with more than .05% of the premium. This gives a sample of between 43 and 51 company groups for the ten year period. A unique feature of the Massachusetts data is the fact that for (almost[19]) all of that time period, all companies had to charge the same rate to the same policyholders. This allows the loss ratio to control for the mix of business according to classifications written. It also allows us to calculate the variance from the target mean allowed by the regulator as well as the variance from the realized mean. The data show no great surprises but it does seem worthwhile to list some features of those variances.

i. Smaller volume company groups (Bottom 25% by premium) exhibited much larger variances then did the large volume company groups (Top 25% by premium).

ii. Workers' Compensation variances were generally significantly higher for similar size samples than the automobile variances (and, therefore, higher than the combined auto and workers' compensation variances).

iii. The regulatory control on the rates, causing the realized mean to differ from the target mean, <u>increased</u> the variance calculated in all categories by about 20%.

iv. The combination of auto liability and physical damage coverages, which about double the premium volume, or with workers' compensation, which triples the premium volume, lower the variances by only a small amount. This is consistent with the prior findings of Hammond, Shilling and Shapiro ([14], p.55) which showed private passenger auto liability, private passenger physical damage and <u>all lines</u> standard deviations of loss ratios to be approximately the same (.104, .110 and .094 respectively).

v. Since the variances were calculated as deviations from each annual realized or target mean, the resulting variance should be independent of the general inflationary variance (.0016) calculated by Cummins for the entire industry and assumed for each company ([8], footnote 9 and compare Kraus & Ross [20], p.1023).

vi. The variances calculated here, and added to the Cummins' inflationary variance, may be more typical of the unanticipated changes in the value of L expected in the rates, faced by <u>individual</u> companies (Cummins [8], p.29).

C. <u>Payout Parameter</u>

The payout parameter $\theta$ plays an important role within the Cummins' model. The parameters used in our examples represent an estimate of $\theta$ obtained by calculating an estimate of the inverse of $\theta$, the average time of claim payouts for the actual payment flows, rather than as the elasticity in the exponential runoff model. In any event, the two methods of estimating Θ should be close. We estimate the following payout parameters Θ.

| | |
|---|---|
| Workers' Compensation | 0.5 |
| P.P. Auto Liability[20] | 1.0 |
| P.P. Auto Physical Damage | 1.6 |
| P.P. Auto Total | 1.2 |
| P.P. Auto & W.C. | 0.8 |

Tables V-2a,b,c and V-3a,b,c following show the results of choosing a required solvency margin, actually the asset/liability ratio and thus the solvency margin at the writing of the policy cohort, based on the fully guaranteed criterion of the last section (IV-29).

For discussion purposes we reproduce here an abbreviated table for the "Top 25%" large writers in the sample and compare those results to the results using the Cummins' inflationary liability variance alone.

**Table V-4**

Required Risk Premium Ratios to Expected Liabilities

| Line of Insurance | From Realized Means r* = .025 | .014 | .000 |
|---|---|---|---|
| W.C. | 2.29 | 2.37 | 2.46 |
| Auto Liab. | 1.43 | 1.44 | 1.47 |
| Auto P.D. | 1.33 | 1.34 | 1.36 |
| All Auto | 1.33 | 1.34 | 1.36 |
| Auto & W.C. | 1.46 | 1.49 | 1.52 |
| Cummins Liab. Variance | 1.28 | 1.32 | 1.38 |

| Line of Insurance | From Target Means r* = .025 | .014 | .000 |
|---|---|---|---|
| W.C. | 2.5+ | 2.5+ | 2.5+ |
| Auto Liab. | 1.73 | 1.76 | 1.79 |
| Auto P.D. | 1.49 | 1.51 | 1.52 |
| All Auto | 1.53 | 1.55 | 1.57 |
| Auto & W.C. | 1.76 | 1.79 | 1.84 |
| Cummins Liab. Variance | 1.28 | 1.32 | 1.38 |

Three results stand out in comparison to the Kenney-type overall rule of thumb and the New York Department's allocation of surplus by reserves discussed in Section II.

Table V - 1a

Massachusetts Log Loss Ratio Variances and Guaranty Fund Risk Premiums
Private Passenger Automobile and Workers' Compensation
1976 - 1985

$r - r_L = .025$

| Insurance | Sample | From Annual Realized Means | | From Annual Target Means | |
|---|---|---|---|---|---|
| | | Variance($\sigma^2$) | Risk-Premium $\pi(1)$ | Variance($\sigma^2$) | Risk-Premium $\pi(1)$ |
| Workers' Compensation $\Theta = .5$ | All (44) | .12416 | .12014 | .14460 | .13064 |
| | Top 25% (11) | .03876 | .06240 | .09261 | .10208 |
| | Bottom 25% (11) | .22208 | .16477 | .25320 | .17665 |
| P.P. Auto Liability $\Theta = 1.0$ | All (43) | .07050 | .06639 | .07925 | .07066 |
| | Top 25% (11) | .01529 | .03027 | .03750 | .04751 |
| | Bottom 25% (11) | .09817 | .07921 | .12082 | .08846 |
| P.P. Auto Physical Damage $\Theta = 1.6$ | All (47) | .05599 | .04825 | .08006 | .05805 |
| | Top 25% (12) | .01686 | .02676 | .03397 | .03744 |
| | Bottom 25% (12) | .06604 | .05254 | .17199 | .08637 |
| P.P. Auto Total $\Theta = 1.2$ | All (44) | .04277 | .04733 | .05222 | .05252 |
| | Top 25% (11) | .01143 | .02497 | .02793 | .03806 |
| | Bottom 25% (11) | .05996 | .05647 | .09504 | .07198 |
| P.P. Auto & Workers' Compensation Combined $\Theta = .8$ | All (51) | .05311 | .06242 | .05861 | .06584 |
| | Top 25% (13) | .01361 | .03079 | .03137 | .04705 |
| | Bottom 25% (13) | .09332 | .08471 | .10677 | .09110 |
| All Industry $\Theta = .4$ | Cummins | .00000 | .01285 | .00000 | .01285 |

Notes:

1. The sample consists of the natural log of the Annual Statement Loss Ratios by all company groups writing in Massachusetts by years 1976-1985 subject to certain minimum (greater than .05% of total premium) combined premium volume. The number of company groups is shown in parentheses. Top and Bottom 25% selected according to premium volume for all ten years.
2. Variance calculated using individual annual realized or target means for each of the ten years. Target mean is that underlying the approved rates charged by all companies.
3. Risk premium calculated according to Cummins's Policy Cohort Model for Guaranty Fund Premium using Asset variance with 1980 portfolio weights (.0047), Liability variance (.0016 + $\sigma^2$ above), $r - r_L$ (.025), and Payout Parameter $\Theta$ (W.C. 0.5, Liability 1.0, Physical Damage 1.6, Auto Total 1.2, Combined 0.8) and expressed as a fraction of liabilities.

Table V - 1b

Massachusetts Log Loss Ratio Variances and Guaranty Fund Risk Premiums
Private Passenger Automobile and Workers' Compensation
1976 - 1985

$r - r_L = .014$

| Insurance | Group Sample | | From Annual Realized Means Variance($\sigma^2$) | From Annual Realized Means Risk-Premium $\pi(1)$ | From Annual Target Means Variance($\sigma^2$) | From Annual Target Means Risk-Premium $\pi(1)$ |
|---|---|---|---|---|---|---|
| Workers' Compensation $\Theta = .5$ | All | (44) | .12416 | .12966 | .14460 | .14019 |
| | Top 25% | (11) | .03876 | .07150 | .09261 | .11153 |
| | Bottom 25% | (11) | .22208 | .17433 | .25320 | .18620 |
| P.P. Auto Liability $\Theta = 1.0$ | All | (43) | .07050 | .07131 | .07925 | .07560 |
| | Top 25% | (11) | .01529 | .03488 | .03750 | .05233 |
| | Bottom 25% | (11) | .09817 | .08417 | .12082 | .09344 |
| P.P. Auto Physical Damage $\Theta = 1.6$ | All | (47) | .05599 | .05139 | .08006 | .06120 |
| | Top 25% | (12) | .01686 | .02977 | .03397 | .04053 |
| | Bottom 25% | (12) | .06604 | .05568 | .17199 | .08956 |
| P.P. Auto Total $\Theta = 1.2$ | All | (44) | .04277 | .05141 | .05222 | .05663 |
| | Top 25% | (11) | .01143 | .02882 | .02793 | .04207 |
| | Bottom 25% | (11) | .05996 | .06059 | .09504 | .07615 |
| P.P. Auto & Workers' Compensation Combined $\Theta = .8$ | All | (51) | .05311 | .06843 | .05861 | .07187 |
| | Top 25% | (13) | .01361 | .03638 | .03137 | .05292 |
| | Bottom 25% | (13) | .09332 | .09082 | .10677 | .09722 |
| All Industry $\Theta = .4$ | Cummins | | .00000 | .02079 | .00000 | .02079 |

Notes:

1. The sample consists of the natural log of the Annual Statement Loss Ratios by all company groups writing in Massachusetts by years 1976-1985 subject to certain minimum (greater than .05% of total premium) combined premium volume. The number of company groups is shown in parentheses. Top and Bottom 25% selected according to premium volume for all ten years.
2. Variance calculated using individual annual realized or target means for each of the ten years. Target mean is that underlying the approved rates charged by all companies.
3. Risk premium calculated according to Cummins's Policy Cohort Model for Guaranty Fund Premium using Asset variance with 1980 portfolio weights (.0047), Liability variance (.0016 + $\sigma^2$ above), $r - r_L$ (.014), and Payout Parameter $\Theta$ (W.C. 0.5, Liability 1.0, Physical Damage 1.6, Auto Total 1.2, Combined 0.8) and expressed as a fraction of liabilities.

Table V - 1c

Massachusetts Log Loss Ratio Variances and Guaranty Fund Risk Premiums
Private Passenger Automobile and Workers' Compensation
1976 - 1985

$r - r_L = .000$

| Insurance | Group Sample | From Annual Realized Means | | From Annual Target Means | |
|---|---|---|---|---|---|
| | | Variance($\sigma^2$) | Risk-Premium $\pi(1)$ | Variance($\sigma^2$) | Risk-Premium $\pi(1)$ |
| Workers' Compensation $\Theta = .5$ | All (44) | .12416 | .14254 | .14460 | .15304 |
| | Top 25% (11) | .03876 | .08437 | .09261 | .12444 |
| | Bottom 25% (11) | .22208 | .18706 | .25320 | .19889 |
| P.P. Auto Liability $\Theta = 1.0$ | All (43) | .07050 | .07793 | .07925 | .08222 |
| | Top 25% (11) | .01529 | .04141 | .03750 | .05893 |
| | Bottom 25% (11) | .09817 | .09078 | .12082 | .10005 |
| P.P. Auto Physical Damage $\Theta = 1.6$ | All (47) | .05599 | .05557 | .08006 | .06539 |
| | Top 25% (12) | .01686 | .03392 | .03397 | .04471 |
| | Bottom 25% (12) | .06604 | .05987 | .17199 | .09373 |
| P.P. Auto Total $\Theta = 1.2$ | All (44) | .04277 | .05695 | .05222 | .06217 |
| | Top 25% (11) | .01143 | .03427 | .02793 | .04759 |
| | Bottom 25% (11) | .05996 | .06613 | .09504 | .08169 |
| P.P. Auto & Workers' Compensation Combined $\Theta = .8$ | All (51) | .05311 | .07664 | .05861 | .08008 |
| | Top 25% (13) | .01361 | .04446 | .03137 | .06109 |
| | Bottom 25% (13) | .09332 | .09903 | .10677 | .10543 |
| All Industry $\Theta = .4$ | Cummins | .00000 | .03538 | .00000 | .03538 |

Notes:

1. The sample consists of the natural log of the Annual Statement Loss Ratios by all company groups writing in Massachusetts by years 1976-1985 subject to certain minimum (greater than .05% of total premium) combined premium volume. The number of company groups is shown in parentheses. Top and Bottom 25% selected according to premium volume for all ten years.
2. Variance calculated using individual annual realized or target means for each of the ten years. Target mean is that underlying the approved rates charged by all companies.
3. Risk premium calculated according to Cummins's Policy Cohort Model for Guaranty Fund Premium using Asset variance with 1980 portfolio weights (.0047), Liability variance (.0016 + $\sigma^2$ above), $r - r_L$ (.000), and Payout Parameter $\Theta$ (W.C. 0.5, Liability 1.0, Physical Damage 1.6, Auto Total 1.2, Combined 0.8) and expressed as a fraction of liabilities.

Table V - 2a

Solvency Requirements for Fully Guaranteed Contract
Using Massachusetts Data 1976 - 1985

$r - r_L = .025$

| Line of Insurance | Group Sample | | From Annual Realized Means: variance($\sigma^2$) | Risk Premia ($\pi$) | | | | | | | Required Solvency Level ($x^*$) |
|---|---|---|---|---|---|---|---|---|---|---|---|
| | | | | x = 1 | 1.2 | 1.4 | 1.6 | 1.8 | 2.0 | 2.2 | |
| Workers' Comp. $\theta = .5$ | All | (44) | .12416 | .12014 | .06449 | .03495 | .01935 | .01100 | .00643 | .00386 | 2.2+ |
| | Top 25% | (11) | .03876 | .06240 | .01726 | .00428 | .00103 | .00025 | .00006 | .00002 | 2.2+ |
| | Bottom 25% | (11) | .22208 | .16477 | .10791 | .07226 | .04956 | .03479 | .02496 | .01827 | 2.2+ |
| P.P.Auto Liab. $\theta = 1.0$ | All | (43) | .07050 | .06639 | .01720 | .00383 | .00080 | .00017 | .00004 | 8E(-6) | 2.18 |
| | Top 25% | (11) | .01529 | .03027 | .00114 | 2E(-5) | 1E(-7) | 8E(-10) | 5E(-12) | 3E(-14) | 1.43 |
| | Bottom 25% | (11) | .09817 | .07921 | .02639 | .00810 | .00243 | .00074 | .00023 | .00008 | 2.2+ |
| P.P.Auto Phys.Dam. $\theta = 1.6$ | All | (47) | .05599 | .04825 | .00597 | .00047 | .00003 | 2E(-6) | 1E(-7) | 6E(-9) | 1.68 |
| | Top 25% | (12) | .01686 | .02676 | .00038 | 1E(-6) | 1E(-9) | 8E(-13) | 5E(-16) | 4E(-19) | 1.33 |
| | Bottom 25% | (12) | .06604 | .05254 | .00797 | .00084 | .00007 | 6E(-6) | 5E(-7) | 5E(-8) | 1.77 |
| P.P.Auto Total $\theta = 1.2$ | All | (44) | .04277 | .04733 | .00608 | .00051 | .00004 | 2E(-6) | 1E(-7) | 1E(-8) | 1.70 |
| | Top 25% | (11) | .01143 | .02497 | .00035 | 9E(-7) | 1E(-9) | 8E(-13) | 5E(-16) | 4E(-19) | 1.33 |
| | Bottom 25% | (11) | .05996 | .05647 | .01062 | .00153 | .00020 | .00002 | 3E(-6) | 4E(-7) | 1.90 |
| P.P.Auto & Workers' Comp. Combined $\theta = .8$ | All | (51) | .05311 | .06242 | .01534 | .00321 | .00063 | .00012 | .00003 | 5E(-6) | 2.13 |
| | Top 25% | (13) | .01361 | .03079 | .00149 | .00003 | 4E(-7) | 5E(-9) | 6E(-11) | 7E(-13) | 1.46 |
| | Bottom 25% | (13) | .09332 | .08471 | .03146 | .01108 | .00387 | .00138 | .00051 | .00019 | 2.2+ |
| All Industry $\theta = .4$ | Cummins | | .00000 | .02185 | .00010 | 2E(-7) | 1E(-10) | 1E(-13) | 6E(-17) | 4E(-20) | 1.28 |

Notes:

1. The sample consists of the natural log of the Annual Statement Loss Ratios by all company groups writing in Massachusetts by years 1976-1985 subject to certain minimum (greater than .05% of total premium) combined premium volume. The number of company groups is shown in parentheses. Top and Bottom 25% selected according to premium volume for all ten years.
2. Variance calculated using individual annual realized or target means for each of the ten years. Target mean is that underlying the approved rates charged by all companies.
3. Risk premium calculated according to Cummins's Policy Cohort Model for Guaranty Fund Premium using Asset variance with 1980 portfolio weights (.0047), Liability variance (.0016 + $\sigma^2$ above), $r - r_L$ (.025), and Payout Parameter $\theta$ (W.C. 0.5, Liability 1.0, Physical Damage 1.6, Auto Total 1.2, Combined 0.8) and expressed as a fraction of liabilities.
4. The "required solvency level" employs the criterion that $\pi(x^*) < 1E(-5)$.

Table V - 2b

Solvency Requirements for Fully Guaranteed Contract
Using Massachusetts Data 1976 - 1985

$r - r_L = .014$

| Line of Insurance | Group Sample | From Annual Realized Means: variance($\sigma^2$) | Risk Premia ($\pi$) x = 1 | 1.2 | 1.4 | 1.6 | 1.8 | 2.0 | 2.2 | Required Solvency Level (x*) |
|---|---|---|---|---|---|---|---|---|---|---|
| Workers' Comp. | All (44) | .12416 | .12966 | .07114 | .03933 | .02218 | .01282 | .00761 | .00464 | 2.2+ |
|  | Top 25% (11) | .03876 | .07150 | .02107 | .00555 | .00141 | .00036 | .00010 | .00003 | 2.2+ |
| $\theta = .5$ | Bottom 25% (11) | .22208 | .17433 | .11563 | .07832 | .05428 | .03847 | .02784 | .02054 | 2.2+ |
| P.P.Auto Liab. | All (43) | .07050 | .01731 | .01916 | .00442 | .00096 | .00021 | .00005 | .00001 | 2.2+ |
|  | Top 25% (11) | .01529 | .03488 | .00150 | .00002 | 2E(-7) | 2E(-9) | 1E(-11) | 8E(-14) | 1.44 |
| $\theta = 1.0$ | Bottom 25% (11) | .09817 | .08417 | .02881 | .00907 | .00279 | .00087 | .00028 | .00009 | 2.2+ |
| P.P.Auto Phys.Dam. | All (47) | .05599 | .05139 | .00666 | .00055 | .00004 | 2E(-6) | 1E(-7) | 8E(-9) | 1.70 |
|  | Top 25% (12) | .01686 | .02977 | .00049 | 2E(-9) | 2E(-9) | 1E(-12) | 1E(-15) | 8E(-19) | 1.34 |
| $\theta = 1.6$ | Bottom 25% (12) | .06604 | .05568 | .00879 | .00096 | .00009 | 8E(-6) | 7E(-7) | 6E(-8) | 1.79 |
| P.P.Auto Total | All (44) | .04277 | .05141 | .00700 | .00062 | .00005 | 3E(-6) | 2E(-7) | 1E(-8) | 1.72 |
|  | Top 25% (11) | .01143 | .02882 | .00048 | 1E(-6) | 2E(-9) | 2E(-12) | 1E(-15) | 1E(-18) | 1.34 |
| $\theta = 1.2$ | Bottom 25% (11) | .05996 | .06059 | .01190 | .00179 | .00024 | .00003 | 4E(-6) | 5E(-7) | 1.92 |
| P.P.Auto & Workers' | All (51) | .05311 | .06843 | .01763 | .00386 | .00079 | .00016 | .00003 | 7E(-6) | 2.17 |
| Comp. | Top 25% (13) | .01361 | .03638 | .00205 | .00005 | 8E(-7) | 1E(-8) | 1E(-10) | 2E(-12) | 1.49 |
| Combined $\theta = .8$ | Bottom 25% (13) | .09332 | .09082 | .03470 | .01255 | .00450 | .00164 | .00061 | .00024 | 2.2+ |
| All Industry $\theta = .4$ | Cummins | .00000 | .02079 | .00027 | 8E(-7) | 1E(-9) | 1E(-12) | 9E(-16) | 9E(-19) | 1.32 |

Notes:

1. The sample consists of the natural log of the Annual Statement Loss Ratios by all company groups writing in Massachusetts by years 1976-1985 subject to certain minimum (greater than .05% of total premium) combined premium volume. The number of company groups is shown in parentheses. Top and Bottom 25% selected according to premium volume for all ten years.
2. Variance calculated using individual annual realized or target means for each of the ten years. Target mean is that underlying the approved rates charged by all companies.
3. Risk premium calculated according to Cummins's Policy Cohort Model for Guaranty Fund Premium using Asset variance with 1980 portfolio weights (.0047), Liability variance (.0016 + $\sigma^2$ above), $r - r_L$ (.014), and Payout Parameter $\theta$ (W.C. 0.5, Liability 1.0, Physical Damage 1.6, Auto Total 1.2, Combined 0.8) and expressed as a fraction of liabilities.
4. The "required solvency level" employs the criterion that $\pi(x^*) < 1E(-5)$.

Table V - 2c

Solvency Requirements for Fully Guaranteed Contract Using Massachusetts Data 1976 - 1985

$r - r_L = .000$

| Line of Insurance | Group Sample | From Annual Realized Means: variance($\sigma^2$) | Risk Premia ($\pi$): x = 1 | 1.2 | 1.4 | 1.6 | 1.8 | 2.0 | 2.2 | Required Solvency Level (x*) |
|---|---|---|---|---|---|---|---|---|---|---|
| Workers' Comp. $\Theta = .5$ | All (44) | .12416 | .14254 | .08037 | .04558 | .02631 | .01554 | .00940 | .00583 | 2.2+ |
| | Top 25% (11) | .03876 | .08437 | .02690 | .00765 | .00209 | .00057 | .00016 | .00005 | 2.2+ |
| | Bottom 25% (11) | .22208 | .18706 | .12607 | .08665 | .06085 | .04365 | .03194 | .02381 | 2.2+ |
| P.P.Auto Liab. $\Theta = 1.0$ | All (43) | .07050 | .07793 | .02192 | .00528 | .00120 | .00027 | .00006 | .00001 | 2.2+ |
| | Top 25% (11) | .01529 | .04141 | .00212 | .00004 | 4E(-7) | 3E(-9) | 3E(-11) | 2E(-13) | 1.47 |
| | Bottom 25% (11) | .09817 | .09078 | .03214 | .01045 | .00331 | .00106 | .00035 | .00012 | 2.2+ |
| P.P.Auto Phys.Dam. $\Theta = 1.6$ | All (47) | .05599 | .05557 | .00763 | .00066 | .00005 | 3E(-6) | 2E(-7) | 1E(-8) | 1.72 |
| | Top 25% (12) | .01686 | .03392 | .00065 | 2E(-6) | 3E(-9) | 3E(-12) | 2E(-15) | 2E(-18) | 1.36 |
| | Bottom 25% (12) | .06604 | .05987 | .00993 | .00114 | .00011 | .00001 | 9E(-7) | 9E(-8) | 1.81 |
| P.P.Auto Total $\Theta = 1.2$ | All (44) | .04277 | .05695 | .00834 | .00080 | .00006 | 4E(-6) | 3E(-7) | 2E(-8) | 1.75 |
| | Top 25% (11) | .01143 | .03427 | .00070 | 3E(-6) | 4E(-9) | 4E(-12) | 4E(-15) | 4E(-18) | 1.36 |
| | Bottom 25% (11) | .05996 | .06613 | .01370 | .00217 | .00030 | .00004 | 6E(-6) | 8E(-7) | 1.95 |
| P.P.Auto & Workers' Comp. Combined $\Theta = .8$ | All (51) | .05311 | .07664 | .02096 | .00487 | .00106 | .00023 | .00005 | .00001 | 2.2+ |
| | Top 25% (13) | .01361 | .04446 | .00301 | .00009 | 2E(-6) | 2E(-8) | 4E(-10) | 6E(-12) | 1.52 |
| | Bottom 25% (13) | .09332 | .09903 | .03920 | .01466 | .00542 | .00203 | .00078 | .00031 | 2.2+ |
| All Industry $\Theta = .4$ | Cummins | .00000 | .03538 | .00086 | 4E(-6) | 1E(-8) | 2E(-11) | 2E(-14) | 4E(-17) | 1.38 |

Notes:

1. The sample consists of the natural log of the Annual Statement Loss Ratios by all company groups writing in Massachusetts by years 1976-1985 subject to certain minimum (greater than .05% of total premium) combined premium volume. The number of company groups is shown in parentheses. Top and Bottom 25% selected according to premium volume for all ten years.
2. Variance calculated using individual annual realized or target means for each of the ten years. Target mean is that underlying the approved rates charged by all companies.
3. Risk premium calculated according to Cummins's Policy Cohort Model for Guaranty Fund Premium using Asset variance with 1980 portfolio weights (.0047), Liability variance (.0016 + $\sigma^2$ above), $r - r_L$ (.000), and Payout Parameter $\Theta$ (W.C. 0.5, Liability 1.0, Physical Damage 1.6, Auto Total 1.2, Combined 0.8) and expressed as a fraction of liabilities.
4. The "required solvency level" employs the criterion that $\pi(x^*) < 1E(-5)$.

Table V - 3a

Solvency Requirements for Fully Guaranteed Contract
Using Massachusetts Data 1976 - 1985

$r - r_L = .025$

| Line of Insurance | Group Sample | From Annual Target Means: variance($\sigma^2$) | Risk Premia ($\pi$): x = 1 | 1.2 | 1.4 | 1.6 | 1.8 | 2.0 | 2.2 | Required Solvency Level (x*) |
|---|---|---|---|---|---|---|---|---|---|---|
| Workers' | All (44) | .14460 | .13064 | .07438 | .04297 | .02540 | .01541 | .00959 | .00613 | 2.2+ |
| Comp. | Top 25% (11) | .09261 | .10208 | .04816 | .02261 | .01078 | .00528 | .00267 | .00139 | 2.2+ |
| $\theta$ = .5 | Bottom 25% (11) | .25320 | .17665 | .11995 | .08335 | .05930 | .04314 | .03203 | .02423 | 2.2+ |
| P.P.Auto | All (43) | .07925 | .07066 | .02012 | .00506 | .00122 | .00029 | .00007 | .00002 | 2.2+ |
| Liab. | Top 25% (11) | .03750 | .04751 | .00654 | .00061 | .00005 | 4E(-6) | 3E(-7) | 2E(-8) | 1.73 |
| $\theta$ = 1.0 | Bottom 25% (11) | .12082 | .08846 | .03373 | .01222 | .00440 | .00161 | .00061 | .00024 | 2.2+ |
| P.P.Auto | All (47) | .08006 | .05805 | .01091 | .00155 | .00019 | .00002 | 3E(-6) | 4E(-7) | 1.89 |
| Phys.Dam. | Top 25% (12) | .03397 | .03744 | .00220 | .00006 | 9E(-7) | 1E(-8) | 2E(-10) | 3E(-12) | 1.49 |
| $\theta$ = 1.6 | Bottom 25% (12) | .17199 | .08637 | .03080 | .01022 | .00333 | .00110 | .00037 | .00013 | 2.2+ |
| P.P.Auto | All (44) | .05222 | .05252 | .00852 | .00100 | .00010 | .00001 | 1E(-6) | 1E(-7) | 1.81 |
| Total | Top 25% (11) | .02793 | .03806 | .00271 | .00009 | 2E(-6) | 5E(-8) | 1E(-9) | 2E(-11) | 1.53 |
| $\theta$ = 1.2 | Bottom 25% (11) | .09504 | .07198 | .02053 | .00515 | .00124 | .00030 | .00007 | .00002 | 2.2+ |
| P.P.Auto & | All (51) | .05861 | .06584 | .01756 | .00408 | .00091 | .00020 | .00005 | .00001 | 2.2+ |
| Workers' | Top 25% (13) | .03137 | .04705 | .00689 | .00072 | .00006 | 5E(-6) | 5E(-7) | 4E(-8) | 1.76 |
| Comp. | Bottom 25% (13) | .10677 | .09110 | .03667 | .01422 | .00552 | .00219 | .00089 | .00038 | 2.2+ |
| Combined | | | | | | | | | | |
| $\theta$ = .8 | | | | | | | | | | |
| All | Cummins | .00000 | .01285 | .00010 | 2E(-7) | 1E(-10) | 1E(-13) | 6E(-17) | 4E(-20) | 1.28 |
| Industry | | | | | | | | | | |
| $\theta$ = .4 | | | | | | | | | | |

Notes:

1. The sample consists of the natural log of the Annual Statement Loss Ratios by all company groups writing in Massachusetts by years 1976-1985 subject to certain minimum (greater than .05% of total premium) combined premium volume. The number of company groups is shown in parentheses. Top and Bottom 25% selected according to premium volume for all ten years.
2. Variance calculated using individual annual realized or target means for each of the ten years. Target mean is that underlying the approved rates charged by all companies.
3. Risk premium calculated according to Cummins's Policy Cohort Model for Guaranty Fund Premium using Asset variance with 1980 portfolio weights (.0047), Liability variance (.0016 + $\sigma^2$ above), $r - r_L$ (.025), and Payout Parameter $\theta$ (W.C. 0.5, Liability 1.0, Physical Damage 1.6, Auto Total 1.2, Combined 0.8) and expressed as a fraction of liabilities.

Table V - 3b

Solvency Requirements for Fully Guaranteed Contract
Using Massachusetts Data 1976 - 1985

$r - r_L = .014$

| Line of Insurance | Group Sample | From Annual Target Means: variance ($\sigma^2$) | Risk Premia ($\pi$): x = 1 | 1.2 | 1.4 | 1.6 | 1.8 | 2.0 | 2.2 | Required Sólvency Level (x*) |
|---|---|---|---|---|---|---|---|---|---|---|
| Workers' Comp. $\theta = .5$ | All (44) | .14460 | .14019 | .08134 | .04781 | .02871 | .01767 | .01115 | .00721 | 2.2+ |
| | Top 25% (11) | .09261 | .11153 | .05416 | .02611 | .01276 | .00639 | .00329 | .00175 | 2.2+ |
| | Bottom 25% (11) | .25320 | .18620 | .12786 | .08976 | .06445 | .04728 | .03537 | .02694 | 2.2+ |
| P.P.Auto Liab. $\theta = 1.0$ | All (43) | .07925 | .07560 | .02224 | .00577 | .00143 | .00036 | .00009 | .00002 | 2.2+ |
| | Top 25% (11) | .03750 | .05233 | .00769 | .00077 | .00006 | 5E(-6) | 4E(-7) | 3E(-8) | 1.76 |
| | Bottom 25% (11) | .12082 | .09344 | .03642 | .01347 | .00494 | .00184 | .00071 | .00028 | 2.2+ |
| P.P.Auto Phys.Dam. $\theta = 1.6$ | All (47) | .08006 | .06120 | .01188 | .00175 | .00023 | .00003 | 4E(-6) | 5E(-7) | 1.91 |
| | Top 25% (12) | .03397 | .04053 | .00256 | .00007 | 1E(-6) | 2E(-8) | 3E(-10) | 4E(-12) | 1.51 |
| | Bottom 25% (12) | .17199 | .08956 | .03244 | .01092 | .00361 | .00121 | .00041 | .00015 | 2.2+ |
| P.P.Auto Total $\theta = 1.2$ | All (44) | .05222 | .05663 | .00965 | .00119 | .00013 | .00001 | 1E(-6) | 1E(-7) | 1.83 |
| | Top 25% (11) | .02793 | .04207 | .00326 | .00012 | 3E(-6) | 8E(-8) | 2E(-9) | 4E(-11) | 1.55 |
| | Bottom 25% (11) | .09504 | .07615 | .02233 | .00575 | .00141 | .00035 | .00009 | .00002 | 2.2+ |
| P.P.Auto & Workers' Comp. Combined $\theta = .8$ | All (51) | .05861 | .07187 | .02002 | .00486 | .00112 | .00026 | .00006 | .00002 | 2.2+ |
| | Top 25% (13) | .03137 | .05292 | .00837 | .00094 | .00009 | 8E(-6) | 8E(-7) | 7E(-8) | 1.79 |
| | Bottom 25% (13) | .10677 | .09722 | .04012 | .01592 | .00632 | .00255 | .00106 | .00046 | 2.2+ |
| All Industry $\theta = .4$ | Cummins | .00000 | .02079 | .00027 | 8E(-7) | 1E(-9) | 1E(-12) | 9E(-16) | 9E(-19) | 1.32 |

Notes:

1. The sample consists of the natural log of the Annual Statement Loss Ratios by all company groups writing in Massachusetts by years 1976-1985 subject to certain minimum (greater than .05% of total premium) combined premium volume. The number of company groups is shown in parentheses. Top and Bottom 25% selected according to premium volume for all ten years.
2. Variance calculated using individual annual realized or target means for each of the ten years. Target mean is that underlying the approved rates charged by all companies.
3. Risk premium calculated according to Cummins's Policy Cohort Model for Guaranty Fund Premium using Asset variance with 1980 portfolio weights (.0047), Liability variance (.0016 + $\sigma^2$ above), $r - r_L$ (.014), and Payout Parameter $\theta$ (W.C. 0.5, Liability 1.0, Physical Damage 1.6, Auto Total 1.2, Combined 0.8) and expressed as a fraction of liabilities.

Table V - 3c

Solvency Requirements for Fully Guaranteed Contract
Using Massachusetts Data 1976 - 1985

$r - r_L = .000$

| Line of Insurance | Group Sample | | From Annual Target Means variance ($\sigma^2$) | Risk Premia ($\pi$) x = 1 | 1.2 | 1.4 | 1.6 | 1.8 | 2.0 | 2.2 | Required Solvency Level (x*) |
|---|---|---|---|---|---|---|---|---|---|---|---|
| Workers' Comp. $\Theta = .5$ | All | (44) | .14460 | .15304 | .09093 | .05463 | .03347 | .02098 | .01347 | .00884 | 2.2+ |
| | Top 25% | (11) | .09261 | .12444 | .06263 | .03122 | .01574 | .00811 | .00429 | .00233 | 2.2+ |
| | Bottom 25% | (11) | .25320 | .19889 | .13852 | .09850 | .07155 | .05305 | .04008 | .03080 | 2.2+ |
| P.P.Auto Liab. $\Theta = 1.0$ | All | (43) | .07925 | .08222 | .02521 | .00681 | .00175 | .00045 | .00012 | .00003 | 2.2+ |
| | Top 25% | (11) | .03750 | .05893 | .00940 | .00102 | .00009 | 8E(-6) | 7E(-7) | 6E(-8) | 1.79 |
| | Bottom 25% | (11) | .12082 | .10005 | .04009 | .01522 | .00572 | .00218 | .00085 | .00035 | 2.2+ |
| P.P.Auto Phys.Dam. $\Theta = 1.6$ | All | (47) | .08006 | .06539 | .01323 | .00202 | .00027 | .00004 | 5E(-6) | 6E(-7) | 1.93 |
| | Top 25% | (12) | .03397 | .04471 | .00309 | .00009 | 2E(-6) | 3E(-8) | 4E(-10) | 7E(-12) | 1.52 |
| | Bottom 25% | (12) | .17199 | .09373 | .03462 | .01188 | .00399 | .00136 | .00047 | .00017 | 2.2+ |
| P.P.Auto Total $\Theta = 1.2$ | All | (44) | .05222 | .06217 | .01126 | .00147 | .00016 | .00002 | 2E(-6) | 2E(-7) | 1.86 |
| | Top 25% | (11) | .02793 | .04759 | .00410 | .00017 | 5E(-6) | 1E(-7) | 3E(-9) | 8E(-11) | 1.57 |
| | Bottom 25% | (11) | .09504 | .08169 | .02480 | .00661 | .00168 | .00042 | .00011 | .00003 | 2.2+ |
| P.P.Auto & Workers' Comp. Combined $\Theta = .8$ | All | (51) | .05861 | .08008 | .02356 | .00602 | .00146 | .00035 | .00009 | .00002 | 2.2+ |
| | Top 25% | (13) | .03137 | .06109 | .01063 | .00131 | .00014 | .00001 | 1E(-6) | 1E(-7) | 1.84 |
| | Bottom 25% | (13) | .10677 | .10543 | .04489 | .01835 | .00748 | .00310 | .00132 | .00058 | 2.2+ |
| All Industry $\Theta = .4$ | Cummins | | .00000 | .03538 | .00086 | 4E(-6) | 1E(-8) | 2E(-11) | 2E(-14) | 4E(-17) | 1.38 |

Notes:

1. The sample consists of the natural log of the Annual Statement Loss Ratios by all company groups writing in Massachusetts by years 1976-1985 subject to certain minimum (greater than .05% of total premium) combined premium volume. The number of company groups is shown in parentheses. Top and Bottom 25% selected according to premium volume for all ten years.
2. Variance calculated using individual annual realized or target means for each of the ten years. Target mean is that underlying the approved rates charged by all companies.
3. Risk premium calculated according to Cummins's Policy Cohort Model for Guaranty Fund Premium using Asset variance with 1980 portfolio weights (.0047), Liability variance (.0016 + $\sigma^2$ above), $r - r_L$ (.000), and Payout Parameter $\Theta$ (W.C. 0.5, Liability 1.0, Physical Damage 1.6, Auto Total 1.2, Combined 0.8) and expressed as a fraction of liabilities.

i. If we grant that some of the variance facing individual companies is appropriate to include in addition to the inflation variance calculated by Cummins then the overall Kenney Rule of 2 to 1 premium/surplus ratio ($x^* = 1.50$) looks comparable to the results above.

ii. The use of differing premium/surplus ratios by line according to reserves seems to hold up for workers' compensation[21] as compared to either the N.Y. Insurance Department 1.0 or the prior Massachusetts estimated using constant risk adjustments (Section II) of 1.0 ($x^* = 2.0$).

iii. Private Passenger Auto Physical Damage, however, does not show the simple relationship to reserves which yields about 5 to 1 for the New York study and 3 to 1 for the constant risk premium model of Section II. Rather, this shows that the liability and physical damage ratios are about the same <u>and</u>, moreover, the combined coverage ratios are <u>not</u> lower than either individual one, as their variance is, apparently due to the relative weighting of the payout parameters $\theta$.

iv. The effect of the differing interest rates for liabilities seem negligible for all but the Cummins inflationary variance alone. The Cummins risk premiums nearly triple as $r^*$ goes from .025 to 0 (see Table VI-1).

We next turn to the implications of the previous discussions and Massachusetts examples for fully guaranteed policy cohort contracts.

## VI. Implications for Premium Calculations

It is a fact that with the regulatory control exercised by the Commonwealth of Massachusetts, the policies issued for automobile and workers' compensation insurance are virtually guaranteed to have all claims paid. Currently in 1986, Commonwealth Automobile Reinsurers (CAR), the residual market pool, writes more than 50% of the automobile business, thereby automatically spreading the "bad risk" loss payouts to the industry as a whole. For all intents and purposes, these lines should be priced as though they were fully guaranteed or default-free. If that is the case, we can take the Cummins' framework of Section III and combined it with the general options pricing format[22] of Section II in order to arrive at a premium requirement for these (fully guaranteed) lines. In particular, we propose that, unless the policyholder directly bears some default-risk, the appropriate premium charge is (to a first approximation)

$$P(0) = (1 + \pi(1))\ L(0) \tag{34}$$

where L(0) is the present value of the fully guaranteed loss payouts L. If, further, we observe that for any individual company devoting some asset/liability ratio $x_c$ to this policy cohort, a fully guaranteeing reinsurer would effectively supply the remaining non-trivial assets/liability ratio $x^* - x_c$ in such a way that we have the premium charged to the insured remain unchanged but equal to the sum of the direct $P_c$ and the reinsurance charges $P_r$.

$$\begin{aligned} P(0) &= (1 + \pi(1))\ L(0) \\ &= [(1 + \pi(1) - \pi(x_c)) + \pi(x_c)]\ L(0) \\ &= P_c(0) + P_r(0) = (1 + \pi(1) - \pi(x_c))\ L(0) + \pi(x_c)\ L(0) \end{aligned} \tag{35}$$

or rearranging and adding the underlying surplus quantities, $S_c$ and $S_r = S^* - S_c$, for the direct writer and reinsurer, respectively, we get

$$\begin{aligned} P(0) + S^*(0) &= [P_c(0) + S_c(0)] + [P_r(0) + S_r(0)] \\ &= L(0) + [(\pi(1) - \pi(x_c))\ L(0) + S_c(0)] \\ &\quad + [\pi(x_c)\ L(0) + S_r(0)] \end{aligned} \tag{36}$$

Verbally, we have reproduced the type of option equation seen in III-15 whereby the assets $A(0) = P(0) + S^*(0)$ backing the fully guaranteed policy cohort decompose naturally into[23]

$$\text{Assets} = \text{Policyholders Claim} + \text{Direct Insurer Claim} + \text{Reinsurers Claim} \tag{37}$$

If equation (35) is to be a viable pricing equation then Cummins' 2nd boundary condition (IV-4b) must be replaced by a condition such as

$$\pi(0+) = 1 + \pi(1) \tag{38}$$

Otherwise, we encounter the peculiar result that one should always write policy cohorts with <u>negative</u> surplus requirements since $MIN(x + \pi(x))$ occurs with $0 < x < 1$. (See Cummins [8], p.27).

The more desirable use to make of the Cummins framework is to restrict the premium solution set to $x \geq 1$ on the grounds that all regulators would require the direct writer to hold <u>at least</u> the discounted value of reserves as assets as a condition of writing business. With that assumption, equation (2) becomes a viable pricing equation.

A word about the reasonableness of the estimates of equation (35) is in order. If, indeed, $\pi(1)$ represents an expected percentage of discounted liabilities, which to a first approximation is the premium, then $\pi(1)$ should be (very) roughly all post-tax income in excess of the pre-tax income on surplus. For the entire industry during the 10-year period, 1975-1984, such excess income averaged to approximately 2.47% of annual premium.[23]

It is then worthwhile to compare that realized percentage return with the risk premium calculated for a company with the "Top 25%" average variance parameter.

**Table VI-1**

Required Risk Premium Ratios to Expected Liabilities

| Line of Insurance | From Realized Means r* = .025 | .014 | .000 |
|---|---|---|---|
| W.C. | .062 | .072 | .084 |
| Auto Liab. | .030 | .035 | .041 |
| Auto P.D. | .027 | .030 | .034 |
| All Auto | .025 | .029 | .034 |
| Auto & W.C. | .031 | .036 | .044 |
| Cummins Liab. Variance | .013 | .021 | .035 |
| 1975-1984 Realized | .025 | .025 | .025 |

| Line of Insurance | From Target Means r* = .025 | .014 | .000 |
|---|---|---|---|
| W.C. | .102 | .112 | .124 |
| Auto Liab. | .048 | .052 | .059 |
| Auto P.D. | .037 | .041 | .045 |
| All Auto | .038 | .042 | .048 |
| Auto & W.C. | .047 | .053 | .061 |
| Cummins Liab. Variance | .013 | .021 | .035 |
| 1975-1984 Realized | .025 | .025 | .025 |

This comparison may indicate that the effect of introducing taxes into the model is to reduce the relative size of the appropriate risk premium $\pi(1)$, because of the smoothing effect of taxes, as we increase the size of the liabilities to accommodate the value of the expected tax liability passed on to policyholders. That will be the subject of a follow-up study to the current effort.

## VII. Concluding Remarks

The discussion in the preceeding sections has concentrated on the results of applying financial theory concepts, specifically options pricing, to the question of required solvency margins. A simple risk premium - solvency margin relation was derived in Section II showing that allocation of surplus by line should be in proportion to discounted reserves if and only if the systematic risk in each period of the life of the policy is constant. That result is a direct consequence of the financial principle of equal rates of return for equal risk. A financial criterion for required solvency margins was proposed as a replacement for the usual statistical ruin criteria in Section III. Verbally, a company with an asset/liability ratio of x is solvent at a level $\epsilon > 0$ if the premium $\pi$ necessary to reinsure its outstanding liabilities is less than $\epsilon$.

Section IV described the Cummins' guaranty fund premium model for a policy cohort based upon the modelling assumption of assets and liabilities as diffusion processes. Section V reviewed examples of Cummins' model calculation using more realistic values for the liability variance facing individual companies. Massachusetts data for the workers' compensation and private passenger automobile lines of insurance for 1976-1985 were used to estimate appropriate company variances. Required solvency margins for the "Top 25%" companies by premium volume variances showed overall similarity with the Kenney 2 to 1 rule of thumb while the margin for physical damage coverages showed to be much greater than the simple proportion to reserves.

Finally, all the ideas were brought together in Section VI to suggest a pricing model based upon the Cummins' model calculation. It remains then to assess where this may lead us.

First, there is no doubt that the notions of options pricing should work their way into the fundamental analysis of the insurance pricing problem. The models discussed here may turn out to be somewhat crude approximations but the underlying appropriateness of the concepts does not seem to be in doubt.

Second, these models have finally reconciled the ruin theoretic dependence on the variance of the loss process with the finance theoretic dependence upon systematic risk alone. The good news is that there is a fundamental role for process variance to play in pricing insurance contracts.

Third, the method used in this paper to assess the liability variance through Massachusetts Annual Statement data should be viewed as a rough cut at calculating the true relevant liability process variance. It is hoped that simulation techniques can be applied to produce better, and more relevant, estimates of the process variance. We look forward to that advance.

Finally, all of the ideas presented here should be reviewed for the effect of taxes. Prior research has shown that the tax effect is quite important[25] and its effect within the continuous model needs to be known.

# NOTES

1. An asset/written premium ratio of 3/2 translates to the "two to one" Kenney Rule when assets less premiums are interpreted as surplus.

2. Brackets refer to numbered references to be found at the end of the paper.

3. For a description of the regulatory use of financial models in Massachusetts automobile and workers' compensation ratemaking, see Derrig [11].

4. This relation is not surprising considering that "the allocation of ... net worth ... shall be in the proportion that the investable funds for the line bears to the investable funds for all lines (Reg 70, p. 4).

5. Full details were presented in companion position papers prepared by the author and the Bureau Counsel ([3], [4]).

6. Hill and Modigliani ([16], pp. 46-49) decompose the liability beta into frequency and severity components which in all likelihood would produce unequal liability betas during the time of policy exposure as compared to the time periods after the policy expires.

7. This promise of certainty for bond payments exists unless there are option provisions, such as a call premium, which provide for uncertain payments.

8. The approach in Doherty and Garven [12] considers the tax claims as well.

9. Note that we are implicitly assuming that the stochastic process $L(\tau)$ is random in magnitude but certain given that magnitude. See also Section IV.

10. Compare Cox and Ross ([7], p. 387).

11. This author acknowledges the generosity of those authors in providing preliminary copies of their papers as well as the several helpful discussions of the subject matter.

12. The alternate view of default, which Hill may have had in mind, is that the present value of the nominal claim payments should be reduced by the present value of the expected defaulted payments.

13. This assumption is equivalent to assuming the total <u>expected</u> value of claims and the claim payment flow pattern is known.

14. These calculations are shown in the technical appendix.

15. The function M or ${}_1F_1$ is also known as the confluent hypergeometric function ([1], pp. 503-535). Series of the form M were first investigated by Kummer in 1836 [21].

16. This is equivalent to Cummins's equation ([8], Eq.(27), p. 17) with $r = r^* = r - r_L$ and $\pi(0+) = 1$ since $\Gamma(2) = 1$.

17. This derives from the Hill-Modigliani ([16], pp. 35, 43) estimates for liability betas (.21), market risk premiums (.09) and average effective underwriting tax rates (.24) giving .014 = (.21)(.09)(1 - .24).

18. There is a possibility that the two components of variance are not completely independent slightly overstating the liability variance.

19. Private passenger automobile had a short-lived experiment with competitive rating in 1977. Rate deviations are allowed, but only downward, and given the general rate inadequacies, deviations are in place for only an insignificant portion of the market.

20. This represents the combined bodily injury and property damage liability for Massachusetts policies rather than the (bodily injury) liability parameter estimated by Cummins ([8], p.22).

21. The estimates using the variation from the target means are hampered by the fact that (a) rates were grossly inadequate during most of the ten-year period and (b) only four general changes in target ratios were implemented (1978, 1980, 1983 twice).

22. Unfortunately, unlike Doherty and Garven [12], this formulation does not explicitly include the effect of taxes on the calculation.

23. Doherty has suggested (NCII Conference 1985) that equation (4) may not hold in the presence of a differential tax system if value can be created in the reinsurance transaction purely by the relative tax status of the direct reinsuring carriers.

24. Source: A.M. Best & Co. Special Study.

25. See Derrig [10].

# APPENDIX

**Solution of the Policy Cohort Ordinary Differential Equation By the Method of Frobenius**

## I. The Policy Cohort Equation

Assume the policy cohort system of stochastic differential equations (Cummins, Eq 20a, 20b) can be reduced to an ordinary 2nd order linear differential equation with independent variable x = G/L = Market Value of Premium/Market Value of Loss and dependent variable $\pi$ denominated in units of losses L (Cummins, Eq 25).
The ODE is:

$$\pi(r-r_L+\Theta) = \pi_x\,[x(r-r_L+\Theta) - \Theta] + \tfrac{1}{2}\,x^2\,\pi_{xx}\,(\sigma_A^2+\sigma_L^2) \qquad (1)$$

with boundary conditions

* $\lim_{x \to 0} \pi(x) = 1$    *[This requires that the market value of L <u>includes</u> a guarantee premium] (1a)

$\lim_{x \to \infty} \pi(x) = 0$ (1b)

where $r$ = risk-free rate, assumed constant
$r_L$ = rate of return on liabilities, assumed constant
$\Theta$ = rate of payment of liabilities, assumed constant
$\sigma_A{}^2$ = variance of returns on assets, assumed constant
$\sigma_L{}^2$ = variance of returns on liabilities, assumed constant

For convenience, we set new constants a and b as

$$a = (r - r_L + \Theta)/(\sigma_A{}^2 + \sigma_L{}^2)/2$$

$$b = \Theta/(\sigma_A{}^2 + \sigma_L{}^2)/2$$

and obtain

$$x^2 \pi_{xx} + [ax - b] \pi_x - a\pi = 0 \qquad (1)'$$

Equation (1)' has a singular point (Spiegel, p.292) at x = 0. This point would be a regular singular point if

$$\frac{x\ (ax - b)}{x^2} \quad \text{and} \quad \frac{x^2\ (-a)}{x^2}$$

are both analytic functions at 0 (see Spiegel, p.292 footnote).

The first function, however, is a - b/x which has a simple pole at x = 0 and, therefore, is not analytic.

Equation (1)' has no other singular points in the plane. It has a singular point at $x = \infty$ that is regular as we see below ($x = \infty$ is a regular singular point of (1)' $\Leftrightarrow$ Z = 0 is a regular singular point of (1)' transformed by Z = 1/x)

Let us transform equation (1)' by letting

$$Z = 1/x, \quad \nu(Z) = \pi(1/Z) = \pi(x)$$

then[1], $\nu'(Z) = \pi'(1/Z)\ (-1/Z^2) = \pi'(x)(-x^2)$

$$\nu''(Z) = \pi''(1/Z)\ (1/Z^4) + \pi'(1/Z)(2/Z^3)$$

$$= \pi''(x)\ x^4 + \pi'(x)\ 2x^3$$

so, $\pi'(x) = -Z^2\ \nu'(Z)$

$$\pi''(x) = Z^4\ \nu''(Z) + 2Z^3\ \nu'(Z)$$

and, (1)' becomes, for $Z \neq 0$

(2) $\frac{1}{Z^2}[Z^4\nu''(Z)+2Z^3\nu'(Z)] + [\frac{a}{Z}-b](-Z^2\nu'(Z)) - a\nu(Z) = 0$ or,

(2)' $Z^2\nu''(Z) + [2Z - aZ + bZ^2]\nu'(Z) - a\nu(Z) = 0$

Then since both

$$Z\left[\frac{(2-a)Z + bZ^2}{Z^2}\right] \quad \text{and} \quad \frac{Z^2(-a)}{Z^2}$$

are analytic at $Z = 0$, $Z = 0$ is a regular singular point of (2)'

It follows from general theorems (Spiegel pp. 292,294) that there always exists a solution in the form of a Frobenius Series, i.e., one of the type

$$\nu(Z) = Z^r(a_0 + a_1 Z + a_2 Z^2 + \ldots\ldots)$$

with $\nu(Z)$ convergent for all values of Z, and hence, analytic in the entire plane.

(since $Z = 0$ is a regular singular point and there are no others in the finite plane).

Series of Frobenius type may provide a basis for the space (2 dimensional) of all solutions. This will happen if there are two distinct values of r in the Frobenius Series.

## II. The Frobenius Solutions

Assume $\nu(Z) = Z^r(a_0+a_1Z+a_2Z^2+\ldots), \; a_0 \neq 0$

then $\nu'(Z) = r\,a_0Z^{r-1}+(r+1)a_1Z^r+(r+2)a_2Z^{r+1}+\ldots$

$\nu''(Z) = r(r-1)a_0Z^{r-2}+(r+1)ra_1Z^{r-1}+(r+2)(r+1)a_2Z^r+\ldots$

It follows that

$$Z^2\nu''(Z) = r(r-1)a_0Z^r+(r+1)\,r\,a_1\,Z^{r+1}+(r+2)(r+1)a_2Z^{r+2}$$

$$(2-a)Z\nu'(Z) = r(2-a)a_0Z^r+(r+1)(2-a)a_1Z^{r+1}+(r+2)(2-a)a_2Z^{r+2}$$

$$bZ^2\nu'(Z) = \qquad rba_0Z^{r+1}+ \quad (r+1)ba_1Z^{r+2}$$

$$-a\nu(Z) = -a\,a_0\,Z^r+ \quad -aa_1Z^{r+1}+ \quad -aa_2Z^{r+2}$$

→ since $a_0 \neq 0$, equation (2)' implies

$$r(r - 1) + r(2 - a) - a = 0$$

→ $r^2 + (1 - a)r - a = 0$ or

$$r = \frac{a-1 \pm \sqrt{(1-a)^2+4a}}{2} = \frac{a-1 \pm (1+a)}{2} = -1,\ a$$

<u>Case I</u> $r = -1$

Setting the coefficient of $Z^{r+1} \equiv 0$, we have

$$-b\ a_0 = +a\ a_1 \quad \text{or} \quad a_1 = (-b/a)\ a_0$$

Setting the coefficient of $Z^{r+2} \equiv 0$, we have

$$(2 - a)\ a_2 - a\ a_2 = 0 \quad \text{or } a_2 = 0$$

It can easily be shown that $a_k = 0$ if $k \geq 2$.

Therefore, a solution is

$$\nu_1(Z) = Z^{-1}(a_0 + a_1 Z) = a_1 + a_0 Z^{-1}$$
$$= (-a_0)\ (1 - b/a\ Z^{-1})$$

which is analytic in the punctured plane C-{0}, with a simple pole at Z = 0.

For the original equation (1)', this represents the solution

$$\pi(x) = c\ (1 - (\theta/r - r_L + \theta)\ x)$$

so if $r^* = r - r_L > 0$ then $(r^* + \theta)/\theta > 1$ and solution is

(for real values of x)

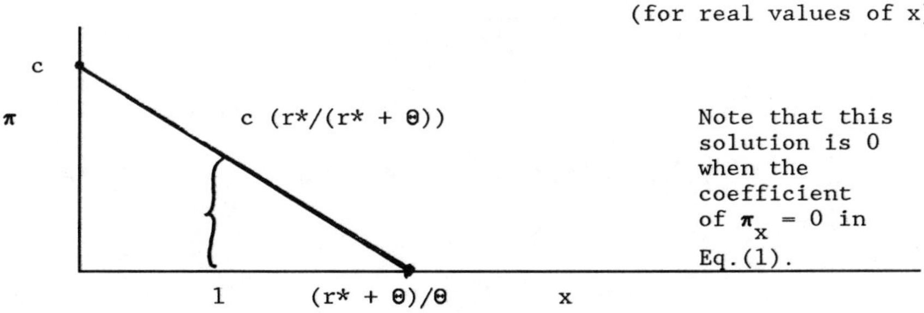


This solution, however, it not the promised solution entire in 1/x.

Case II $r = a$

Setting the coefficient of $Z^{a+1} \equiv 0$, we have[2]

$$(a + 1)a\ a_1 + (a + 1)(2 - a)a_1 + ab\ a_0 + (-a)a_1 = 0$$

$$[(a + 1)2 - a]\ a_1 + ab\ a_0 = 0$$

$$a_1 = \frac{-a\ b}{a + 2}\ a_0 \qquad a \neq -2$$

Setting the coefficient of $Z^{a+2} \equiv 0$, we have

$$[(a + 2)(a + 1) + (a + 2)(2 - a) - a]a_2 + (a + 1)b\ a_1 = 0$$

$$[(a + 2)(3) - a]a_2 = -(a + 1)b\ a_1$$

$$(a + 3)2\ a_2 = -(a + 1)b\ a_1$$

$$a_2 = \frac{(a + 1)(-b)a_1}{(a + 3)2}$$

$$= \frac{(a + 1)a\ b^2}{(a + 3)(a + 2)2}\ a_0 \qquad a \neq -2, -3$$

Generally, setting the coefficient of $Z^{a+i} \equiv 0$, we have

$$a_i = \frac{(a + i - 1)\ (-b)}{(a + i - 1)\ i}\ a_{i-1}$$

$$= \frac{(a + i - 1)(a + i - 2)(-b)^2}{(a + i + 1)(a + i)\ i(i - 1)}\ a_{i-2}$$

$$= \frac{(a + i - 2)(a + i - 3)(-b)^3}{(a + i + 1)(a + i)\ i(i-1)(i-2)}\ a_{i-3}$$

$$= \ldots\ldots$$

$$= \frac{(a+1)a(-b)^i}{(a+1+i)(a+i)i!}\ a_0 \qquad a \neq -n, \text{ n a positive integer.}$$

Thus, the Frobenius Series Solution is:

$$\nu_2(Z) = a_0 \sum_{i=0}^{\infty} \frac{(a+1)a\ (-bZ)^i\ Z^a}{(a+i+1)(a+1)\ i!}$$

which can be shown by the ratio test to be convergent in the entire plane and thus is the entire (analytic in the entire plane) solution promised by the theorem.

It can be observed that $\nu_2(Z)$ can be expressed using a Kummer[3] function, also known as a confluent hypergeometric function

$$\nu_2(Z) = a_0\ Z^a \sum_{i=0}^{\infty} \frac{(a+1)a\ (-bZ)^i}{(a+1+i)(a+i)\ i!}$$

$$= a_0\ Z^a\ M\ (a,\ a+2,\ -bZ)$$

where the general Kummer function M (a,b,Z) is

$$M(a,b,Z) = {}_1F_1\ (a,b,Z) = \sum_{i=0}^{\infty} \frac{(a)_i}{(b)_i} \frac{Z^i}{i!}$$

where $(a)_i = a(a+1)\ldots(a+i-1)$ (a product of i terms)

Thus, the general solution in the punctured plane C-{0} is:

$$\nu(Z) = c_1\ \nu_1(Z) + c_2\ \nu_2(Z) \qquad Z \neq 0$$

or for the transformed equation

$$\pi(x) = c_1\ (1 - b/a\ x) + c_2\ x^{-a}\ M(a,\ a+2,\ -b/x) \qquad (3)$$

Since $\lim_{x\to\infty} \pi(x) = 0 \rightarrow c_1 = 0$ (since $\lim_{Z\to 0} \nu_2(Z) = 0$)

therefore, the solution is of the form

$$\pi(x) = c\ x^{-a}\ M(a,\ a+2,\ -b/x) \qquad (4)$$

## III. The Second Boundary Value

The second boundary value set by Cummins (1a) has $\lim_{x\to 0} \pi(x) = 1$. Alternately, $\lim_{Z\to\infty} \nu(Z) = 1$. But $\nu_2(Z)$ is entire, if $\lim_{Z\to\infty} \nu_2(Z) = 1$, this implies a fortiori that $|\nu_2(Z)|$ is bounded. By Liouville's Theorem (Ahlfors, p.122) this would imply that $\nu_2(Z)$ is constant; i.e., $c_2 = 0$. Thus we must have either a new boundary equation or restrict the $\lim_{x\to 0}$ process.

Consider the general solution

$$\nu(Z) = c\,\nu_2(Z)$$
$$= c\,Z^a\,M(a,\ a + 2,\ -bZ)$$

As $Z \to\infty$, $a > 0$, $b > 0$

As the (complex) argument $Z \to\infty$, there are two asymptotic formulas for Kummer functions which involve the Gamma function.

From the Handbook of Mathematical Functions, p. 504,

#13.1.4 if Re $Z > 0$ $\quad M(a,b,Z) = \dfrac{\Gamma(b)}{\Gamma(a)}\, e^Z\, Z^{a-b}\, [1+O(|Z|^{-1})]$

#13.1.5 if Re $Z < 0$ $\quad M(a,b,Z) = \dfrac{\Gamma(b)}{\Gamma(b-a)}\, (-Z)^{-a}\, [1+O(|Z|^{-1})]$

Using 13.1.5 first we have, if Z is in the right half plane, Re $(-bZ)<0$

$$\lim_{\substack{Z\to\infty \\ Z\in RHP}} \nu(Z) = \lim_{\substack{Z\to\infty \\ Z\in RHP}} c\,Z^a\,\frac{\Gamma(a + 2)}{\Gamma(2)}\,(bZ)^{-a}\,[1 + O(|Z|^{-1})]$$

$$= \lim_{\substack{Z\to\infty \\ Z\in RHP}} c\,\frac{\Gamma(a + 2)}{\Gamma(2)}\,b^{-a}\,[1 + O(|Z|^{-1})]$$

$$= c\,\frac{\Gamma(a + 2)}{\Gamma(2)}\,b^{-a}$$

using the first Kummer transformation (Handbook, #13.1.27)

$$M(a,b,Z) = e^{Z} M(b - a, b, -Z)$$

then

$$\nu(Z) = c\, Z^{a}\, e^{-bZ} M(2, a + 2, bZ)$$

Now applying #13.1.4

$$\lim_{\substack{Z\to\infty \\ Z\in RHP}} \nu(Z) = \lim_{\substack{Z\to\infty \\ Z\in RHP}} c\, Z^{a}\, e^{-bZ} \frac{\Gamma(a + 2)}{\Gamma(2)} e^{bZ} (bZ)^{-a} [1+O(|Z|^{-1})]$$

$$= \lim_{\substack{Z\to\infty \\ Z\in RHP}} c \frac{\Gamma(a + 2)}{\Gamma(2)} b^{-a} [1 + O(|Z|^{-1})]$$

$$= c \frac{\Gamma(a + 2)}{\Gamma(2)} b^{-a}$$

so if we denote $\lim_{x\to 0+} \pi(x) = \pi(0+)$, then $c = \frac{\Gamma(2)\ \pi(0+)}{\Gamma(\ a + 2)} b^{a}$

and the general solution is, for $x > 0$

$$\pi(x) = \frac{\pi(0+)}{\Gamma(a + 2)} (b/x)^{a}\, e^{-b/x} M(2,a+2,b/x) \quad (\text{since } \Gamma(2) = 1). (5)$$

As shown in Cummins' equation (27) [with $r = r^*$, $\pi(0+) = 1$].

## IV. The Derivatives

Proposition 1 $\pi'(x) < 0$, for all $x > 0$

Proof
It is clear that $\pi'(x) < 0 \iff \nu_2'(Z) > 0$, $Z = 1/x$.

Since

$$\nu_2(Z) = a_0 \sum_{i=0}^{\infty} \frac{a(a + 1)(-b)^{i}\, Z^{a+i}}{(a + 1 + i)(a + i)\ i!}$$

$$\nu_2'(Z) = a_0 \sum_{i=0}^{\infty} \frac{a(a+1)(-b)^i Z^{a+i-1}}{(a+1+i)\, i!}$$

$$\text{so } \nu_2'(Z) = a_0\, a\, Z^{a-1} \sum_{i=0}^{\infty} \frac{(a+1)(-bZ)^i}{(a+1+i)\, i!}$$

$$= a_0\, a\, Z^{a-1}\; M(a+1,\ a+2,\ -bZ)$$

$$= a_0\, a\, Z^{a-1}\; e^{-bZ}\, M(1,\ a+2,\ bZ) > 0$$

<u>Proposition 2</u> $\pi''(x) > 0$, for all $x > 0$

<u>Proof</u>

$\pi''(x) = Z^3[Z\nu_2''(Z) + 2\nu_2'(Z)]$ for $Z = 1/x$

But from above,

$\nu_2'(Z) = a_0\, a\, Z^{a-1}\, M(a+1,\ a+2,\ -bZ)$

Therefore,

$$\nu_2''(Z) = a_0\, a(a-1)\, Z^{a-2}\, M(a+1,\ a+2,\ -bZ) + a_0\, a\, Z^{a-1}\, (-b)\, M'(a+1,\ a+2,\ -bZ)$$

And so by using the <u>Handbook</u> Kummer function identity 13.4.10

$$Z\,\nu_2''(Z) + 2\nu_2'(Z) = a_0\, a\, Z^{a-1}\, (a-1)\, M(a+1,\ a+2,\ -bZ) + (-bZ)\, M'(a+1,\ a+2,\ -bZ) + 2\, M(a+1,\ a+2,\ -bZ)$$

$$= a_0\, a\, Z^{a-1}\; (a+1)\, M(a+1,\ a+2,\ -bZ) + (-bZ)\, M'(a+1,\ a+2,\ -bZ)$$

$$= [a_0\, a\, Z^{a-1}\, (a+1)\, M(a+2,\ a+2, -bZ)]$$

But $M(a+2,\ a+2,\ -bZ) = e^{-bZ}$

so

$\pi''(x) = Z^3[Z\,\nu_2''(Z) + 2\nu_2'(Z)]$

$\pi''(x) = a_0\, a(a+1)\, Z^{a+2}\, e^{-bZ} > 0$, for all $Z = 1/x$

Thus we have the shape of $\pi$ as:

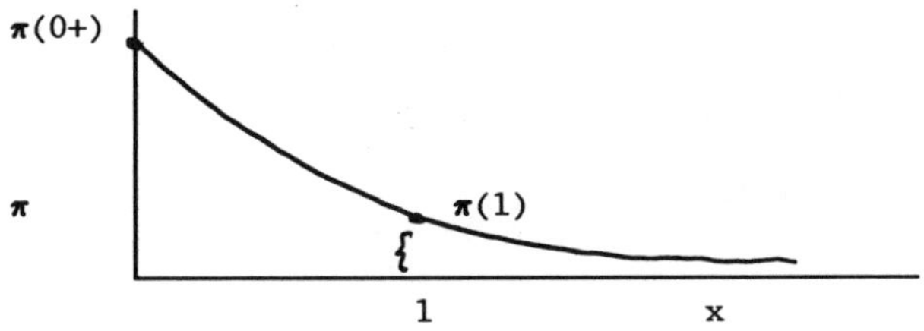


<u>Proposition 3</u> $\quad \lim_{x\to 0+} \pi'(x) = \pi'(0+) = -a\, b^a\, \pi(0+)$

<u>Proof</u>:

$$\lim_{x\to 0+} \pi'(x) = \lim_{\substack{Z\to\infty \\ \mathrm{Re}Z>0}} - Z^2\, \nu_2'(Z)$$

$$= \lim_{x\to 0+} -a_0\, a\, Z^{a+1}\, e^{-bZ}\, M(1,\ a + 2,\ bZ)$$

Using <u>Handbook</u> 13.1.4 again we have

$$\lim_{x\to 0+} \pi'(x) =$$

$$\lim_{\substack{Z\to\infty \\ \mathrm{Re}Z>0}} -a_0 a Z^{a+1}\, e^{-bZ}\, \frac{\Gamma(a+2)}{\Gamma(1)}\, e^{bZ}\, Z^{-(a+1)}[1+0(|Z|^{-1})]$$

$$= \ -a_0\ a\ \Gamma(a + 2) \quad \text{but } a_0 = \frac{\pi(0+)}{\Gamma(a + 2)}\, b^a$$

Therefore

$$\pi'(0+) = -a\, b^a\, \pi(0+)$$

<u>Proposition 4</u> $\quad \lim_{x\to 0+} \pi''(x) = \pi''(0+) = 0$

<u>Proof</u>:

From above, $\pi''(x) = a_0\ a(a + 1)\ Z^{a+2}\ e^{-bZ}$ for $Z = 1/x$

So,

$$\lim_{\substack{x \to 0+}} \pi''(x) = \lim_{\substack{Z \to \infty \\ Z > 0}} a_0 \, a(a + 1) \, Z^{a+2} e^{-bZ}$$

But $\mathrm{Log}\,(Z^{a+2} e^{-bZ}) = (a + 2) \,\mathrm{Log}\, Z - bZ$

and so $$\frac{\mathrm{Log}\,(Z^{a+2} e^{-bZ})}{Z} = (a + 2) \frac{\mathrm{Log}\, Z}{Z} - b$$

Therefore,

$$\lim_{\substack{Z \to \infty \\ Z > 0}} \frac{\mathrm{Log}\,(Z^{a+2} e^{-bZ})}{Z} = -b$$

Hence $$\lim_{\substack{Z \to \infty \\ Z > 0}} Z^{a+2} e^{-bZ} = \lim_{\substack{Z \to \infty \\ Z > 0}} e^{-bZ} = 0$$

## V. Approximations to $\pi(x)$

It will be useful to establish estimates for the number N of terms needed from the Frobenius Series for $\pi$ in order to approximate $\pi(x)$ for a given x. The solution given in (5) is:

$$\pi(x) = \frac{\pi(0+)}{\Gamma(a + 2)} (b/x)^a e^{-b/x} M(2, a + 2, b/x), \quad x>0.$$

Writing $$M(2, a + 2, b/x) = \sum_{i=0}^{\infty} \frac{(2)_i}{(a + 2)_i} \frac{(b/x)^i}{i!}$$

and using the fact that $$(c)_i = \frac{\Gamma(c + i)}{\Gamma(c)}$$

we get

$$M(2, a + 2, b/x) = \sum_{i=0}^{\infty} \frac{\Gamma(2 + i)}{\Gamma(2)} \frac{\Gamma(a + 2)}{\Gamma(a + 2 + i)} \frac{(b/x)^i}{i!}$$

so,

$$\pi(x) = \pi(0+)(b/x)^a e^{-b/x} \sum_{i=0}^{\infty} \frac{\Gamma(2 + i)}{\Gamma(a + 2 + i)} \frac{(b/x)^i}{i!}$$

Now if we let $$S_N(a,b,x) = \sum_{i=0}^{N-1} \frac{\Gamma(2 + i)}{\Gamma(a + 2 + i)} \frac{(b/x)^i}{i!}$$

Then, letting $\rho$ = the error in using the approximation of N terms of the series, i.e.

$$\rho_N = |\pi(x) - \pi(0+)(b/x)^a e^{-bx} S_N(a,b,x)| \text{ or,}$$

$$\rho_N = |\pi(0+)(b/x)^a e^{-b/x} \sum_{i=N}^{\infty} \frac{\Gamma(2+i)}{\Gamma(a+2+i)} \frac{(b/x)^i}{i!} |$$

but $\displaystyle\sum_{i=N}^{\infty} \frac{\Gamma(2+i)}{\Gamma(a+2+i)} \frac{(b/x)^i}{i!}$

has terms satisfying for j=0, 1, 2...

$$\frac{\Gamma(2+N+j)}{\Gamma(a+2+N+j)} \frac{(b/x)^{N+j}}{(N+j)!} = \frac{\Gamma(2+N)}{\Gamma(a+2+N)} \frac{(b/x)^N}{N!} \frac{(N+2)_j}{(a+N+2)_j} \frac{(b/x)^j}{(N+1)^j}$$

Therefore, if $a > 0$, $(N+2)_j \leq (a+N+2)_j$ and $(N+1)^j \leq j!$, hence

$$\rho_N \leq \frac{\pi(0+)(b/x)^{N+a}}{N!} \frac{\Gamma(2+N)}{\Gamma(a+2+N)} = \frac{\pi(0+)(N+1)}{(a+N+1)\ \Gamma(a+N+1)} (b/x)^{N+a}$$

Therefore,

$$\rho_N \leq \frac{\pi(0+)(b/x)^{N+a}}{\Gamma(N+a+1)} = \frac{\pi(0+)}{(b/x)^{-(N+a)} \int_0^{\infty} e^{-t}\ t^{N+a}\ dt}$$

or

$$\rho_N \leq \frac{\pi(0+)}{\int_0^{\infty} e^{-t}\ (xt/b)^{N+a}\ dt}$$

Thus we have

<u>Proposition 5</u> The approximation $A_N$ to $\pi(x)$ using N terms of the Kummer Function of the solution with 2nd boundary value $\pi(0+)$ satisfies

$$|\pi(x) - A_N(x)| \leq \pi(0+)(b/x)^{N+a}/\Gamma(N+a+1) \qquad (6)$$

or equivalently,

$$|\pi(x) - A_N(x)| \leq \pi(0+)[\int_0^{\infty} e^{-t}\ (xt/b)^{N+a}\ dt]^{-1} \qquad (6)'$$

Using the inequality of (6) and an identity for the factorial function analogous to Sterling's formula for the Gamma function we can show:

Proposition 6  The approximation $A_N$ to $\pi(x)$ using N terms of the Kummer function of the solution with 2nd boundary value $\pi(0+)$ satisfies:

$$|\pi(x) - A_N(x)| < \frac{\pi(0+)}{\sqrt{2\pi(N+a)}} \left[\frac{be}{x(N+a)}\right]^{N+a} \quad (7)$$

Proof:

Now from Handbook, 6.1.38, for any positive m, there is a $\psi$, $0<\psi<1$, such that

$$\Gamma(m + 1) = m! = \sqrt{2\pi} \quad m^{m+\frac{1}{2}} \exp(-m + \frac{\psi}{12m}) \quad (8)$$

Thus, since for some $\psi$, $0<\psi<1$,

$$\Gamma(N + a + 1) = (N + a)!$$
$$= \sqrt{2\pi} \; (N + a)^{N+a+\frac{1}{2}} \exp(-(N + a) + \frac{\psi}{12(N+a)})$$
$$> \sqrt{2\pi(N + a)} \; (N + a)^{N+a} \exp(-(N + a))$$

and we have from (6),

$$|\pi(x) - A_N(x)| \leq \pi(0+)(b/x)^{N+a}/\Gamma(N + a + 1)$$
$$< \pi(0+)(b/x)^{N+a}/\sqrt{2\pi(N+a)} \quad (N+a)^{N+a} \exp(-(N+a))$$
$$= \frac{\pi(0+)}{\sqrt{2\pi(N + a)}} \left[\frac{be}{x(N + a)}\right]^{N+a}$$

For example, if we use Cummins's estimates for the relevant parameters (Cummins, Table 2)

| Parameter | Sample Period 1926-1980 | 1959-1980 |
|---|---|---|
| Asset portfolio risk ($\sigma_A{}^2$) | .0051 | .0047 |
| Liability risk ($\sigma_L{}^2$) | .0048 | .0016 |
| $r - r_L$ ($r^*$) | .025 | .025 |
| Payout Parameter ($\theta$) (Mass Auto BI) | .4 | .4 |
| 2nd Boundary Value $\pi(0+)$ | 1 | 1 |

Then since $a = \frac{2(r^* + \theta)}{\sigma_A{}^2 + \sigma_L{}^2}$ and $b = \frac{2\theta}{\sigma_A{}^2 + \sigma_L{}^2}$

We have $a = \begin{cases} 85.8586 & (1926\text{-}80) \\ 134.9206 & (1959\text{-}80) \end{cases}$

$b = \begin{cases} 80.8081 & (1926\text{-}80) \\ 126.9841 & (1959\text{-}80) \end{cases}$

Then, for this case, since $\pi(0+) = 1$

$$\rho_N = \frac{1}{\sqrt{2\pi(N + a)}} \left[\frac{be}{x(N + a)}\right]^{N+a}$$

For a good approximation we would at least want N to satisfy $be < x(N + a)$ or $(b/x)e - a < N$. For example, using the 1926-1980 data and $x = 1$ we would have, $(b/x)e - a = 133.8$. Taking $N > 134$ gives

| | |
|---|---|
| $N = 135$ | $\rho_N < 8.1\ E(-3)$ |
| $N = 140$ | $\rho_N < 5.0\ E(-5)$ |
| $N = 150$ | $\rho_N < 1.4\ E(-9)$ |

or for $x = 2$ we would have, $(b/x)e - a = 24.0$. Taking $N > 24$ gives

| | |
|---|---|
| $N = 25$ | $\rho_N < 1.4\ E(-2)$ |
| $N = 30$ | $\rho_N < 7.6\ E(-5)$ |
| $N = 40$ | $\rho_N < 1.3\ E(-9)$ |

or for $x = \frac{1}{2}$, $(b/x)e - a = 380.9$. Taking $N > 381$ gives

| | |
|---|---|
| $N = 381$ | $\rho_N < 8.7\ E(-15)$ |

So, in the asset/liability ratio interval of interest $\frac{1}{2}<x<2$, N can be taken to be about 500 insuring a good approximation to $\pi(x)$ by using 500 terms of the Kummer function. The convergence, however, is often more rapid than this approximation shows.

The above examples do illustrate the extremely rapid convergence of these Kummer function values once a suitable threshold number of terms are used. The number of terms, however, depend inversely on x, the asset/liability ratio, causing the convergence to be somewhat slower as x goes from 1 to 0.

## VI The Alternative to the Second Boundary Condition

Cummins second boundary condition was given as (1b) $\pi(0+) = 1$. An alternative to Cummins second boundary condition described in the text at equation (38) is

$$\pi(0+) = 1 + \pi(1) \tag{9}$$

The general solution without using this boundary value was given in (4) as

$$\pi(x) = c\, x^{-a} M(a,\ a + 2,\ -b/x) \tag{4}$$

But we know from the argument preceeding the general solution (5) using the Cummins's boundary value (1b) that

$$\pi(0+) = c\, \Gamma(a + 2)\, b^{-a} \qquad \text{(since } \Gamma(2) = 1) \tag{10}$$

Then since

$$\pi(1) = c\, M\, (a,\ a + 2,\ -b)$$

The alternative boundary value equation (9) gives us

$$c\, \Gamma(a + 2)\, b^{-a} = 1 + c\, M\, (a,\ a + 2,\ -b)$$

or

$$c = \frac{1}{\Gamma(a + 2)\, b^{-a} - M(a,\ a + 2,\ -b)} \tag{11}$$

so if we let

$$\gamma = \frac{M(a,\ a + 2,\ -b)\, b^{a}}{\Gamma(a + 2)} \tag{12}$$

Then $0<\gamma<1$ and

$$\pi(0+) = \frac{\Gamma(a + 2)\, b^{-a}}{\Gamma(a + 2)\, b^{-a} - M(a,\ a + 2,\ -b)} \tag{13}$$

$$= \frac{1}{1 - \gamma} > 1$$

and

$$\pi(1) = \frac{M(a,\ a + 2,\ -b)}{\Gamma(a + 2)\, b^{-a} - M(a,\ a + 2,\ -b)} \tag{14}$$

$$= \frac{\gamma}{1 - \gamma}$$

and the general solution is

$$\pi(x) = \frac{(b/x)^a M(a, a + 2 - b/x)}{\Gamma(a + 2) - b^a M(a, a + 2, -b)} \tag{15}$$

This solution also will have a negative derivative on the positive real axis with

$$\lim_{x \to 0+} \pi'(x) = \frac{-b\ a^b}{1 - \gamma} \tag{16}$$

Thus, under this alternative second boundary value the y-intercept is larger than 1 with the downward slope larger than Cummins's value by a factor of $1/(1 - \gamma)$.
Since generally $a > 0$, at least when $r > r_L$, $a_1$ can be solved in terms of $a_0$.

**NOTES**

1. Kummer considered series of this type in 1836 (see References).
2. This solution assumes the Cummins' 2nd boundary value of $\pi(0+) = 1$.
3. In this presentation the usual prime (') notation will denote differentation when a single variable is involved instead of the "sub x" notation of equation (1) and (1)'.

# REFERENCES


1. Abramowitz, Milton and Irene A. Stegun, 1971, Handbook of Mathematical Functions with Formulas, Graphs and Tables, National Bureau of Standards Applied Mathematics Series #55, U.S. Department of Commerce.

2. Ahlfors, Lars V., 1979, Complex Analysis, 3rd Ed., McGraw-Hill, New York.

3. Callaghan, Acheson H. Jr. and Richard A. Derrig, 1982, Position Paper on Surplus, Hearing on Massachusetts Workers' Compensation Rates Exhibit 69, June 1982.

4. Callaghan, Acheson H. Jr. and Richard A. Derrig, 1982, Position Paper on the Reward and Risk for Underwriting, Hearing on Massachusetts Workers' Compensation Rates Exhibit 70, June 1982.

5. Carlson, B.C., 1977, Special Functions of Applied Mathematics, Academic Press, New York.

6. Coutts, S.M., E.R.F. Devitt, and G.A.F. Ross, 1983, "A Practical Approach to Solvency," Working Paper, Institute of Actuaries, December.

7. Cox, John C. and Stephen A. Ross, 1976, "A Survey of Some New Results in Financial Option Pricing Theory," Journal of Finance, v. 31, May: 383-402.

8. Cummins, J. David, 1986, "Risk-Based Premiums for Guaranty Funds," International Conference on Insurer Solvency, University of Pennsylvania.

9. Cummins, J. David, 1985, "Risk-Based Premiums for Guaranty Funds," NCCI Economic Issues in Workers' Compensation, New York Conference Papers.

10. Derrig, Richard A., 1985, "The Effect of Federal Taxes on Investment Income in Property-Liability Ratemaking," ARIA 1985, Annual Meeting, Vancouver, British Columbia, Canada.

11. Derrig, Richard A., 1987, "The use of Investment Income in Massachusetts Private Passenger Automobile and Workers' Compensation Ratemaking," in J. D. Cummins and S. E. Harrington, eds., Fair Rate of Return in Property-Liability Insurance, Kluwer-Nijhoff, Boston.

12. Doherty, Neil A. and James R. Garven, 1986, "Price Regulation in Property-Liability Insurance: A Contingent Claims Approach," Journal of Finance, v. 41, 1031 - 50.

13. Fairley, William B., 1979, "Investment Income and Profit Margins in Property-Liability Insurance: Theory and Empirical Results." Bell Journal of Economics 10, No. 1 (Spring): 192-210. Reprinted in J. D. Cummins and S. E. Harrington, eds., Fair Rate of Return in Property-Liability Insurance. Kluwer-Nijhoff, Boston.

14. Hammond, J.D., Arnold F. Shapiro, and N. Shilling, 1978, The Regulation of Insurer Solidity Through Capital and Surplus Requirements, Technical Report, NSF APR75-16550 A01.

15. Hill, R.D., 1979, "Profit Regulation in Property-Liability Insurance." Bell Journal of Economics 10, No. 1 (Spring): 172-191.

16. Hill, R.D. and Franco Modigliani, 1986, "The Massachusetts Model of Profit Regulation in Non-Life Insurance: An Appraisal and Extension," in J. D. Cummins and S. E. Harrington, eds., Fair Rate of Return in Property-Liability Insurance. Kluwer-Nijhoff, Boston.

17. Hofflander, Alfred E., 1969, "Minimum Capital and Surplus Requirements for Multiple Line Insurance Companies: A New Approach," Insurance, Government, and Social Policy, Spencer L. Kimball and Herbert S. Devenberg eds., Irwin Inc., pp. 63-94.

18. Houston, D.B., 1964, "Risk, Insurance, and Sampling," The Journal of Risk and Insurance, Vol. 31, pp. 511-532.

19. Ibbotson Associates, 1986, Stocks, Bonds, Bills and Inflation 1986 Yearbook, Chicago.

20. Kraus, Alan and Stephen A. Ross, 1982, "The Determinants of Fair Profits for the Property-Liability Insurance Firm." Journal of Finance, 37 (September): 1015-1028. Reprinted in J. D. Cummins and S. E. Harrington, eds., Fair Rate of Return in Property-Liability Insurance. Kluwer-Nijhoff, Boston.

21. Kummer, E.E., 1836, "Uber die hypergeometrische Reihe..," J. Reine Angew Math, v.15: 39-83, 127-172.

22. Myers, Stewart and Richard Cohn, 1987, "A Discounted Cash Flow Approach to Property-Liability Insurance Rate Regulation," in J. D. Cummins and S. E. Harrington, eds., Fair Rate of Return in Property-Liability Insurance. Kluwer-Nijhoff, Boston.

23. Stone, James M., 1973, "A Theory of Capacity and Insurance of Catastrophic Risks," The Journal of Risk and Insurance, Vol. 40, (Part I), pp. 231 ff and (Part II) p. 339 ff.

24. Spiegal, Murray R., 1967, Applied Differential Equations, 2nd Ed., Prentice-Hall, Englewood Cliffs.

25. Williams, C. Arthur Jr., 1983, "Regulatory Property and Liability Insurance Rates Through Excess Profits Statutes," Journal of Risk and Insurance, v.50, September: 445-472.

# Subject Index

# Author Index